# TIME
for **LIFE**

The Pennsylvania State University Press
University Park, Pennsylvania

# TIME
## for LIFE

## The Surprising Ways
## Americans Use
## Their Time

### Second Edition

### John P. Robinson
### and Geoffrey Godbey
With a Foreword by Robert D. Putnam

Library of Congress Cataloging-in-Publication Data

Robinson, John P.
　　Time for life: the surprising ways Americans use their time /
John P. Robinson and Geoffrey Godbey; with a foreword by Robert D.
Putnam.—2nd ed.

　　　　p.　　　cm.
　　Includes bibliographical references and index.
　　ISBN 0-271-01970-0 (pbk.: alk. paper)
　　1. Time management surveys—United States.　2. Hours of
labor—United States.　3. Leisure—United States.　4. Stress
management—United States.　I. Godbey, Geoffrey.　II. Title.
HN90.T5R66　1999
640'.43'0973—dc21

99-16903
CIP

It is the policy of The Pennsylvania State University Press to use acid-free paper for the
first printing of all clothbound books. Publications on uncoated stock satisfy the minimum requirements of American National Standard for Information Sciences—
Permanence of Paper for Printed Library Materials, ANSI Z39.48–1992.

The study of time, which is an intellectual endeavor, may . . . be compared with trying to identify the patterns on a jigsaw puzzle whose pieces grow, change and become more complex while the puzzle is being assembled. . . . We are charting a land that is being created by the act of its discovery.

—J. T. Fraser

# Contents

## Part One: Introduction and Methods

## Part Two: Work and Other Obligations

## Part Three: Free Time

## Part Four: The Demographics of Time Use

# List of Tables

# List of Figures

# Foreword by Robert D. Putnam

Time and its uses have unexpectedly become matters of high politics in contemporary America. Only a few decades ago, *Life* magazine was wringing its hands over the prospect that time-saving technologies and economic progress would leave the nation with time on its hands and little to do. "Americans now face a glut of leisure," ran the headline, "The Task Ahead: How to Take Life Easy" (February 21, 1964). Now presidential candidates debate how to allow American workers more flexibility to juggle the seemingly irreconcilable time pressures of family, community, and professional responsibilities. As Baby Boomers enter the demanding years of the "shoulder generation," balancing obligations to partners, children, and aging parents, time has become the content, context, and coinage of myriad intimate negotiations. More Americans than ever before, it seems, feel harried and rushed. What is to be done?

The first priority is to get the facts straight. Against this backdrop, it is hard to imagine a more timely and important book than this one, harvesting as it does the long-awaited fruits of three decades of careful assessment of how Americans spend their days and nights. Once a decade, beginning in 1965, samples of ordinary Americans have obliged curious social scientists by keeping minute-by-minute diaries of how they spent a single 24-hour period. John Robinson and Geoffrey Godbey have painstakingly analyzed the results of these "time diary" studies. Their surveys provide a uniquely valuable insight into how we have "saved," "invested," "spent," and "wasted" time. ("Time is money" is a peculiarly American maxim, so our penchant for monetary metaphors when discussing time is hardly surprising.) And because these researchers have carefully replicated their original research design in successive surveys, their evidence offers a nearly unparalleled opportunity to explore how Americans' use of time has changed—or not changed—across these decades.

The central and paradoxical finding of this research will inevitably occasion controversy. Subjectively, Americans today undeniably "feel" more rushed now than a generation ago. By the clock, however, and by their own minute-by-minute chronologies, Americans since 1965 appear to have gained nearly an hour more free time per day. We seriously overestimate how much time we spend on work (both on the job and at home), and we dramatically underestimate how much free time we have at our disposal. (We estimate, on average, that we have about 18 hours of free time per week, but our time diaries suggest that we actually have more than twice that amount.) Compared with our counterparts in Japan, Russia, and elsewhere, we report that our lives are busier and more rushed—but our time diaries imply, by contrast, that we have much more free time than they.

Where has the added free time come from, and where has it gone? Robinson and Godbey chart the intriguing details in successive tables and graphs, but the basic outline of their account is fairly straightforward. The momentous movement of women into the paid labor force has, in itself, increased the hours that half of us spend on the job. However, in the aggregate that factor has been more than offset by two other equally important but less widely discussed trends.

- Fewer Americans today are married than a generation ago, and fewer still are parents. Since family obligations are demonstrably time-consuming, nearly everyone (both employed and unemployed, both men and women) is spending less time on housework and child care.
- More and more Americans are retiring (or cutting back on work hours) at earlier and earlier ages—some of them involuntarily, of course. As a result, those of us over age 55 have made major gains in free time. (Since 1965, men and women aged 55–64 have gained about 10 hours a week in additional free time, compared with a gain of less than one hour a week for those aged 25–34.)

Robinson and Godbey show that the smallest gains in free time have been experienced by middle-aged, college- (and graduate-) educated, married parents. This pattern, of course, is consistent with the stereotype of the harried, two-career middle-class family. (Since that is precisely the sociological category that has traditionally supplied disproportionate civic energy for American community institutions, this pattern may also help explain why the growth in aggregate "free time" has coincided with an apparently paradoxical decline in the aggregate time we devote to civic and social activities.) On the other hand, that category accounts for only a small and diminishing fraction of the American population, and it is a serious optical illusion to generalize from their experience.

The authors' answer to the question "Where has all this free time gone?" will be as contentious as it is simple: television. To their own surprise, successive surveys have revealed that virtually all the added "leisure" gained over the last 30 years has been spent on the couch in front of the tube. The increase in TV-watching has in fact cut into the time we have allocated to almost everything else in our lives—but most especially to activities outside the home. Television-viewing now occupies, Robinson and Godbey calculate, 40 percent of the free time of the average American adult.

Yet another paradox is that the respondents in the time-diary studies seem not to enjoy watching television as much as many alternatives. (On a scale that runs from sex to the dentist, TV-watching ranks somewhere in the middle.) If the pleasures of television-watching are so questionable, why then do we spend so much time at it? The answer, Robinson and Godbey argue, is that the costs are even lower. Television is ubiquitous, convenient, undemanding, virtually free (at least at the margin), and perhaps even addictive. Our extra "free time" has arrived (and then disappeared) in tiny packets scattered across the workweek—long enough to channel-surf but not enough for deep relaxation and leisure of the sort that (as their data also show) we do enjoy during vacations, and not enough for social intimacy and civic engagement, both of which are declining, according to these time studies. Whatever the interpretation, the increasing incursion of television into our daily schedule represents the most drastic change in the way we have allocated our hours over the last three decades.

The list of timely topics that are illuminated by this research is diverse and endlessly fascinating, and the conclusions of this study run counter to much conventional wisdom.

- Sleepless in America? The results reported here suggest surprisingly little change in the amount of time we spend abed—almost exactly 8 hours on average in 1965 and today.
- National productivity? The authors detail striking evidence that existing government measures exaggerate the number of hours that Americans actually spend on the job. Since productivity is the ratio of output to hours worked, if the denominator of that fraction is lower than previously thought, then U.S. workers may be more productive than we had believed.
- Neglected children? The evidence here suggests that the amount of time parents spend per child has remained essentially constant over these dec-

ades. The widely discussed reduction in aggregate time spent in child care appears to be almost entirely attributable to declines in the proportion of children in the population.

- Husbands and "the second shift"? Perhaps the finding in this study destined to generate most debate in households around the country is the authors' claim that, at least in terms of time allocations, "there is solid evidence that America is indeed moving toward a gender-less or androgynous society."

- Class differences? The most worrisome social trend in America over the last several decades has been the widening gap in wealth and income between the social classes. Robinson and Godbey report a less noticed counterpart trend: Less well educated Americans appear to be "enjoying" more free time, whereas their college-educated counterparts, for the most part, are not. Paradoxically, as the authors put it, the "working class" is spending fewer hours at work, while the erstwhile "leisure class" has less leisure. Whether this implicit trade-off in the distribution of time and money is psychologically or morally satisfying for either group is a perplexing question.

No interesting account of contemporary social change is uncontroversial, of course, and that truism applies above all to issues as intimate as how we spend our lives. Other distinguished experts, like Juliet Schor and Arlie Hochschild, have offered accounts of American time allocations that differ sharply from the interpretation offered by Robinson and Godbey. This book will trigger a clarifying debate about the facts, and its careful assessment of quantitative evidence has set admirably high standards for that discussion.

A superficial interpretation of the evidence gathered by Robinson and Godbey—and of the central paradox that Americans apparently have more time but feel more harried—might seem to be that we have become chronic whiners, that the problem of time is "all in our minds." To their credit, the authors eschew this simplistic conclusion. Rather, they point to the need to restructure our lives and our institutions to make our "free" time more usable, more personally rewarding, more civicly productive, and, in a profound sense, "more leisurely." Their research should become an invaluable touchstone for all Americans concerned about reordering our personal priorities and renewing our civic life.

# Preface to the Second Edition

In this updated edition of *Time for Life*, we present the results of studies conducted in the 1990s. These data confront us with perhaps the most sobering of realities about Americans' use of time—namely, its unpredictability. As in the case of the surprise in the 1975 data, noted in the Preface to the First Edition, many of the regularities and constants of daily living found in the time-diary data up to 1985 are in need of revision or qualification. Over the last decade, paid work hours do not show the decline found between 1965 and 1985 (especially for employed women), and men's housework and family-care hours are not increasing. Rather than staying constant, time spent on the personal-care activities of eating and grooming has declined. While as a result free time has generally managed to continue its increase, other free-time activities besides television-viewing, such as fitness and social activities, have now shared in that increase. Although the "invisible hand" keeps men and women continuing to put in much the same hours on all productive activities, and spending their time in increasingly similar and unisex directions, for the first time men's free time since 1965 is notably greater than that for women.

As we try to comprehend and explain the nature and causes of these changes, we find at the same time that the 1990s data do not fundamentally change the general trends since the 1960s noted in Chapters 1 through 21. Paid work hours reported in the time diaries are lower, even as workers' estimated work hours remain virtually constant. Women (both employed and nonemployed) are doing less housework, and hours spent shopping and with child-care have remained virtually unchanged. Free time continues to increase, and television-viewing time along with it. When viewed in the long-term perspective of the updated Figure 11, not that much has changed over the last third of the twentieth century.

To rephrase the old adage, then, the more things stay the same, the more they change. We look forward to seeing what the twenty-first century has in store for us, particularly because the federal government (the U.S. Bureau of

Labor Statistics through the Bureau of the Census) may regularly be collecting large and regular time-diary data from the American people. That will mean that not as much time will have to be spent persuading funding agencies to support such data collection, and it will give us more time to determine how the computer, the Internet, and all the other social changes awaiting us in the new century will reshape the way Americans spend their time.

In addition to the funding support for data collection from the National Science Foundation, Environmental Protection Agency, and the Electric Power Research Institute, we wish to thank the Alfred P. Sloan Foundation for supporting our analyses of these most recent data.

# Preface to the First Edition

This is a book about the structure of daily life in America and how it has been changing. It documents several surprising ways in which everyday life has or has not been changing since the 1960s and earlier, not only in terms of time spent in work and family care, but also in terms of the way we spend our free time. Much of this work has been described in a series of articles that have appeared in the magazine *American Demographics* since 1987, but in this book we are able to portray how these changes fit into a larger and more comprehensive picture of American life.

That picture challenges most other scholarly and popular accounts about how Americans have been spending their time. Perhaps that is the reason we have had difficulty getting this book into print. When we first proposed to counter the findings of *The Overworked American* (Schor, 1991) to the *New York Times Book Review*, we were told by the editor that we had to "draw blood." Even the most vigorous arguments we had to meet this marching order were dismissed as "too technical," a barrier we have encountered throughout the more than five years involved in preparing the present volume through any number of popular presses and book agents. During the same period, however, we have been interviewed by literally hundreds of media reporters who were not only open to our major findings but also usually concluded that our time-diary approach provided the most logical measurements of how Americans were actually spending their time.

What sets this book apart from its predecessors is its more systematic and comprehensive examination of time-use differences and changes within the context of the census of behavior afforded by the time-diary method. Therefore, separate chapters are devoted to the more complete dynamics of how women and men, older and younger people, white and black, and higher status and lower status individuals differ in use of their time. Other chapters are devoted to the interpretation and meaning of simple time-use figures— how time-pressured Americans feel, how much they enjoy various activities, and what tangible benefits they derive from the time they invest in different activities.

Previous books using data from the Americans' Use of Time Project include *The Use of Time* (Szalai et al., 1972), *How Americans Use Time* (Robinson, 1977a), *Time, Goods, and Well-Being* (Juster and Stafford, 1985), and *The Rhythm of Everyday Life* (Robinson, Andreyenkov, and Patrushev, 1989). The first two works described results from the 1965 study, the Juster and Stafford volume described results from the 1975 study, and the last work looked at early results from the 1985 study, along with a direct comparison with data from the former Soviet Union.

We are grateful that Penn State Press now affords us a venue for publishing our controversial ideas in all of their quantitative splendor and detail. In particular, we are grateful to Peter Potter, social science editor, for his continuing encouragement throughout the project, and to Peggy Hoover, manuscript editor, for struggling through blizzards of early drafts to ensure whatever coherence and persuasiveness with which the present work is blessed.

We also need to express our appreciation to the National Science Foundation, which has provided funding for the Americans' Use of Time Project from the beginning. In particular, the foresight and persistence of Dr. Murray Aborn has been responsible for ensuring the continuity and scientific integrity of this research methodology. More recent support from Leonard Lederman and Jon McAdams has allowed us to pursue our interests in the technological, communication, and psychological implications of the diary data. The many methodological contributions of Drs. Philip Converse and F. Thomas Juster in the early years of the project at the University of Michigan are also acknowledged. In particular, Dr. Juster's legendary skepticism provided a persistent goad to acquiring more demanding evidence of the scientific quality of various time measures.

The resulting quantitative evidence of the accuracy of the time-diary method that we are now able to describe in this work provides the basis for the overall confidence we have in the controversial conclusions presented in this volume. We have tried to minimize the amount of statistical material in this work, and we hope that the many tables and charts do not distract the reader from following our line of reasoning in drawing conclusions. We fully expect that many readers will thumb past the longer methodological/statistical passages to reach our conclusions, but they can return to those more technical passages to realize their quantitative basis. We again are grateful to

Penn State Press for including as much of this necessary documentation as it has.

The reader may be disappointed that the book does not contain any general predictions about future changes in time use. That is because, as we point out in different chapters, we have been unpleasantly surprised by the failure of many regularities in diary data to persist across time. Thus, the initial 1965 data provided convergent evidence that American society had reached plateaus in time devoted to doing housework and watching television. One implication from such results was that it was not necessary to repeat these studies at frequent intervals. Yet the two most striking findings in the subsequent 1975 study were that time spent on housework and watching television had changed dramatically (housework going down, and television having gone up), and these trends were verified again in the 1985 data. In neither case could these changes have been anticipated simply on the basis of demographic changes. Thus, we have encountered enough problems predicting the past that we hesitate to venture any guesses about the future— although it does appear that changes in time use since 1975 are less severe than those occurring between 1965 and 1975. That is further evidence that the 1960s were a pivotal decade of social change.

We plan in future works to incorporate analysis of the many other aspects of time use measured by our time diaries, such as the "secondary activities" that accompany primary activities and that reflect the important modern phenomenon of time-deepening we discuss in Chapters 2 and 3. The same is true about the important issues surrounding the timing and coordination of activities and the social partners involved, such as family meals and supervision of children. It is important to remember that while parents spend less than an hour a day with their children (and fathers less than 20 minutes) as a primary activity, earlier diary studies established that total time with children was closer to 25 hours a week, which more accurately reflects the time commitment that having a child brings with it.

We wish to thank the many colleagues and friends who have helped in various ways to critique and improve this work, including Cynthia Costell, Rich Yocum, Tom Goodale, Mike Csikszentmihalyi, Stanley Presser, Robert Kubey, and Elihu Katz. We have been enriched by their comments and suggestions and have ignored some of their suggestions at our peril. We are also indebted to our co-authors, Ronica Rooks in Chapter 15, and Vladimir Andreyenkov, Stephen McHale, Anna Andreyenkova, and Ilona Andreyenkova in Chapter 19.

If we seem overly critical of contemporary American society, that is proba-bly because we spend most of our time in this part of the planet. Our travels abroad have made us aware of equally serious and questionable time practices in other societies, such as the death from overwork (*karoshi*) and attempts to economize on sleep (*enamuri*) in Japan, the insane speeds on the autobahns of Germany, and the track-meet pace of life and cellular-phone tyranny in Hong Kong and Korea. While we find much to admire in the time-use pat-terns in Holland, a recent visit there indicates that even Dutch life is being threatened by the time crunches accompanying the 24-hour global economy described by Presser (1996).

Our counterintuitive findings have sometimes made us feel like the iso-lated boy who dared to point out that the emperor marching in the parade was wearing no clothes, but we are encouraged by many other scholars who have begun to accept the findings of this book. If we have been able to find the time to write this book, then there must be time for life.

# PART 1

# Introduction and Methods

# 1

# The Use of Time

> Time is a device of the mind to keep every-
> thing from happening at once.
>
> —Anonymous

> Life is what happens while you're making
> other plans.
>
> —John Lennon

This book is about how Americans spend their time and the surprising ways in which their use of time has changed. It also examines how people feel about time: the pace of life, satisfaction with daily activities, and people's perceptions of changes in their hours of work and free time. Based on time-diary and other research conducted over the last 30 years, we propose that issues and trends concerning people's use of time have been interpreted incorrectly by many authors, by the American media, and by the American public. This has led to serious misunderstandings about how Americans lead their everyday lives. Among such misunderstandings are:

1. The questionable belief that most Americans are working longer hours than a few decades ago (Schor, 1991; Cross, 1993).
2. The questionable belief that women have been particularly hard hit by these work pressures and continue to put in the same time doing housework while having to work outside the home (Hochschild, 1989).
3. The questionable belief that men's contribution to housework is insignificant and shows no sign of improving the gender imbalance in housework (Hochschild, 1989).
4. The questionable belief that as a result of these and other pressures, today's children receive less time and attention from their parents (Mattox, 1990).
5. The questionable belief that household technology has helped to relieve some of these time pressures, making it possible to reduce time spent on such core housework chores as cooking and cleaning, and allowing women to work outside the home (Bose, 1979).
6. The questionable belief that in order to keep up with these changes in technology, Americans need to spend more time in related shopping and repair service activities (Linder, 1970).
7. The questionable belief that to make up for the previous sources of lost time, Americans are spending less time sleeping and eating meals (Burns, 1993).

There have also been misunderstandings about the things Americans do in their free time, such as:

8. The questionable belief that Americans have turned away from religion and are no longer as active in religious observance (Burns, 1993).
9. The questionable assertion that reading has become a lost art and print media are becoming obsolete in an age dominated by the TV screen (Postman, 1985).
10. The questionable belief that Americans no longer have the time or interest in participating in the arts, particularly art forms that are demanding of time, such as opera, concerts, or art exhibitions (Postman, 1985; Burns, 1993).
11. The questionable belief that in order to stay healthy, Americans have

become involved in an increasing spiral of fitness activity (Groff, quoted in Capra, 1988).

12. The questionable belief that participation in organizational and volunteer activity has suffered, as busy people look instead to government action to fill in the holes in the social safety net (Burns, 1993).

13. The questionable belief that video and computer games are luring adults and children away from more serious and enduring cultural involvement (Postman, 1985; Kubey and Csikszentmihalyi, 1990).

14. The questionable belief that home computers and Internet use have reduced Americans' use of print and broadcast media. (Gilder, 1994)

In the chapters that follow, we challenge these beliefs and assumptions, in particular the widespread belief that Americans have run out of time, or even that they have less free time (Harris and Associates, 1988; Schor, 1991). Instead, we argue that Americans have *more* free time than they did 30 years ago and that free time is likely to increase even more in the future. We believe this book presents a different and more accurate picture of everyday life in America because that picture is based on data gathered by the time-diary method.

## The Time Diary

The "time diary" is a sort of social microscope that allows us to examine facets of daily life that are not otherwise observable. Like early discoveries with the microscope, the data we gathered by this method challenge widely held beliefs about how the daily lives of Americans are structured.

Time diaries filled out by cross-section samples of Americans provide complete accounts of what they did on a particular day, for the entire 24 hours. They take us step-by-step through a day, by describing what they were doing at midnight as the new day began, when they got up and started the new day, the various things they did throughout the day, and then how they ended the day the following midnight. These time-diary studies also include where these people spent their day, who they were with, what other activities they were doing to accompany these activities, and how they felt about these activities. A sample time-diary form covering the hours from midnight to midnight is shown in Figure 1.

One of the most valuable features of these time-diary accounts is that the reports are in the respondent's own words. Respondents describe their day as

**Figure 1.** Basic Time-Diary Format

| Time Began | Time Ended | What Did You Do? | Where? | List Other Persons With You | Doing Anything Else? |
|---|---|---|---|---|---|
| Midnight | | | | | |
| | | | | | |
| | | | | | |
| | | | | | |
| | | | | | |
| | | | | | |
| | | | | | |
| | | | | | |
| | | | | | |
| | | | | | |
| | | | | | |
| | | | | | |
| | | | | | |
| | | | | | |
| | | | | | |
| | | | | | |
| | | | | | |
| | | | | | |
| | | | | | |
| | | | | | |
| | | | | | |
| | | | | | |
| | | | | | |
| | | | | | |
| | | | | | |
| | | | | | |
| | | | | | |
| | | | | | |
| | | | | | |
| | | | | | |
| | | | | | |
| | | | | | |
| | | | | | |
| | | | | | |
| | | | | | |
| | Midnight | | | | |

SOURCE: Americans' Use of Time Project.

they experience or recall it, rather than being limited by prearranged categories devised by us. That allows us to be sensitive to changes across time in the language and context in which people describe their lives. The diary entries are then coded into categories of activity that are based on the various activities the respondents report.

Thus, these time-diary accounts provide a unique historical documentation of "a day in the life of America" in quantitative terms. However, the diary reporting technique is not without its limitations. For example,

- We know no more than what people are able or willing to tell us in this reporting framework. If they want to distort their accounts, we have only limited ability to control or correct them. Thus, few respondents report engaging in sexual or other personal biological activity in their diary accounts.
- Respondents vary in their accounts of the day. In the sample diary account shown in Chapter 4, the respondent describes 31 activities, which is well above average. While some respondents describe more than 40 activities, others report fewer than 10, even when probed for additional details.
- These accounts are collected for a single day only, so for a respondent who is taking an occasional day off or taking care of some family emergency, the day could be quite atypical. Conversely, though, when 40 percent of respondents tell us that the diary day about which we interviewed them was not typical, it may not make sense to think of time in terms of "typical days."

Most of these limitations are not inherent in the time-diary method and could be overcome by more ambitious formats (and more costly research funding). Despite the limitations, however, we found that these single-day accounts, when cumulated across fairly large representative samples, provide a robust base for measuring long-term societal changes in how Americans spend their time. Statistically, at least, we can expect in large samples that respondents who spend more time than usual at work or at home on their diary day should be balanced by others who are spending less time than usual—and that seems to be borne out in our data. We present evidence in Chapters 4 and 5 that these diary accounts seem both valid (in the sense of being corroborated by observational data) and reliable (in the sense of producing consistent results from one sample to another and from one time-diary study to another). That enhances our confidence in the accuracy of these diary "time-and-motion" studies of American daily life and the often counterintuitive results they produce.

In particular, these results seem to be seriously at odds with the time patterns that many social observers have reported and that many of our own respondents report are affecting their lives—such as the faster pace of American life. Before examining our controversial results, however, it is important to consider them within the larger social context in which they are embedded. One must remember that the structure of America's population has been undergoing some fundamental structural and compositional shifts across the periods of our study and that it is impossible to report changes in time use without taking such shifts into account.

## Demographic Shifts Since the 1960s

Since the end of World War II, U.S. Census Bureau figures have documented several important shifts in the structure and composition of the American population. In the first phase, between the mid-1940s and the 1960s, they describe the dramatic "Baby Boom" that began shortly after the war and that led, in part, to the growth of the suburbs, to the return of women to the role of full-time mothers and housewives, and to a greatly stimulated economy.

Since the 1960s, however, we have witnessed a different chain of events, particularly in regard to women. For both economic and social reasons, more women have entered the paid labor force—and hold more responsible positions in that labor force, reflecting an increase in career-seeking behavior rather than episodic employment. From the 34 percent of women aged 18–64 who were employed full-time in 1960, more than 60 percent were employed in 1990—almost twice the percentage. That has meant a marked change in how women spend their time—both at work and in terms of home and family care (see Chapter 6).

Simultaneously, however, other demographic changes in women's lives have made up for this loss in free time. The first is the factor of marriage. Not only are 1990s women (and men) getting married later in life than in the 1960s, but they are involved in more partnerships and longer periods of subsequent marriage breakups. Our data indicate that less time being married leads to less time devoted to housework, and less housework time usually means more free time.

Another demographic factor affecting women's free time is the presence of young children, and here also Census Bureau figures document that today's

women are having fewer children than in the 1960s. How much this is a conscious time choice—potential parents realizing that having a child has severe
and long-term consequences for their free time—is not clear, but we sense that
time must be a relevant concern. Whatever the ultimate motivation, having
fewer children means increases in free time, and that would also offset the
decline in women's free time brought on by joining the paid labor force.

Further factors leading to increases in free time among the age 18–64 segment
of the public are changes related to participation in the paid labor market by
those at both ends of this age distribution. First, more young adults are in college
or other educational institutions, and most students have more free time than
average. More important, however, is that more men in the "empty nest" years
of 55–64 are taking advantage of early retirement opportunities or are otherwise
anticipating retirement by working fewer hours than in previous decades.

The nature of these changes is reflected in the compositions of the 1970 U.S.
adult population and the 1990 adult population, as shown in Figure 2. This
breakout uses the eight different categories into which women and men aged
18–64 fall based on their employment, marriage, and parental statuses. We
concentrate on this age segment because it is the most economically active
segment of the population.

As might be expected, one of the biggest shifts for adult males involved men
with the triple role responsibilities of worker, spouse, and parent. That category
dropped from 44 percent of men in 1970 to 36 percent in 1990. Even more
dramatic is the 50 percent decline in women in the stereotypical full-time
housewife role, from 30 percent in 1970 to 14 percent in 1990. In contrast, the
biggest increases are found for the percentages working but having *neither* marital nor parental responsibilities—from 10 percent of women and 11 percent of
men in the 1970s to 16 percent and 21 percent most recently.

Of particular interest is the social category, which media accounts typically use to illustrate the severe time pressures under which Americans now
find themselves—the employed single mother. The percentage of women in
that category has increased from the 1970 figure of 6 percent to 9 percent
today—an increase of 50 percentage points: But that 9 percent is still less
than one-third as large as the 32 percent of working women with no parental
responsibilities, about half of whom are also not married.

Figure 2 thus identifies some of the factors that have mitigated the effects
of women's participation in the paid labor force, which might otherwise have
resulted in dramatic declines in the free time they have available. We assume
that Americans are rather flexible and reasonable people (even if somewhat
short of complete rationality in the economists' sense) and that if they feel

**Figure 2.** Demographic Shifts in the Composition of the American Population Aged 18–64, 1970–1990

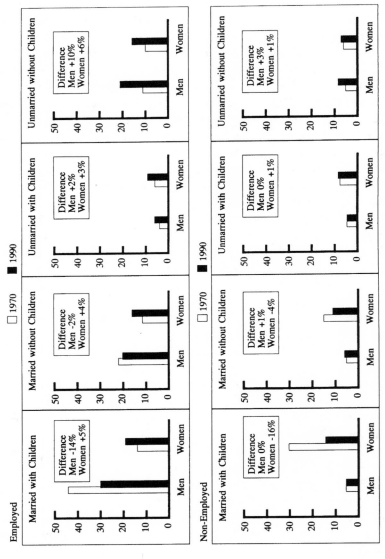

SOURCE: U.S. Census Bureau, Current Population Survey, 1970 and 1990.

pressures from one part of life (for example, women's employment), they will take appropriate time-saving countermeasures (for example, have fewer children or delay/avoid marriage). Indeed, many of these decisions can be the direct result of the realization that having children entails serious short-term and long-term time obligations and that being married usually means living in a larger house with more household maintenance time demands and more people for whom to care and shop.

Figure 2 also helps us see how increasingly fragmented and diverse the U.S. population has become, and how difficult it is to speak in generalities about the population as a whole when it is made up of so many diverse elements. Most important, it reminds us of two main strategies—fewer children, later marriages—that Americans can employ to counter the declines in free time that result from women entering the paid labor force.

## Four Types of Time

Time-diary researchers have found it convenient to distinguish four types of time: (1) paid work (contracted time), (2) household/family care (committed time), (3) personal time, and (4) free time (see Figure 3). These are strongly related to the role distinctions of worker, spouse, and parent and can further complicate the ways in which paid work time and free-time activities can interact. The first type involves the time Americans spend at paid work and is called "contracted time" to connect it to the contractual work arrangements implicit in the schedules that workers make with their employers. This includes paid work done at home, as well as work breaks and other nonwork activities at the place of work. Commuting time is considered separately below as travel.

The second type of time use covers housework, child care, and shopping and is referred to as "committed time" to reflect the family and household role commitments usually associated with such activities. Most economists today probably recognize that committed time needs to be added to contracted time, to reflect the most economically productive of activities, and that they thus capture the two main types of "work" in a society: paid and unpaid.

The third category of time refers to the biological necessities of human existence and includes mainly sleeping, eating, and grooming. These maintenance and care activities are referred to as "personal time," implying that it is time that everyone needs in order to function effectively in society. However, "personal time" has considerable flexibility or elasticity about it—that is, for

**Figure 3.** Interrelations Across the Four Types of Time

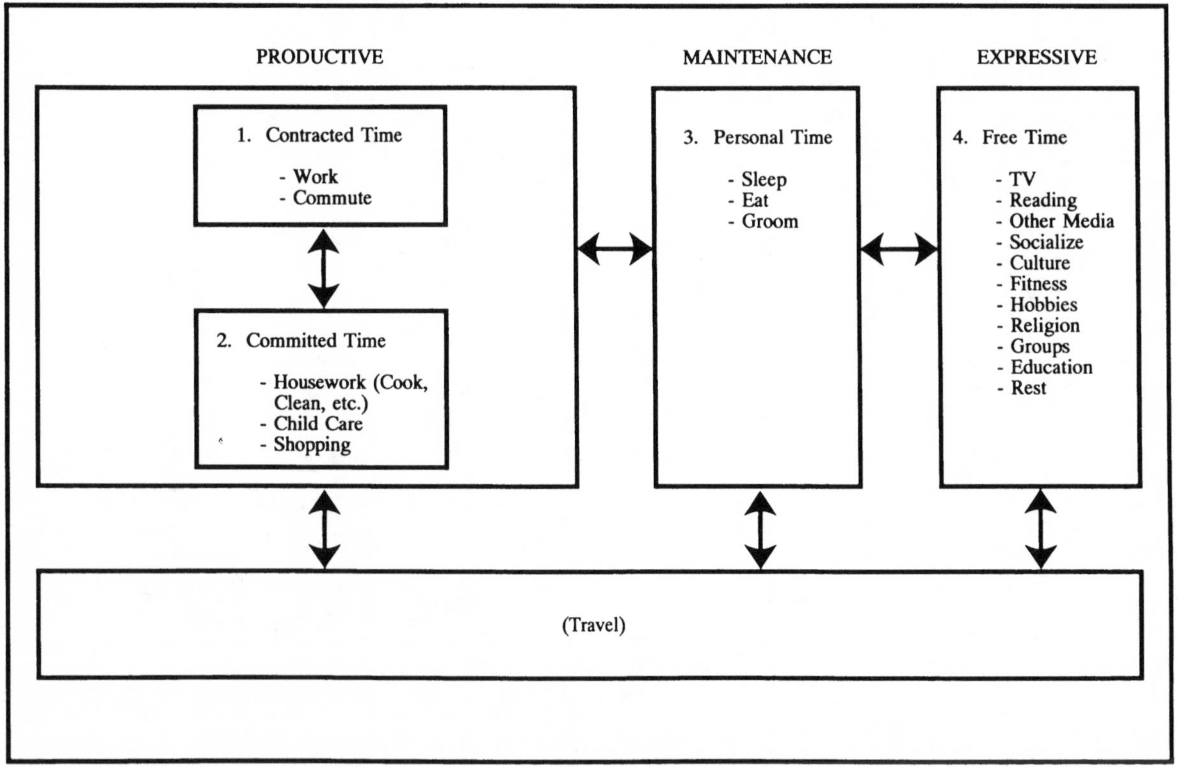

| PRODUCTIVE | MAINTENANCE | EXPRESSIVE |

**1. Contracted Time**
- Work
- Commute

**2. Committed Time**
- Housework (Cook, Clean, etc.)
- Child Care
- Shopping

**3. Personal Time**
- Sleep
- Eat
- Groom

**4. Free Time**
- TV
- Reading
- Other Media
- Socialize
- Culture
- Fitness
- Hobbies
- Religion
- Groups
- Education
- Rest

(Travel)

SOURCE: Americans' Use of Time Project.

example, humans can function adequately whether they wash their hair every day or only once a month, or whether they take one hour or three hours to eat meals. Thus, much personal-care activity can have a discretionary quality about it, motivated by both pleasure-seeking and lifestyle.

The fourth category, "free time," involves any remaining activities and activities that presumably involve maximum choice on the part of the individual. Individuals have comparatively little choice about paid work time or household and personal-care time—which is not to say that people have no choice or find no enjoyment in these activities, but rather that the time spent often involves less perceived freedom or internal locus of control.

Free-time activities involve not only the things we usually think of as free time—such as using the media, socializing, culture, hobbies, and other recreation—but also the "semi-leisure" activities of adult education, religion, and other organizational activity. While education and organizational activity may be "forced" on the individual by other role obligations, these are also activities that most people feel they have some choice in, as supported by empirical study (for example, Robinson, 1977a).

While any division of time use into categories is arbitrary or debatable, the time-diary method we used allows analysts who disagree with the codings to recombine the data in ways that are more suitable for them. Our concentration on four time categories allows us to broaden our understanding of the determinants of free time, and we can readily see how an increase (decrease) in paid work time may not necessarily mean a decrease (increase) in free time. Time in committed activities or personal care could also be reduced as a way to maintain levels of free time. The quality of that free time might be affected if sleep or laundry time were sacrificed, but the amount of free time would be maintained.

The four types of time relate to one another in a number of ways. The far-left portion of Figure 3 has the "productive" activities of paid work and household/family care and the main components of each type of work. The middle part has the personal-care, or maintenance, activities of sleeping, eating, and grooming. At the far right are the more "expressive" free-time activities people can choose. For many people, particularly those who do not enjoy their jobs or family care, free-time activities provide opportunities to express their personal attitudes and personalities.

A "floating," fifth time category is travel, which can be seen either as a separate maintenance activity connecting the four other types of time or as a necessary adjunct to each type. We look at time spent on all travel in Chapter 7, and in Chapter 6 we separately add the commute to work and travel for children and for shopping into our measures of total "productive time."

We recognize that the model in Figure 3 is not a very ambitious or sophisticated model of everyday human behavior. People engage in the same activities for many different motives and goals, and the same work or meal that is the highlight of one day may be quite unpleasant on another day. Nonetheless, we present evidence that the broad outlines of the model have some basis in how people feel about their activities, while also reflecting the variation in motivations and feelings across days and individuals that we have just described (see Chapter 17).

We also believe that this is about as far as most time-diary data can go in describing human behavior. We may know what people do and where they do it, but the diary data are virtually silent about the *reasons* behind the activity, the energy or effort behind the activity, or how "productive" the activity is.

Thus, in Chapters 5 and 6, we show decreases in work and housework activities and treat those decreases as if they indicate a decline in related output. But there are large differences across individuals and days in how much a person can accomplish per unit of time. A decline in paid work time or household/family care time might be a result of someone learning a new and more efficient way of doing a task or tasks, as much as from wanting to use that time to do something else. We do not wish to discourage researchers who want to develop more elegant models of time use, but we do caution that our own efforts in this direction have been stymied by the unpredictable nature of important time-diary variables (especially across time) and by the perverse presence of "Parkinson's Law"—that work expands to fill the time available to do it—in our attempts to relate the time data to output measures (see Chapter 18).

The problem with analyzing time-diary data in this straightforward way was put succinctly and eloquently by De Grazia (1962):

> By using a strictly quantitative, assembly-belt conception of time—time as a moving belt of equal units—one ignores the significance of most activity. A moment of awe in religion or ecstasy in love or orgasm in intercourse, a decisive blow to an enemy, relief in a sneeze or death in a fall is treated as equal to a moment of riding on a bus, shoveling coal, or eating beans. (P. 142)

All time-diary analysts must continually remind themselves that the convenience and elegance of the quantitative diary measures may not translate easily or straightforwardly into conclusions about the ultimate meaning of human behavior, either in terms of what they mean subjectively to individuals or objectively in terms of what is produced as a result. For example, an increase in such a simple activity as watching television can represent a shift toward increased laziness, a reaction to the dangers that lie outside the confines of one's home, an improvement in television's ability to meet audience needs, the use of a more efficient medium to learn about human behavior, or the only activity left to the individual after more-exhausting aspects of life. It could also simply reflect the aging of the population as retired people watch more television. Linder (1970) pointed out that Americans now act "to increase the yield on all aspects of their daily life, not just productive activities." This may apply to TV viewing as well.

Our time-diary records can therefore be seen as something akin to the physical artifacts, such as bones and tools, available to archeologists. In their patterns and traces, they invite insightful speculations about the nature of human behavior. In the same way, evidence of decreases in household/family care time or increases in television-watching time are consistent with models of America becoming a more sedentary or unimaginative society. But the same data could be used to argue that Americans have become more adept at reducing time spent on less-important aspects of their lives. While we shall present evidence that is mainly critical of the amounts of time Americans spend watching television, it is our goal to stimulate readers and other researchers to see how well these interpretations square with their own observations about contemporary life. The great advantage we have over archeologists is that we are able to ask other questions of our respondents or to conduct more in-depth studies of what current uses of time seem to mean and represent.

One type of output from time-diary studies that can be particularly revealing and persuasive comes from the "zero-sum" property of time. Simply put, if one increases time spent on some new activity, such as computer usage, yoga classes, or rollerblading, time on some other activity must show a decrease. Sometimes these exchanges are straightforward, such as the decreases in the "functionally equivalent" activities of movie-going, radio-listening, and fiction-reading that accompanied the arrival of television (see Chapter 9 and Robinson, 1972b). Other changes in societal behavior followed less clearly from the functional-equivalence argument, such as the decrease in sleep or yard/garden activities of television owners. In the same way, the declines in women's housework we describe in Chapter 6 follow not only from the increased time they spend at paid work but also from the decreases in marriage and parenthood described above and as a response to changed norms and expectations.

This highlights another important feature of time-diary data—namely, that they are complete. When all 24 hours of the day are reported in a time diary, potentially all human behavior is captured and represented. Anything that people can do, they must do in time. Because "everybody has to be somewhere," the time diary allows us to compare activities directly in terms of the time devoted to them. Such interpretations are subject to multiple explanations, but there can be little argument over the common yardstick applied to each activity.

Nonetheless, we agree with Heirich (1964) that "to be conceptually useful, allocation of time (an input) must be linked to output from time use." While we make some efforts in that direction in Chapter 18, they seem to be bedeviled by the operations of Parkinson's ever-present law. While it may increasingly be the case in American society that time is treated as money, it is not at all clear how to calculate exchange ratios between the two, except in market terms for paid work. That is the way many economists have chosen to analyze time, but their predictions from these assumptions—such as that men will do more of the housework in homes where the wife's wage rate is high relative to the husband's—have generally not been supported in empirical analyses (Robinson, 1977b; Berk, 1985). Nor do other assumptions that flow from this approach—such as that women's housework is valued more if the person doing it has a higher working wage-rate, or that an hour of television viewed by a wealthy person is worth more than an hour viewed by a poor person—have much empirical support or intuitive appeal.

We also agree with Levine's insightful analysis of the way time can translate to power through the phenomenon of waiting, according to "the general rules of economics":

> The greater the demand, the scarcer the supply, the longer the line. So we wait in line to hear people perform, in traffic to reach favorite beaches and in offices to consult prestigious lawyers. (Levine, 1985, p. 12)

Those who have power are waited on, while those who don't do the waiting. It is not by accident that people who are in the hospital are called "patients." At the same time, the exact translation costs are not clearly established for most everyday situations, and the problem becomes far more difficult when all uses of time (including sleep) are factored into the equation.

## A Larger Model

The factors that are most important in predicting people's daily behaviors are identified in Figure 4. We have already described several demographic factors that are helpful to understanding time use. Most prominent is the variable of gender (sex), not only because large gender differences are found in the uses of time (which, we argue in Chapter 13, are becoming less pronounced across time), but also because of the sociopolitical sensitivities surrounding gender differences. Thus, gender is at the heart of Figure 4, which shows the various demographic and background factors that affect how time is spent.

Other biological factors—those that mark us at birth, such as age and race

**Figure 4.**   Basic Background Factors in the Model Underlying Activity Participation

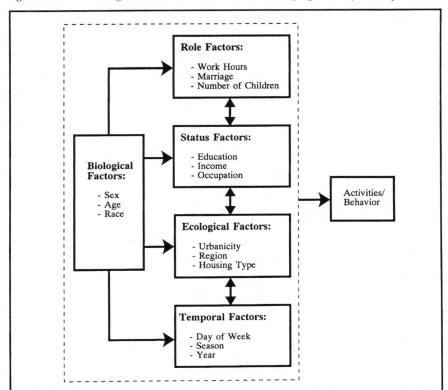

Source: Americans' Use of Time Project.

or ethnic origin—also predict interesting and important differences in how people spend time. First, there are clear and familiar differences in how time use changes across the life cycle that are prescribed by most societies. In Western societies, early life is expected to be a period of learning and socialization, largely in preparation for the "work" expected of individuals in the middle part of their lives. After a certain age, people move into the retirement phase of life, in which they are freed of the necessity of doing most forms of work. If for no other reason than these societal expectations about appropriate activity across the life cycle, age differences can play a large role in how time is spent.

The other factor is nationality or race. Although there are large differences across peoples of various ethnic backgrounds in America, the most visible and problematic differences are between African Americans and the predominant white population. In examining these racial differences in time use, it is important that the analyst recognize that these differences are confounded by a host of other demographic differences, such as parenthood, marriage, urban or rural residence, and, most important for time use, level of education. Thus we take care to separate differences by race from these other confounding factors. Nonetheless, there is another problem in analyzing racial differences in these diary studies—namely, the relatively small sample sizes in a data collection in which behavior for only one day is examined. Thus, in a cross-section sample of 1,500 people, we will find only 150–200 African Americans, or fewer than 30 African Americans a day. The problem becomes even more acute for other important but smaller minorities, such as Hispanics, Native Americans, and Asian Americans.

Demographic variables make up the middle of Figure 4. These include three main indicators of a person's social status: education, income, and occupation. Achieving higher levels on such measures of such status means increased access to skills and resources. That is most apparent in the case of income, because it directly affects one's ability to purchase technology or services to do things one wants to do. But the factors of education and occupation also provide important resources of "cultural capital," which allow individuals access to more specialized and varied ways of spending time—such as being able to derive meaning, insight, and satisfaction from reading a book, enjoying a gourmet meal, or attending the opera.

The three status factors are highly intercorrelated, so that more highly educated people are not only more likely to have the skills and vocabulary to find and enjoy these activities, but also have the income to pay for them, and the co-workers with whom to share these experiences and to reinforce their value. While the factors of education and income have been regularly measured in time-diary studies done to date, the factor of occupational status is more difficult to measure in a standardized way and cannot be analyzed in as systematic a fashion at the present time. In the diary studies that have examined the factor, however, differences in type of occupation in time use can be largely explained by education and income. Nonetheless, that may not be the case in future studies in which larger sample sizes would allow for more fine-tuned categories of occupation to be examined (as in Robinson et al., 1969).

Another important set of demographic factors in Figure 4 are role factors, which include work hours, marital status, and parenthood. Role factors usually imply strong commitments of time—to the job, to the marriage, and to children. They are therefore extremely important factors to control and adjust for in examining differences and trends in different ways of spending time. We shall see that their function in predicting time use varies widely, depending on the activity in question. In this context, we shall also see that an hour devoted to paid work does not necessarily result in an hour of lost free time, and that marriage and parenthood affect not only work and housework differently, but also the things people do in their free time. In general, these role factors are the most important factors affecting the amount of free time that people have available.

The temporal (chronological) factors described in Figure 4 greatly affect how time is spent. Obviously, time use also varies across days of the week. While work is usually done on Mondays through Fridays, we find increasing evidence of work time being more equally distributed across days of the week, especially Sundays (Robinson, 1989d). Activities also vary by month or season of the year, and this is largely a function of more moderate temperatures in the spring and fall months, which allow people to spend more time outdoors. Activities also vary across years, and this is a major focus of this book. However, we see this as a function of irregular social trends rather than of the predictable weekly or daily cycles of activities that recur regularly in society. There are interesting cross-time trends as well in another temporal way in which activities differ—namely, by time of day. Although not reviewed extensively in this book, more detailed analysis of time-of-day differences can be found in Robinson (1993d) and Stone (1972b).

Another set of variables that can affect time use involves locational, ecological, or geographic factors. We mainly distinguish three types of these ecological factors in our research: region of the country, size of place or urban area, and type of housing. Region can reflect distinct lifestyles, such as in the

South or on the West Coast, but regional differences can also arise from different types of inhabitants of that region or from different climate and weather conditions. Except for weather, much the same is true for differences among residents of urban, suburban, and rural locations, although those differences can arise because of differential access to facilities as well. Type of housing can also affect behavior, with residents of single-family houses having more internal space in which to spread out for technology and activities, but that means there is more area to clean and more outdoor space to maintain as well. A related factor here is the permanence of the space, in the sense that renters of a housing unit might invest less time and effort in upkeep than an owner would. Another major "locational" factor is society itself, and we devote attention to differences in time use in Japan, Russia, and Canada in Chapter 19.

Of the myriad other factors that can affect time, we examine home technology in particular detail. Technology is often cited as an important factor because of the presumed time-saving features of new household appliances related to production. While we have been less impressed with the time-saving features of technology as a result of our analyses, the time-diary studies make it clear that at least one piece of household technology—television— has truly revolutionized life in America and in the rest of the world.

Television's impact on society is evident not only in that it takes up close to half of Americans' free time, but also in the ways in which it is making continued inroads into what people do with their time. Television is clearly the 800-pound gorilla of free time, and its effects spill over to nonleisure activities as well. While some of its functions and roles have now been joined with the computer, it will be interesting to see whether the computer will have as clear and monumental impact on daily behavior as television has. Other pieces of technology we had the opportunity to study in this way include cable TV, VCRs, home laundry equipment, dishwashers, vacuum cleaners, and the microwave oven. In no case do we find anywhere near the differences in time associated with these technologies as those found for television.

All these factors are brought together into a single multivariate model (in Figure 4), to remind us of the many cross-cutting variables that can affect time use, and of the need to take them into account in describing patterns and trends in time use. In light of the many interesting trends we shall examine, the context of the multiple determinants of time use identified in Figure 4 are particularly important.

## An Outline of the Book

This book is divided into six parts:

1. Introduction and Methods (Chapters 1–4)
2. Work and Other Obligations (Chapters 5–7)
3. Free Time (Chapters 8–11)
4. The Demographics of Time Use (Chapters 12–15)
5. Subjective Time (Chapters 16–19)
6. Only Time Will Tell (Chapters 20–21)

Part One continues with Chapters 2 and 3, which examine time histori-cally—in particular, the potentially dysfunctional and presumably accelerat-ing pace of American life, as reflected in the various models and strategies of spending time that have been advanced by other authors. In Chapter 4 we examine methodological options to measure how people spend time, as well as the basic time-diary method on which our work is based. We describe the advances in measurement brought about by this method, and we illustrate its functions with a real-life example of how one of our respondents reported his diary day.

Part Two focuses on what the time-diary data reveal about the more "obligatory" side of daily life: the activities of paid work, household care, and personal care. Chapter 5 begins with evidence that raises questions about the widely accepted government figures on time Americans spend at work and the trends in these figures. In Chapter 6 we look at an aspect of time use that has come to be of increasing interest as more women are working: house-hold care and family care. Family care is broken down into three separate components (housework, child care, and shopping), each of which shows different determinants, dynamics, and trends. Chapter 7 examines changes in personal care and travel time, both for productive activities and for free-time activities. We also review the implications of a recent survey of sexual behavior for time-diary studies, because diaries may seriously underreport such activities.

Part Three begins with an analysis of trends in overall free time and a look at how the various factors in Figure 4 relate to the amount of free time people have (Chapter 8). Chapter 9 is devoted to an examination of TV viewing, the predominant free-time activity. Television is also the activity that has shown the greatest increase since the 1960s. In this connection, reading, radio-listening, and time spent with other media are also examined. Television viewing is likely to be affected by the newer technology of the computer. Recent data on how owners of new home computer technology are and are not using various media differently from nonowners of personal computers is reviewed in Chapter 10. Other nonmedia uses of free time, many of which have been described as "social capital," are the focus of Chapter 11. These include socializing, recreation, participation in the arts, other cultural pursuits, hobbies, sports, religion, other organizational activity, and adult education.

Part Four begins with an analysis in Chapter 12 of the interplay between various background factors (Figure 4) and different uses of time (Figure 3). Thus, both simple and multivariate relations with different uses of time are discussed in these chapters. Because gender continues to be a major factor emerging from these analyses, gender differences are the subject of Chapter 13. We note that women have enjoyed as much of an increase in free time as men have since 1965, even after women's increased employment is taken into account. The factor of age is discussed in Chapter 14, as is the question of whether there are increasing age gaps in how time is used. Chapter 15 concludes our analysis of demographic predictors of time use by examining the influence of education, race, and other status factors.

In Part Five we look at three important *subjective* aspects of how people use time, in terms of pace, affect, and output. Chapter 16 examines subjective data related to how much time pressure people feel. An analysis of how much people enjoy or dislike various daily activities is in Chapter 17. In Chapter 18, we consider the degree to which various uses of time can be considered as productive; four disparate measures of output or productivity that show little relation to inputs of time are discussed. Comparative time data from other countries is presented in Chapter 19, with particular reference to comparable data we collected in Japan, Canada, and Russia.

Part Six concludes the book with summary comments and observations and a look at the future. In Chapter 20, we review findings and conclusions from the main topics covered in this book: (1) the methodology of time measurement, (2) current time expenditure patterns, and historical changes since the 1960s, (3) differences and inequalities within various demographic segments of the population, (4) comparisons with other countries, and (5) the gap between how people feel about time and how they use it.

*Time for Life* concludes with an examination of some broader implications and observations from our findings (Chapter 21): the need to redistribute time across the life cycle and to redefine leisure in terms of human values rather than in terms of time and the clock, the implications of declining work time for our use of free time, the prospects for slowing down the pace of life, future predictions concerning further declines in the time spent in work activities, and the issue of "enforced" leisure. We also consider the implications of the divergence of our internal and external worlds for judging what we do in time and space.

In general, then, this book looks at a broad array of diverse measures of changes in the experience of everyday life in America since the 1960s. While mainly documenting changes in the amounts of time devoted to various activities, we try to add meaning to these numbers by describing differences in time use across different segments of the public, by making some international comparisons, and by analyzing social-psychological measures that reflect on the quality of everyday experience. That provides us with a rather different and, we believe, more accurate and optimistic interpretation of how American life has been changing and may continue to change in the decades ahead.

# 2

# The Speedup of Life: Time-Deepening

> To every thing there is a season, and a
> time to every purpose under heaven.
> —Ecclesiastes 3:1

Americans tend to an open-ended view of the world. In American society, "more" is almost always admirable; it doesn't seem odd to us, or immoral, that people can afford to routinely build 10,000-square-foot homes and own many automobiles.

The professionalism to which many aspire in their work is also open-ended. There is always one more thing to be done to enhance our résumé. In sports, we admire athletes who give "110 percent." Even the play-time activities of children have become open-ended. Throwing a Frisbee has become so specialized that some people now make it a living.

The progression of open-end living has moved from the endless consumption of things to endless experiences, communication, and our very concept of ourselves. Time is the critical variable in this equation. Because our time on this planet is limited, however, such endless expectations have made efficiency (doing more with less in a shorter time) a dominant value in American culture.

Time has become the most precious commodity and the ultimate scarcity for millions of Americans. A 1996 *Wall Street Journal* survey found 40 percent of Americans saying that lack of time was a bigger problem for them than lack of money (Graham and Crossan, 1996). For the vast majority of people who have ever lived on earth, this situation would have seemed unimaginable—the most valuable and scarce commodity is not food, water, shelter, safety from disease, or war—but time. The problem of lack of time is, in most senses, a perceptual problem, but it has real consequences for the mind, body, and spirit. How did things get so rushed?

## Time as a Creation of Society

Every living thing on earth has its own sense of time as part of its genetic endowment. At a cellular level, there is one point at which male sperm become capable of making their incredible dark journey toward an unfertilized egg, and another point when nutrition can no longer be metabolized. The way humans think about time, however, is based largely on their way of life and how they view the world, rather than on the events of nature. Although all notions of time have in some way been related to change, vastly different concepts have historically conditioned the individual to behave in a certain way and affect his or her understanding of others.

Our very definition of a situation is directly shaped by how we view time. If a resident of Manhattan and one from Mexico City are both standing at a bus stop, one may define the situation as "waiting" for a bus that is "thirteen minutes late," while the other is "being" there for a bus that is "coming." In some cultures, rushing is a sign of rudeness and poverty of spirit, while in others it is a sign of intelligence and importance. Arriving on time for dinner at a neighbor's house may be considered either necessary or an unthinkable insult. A rural Turk might invite you to dinner "this evening," while for a resident of Boston a term like "this evening" contains insufficient information as to time.

Time and how we think about it are expressions of what we think is real and what we believe is important. For example, although Hindus have a wide variety of beliefs and practices, they tend to share a belief in inborn duty or virtue (Dharma), a belief in a cosmic law of credits and debits for good and evil acts (Kharma), a belief in the transmigration of souls and their eventual release from time (Moksha), and a belief in the ultimate ground of reality (Brahma). Their sacred hymns describe the world as one in which creation and destruction act simultaneously. As a defense against such a world, the passage of time is judged to be insignificant. While real enough for daily chores, time has little bearing on the workings of the universe (Fraser, 1987).

The Chinese have historically had a preference for organic naturalism in which time and nature are conceived as aspects of dynamic, living systems that are to be qualitatively explored. Both the Hindu judgment of time as unimportant and the Chinese preference for thinking of time in natural, qualitative terms, however, are systematically changed when a culture begins to "modernize." To become "modern" means that time becomes more ordered by *human* activity than by the acts of nature.

Thus, time is a diverse concept that is redefined in each culture—and by each individual. There are, of course, extremes. As a homeless man told us, "I don't think there's any such thing as time." At the other extreme, one of our colleagues calculated how many hours of his life he would spend tying his shoes and putting on a belt and, having decided the investment was too great, henceforth wore only shoes that could be closed with a Velcro fastener and bought pants that were "Sansabelt."

## Living in a Circle

In ancient and traditional societies, time had to do with the ebb and flow of tides, the orbits of sun and moon, and the passing of seasons. It was marked by thinning light, the gradual thawing of ice, or the birth of lambs in the endlessly recurring seasons. Time was a circle within which humans lived. Not only was there an element of recreation in the economic activities of most preindustrial cultures, but in many the amount of time available for leisure appears to have been as great or greater than our own.

Anthropologists Johnson and Johnson (1978) found this to be the case among the Machiguenga Indians of Peru. These Indians survive by growing food in gardens, hunting, fishing, and collecting wild foods. "They are self-sufficient; almost everything they consume is produced by their own labors using materials that are found close at hand." When the Johnsons divided the time of the Machiguenga into production time (work), consumption time (using consumer goods for pleasure, eating), and free time (idleness, rest, sleep, chatting) and then compared these time expenditures to those in current French society, they discovered that French men and women (both working and housewives) spent more time in productive activities than the Machiguenga. The French also spent from three to five times more hours in the consumption of goods than the Indians.

The Machiguenga's free time, however, was found to surpass that of the French by more than four hours a day. The Johnsons argued that while technological progress has provided us with more goods, it has not resulted in more free time for most people living in industrial society. They also pointed out that the pace of life for the Peruvian Indians was leisurely; daily activities never seemed hurried or desperate. "Each task was allotted its full measure of time, and free time is not felt to be boring or lost but is accepted as being entirely natural" (p. 55). Anthropologists have found that many hunter-gatherer societies, such as the Australian aborigines, require only three or four hours of work a day to provide the material requirements for their simple way of life (Sahlins, 1972).

Thus, there are two ways to reach affluence: our own way, which is to produce more, or to be satisfied with less. It is difficult for us to appreciate the advantages of hunter-gatherer societies when we simply think of such societies as being comprised of ignorant savages. Nevertheless, "hunters and gatherers are not foolish. As recent studies show, their unique economy gives them all the time they need to build culture." Lewin (1980, p. 16) made this point dramatically by reporting that the bushmen known as the Kung San work, on average, two and a half days a week for an average of six hours a day; yet their diet exceeds recommended allowances set by the U.S. Food and Drug Administration.

Even when mechanical means began to be used to measure time many centuries ago, it did not signal drastic changes in the organization of society. Such early devices as the sundial, the hourglass, the water clock, and the timing candle or lamp were operated independently of any standardized time. There was no fixed moment to which the hourglass could be synchronized. Precision in the use of time was rare, and if rain rendered the sundial useless it did not matter.

# Church and Commerce

Concepts of time that were circular and less precise gradually changed to linear concepts in the Western world. Time became a straight line with a fixed beginning and a fixed end. Early emperors such as Alexander and Augustus declared that Year One began with their rule. Judaism replaced the reoccurring events of nature as a basis for conceiving time with specific non-reoccurring events, thus constructing a past, a present, and a future.

History no longer repeated itself. "The Creation," which was the start of time, was thought to be the work of a single God. The passage of time was marked by the events of humans rather than nature. In Judaism and Christianity as well, there was an imagined end of time—a day of judgment, of potential salvation. Individual behavior would shape the outcome. Thus, the notion of "free will" was born, and with it the measurement of time in terms other than those of nature.

For Christians, the linear progression of history—from the fall of Adam and Eve in the Garden of Eden, to the birth, death, and resurrection of Jesus, and from there to the Last Judgment—became the foundation of the Christian faith. Ancient Hebrews preferred to believe in linear progress toward the Promised Land. Time became a line of finite but indeterminate length.

In spite of the biblical sentiments of Ecclesiastes, "the Preacher," the transformation of concepts of time from cyclic (a circle) to linear (a straight line) was wrapped up in changes in religious belief. The mechanical measurement of time by clocks helped reinforce the linear concept of time. It allowed more accurate measurements of time to be made and shared among people. This was necessary as people began to earn their living in ways other than hunting and gathering, farming, or individual production of goods. Mechanical measurement of time was to pave the way for industrialization and for dividing the day into segments of work and leisure.

Viewing time as a line with a beginning and an end made it a finite commodity. As an expert in the study of time, philosopher J. T. Fraser (1987, p. 22) pointed out, "With the meteoric advance of science and technology—made possible by the linear view of time and history—the relationship between God-the-timer and man-the-timed has changed. In our epoch, carrying out the promise of salvation history became a responsibility of the created and not of the Creator."

Eventually, "man-the-timed" was timed more closely, not only by God but also by employers, schools, stoplights, parking meters, and stopwatches; by the actuarial tables of insurance companies and the whistles of referees in sporting events; by the regularity with which the ghost images of television appeared, dancing in another world; by sex manuals, aerobic dance instructors, the coming and going of planes and trains; by digital clocks all over the house; by the beep of telephone answering machines; and finally by the precise unfolding of events as various as the firing of nuclear missiles to the cooking of french fries made possible by the computer's rhythms. But we are (characteristically) rushing ahead of the story.

## The Industrialization of Work

Little by little, humans have become runners on the straight line of time. From the Middle Ages through the Industrial Revolution, the pace of life began an unprecedented process of speeding up. Not only was there a speedup of work in factories, but there were also related changes that reflected the new values ascribed to speed and efficiency: the standardization of hours during which pubs could be open, the mass production of watches, the legislation against loitering. While the idea of democracy had caught hold in Europe and North America, rejecting the tyranny of humans, there was increased willingness to accept the tyranny of the clock. Slowly, time became the ultimate organizing mechanism of the modern world—the ultimate scarce commodity.

Not only did industrial capitalism create a small "leisure class" that had both time and money, it also brought about a class of workers who were forced into a new kind of labor and eventually enticed into a model of open-ended consumption. One movement, the "Luddite" movement, sought to destroy the machines that were introduced into the workplace—until its leaders were shot, hanged, and deported into submission. Such protest groups were mistaken in their attacks. What really changed and came to rule their lives was not the machines on the shop floor but what hung over them from the ceiling—the clock.

Before the factory system, the work of peasants and life in general was less time-bound and organized. The clock, which made industrial work possible, fundamentally changed the nature of work and, subsequently, the rest of life, making time scarce. In the seventeenth century, the poet Ciro di Pers (quoted by De Grazia, 1962, p. 310) described when clocks became more than a bauble for the rich, making time scarce for the rest of society:

Noble machine with toothed wheels
Lacerates the day and divides it in hours . . .
Speeds on the course of the fleeing century.
And to make it open up,
Knocks every hour at the tomb.

By the late 1800s, inexpensive Swiss- and then U.S.-made watches were organizing the day for millions. By 1888 the Waterbury Company in Connecticut was selling 500,000 watches a year. While earliest clocks had only an hour hand, the minute hand was added as time became more precious—and then a sweeping second hand, which moved in endless circles as if time were still a circle of seasons. Seconds were divided by the "stopwatch," first into tenths and then into hundreds. Ultimately, the computer provided a further division of time beyond human perception—the nanosecond, one billionth of a second.

## Scientific Management

While industrialization and the clock profoundly altered life and sped up its pace dramatically, Frederick Taylor, creator of scientific management, may have been more responsible for the time famine in American culture than anyone else. In 1899, Taylor established a company whose service was to provide advice on how to make enterprises more efficient. Among the services were time-and-motion studies of workers on the shop floor. Taylor called his system the "piece-rote" system; each man performed by rote in the most efficient (usually meaning the fastest) way. Taylor's techniques controlled each of six time dimensions on the shop floor—sequence, duration, schedule, rhythm, synchronization, and time perspective—stripping the individual worker of control of the work processes and making him a servant of the machine. As Bell (1976) observed: "If any social upheaval can ever be attributed to one man, the logic of efficacy as a mode of life is due to Taylor. With scientific management as formulated by Taylor in 1895, we pass the old rough computations of the division of labor and move into the division of time itself" (p. 55).

The ultimate impact of scientific management was not only to wrest control of the work process from the worker but also to make the worker more efficient. In doing so, Taylor unwittingly reshaped the use of time in every aspect of our lives. Modern homemaking began to reflect these values and processes. For example, kitchens were designed increasingly in standardized ways based on the same time and motion studies that Taylor helped introduce, and the methods of coaching many sports came to be indistinguishable from the methods employed by Henry Ford to produce his Model T automobile. Largely because of the economic success of scientific management in the workplace, time and attitudes toward time have slowly been reorganized in the rest of life, with the ultimate result being a perceived scarcity of time.

## The Industrialization of Free Time

As work became more ordered and time became the ordering device for many workers, the remainder of the day became "free time," an empty container that could no longer be filled with the old forms of play and holy days that characterized peasant life. New work patterns, the emergence of capitalism, and the urban environment, which was largely an unplanned phenomenon accompanying the factory system, made former ways of life and leisure obsolete.

If the factory system was a catastrophe for peasant culture, peasant culture also was initially a catastrophe for the factory system. Peasants often preferred idleness and drinking, working only when the mood struck them, and the pleasures of the body over the pleasures of the mind. In both Europe and North America, gambling and drinking either accompanied or had been the source of most leisure activity of adult males and some females. Such preferences led to a series of attempts to reform the leisure activities of the peasants, because employers and managers believed it was necessary to change such habits for industrialism to succeed. Many, including Charles Dickens, also recognized that leisure time was the only arena for the "re-creation" of the physical and psychological capacity to work (Cross, 1990, p. 87).

By the 1830s, reformers understood that new work patterns had deprived members of society of the means to express their religious and family values. The "rest of life," in many senses, had to be reinvented. Such reformers believed leisure was the best place to promote the personal values essential for a growing commercial economy: self-control, family values, and "respectability."

The various reform movements did not only want to suppress various leisure behaviors that were considered evil. They also wanted to transform leisure behavior, replacing play that was public, inconclusive, and improvised with play that was more highly ordered and planned. In doing so, the intent was to make the working class more "respectable, more predictable, less dangerous to others, and more amenable to industrial working conditions." In all such change, the ability to treat time as a scarce resource was critical.

The means of achieving these ends were as diverse as promotion of reading, choral societies, structured sports experiences, adult education, and a variety of other nonwork experiences. The nature of many such efforts had descended from the techniques of industrial work. Modern sports, for instance, was born in the nineteenth century during the transformation of work to the industrial system. In Britain, sports such as track and field, swimming, rowing, and soccer became regulated contests with techniques drawn from industrial production and from the unfolding world of capitalistic market relationships. Increasingly, athletics were measured, timed, specialized, and synchronized in ways that would have made Taylor proud. And to reform the habits of working-class women, the "rational domesticity" movement featured visits to workers' homes by upper-class females who taught handcrafts, child-rearing, ways to improve housework, improved hygiene, and ways to be more efficient, punctual, and productive.

The transformation of work caused the transformation of leisure. Free time became industrialized. Many traditions of preindustrial life were lost forever.

## The Further Ordering of Time

Time not only became more ordered in the daily lives of those in individual communities, it became standardized throughout the world. Historically, different communities had set their own time based on tradition, the local economy, or nature, as late as the beginning of the twentieth century. In 1870, a rail passenger traveling from Washington to San Francisco would have traveled through roughly 200 different time systems on the journey. The British, however, had set a standardized time system for their railroads, and soon countries with large rail systems wanted to do the same.

An International Conference on Time held in Paris in 1912 ratified the agreement of an earlier conference in which Greenwich, England, became the timekeeper for the world—the prime meridian. Thus, all the world became, to some extent, subject to a uniform system of time, a system that was removed from nature, and based completely on utilitarian considerations. The stage was set for time to become a new form of tyranny, an unrecognized imperialism.

Today, the computer has joined the clock as the new time-ordering device. Computer programs predetermine how the future will unfold, and they control the sequence, duration, tempo, and coordination of activities. The computer, however, is different from a clock as a teller of time. While clocks are set in terms of sequence, duration, and rhythm, a computer can manipulate these by changing the program. While an alarm clock can be "programmed" to signal at a particular time, a computer can be programmed to signal under different conditions. Time is no longer a single fixed reference point that exists external to events. It is no longer bound in any way to the rhythms of the natural world, but rather a mathematical abstraction that separates us from the natural world. The sequence of events for which computers can be programmed, from the procedures for landing a jumbo jet to the renewing of insurance policies, has no relationship to the rising of the sun or the ebb and flow of tides.

While time has always been equated with change, and more recently with money (as Ben Franklin observed), it is now equated with information as well. The rate at which such information is calculated, the nanosecond (one billionth of a second) speeds up the rate of change exponentially. Thus, we dance faster and faster just to stay in place. Computers have not so much become "user friendly" as we have had to become "computer friendly."

If the computer increasingly defines and controls time in whatever capacity it is used, it may reshape our inner sense of time. All of us experience time in psychological terms, making qualitative judgments about it. For instance, if you enjoy reading this book, 45 minutes spent reading seem to pass more quickly than if you do not enjoy reading it. Psychological time, or inner time, is our perception or inner sense of the passage of events. In this respect, time can be judged only in terms of personal meaning. As we shall see later, our inner sense of time has been fundamentally reshaped by a computerized world.

Time may now be thought of as relative rather than an absolute, not only because of the computer's ability to "program" time in any way we want it to, but also because of parallel changes in theoretical physics. Einstein's special theory of relativity assumes that space and time are relative and related concepts rather than constant, absolute, and separate. While the speed of light is a constant throughout the universe, our perceptions of time are shaped by how fast we are moving.

Nothing is at absolute rest. If we moved away from a clock tower that said 12 o'clock at the speed of light and continued to view the clock, it would always say 12 o'clock, because the light that carried the image of the clock would be traveling at the same speed we were. Even looking at a wristwatch produces some lag, since light must carry the image to our eyes and then to our brain. Thus, there is no universal "present." People experience events differently, depending on where they are on the planet and how fast they and what they observe are traveling.

Perhaps the psychological equivalent of Einstein's theory is that our world and the events we perceive in it seem to be traveling faster and faster. Americans may perceive time differently from those in other countries, because we and the events we observe are moving faster and faster.

Every culture is haunted by factors that seem to be beyond its control: weather, war, disease, religious prejudice, boredom, starvation. At present, American society is starving—not the starvation of the Somalis or other traditional cultures, who die for lack of food, but for the ultimate scarcity of the postmodern world, time.

Starving for time does not result in death, but rather, as ancient Athenian philosophers observed, in never beginning to live. The examples of time scarcity surround us:

- Condensing of birthday parties into restaurant meals at which the wait staff assemble to sing a quick chorus of "Happy Birthday," perhaps accompanied by a cupcake with a lit candle extinguished within twenty seconds.
- Running red lights, risking life and limb to save a few seconds.
- Gulping food at meals too quickly to savor the flavor, a habit that is a major factor in obesity.
- Using drive-through windows in "fast-food" restaurants: You drive through throwing money at them, and they throw grease, salt, and sugar back at you.
- Advising parents to spend "quality time" with children, which simply means doing more with them in less time.
- Spending rarely more than a few seconds in front of a painting in a museum.
- Complaining by retired couples that they always feel rushed, even though there is almost nothing they have to do.
- Wrecking a car as a result of simultaneously driving, talking on the telephone, listening to a taped lecture, and eating lunch out of a McDonald's bag (as actually happened to a colleague of ours).
- Playing endless and perverse games of "communication tag," made worse by call waiting, fax machines, and "voice mail."
- Following the new social taboos against being late, taking too long to get to "the point" in a conversation, or waiting—for anything.
- Relying increasingly on guns and violence as a quick way to resolve conflicts.

- Experiencing the massive decline of patience in everyday life—except for those who are "patients" in hospitals, but even patients are becoming impatient.

Thus, the quality of experiences has changed dramatically as the pace of life has become faster. Consider a simple trip to the zoo, in the foggy past and now:

---

### A Hypothetical Trip to the Zoo

*The kids had talked about the trip for several weeks. Mom packed a lunch the night before and instructed her children about what clothes to wear—their good clothes. The next day, the entire family drove to the zoo, or took a bus, and once their destination was reached spent all morning just roaming around. After a leisurely lunch on the grass, the father perhaps snoozed a bit, the mother cleaned up, and the kids wandered off to see their favorite animals. Once alone, mother and father might even have talked with each other in hushed tones while slowly pulling blades of grass or staring at the clouds. Lying on their backs, hands folded behind their heads, the couple slowly came to realize that a distant cloud bank looked like dreaming elephants bound for home. They watched other people with a passive receptiveness that occasionally led to insights about the world and their own lives. The children returned. A few arguments were partially settled. The animals were discussed with great enthusiasm as the remains of the picnic basket were depleted. Perhaps blades of grass were pulled from the father's cupped hands to determine who got the last half of a brownie. The family returned home as the sun set, tired but full of wonder.*

And today:

*Mom or Dad (not both) rushes the kids into the car and gets on the Interstate and drives at 65 miles an hour to Animal Safari Park. There they pay $10 per person and drive through taking snapshots through rolled-up windows with an instamatic camera. In just 45 minutes they are back on the Interstate looking for a fast-food place for lunch. The only sense of wonder is what to do next.*

---

## What Does It Mean to Rush?

To "rush" is a bit more sinister than one might suspect. In a culture that is particularly rushed, this may be hard to discern because it takes a good deal of unrushed reflection to recognize what rushing means.

The word "rush" has many related meanings. It can be a swift advance, or it can be an attack or charge. "To rush" means "to move, act, or progress with speed, impetuosity, or violence" (*Random House College Dictionary*, Revised Edition, 1988). Thus, rushing can mean not only speed of action or progression but also rash or unthinking action or an injurious, rough, or destructively forceful action. The range of synonyms for rushing has expanded to include:

> speed, race, hasten, hie, hurry, run, dash, tear, scramble, dart, hustle, scurry, scamper, speed up, accelerate, dispatch, expedite, perform hastily, finish with speed, work against time, hurry, spur, whip, urge, goad, drive, pressure, push, press, keep at, go carelessly, go headlong, act thoughtlessly, leap, plunge, precipitate oneself, attack suddenly, storm, charge, descend upon, have at, run, dash, sprint, haste, speed, dispatch, urgency
>
> (*Random House Thesaurus*, College Edition, 1989)

In most of these meanings, there is the quality of aggression. Aggression is a widely admired trait in America—from business to sports to politics to matters of the heart, aggressiveness is encouraged.

There is also a quality of violence in rushing; it is no accident that the high-speed train system in Japan is called the "bullet train." There is rushing in football, in dating, and in fraternities. In many cases, "rushing" indicates going after some objective independent of the feelings of others. If you move slowly, the other individuals involved have time to consider what you are doing and make judgments about it. If you rush, they might not.

Among the antonyms to "rushing" are "walk," "crawl," "slow," "dawdle"—and "leisure." Leisure requires an absence of rushing, tranquillity, an end to hurrying, a letting go. Thus, data on amounts of "free time" in a society may not tell us much about the extent to which that society experiences leisure.

"Rushing," then, is a complex term. It is easy to see situations in which rushing would be worthwhile and functional. If your house is on fire, you should rush out of the building; if a mugger is chasing you, rush away; if the wind blows your hat across the field, rush after it. As a way of life, however, rushing doesn't sound very inviting or even functional.

Effortless speed is something very different from rushing. The leopard does not "rush" after its prey. Mozart did not rush to create music—it simply poured out. One who is a "quick study" does not have to necessarily "rush" for answers, and a savant seems to receive his or her magical skills as a gift from God. Indeed, much of what we can do quickly without rushing appears to be a gift from God. Barry Sanders of the Detroit Lions is remarkably gifted at "rushing," yet like most highly talented running backs he never seems to be in a hurry. Rushing, then, is something different from speed; it is an attempt at greater control, often after control appears to be lost. If you stomp an anthill with your boot, the ants will rush around. Sometimes American culture resembles one big stomped anthill.

## Of Time Pressure, Good and Bad

Not all time pressures are unnatural or dysfunctional. All living things are subject to daily (diurnal) and annual cycles and processes, and humans are not exempt from such processes. All the organs of the human body are subject to the influences of the biological diurnal clock. These biological cycles are not caused by the alteration of sleeping and waking. Just as sleeping and waking, they are an expression of our genetic makeup. A large body of research shows that our performance ability is greatly influenced by the time of day.

For instance, the performance of industrial workers reaches its first peak in the morning, and then reaches another, slightly lower, peak in the afternoon, following a midday low. Performance in the evening drops off quickly and reaches a pronounced low in the early hours of the next morning. This pattern applies to both day-shift and nightshift workers. Alcohol is absorbed into the bloodstream faster at some times of the day than others. And suicide rates, conception of illegitimate children, the number of books loaned by libraries, and even the effects of exercise vary by the time of year (Aschoff, 1974).

There is also a social element to time pressures that is highly desirable for humans. Being "unemployed" means not only not having an income but also the destruction of a time routine, even when income is provided by government. The absence of a succession of events and "intentionality of action" makes workless days forgettable and destructive for many of the unemployed. As historian Cross (1993) observed about the "Depression":

> To the jobless male, in particular, unemployment destroyed the oppositional character of time: it obliterated the division between public "obligation," which justified the individual with a wage, and private freedom, where men displayed themselves as chums and providers.

Those who cope with unemployment successfully were generally those who established new routines with new time pressures around which the rest of life could unfold.

All these examples demonstrate that we are shaped by time and time pressures that are part of our makeup. This time pressure can be a good thing.

> Temporal pressure is constricted, but it is also the framework within which our personality is organized. When it is absent we are disoriented. There is nothing to bind the sequence of activities: we are alone. Human equilibrium is too precarious to do without fixed positions in space and regular cues in time. (Fraisse, 1964, p. 141)

There are, in other words, advantages to time pressure. It is a natural and healthy part of our lives. There are also time patterns in the natural world that shape us because we are a part of nature. More recently, however, time pressures have intensified to the point where millions of Americans are starving for time.

## Time-Deepening

How do we explain the time famine? Economist Staffan Linder theorized that the speedup of the pace of life in America came about as follows. At one point, there was an equilibrium between the work time and leisure time of Americans in terms of what they accomplished during each time frame. As output per worker increased, however, the time of each worker became more valuable, and therefore was considered more scarce. This destroyed the balance between work and leisure, because people had increased the "yield" on their work but not their leisure. People then began to attempt to increase the "yield" on their leisure, both by speeding up participation in various activities and by combining given activities with additional material goods. This caused a shift away from leisure activities that could not be speeded up or easily combined with additional material goods (for example, contemplation, singing, dancing, writing poetry) and increased time spent in activities that could be speeded up and combined with material goods (such as driving a car for pleasure, shopping, tourism). Linder (1970) argued that this situation has led to a generally perceived scarcity of time. Burns (1993) has provided several more recent examples of this principle in action, such as people preferring cats to dogs because they are less time-intensive, and people buying orange juice ready to drink instead of frozen juice concentrate (which takes time to "thaw and mix").

The response to the time famine has been "time-deepening" behavior. Time-deepening assumes that, under pressure of expanded interest and compulsion, people are capable of higher rates of "doing." Rather than thinking of human behavior in "either-or" terms—that is, a person does either one activity or another—some people develop the ability to do both Activity A and Activity B. Time-deepening can occur in at least four ways:

1. Attempting to speed up a given activity: bringing the relief pitcher from the bull pen in a golf cart, visiting a national park without getting out of your car, telling a date your life story in less than two minutes.
2. Substituting a leisure activity that can be done more quickly for one that takes longer: phoning for home-delivered fast food instead of cooking it yourself, substituting faster-paced, step-intensive racquetball or squash for tennis.
3. Doing more than one activity at once: watching television while reading the newspaper and eating dinner, eating and drinking and doing your income tax while watching a movie on an airplane trip.
4. Undertaking a leisure activity with more precise regard to time: perhaps planning an evening with friends for cocktails, dinner, and theater with only a five-minute tolerance in the schedule, or politicians planning bathroom time in their daily schedules.

Time-deepening is probably more likely to occur among upwardly mobile Americans who are middle class or upper class. While it may have some advantages in terms of accomplishment, it has many disadvantages. It may produce great stress, and it also means that many Americans never experience anything fully, never live in the moment. Leisure activities that require a long time to learn necessary skills are avoided. Sand traps and hazards are removed from both real and miniature golf courses to speed play.

The desire to speed things up extends even to sexual activity. Pornography is, in effect, a sped-up substitute for more time-intensive forms of sexual involvement. Prostitutes operate in alleys or out of parked cars for "quickies." The practice of taking a mistress, as Linder observed, is dying out simply because men don't have sufficient unaccounted-for time to develop such a relationship. Even the increase in sexual intercourse outside marriage may represent not so much a change in morals but rather an attempt to obtain the only type of intimacy that can be realized quickly. Social or spiritual intimacy is hopelessly time-consuming.

Work activities have been sped up too. Yesterday's typist used to average about 30,000 keystrokes an hour, but today's VDT operator is expected to reach about 80,000 keystrokes in the same amount of time (Rifkin, 1987). The fax machine, electronic mail, and the emerging information highway make communication faster and faster, although rarely more thoughtful. Computers speed up the process of analyzing information. Sony and Panasonic have marketed a variable speech-control cassette tape-recorder that allows the human voice to be speeded up without sounding like a chipmunk. More than 1 million people have already become speed-listeners.

Americans also substitute quicker activities for more time-consuming ones. The Nautilus machine can replace the more time-demanding exercise forms. People debate whether they really want to "invest the time" in learning ballroom dancing or organic gardening. Candidates for a number of jobs are shuttled from interview to interview, scheduled every minute.

Over the last few decades, Americans have become more proficient at devising and adapting to such behaviors. In multinational time-diary studies, Americans were more likely to record multiple activities in their diaries than respondents from other countries. As German sociologist Erwin Scheuch (1972, p. 77) observed about the landmark 12-nation time-diary study of 1965:

> A main problem in recording the use of time derives from the fact that many people during a large part of the day do more than one thing at one time. Our pretests suggest that the more a person is part of an industrial society with a very high density of communication, the more educated a person, the more likely he is to do a number of things simultaneously. While it is generally true that everyone—regardless of status or nationality—has merely the same 24 hours at his disposal, there is actually something like "time deepening" (to coin a term in analogy to capital deepening): if a person develops the ability to do several things simultaneously, he can crowd a greater number of activities into the same 24 hours.

It is difficult to remember that prior to television people sat by the radio and listened, doing nothing else. A child might sit, staring through the window at the darkening trees, hearing only the Lone Ranger's voice and the hooves of horses in the canyon. Today, radio is almost exclusively a secondary activity, something we listen to while doing something else. Television is beginning to go the same route as radio—at least one-quarter of television viewing is combined with other activities. Those who don't do something else while watching can "graze" on the video menu, surfing from channel to channel every few seconds.

We often found that the results of our own research and the research of others about time use can be described in terms of "the more . . . the more . . ." pattern initially described by Meyersohn (1968). Rather than playing either tennis or squash, those who do one are more likely to do the other as well. Rather than either working longer hours or participating in many active leisure pursuits, those who work longer hours show more active participation. Rather than joining one club or another, those who join one are more likely to join others. Rather than hold a part-time job or spend time studying, those who hold part-time jobs are often more likely to spend longer hours studying.

Although "the more . . . the more . . ." principle does not always hold true, especially for television, the activity that intrigued Meyersohn, the pattern is so pronounced that we must consider how people have different rates of "doing." Rather than thinking of time as a given—a rope tied around our activities—it is more like a mysterious rubber band that binds us but that can be stretched and stretched almost infinitely. When we stretch it, the stress created is often transferred to us. Those who use "time-deepening" techniques keep stretching that rubber band to see where the breaking point is.

Many Americans, it appears, have developed the desire and the capacity to live more intensely. In doing so, however, there have been some unanticipated consequences. As the historian Zeldin (1994) observed:

> The wish to live as intensely as possible has subjected humans to the same dilemma as the waterflea, which lives 108 days at 8 degrees Centigrade, but only twenty-six days at 28 degrees, when its heartbeat is almost four times faster, though in either case its heart beats 15 million times in all. Technology has been a rapid heartbeat, compressing housework, travel, entertainment, squeezing more and more into the allotted span. Nobody expected that it would create the feeling that life moves too fast.

Life, however, is moving faster than many Americans would like. Speeding up the pace of life, of history, and of our perception of reality can be a dangerous thing. Things that go faster and faster have less margin for error. If we are flying blind at mach speed, we should know where we are going.

# Interpreting the Time Famine

# 3

> In one heartbeat one could traverse the
> universe.
>
> —Edward Harrison, physicist

How are we to interpret this modern form of time starvation, in which Americans never seem to have the time they need? Certainly, scientific management was not the only factor responsible for the speeding up of life. We must also look to shifts in people's values, as the economy, society, and technology change. One place to start is with changes in assumptions about life made by the Baby Boom generation, those born in the United States between 1946 and 1964.

Baby Boomers were the Americans most affected by the period of optimism that followed World War II. That period saw the gradual development of the idea that progress and the increases in standard of living were infinite. As the United States rose to the position of the world's greatest economic power after the war, Americans began to believe in infinitely expanding economic opportunity. Consumption of goods came to be thought of in open-ended terms—that is, with no ceiling on what could be purchased and owned. Mobility was infinitely upward. What emerged was a "psychology of entitlement," in which such increasing levels of consumption were seen as more or less automatic—and something the system owed the individual (Samuelson, 1995).

As economist John Kenneth Galbraith (1984) observed, the real income of employed American workers was close to the highest on record for the United States in 1939, as well as the highest of any nation in the world. It doubled in the next quarter-century. If that 1939 income level were considered a terminal objective, then enough income was generated to cut work effort in half over the next 25 years. But advertising, easy credit, and rising expectations caused Americans to want more and more things in the short term. The concept "enough" disappeared.

Gradually, this mentality shifted to the consumption of experiences—just as things could be consumed in infinitely increasing progression, so could experiences. Paralleling the insatiable desire to "have" was people's desire to "do." Open-ended consumption of experiences brought into question the very notion of leisure activity as "voluntary." "Voluntary" implies that there is a choice among many alternatives. Such a choice would mean, in effect, that you willingly gave up several other alternatives in order to undertake the most satisfying one. In short, pleasure involved sacrifice.

Today, however, time-deepening fools people into thinking they can avoid sacrificing one activity for another. We seek instead to do it all and see it all, and to do it and see it now. In effect, time has become a commodity, and time viewed as a commodity seems to have made people's lives shorter and less tranquil. The experience of life is increasingly cataloged in terms of a patternless checklist of having "been there, done that."

Parallel to the commodification of experiences was a shift in how individuals define who they are. Many Americans have become virtual walking résumés, defining themselves only by what they do. They depend not so much on their "ascribed" statuses—the status they were born with and did nothing to achieve (such as gender, ethnic heritage, religion)—to convey who they are, and more on their "achieved" statuses, which are based on accomplishments (such as Director of Marketing, Black Belt in karate, wine connoisseur). The existential belief that people are born without a fixed nature and literally create who they are through authenticating acts is increasingly common. From such a perspective, the line between free time and work is largely irrelevant—to do nothing is to be nothing, and both work and free-time activity are important in defining who we are. It is little wonder that the preparation of résumés has become a science and that such résumés now often include information about people's free-time activities as well as their work activities.

## Time and Efficiency

Advances in technology have also contributed to the speedup of life with blind reliance on efficiency. Efficiency—doing or producing more in less time with less expenditure of resources and personnel—is an open-ended and illusive concept. One can always become more efficient. Technology can always find ways to do things more quickly and cheaper.

If scientific management reshaped Americans' notions of time, so did the computer. An estimated one-half of the American labor force now uses electronic computer terminal equipment. The primary time-measure of the computer, a nanosecond (one billionth of a second) is beyond our ability to comprehend. As Rifkin (1987) points out, the development of the computer represented the complete abstraction of time and its separation, not only from the rhythm of nature but also from human experience. No wonder those who live with computer workers cite arguments about time as a major source of conflict.

Thus, the computer culture has an impact on everyday life, and especially on leisure activities. "Efficiency" has never been a friend of leisure, since "leisure" historically has meant behavior undertaken without reference to time. In the ancient Greek notion of leisure, contemplation was an ideal. Later, "leisure" was thought of as "pastimes," but one cannot "pass" the time if efficiency is the primary goal. One can only "spend," "invest," and "save" it, or one will surely "lose" it. While leisure activity has traditionally been slow-paced and luxuriating in time, the cult of efficiency has reshaped the free time of Americans in fundamental ways. In this postmodern era, all human actions are becoming means to some other end—that is, are instrumental behaviors. We walk for fitness, play golf for contacts, and read to improve one's mind. Passing the time in activities that are pleasurable in and of themselves is almost a foreign notion. Efficiency rules both at work and at leisure. As Walter Kerr's book title (1962) put it 35 years ago, Americans are experiencing a "decline of pleasure."

## The Speedup of Change

The pace of life has not only speeded up due to people's adjustment to technological change, it has also become faster just because of simple demographic trends. Almost one-third of the U.S. population, the Baby Boom generation, is between the ages of 32 and 50. This is an unprecedented situation, brought on by the huge increase in marriage and births after the end of World War II. It can be argued that the present Baby Boom generation was historically the most harried in that so many marriages took place, careers were launched and pursued, babies were born and raised, houses were purchased, and debt was incurred.

The unprecedented bulge in the population pipeline contributed mightily to the frantic pace of life. As Americans get older, the pace of life is likely to decrease. A mere 20 years from now, almost one-third of the population will be between the ages of 50 and 68. Life may get slower, even for young people, because the desires of the older, slower-paced people are likely to be considered first, as the society reshapes itself to meet their needs.

In contrast, American society is characterized by a rate of change that is unprecedented. As the population of the world doubles during the next 50 years, Americans will have to stop living off their environmental "capital" and start living on the "interest." According to leading scientists Robert Ornstein and Paul Erlich (1989), the normal pace of cultural evolution is simply too slow to deal with today's dilemmas, with which our biology and history have left us unprepared to address. Problems of global warming, AIDS, and the rapid depletion of animal species increase the sense of urgency to respond quickly.

Such changes add new costs to American society, as sociologist Daniel Bell (1976) observed. There are new costs of information. People must learn more—how to use a microcomputer, for instance, or how to find substitutes for fossil fuels. There are new costs of coordination, as people perpetually reorganize to deal with the conditions and problems of change, from bilingual education to global birth control to radon detection to the collapse of the Soviet Union. These changes make us think of the world as a bomb with a lit fuse. Time is short.

How are we to judge the impact of this massive speedup of life? In one sense, it means that Americans can experience more than any generation in history. They can do more, see more, travel more. The repertoire of experiences for people of means can be enhanced almost indefinitely. Some people appear to thrive on such speeded-up ways of life. For many, however, the benefits are beginning to be outweighed by the costs. People who always feel rushed, for instance, according to our recent nationwide survey, rate their health and life satisfaction lower than whose who feel less rushed. The stress that accompanies such speeded-up styles of life is a major cause of early death. Levine (1984) showed that the faster the pace of life in a city, the higher its rate of coronary heart disease.

Aside from health problems, however, time-deepening often means that people seek to "take" from activity rather than totally "giving" themselves to it. Research by psychologist Mihalyi Csikszentmihalyi (1991) demonstrates that people are deeply refreshed by activities of either a work nature or a leisure nature, which he terms "flow." In flow experiences, which may be as diverse as playing the guitar or performing surgery, the challenge presented by the activity, and the skills of the individual, are closely aligned. When skill exceeds challenge, it produces boredom. When challenge exceeds skill, the result is anxiety.

When the challenge and the skill level of the participant are in balance, however, individuals may totally give themselves to the activity. Flow is more likely to occur in activities where the participant receives feedback from his or her actions, and where there are some rules and regularities that let the individual concentrate on doing the activity rather than on figuring out what is permissible or appropriate. In such cases, there is a constriction of attention to the activity at hand, a tendency for the individual to act with great assurance, and, most telling, a loss of consciousness of *time* itself. For once, time becomes irrelevant.

In a time-famine society, on the other hand, people rarely lose themselves in such activity. The deep refreshment that accompanies letting yourself go, temporarily losing sense of time and self, is almost never experienced. While people in postmodern society seem to do almost everything as a means to an end, flow experience is its own justification. It has been described as "being on automatic pilot" or "being in the zone."

To achieve flow experience requires discipline, the acquisition of skills, and the acceptance of challenges. One must show patience if one is to play Chopin, grow outstanding orchids, or learn to craft furniture. As the pace of life increases, Americans are becoming more likely to avoid activities that require patience, learning, discipline, and total commitment. Instead, they choose activities and styles of participation that lend themselves to their hurried lives and to the endless parade of new technology. People are content to learn to play the stereo, not the piano.

In a sense, as we shall see in succeeding chapters, American society today is characterized by a great gap between interior and exterior worlds. In the exterior world, overall hours of work are declining, and people spend much of their free time in passive ways. In our interior world, however, the operative American prayer might contain only one word: "more." People are constantly asking: What's next? For many, therefore, the benefits of additional free time are being lost as people rush at the world again and again.

## From Tempo to Duration

Time has the qualities of both tempo and duration, akin to velocity and mass of moving objects. People may therefore believe they are working longer if they are working "harder" or at a faster tempo, or both. It is one thing to report on one's activities, but another to report on overall perceptions. In contrast to our time-diary data, we thus find widespread evidence that Americans perceive that they are running out of time because the pace of life is speeding up (see Chapter 16). For example, in a 1992 national survey we conducted, 38 percent of respondents said they had less free time than they had five years ago. Also, more than one out of three "always" felt rushed. In other surveys concerning leisure behavior, lack of time is generally mentioned more than any other factor (including lack of money) that inhibits participation in desired leisure activities.

Such a speedup does not necessarily mean that Americans are working longer or that the time people spend on activities has changed. Indeed, our 1992 survey shows that, while we might assume work obligations are to blame for the hectic pace of life, one-quarter of Americans blamed leisure activities for making them feel rushed. In addition, 38 percent blamed both work and leisure; only 36 percent blamed it on work exclusively (Godbey and Graefe, 1993a). What seems to have changed is that the time conditions under which people's daily activities take place are rather different. Speed and brevity are more widely admired, whether in serving food, in the length of magazine articles, or in conversation.

As the pace of life has speeded up, there has been a natural tendency to assume that other time elements have been reshaped as well. Primary among these assumptions is the notion that hours of work (duration) are increasing and that those who feel most rushed must work the longest hours.

## The Assumption of Longer Work Hours

In her recent book *The Overworked American* (1991), economist Juliet Schor made the most widely noted argument that Americans are working longer, arguing that the average employed person worked, on average, an additional 163 hours a year in 1987, compared with 1969:

> The breakdown for men and women shows lengthening hours for both groups, but there is a "gender gap" in the size of the increase. Men are working nearly one hundred (98) more hours per year, or two and a half extra weeks. Women are doing about three hundred (305) additional hours, which translates to seven and a half weeks, or 38 added days of work each year. The research shows that hours of work have risen across a wide spectrum of Americans and in all income categories—low, middle, and high. The increase is common to a variety of family patterns—people with and without children, those who are married, and those who are not. And it has been general across industries and, most probably, occupations. (P. 29)

The reasons for such changes, Schor suggests, are tied to the endless cycle of work-and-spend produced by industrial capitalism. To be more specific, the "golden age" of the 1950s and 1960s came to an end with the oil price increases, more international competition, a slowdown in productivity growth, and sluggish demand. As hourly rates of pay dropped to accompany such changes, the "culture of resistance" to longer hours declined, resulting in people working longer hours, having less vacation time, and feeling the time squeeze at home.

The central role of a consumer culture in speeding up life and/or limiting free time is a theme that had been advanced earlier by De Grazia (1962), Galbraith (1984), Linder (1970), Cross (1993), and many others. Americans have been socialized into endless material wants, production, and efficiency as ideals both on and off the job. Ease and abundance, rather than tranquillity, have become the ideals of Americans, and the production and consumption of goods have become ends in themselves, not merely means to an end. Shopping is done not just to acquire specific needed items but as a worthwhile process in and of itself. Such arguments have proven enticing to the American public.

However, as we demonstrate in the following chapters, these results are *not* supported by diary data. In constructing her arguments, Schor uses our time-diary data only for 1975, and then mixes those data with time-estimate data—a step we question in Chapter 5. She does not use our 1965 time-diary data—the major benchmark year for our analyses—because rural residents (who don't differ much from urban Americans in their uses of time) were excluded and because of other sampling issues (which we have handled by poststratification and weighting). She also does not take into account our time-diary data and published articles from the 1985 study, relying instead on regression estimates from 1975 data on housework that do not reflect the surprising changes in actual diary housework times we have found since 1965. Finally, Schor averages government data both on work hours and on work-weeks that show increased hours of work, which were not evident to earlier analysts of these data, such as Hedges (1992) of the Bureau of Labor Statistics (BLS) and Owen (1989). For example, there may be no need to weight the BLS workweek data by weeks per year because these data are already collected across the entire year. Moreover, we find serious problems with these BLS work-time estimate data (see Chapter 5), including their failure to show the same trends as the BLS figures collected from organization pay-rolls. Thus, our results and conclusions about trends in hours spent at work are notably different from Schor's.

Like many analysts, Schor also bases her arguments on data from well-publicized 1988 Harris Poll findings that hours of work for Americans had increased as free time declined by 30 percent since 1972. More careful re-analysis of these data by Hamilton (1991), however, shows how these "trends" could be accounted for by changes in Harris's question wording, concluding that:

> There was no dramatic increase in work between 1973 and 1985, nor was there a dramatic decrease in leisure. . . . The Harris workweek "finding" appears to reflect changes in the methods used rather than any real change. The same conclusion appears justified with regard to his finding about free time. (Pp. 354–55)

Arguments similar to Schor's have been proposed by historians Gary Cross (1993) and Benjamin Hunnicutt (1988). Cross argues that in the 1920s and 1930s advanced Western societies chose consumerism rather than more leisure. Life was built around the purchase and use of an ever-expanding array of material goods, even if doing so kept paid work at the center of life. While in 1920 it appeared that mass production would produce not only endless goods but also increased time free from labor, a cultural and institutional ideology of "work and spend" emerged, largely supported by working families.

Cross argues that consumerism is not an inevitable stage in industrial development, but rather a choice, even if that choice negates gains in free time. This follows Riesman's (1958) argument that America was already a culture that felt uncomfortable with leisure and didn't know what to do with it. According to Cross:

> The decline of political and ideological alternatives parallel personal frustration at the absorption of life with work and consumption. What is clearly missing is an understanding of the possibilities of the democratization of leisure. By this, I mean two things: a balance of work with time free from economic obligation and forms of leisure that provide the widest possible choice, access, and participation. I do not suggest that time totally liberated from work is either possible or desirable; nor do I argue that leisure completely beyond the market is even conceivable in an efficient economy (even though public, as opposed to commercial, forms of leisure have an untested democratic potential). The essential irrationality that I am exploring is the relative insignificance of non-economic, self-initiated activities in a society that is laudably productive. (Cross, 1993, p. 3)

Such arguments assume that consumption and free time are antithetical and accept the conclusion that free time is declining.

Hunnicutt (1988) identifies the Great Depression as the pivotal event in shaping attitudes toward work and free time, because it brought increased and unwanted leisure to society in the guise of unemployment. Before the Depression, the solution to unemployment was seen as work reduction, but afterward it was seen as the creation of work to reemploy those who were idle due to technological advances. The new standard for success became full-time employment for everyone. Rather than viewing progress as the transcending of work, work became an end in itself—the supreme measure of progress. In making such arguments, Hunnicutt relies on the same Harris Poll data Schor relied on.

Much the same argument has been advanced by Witold Rybczynski (1991) in *Waiting for the Weekend*. Rybczynski initially credits commercialism with the idea and emergence of personal leisure—that is, free time in which the individual decided what to do rather than having it prescribed by society:

> The energy of entrepreneurs, assisted by advertising, was an impor-tant influence . . . on leisure in general. Hence a curious and appar-ently contradictory situation: not so much the commercialization of leisure as the discovery of leisure, thanks to commerce. Beginning in the eighteenth century with magazines, coffeehouses, and music rooms, and continuing throughout the nineteenth century, with pro-fessional sports and holiday travel, the modern idea of personal leisure emerged at the same time as the business of leisure. The first could not have happened without the second. (P. 121)

However, Rybczynski later assumes, as do the other authors already cited, that commercialism had become antithetical to leisure. Also, like other scholars who argue that free time is declining, he relies very little on studies concerning how people actually use their time. Commuting and decentral-ized suburban life—"which is to say American life" (p. 221) (actually, less than half of Americans live in suburbs)—with its reliance on the automo-bile, fax machines, and other devices that let people communicate faster and work in their homes—have decreased leisure time, Rybczynski argues.

In terms of actual hours of work and leisure, Rybczynski assumes that a compromise between the results of time-diary research and time-estimate research provides the best answer to the question of hours of work:

> Two recent surveys, by the University of Maryland and by Michigan's Survey Research Center, both suggest that Americans enjoy about thirty-nine hours of leisure time weekly. On the other hand, a 1988 [Harris] survey conducted by the National Research Center of the Arts came to a very different conclusion and found that Americans report a median 16.6 hours of leisure time each week. The truth is probably somewhere in between. (P. 217)

Finally, Rybczynski infers that the weekend, which emerged as a way of containing work, continues to be where our free time, almost exclusively, resides. Weekdays and weekends are viewed as polar opposites in regard to leisure: "We pass weekly from one to the other—from the mundane, commu-nal, increasingly impersonal, increasingly demanding, increasingly bureaucratic world of work to the reflective, private, controllable, consoling world of leisure" (p. 234). In spite of this contention, we shall show that the majority of people's free time occurs during weekdays, not during the weekend (see Chapter 8). While they may feel that their only free time occurs on the weekend, this is not really what they report in their time diaries.

## The Assumption That Women Work Longer Hours

A major corollary to the argument that Americans are working longer hours is that women work significantly longer hours than men do. There is, according to Berkeley sociologist Arlie Hochschild (1989), a "leisure gap" between men and women. Hochschild's own research was based on in-depth interviews with 50 couples, starting with "artisans, students and professionals in Berkeley, California," and grew to include 50 working couples who worked full-time jobs and were raising children under the age of 6. They were identified by sending questionnaires to a large, urban manufacturing company.

Hochschild's conclusions are limited by the small sample size and their geographic/lifestyle peculiarities; married couples with young children who both work full-time are an extremely small fraction of the American public, and Northern California is often found to be out of step with mainstream America. For instance, less than one out of five women with two or more young children works "full-time." Thus, the results may provide little basis for generalizing to the larger public, despite the careful and insightful manner in which they were collected. At the same time, if liberating trends are not happening in Northern California, where are they to be found? Hochschild did briefly consider some aspects of time in her arguments:

> But I began with the measurable issue of time. Adding together the time it takes to do a paid job and to do housework and child care, I averaged estimates from the major studies on time done in the 1960s and 1970s, and discovered that women worked roughly fifteen hours longer each week than men. Over a year, they worked an extra month of twenty-four hour days a year. Over a dozen years it was an extra year of twenty-four hour days. More women without children spend much more time than men on housework: with children, they devote more time to both housework and child care. Just as there is a wage gap between men and women in the workplace, there is a "leisure

gap" between them at home. Most women work one shift at the office or factory and a "second shift" at home. (Hochschild, 1989)

At the same time, Hochschild largely ignores our time-diary studies. Only in the appendix does she acknowledge that

> between 1965 and 1975 Robinson and his co-workers found the leisure gap between men and women had virtually disappeared. Men were doing more housework and child care. Women were doing less, and putting in four to five hours less on the job as well. Rather than re-negotiating roles with their husbands, these wives pursued a strategy of cutting back at home and at work. (Pp. 272–73)

Such findings are dismissed as being unrepresentative: "So detailed and repeated were the questions in this study that about a quarter of the people dropped out of it—among them, presumably, the busiest. Ironically, the women most burdened by the very crunch the researchers were investigating probably didn't have time to fill out such a lengthy questionnaire" (p. 273). Arguments like these are not consistent with our experiences and reflect little familiarity with our time-diary data or with survey research in general. Our respondents do not fill out questionnaires, and very few drop out once the diary is begun: an overall 25 percent nonresponse rate (not all of which is due to dropping out) is not unusual for academic surveys and is less than half that found in Harris and most other commercial surveys that we critique in this book. Moreover, busy people are more likely to participate in time-diary surveys, not less likely (see Chapters 4 and 18); nor do we find a leisure gap by gender in 1965, or in subsequent years (see Chapter 7).

The more critical issue for Hochschild may be not the alleged "leisure gap" but rather the difference between men and women in part-time work: "Even if all women could iron out the leisure gap by working part-time, is part-time work a solution if it's just for women?" (p. 273). This division, she argues, makes women more vulnerable in an era in which half of marriages end in divorce: "A better solution might be to share the part-time option or alternate part-time phases of each spouse's work life" (p. 273).

While such solutions have considerable merit, they are not solutions to a gap in free time, but they are solutions to inequalities in other resources, such as income, power, or the comparative value of paid work versus housework. As we show in Chapter 6, American men and women, as in most

Western countries, seem virtually equal in the productive time they have put in.

## Time Perceived and Time Spent

Thus, there seems to be considerable evidence that Americans regard themselves as more rushed than previously and that numerous factors may have contributed to this speedup. But with what have people become so busy? Does a more speeded-up style of life indicate changes in use of time, or merely changes in attitudes toward time? It reminds us of the dimensions of time Taylor studied and sought to control in his studies that led to scientific management: sequence, duration, schedule, rhythm, synchronization, and time perspective.

Much of the argument for increased working hours has received a sympathetic response both from social observers and from the public at large because of problems related to changes in attitudes toward time. This applies as well to synchronization, particularly for working married couples with young children trying to handle conflicting time demands. Some of these problems, as Schor and others observed, could be attributed to an economy that has lost its way. And as Schor correctly observes, too little of people's free time is bundled in the form of true vacation time, time in which they may literally re-create.

Our speeded-up pace of life and open-ended economy are real problems, but the consequences of such problems have been mistakenly assumed to include fewer overall hours of free time and more hours of work. One can still feel quite rushed and stressed while working comparatively few hours, as undergraduate university students often tell us. Similarly, although the time-measurement problems of women, and men, in regard to housework and child care, paid work, and other obligated activity are real, we shall see in coming chapters that such problems do not mean that women work longer hours than men or that they have less free time. While Americans have fewer vacation days than their European counterparts, we know of no solid evidence that suggests that vacation days are on the decline.

In explaining time use and attitudes toward time, the arguments of psychologist Kenneth Gergen (1991) are more persuasive and enlightening. Gergen does not examine time per se, but rather other perceptual characteristics that people have adopted in today's "postmodern" society. Instead of developing a permanent sense of self, individuals in postmodern society find that their sense of self is continually reshaped by an increasingly diverse and expanding chorus of voices with whom they interact. As new technologies proliferate and contacts with other people expand, individuals develop more short-term strategies to deal with the unique problems that result. Thus, Gergen sees the problem of modern life more in the realm of the *perception of what is necessary* than in the realm of what to do with the time available.

In this book we argue that our time-diary data provide similar glimpses into the increasingly fragmented lives of individuals, perhaps in response to an expanding perception of what is necessary. Such perceptions have made people less able to accurately judge how they use their time as they assume more diverse role responsibilities with more spontaneous daily schedules.

We continue to be enormously impressed by the pioneering work of Sebastian De Grazia in his classic *Of Time, Work, and Leisure* (1962). Although strident, preachy, and sexist by today's standards, De Grazia's observations about the overriding dominance of work and the tyranny of the clock in American life seem as apt in the 1990s as thirty-five years ago. His crucial distinction between leisure and free time still seems lost on American culture, and his leisure ideal offers a challenge that our culture seems incapable of addressing, much less meeting. His observation that "TV has the evening whipped into shape" seems most prophetic, although we suspect that even he would be surprised by the extent to which TV has dominated free time in our time diaries.

Finally, our conclusions are in keeping with the recent arguments of media economist Robert Samuelson (1995) and political scientist Robert Putnam (1995b). It is at heart a basically *optimistic* message: America continues to make progress in regard to increasing free time, just as Samuelson says it does in terms of income. Incomes, on average, are increasing rather than decreasing, and the poverty rate has declined by almost 25 percent since 1945. If, as Putnam argues, the "social capital" of Americans is eroding, as people spend more of their free time with television, it is largely because of the choices Americans have made about their free time. People are doing better than they think they are, but their perceptions of what is happening are increasingly flawed. It may be difficult to find or to appreciate, but *there is time for life*.

**4**

# Measuring How People Spend Time

> You have to accept the idea that subjective time with its emphasis on the now has no objective meaning. . . . The distinction between past, present and future is only an illusion, however persistent.
>
> —Albert Einstein

If time has become such a scarce resource for millions of Americans, how they "spend" it or "use" it becomes a question of central importance—and a surprisingly difficult one to answer. How many hours were you in the office last week? How much television do you watch? How often do you work out? Are you spending "quality time" with the kids?

All these questions have a subjective element, and the answers reflect one's "lifestyle" and self-image. There is a good deal of room for self-service, and thus error, in our estimates. (*Of course* I work long hours, spend lots of time with my kids, spend only a few hours with television, and exercise a lot!)

At first glance, the matter of answering these time-estimate questions may seem straightforward. After all, the modern concept of time envisions time as linear, a simple line with a beginning and an end, clearly ticked off in uniform seconds, minutes, and hours. Because time is a universal medium by which our activities are bound together, it should be a simple task to measure how people spend their time.

But time expenditure is actually an extraordinarily complex concept to estimate accurately. Recalling details about time spent involves complicated calculations, and American culture judges people by what they do. People are often called on to construct answers that put them in a positive light.

Chase and Godbey (1983), for instance, asked members of specific swimming and tennis clubs in State College, Pennsylvania, how many times they had used the club during the last 12 months. Their responses were then checked against the sign-in system each club had. These sign-in systems seemed highly accurate, because to get into the locker rooms or onto the courts club members were required to sign their names in a book or on a card used to reserve a court.

In both cases, almost half of all respondents overestimated the actual number of times they participated by more than 100 percent! Such inaccuracies probably reflect both the difficulty with recall and the fact that respondents wanted to believe they played more tennis or swam more frequently than they had, since doing so would not only make them healthier, it would be getting their money's worth at the club.

There is a rich body of historical data from national samples that relies solely on the time-estimate approach—on time spent working (from the U.S. Bureau of Labor Statistics), doing volunteer work (from ACTION, 1975), traveling (from the U.S. Department of Transportation), and watching television (Roper Organization, General Social Survey). A central question concerning such research is whether the answer will be accurate. There is mounting evidence that it won't be.

## Problems with Time Estimates

The various steps survey respondents take in answering time-estimate questions cause problems. Asking someone "How many hours do you work?" or "How many hours do you watch TV?" assumes that each respondent:

- Interprets "work" or "TV" the same way.
- Separates the most important activity (the primary activity) from other activities that are taking place simultaneously but are ancillary or less important (secondary activities).
- Undertakes the work of searching memory for all episodes of work or television yesterday or the last week.
- Is able to properly add up all the episode lengths across the day yesterday or across days in the last week.
- Feels comfortable describing this duration to an interviewer when it may not be a typical day or week.
- Avoids reverting to social norms, stereotypes, or images of themselves about how much a "normal" person ought to work, like the normal 40-hour workweek.

Any of these obstacles may be problematic in obtaining completely accurate responses regarding time use. This is particularly true in the survey context, in which respondents are expected to provide on-the-spot answers in a few seconds. What seems at first to be a simple estimate task turns out to involve several steps that are quite difficult to perform, even for a respondent with regular and clear work hours (or viewing patterns) and a repetitive daily routine.

One consequence is that, when asked to provide daily and weekly estimates of several activities, survey respondents give estimates that add up to considerably more than the 168 hours of time each of us has available each week. In the studies of Verbrugge and Gruber-Baldine (1993), average estimated weekly times totaled 187 hours, and their list of activities did not include time for church-going, shopping for durable goods or professional services, and adult education. In Hawes et al.'s (1975) national survey, estimated weekly activities averaged at more than 230 hours; and in our own studies of college students, the totals reached more than 250 hours. Thus, the estimate approach has a built-in bias toward overreporting, much as described in the analysis of hours at work in Chapter 5 and the analysis of housework in Chapter 6.

Basically, time-estimate questions encounter the same types of problems that arise from expecting respondents in surveys to answer almost any "simple" question put to them. Survey researchers have fallen into the trap of accepting answers from respondents on almost any type of question. Often, these answers provide quite misleading results, as in the case of the survey question "Where do you get most of your information?" to which most respondents say "TV." However, when we conducted more-detailed studies of actual information acquisition, television viewers turned out to be *less* likely than users of other media to have picked up news information (Robinson and Levy, 1986). The simple question, when broken into the constituent information expected of respondents, is beyond the ability of most respondents to answer accurately.

Because of such difficulties, the time-diary studies reported in this book take a "micro-behavioral" approach to such questions, breaking each part of the question into easier and more answerable components of that micro-level behavior. Rather than ask about a vague reference period, such as a week, an "average" week, or a "typical" day, respondents are asked specifically about "yesterday," the complete day freshest in their memory.

As an example, take this popular survey question: "How many hours of TV do you watch on an average day?" The usual average estimate is about 3 hours a day. In the 1970s, when we also asked "How many hours of TV did you watch yesterday?" and looked at all days of the week, the average was closer to 2.5 hours for the average day. The major reason for this response difference in the two questions was that far more respondents reported zero hours "yesterday" than on an average day, indicating that respondents translated the "average day" question into "the average day *that you watch TV*." The "average" day thus became one in which television is viewed, not the occasional day when none was seen. It is these subtle respondent strategies that subvert the ability to provide the accurate estimates that are expected of them—and why we put more faith in the micro-behavioral method of the time diary.

To illustrate the problems with time-estimate data, suppose we ask you on the spot to respond to this question, which government surveys, such as the Current Population Survey of the U.S. Census Bureau, regularly ask the public:

> How many hours did you work last week?
> Your answer: ___ hours.

Most survey respondents come up with an answer in 3 to 10 seconds, although an appropriately thoughtful answer would require at least three times as much response time (see Chapter 5).

There is no guarantee, then, that because the U.S. government collects data about time use it must be correct. Despite the reliance of the federal government on statistics related to time (e.g., years of life expectancy, weeks of work), no government agency is responsible for measuring work time accurately, raising serious questions concerning the productivity of the American worker. Thus, the most commonly quoted sources of information about how long Americans work may be, quite simply, inaccurate.

The tendency to assume we spend a good deal of time behaving admirably and little time with less admirable behavior is strong. At many universities, professors are asked to report their hours of work per week in various categories such as teaching, preparation for teaching, and funded research. The information is then acted on by university administrators and often the state government. At Penn State University, the average hours reportedly worked is 52 hours a week, and almost no professor reports working less than 25 hours a week. A few, however, report working longer than 90 hours a week. Working 90 hours a week would entail working from 7:00 a.m. to 10:00 p.m. six days a week with no breaks for food, the bathroom, or anything else. Then again, how many professors can be expected to recall accurately how long they worked during the last seven days precisely using such arbitrary and vague categories?

## Alternatives to Time Estimates and Time Diaries

Several methods of estimating time durations are likely to produce more accurate estimates than the estimate approach, because, like the time diary, they also are sensitive to the equal property of time across individuals—the recognition that at any instant of time "everyone has to be somewhere," with only one activity or set of activities occurring at a given time. These alternative methods include:

1. The Experience Sampling Method (ESM) of Csikszentmihalyi (1991), in which respondents write down what they are doing when an electronic beeper goes off at random points during the day.
2. Direct observation studies, such as those by anthropologists in Third World countries in which observers rather than respondents keep time records of what natives in a particular society do across the day (McSweeney, 1980). In the same way, we have recently employed American college students to "shadow" a person they know across the day, and then verified later retrospective diary reports against those observations. The classic study of this type is Barker and Wright's (1948) observation of One Boy's Day, which cataloged more than 500 separate activities during that one day.

3. Electronic trackers, such as those used by parole officers to verify whether those out on parole stay within certain locations. More recently, media rating services have developed electronic badges for TV and radio audience members to wear that record when they are within receiving range of an operating television or radio.
4. On-site verification, in which an observer can count the number of people at a particular site (for example, a church, theater, or school) at a particular time, and then project that to the larger population under study (Chapin, 1974; Barker and Barker, 1961; Hadaway et al., 1993).
5. Telephone coincidental studies, in which respondents report what they were doing when the telephone rang. Such studies need to employ careful procedures to appropriately weight the households in which no one was home when the telephone rang, or what the other people in the household were doing when it rang; otherwise, one can generalize only to the population that is both at home and willing to pick up the phone.
6. The random-hour technique, in which respondents report on a smaller segment of the day and not on the full day. By so reducing the descriptive task, respondents can focus more carefully on these smaller periods of behavior.

Each of these techniques requires minimal memory work or recall on the part of the respondent, and as a result is usually considered to provide more "objective" measures of what people do. At the same time, only the shadow technique covers a very long period of time or can give much dynamic insight into where these various activities fit into the overall lifestyles of the individuals being observed.

To some extent, that limitation applies to our one-day diary approach as well. People may be involved in an unusual day as far as their normal activities are concerned. Thus, nearly 40 percent of respondents in our first national time-diary study claimed that our diary day was unusual in some way for them.

One way around this problem is to have respondents keep week-long diaries instead, an approach that has been used in national studies in England and Holland. The problem is one of cooperation rates, however, with the cooperation rate in both countries being only about 40 percent. At the same time, Gershuny and his colleagues (1986) in England report that those who kept diaries differed little from those who did not, in terms of their estimates of how they spent time.

For American samples, the counterintuitive result has been that respondents who agree to cooperate in single-day diary studies are more likely to lead highly active lives than those who refuse. Thus, respondents in the 1975 national survey who agreed to be reinterviewed three months after the initial data collection were more likely to report longer work and housework times in their initial diaries and also less likely to watch television and to sleep.

That result was replicated in the 1985 study, even though the design of the study was different in that respondents were first interviewed by telephone, then mailed another diary to keep on one day for the following week and finally asked to return the completed diary. Again, those who returned the diaries (for a cash reward) differed from those who did not return them, in terms of their busier lifestyles. These results are consistent with "the more, the more" principle of time allocation, in which already busy people are more likely to participate in a given activity (except television) than those who are initially less active. Such results also challenge Hochschild's (1989) assumption that busier women are underrepresented in time-diary studies.

## Features of the Time Diary

The measurement logic behind this approach to time studies follows from that employed in the most extensive and well-known diary study: the Multinational Time Budget Study of Szalai et al. (1972). In that study, roughly 2,000 respondents from each of 12 different counties kept a diary account for a single day. The same diary procedures and activity codes were employed in each country in 1965. Respondents were chosen in such a way that each day of the week was equally represented. That equal-day allocation was very important for several European countries in the study, because many workers in those countries were on 5-1/2-to-6-workday schedules, so that their weekend activities were very different from those in the United States.

Figure 5 illustrates how the diary was filled out by one American respondent in these studies. This respondent was asleep at midnight as the new day began, and he woke up to do exercises at 5:45 A.M. He went to the bathroom and then got his bike out to take a 10-minute trip to the health club. Returning home at 7:10, he took a shower and got dressed until 7:45. After breakfast, he took the bus to work and worked from 8:45 until 1:00 p.m. He took off to buy a birthday present until 1:50, at which time he returned to work and ate lunch for 20 minutes. He then continued working until 4:45, at which time he took a bus home, arriving home at 5:40. Once home, he placed a marathon 2 hours and 20 minutes of phone calls and then went out

**Figure 5.** Sample Completed Time Diary

| Time Began (1) | Time Ended (2) | Duration in Minutes (3) | Activity (4) | Assigned Activity Code (5) | Location Code (6) |
|---|---|---|---|---|---|
| 0:00 (12 Midnight) | 5:45 AM | 345 | Sleeping at Night | 45 | 5 |
| 5:45 AM | 6:00 AM | 15 | Did Stretching Exercise | 80 | 5 |
| 6:00 AM | 6:05 AM | 5 | Went to Bathroom, Used Toilet | 40 | 4 |
| 6:05 AM | 6:10 AM | 5 | Went Out to Backyard to Get Bike | 89 | 11 |
| 6:10 AM | 6:20 AM | 10 | Traveling, Bicycling | 82 | 59 |
| 6:20 AM | 7:00 AM | 40 | Went to Health Club, Exercising | 80 | 31 |
| 7:00 AM | 7:10 AM | 10 | Traveling, Bicycling | 82 | 59 |
| 7:10 AM | 7:15 AM | 5 | Got Home and Put Bike Away | 89 | 11 |
| 7:15 AM | 7:35 AM | 20 | Took Shower | 40 | 4 |
| 7:35 AM | 7:45 AM | 10 | Got Dressed | 47 | 5 |
| 7:45 AM | 8:10 AM | 25 | Eating a Meal or Snack | 43 | 1 |
| 8:10 AM | 8:15 AM | 5 | Traveling, Walking | 9 | 53 |
| 8:15 AM | 8:16 AM | 1 | Waited at Bus Stop | 9 | 54 |
| 8:16 AM | 8:35 AM | 19 | Traveling, in Transit | 9 | 55 |
| 8:35 AM | 8:45 AM | 10 | Traveling, Walking | 9 | 53 |
| 8:45 AM | 13:00 PM | 255 | Working (at Main Job) | 1 | 21 |
| 13:00 PM | 13:10 PM | 10 | Traveling, Walking | 3 | 53 |
| 13:10 PM | 13:40 PM | 30 | Went Shopping for Birthday Gifts | 31 | 24 |
| 13:40 PM | 13:50 PM | 10 | Traveling, Walking | 3 | 53 |
| 13:50 PM | 14:10 PM | 20 | Went into Office Kitchen and Ate Lunch | 6 | 21 |
| 14:10 PM | 16:45 PM | 155 | Working (at Main Job) | 1 | 21 |
| 16:45 PM | 16:55 PM | 10 | Traveling, Walking | 9 | 53 |
| 16:55 PM | 17:00 PM | 5 | Waited for Bus | 9 | 54 |
| 17:00 PM | 17:35 PM | 35 | Traveling, in Transit | 9 | 55 |
| 17:35 PM | 17:40 PM | 5 | Traveling, Walking | 9 | 53 |
| 17:40 PM | 20:00 PM | 140 | Talked on Phone | 96 | 5 |
| 20:00 PM | 20:10 PM | 10 | Traveling, Walking | 49 | 53 |
| 20:10 PM | 22:00 PM | 110 | Eating a Meal or Snack | 44 | 28 |
| 22:00 PM | 22:10 PM | 10 | Traveling, Walking | 49 | 53 |
| 22:10 PM | 22:20 PM | 10 | Changed Clothes | 47 | 5 |
| 22:20 PM | 24:00 PM | 100 | Sleeping at Night | 45 | 5 |
| | Total in Minutes | 1,440 | | | |

Source: Wiley, Robinson, et al., 1991.

for supper. Returning home at 10:10, he got ready for bed and was asleep by 10:20, which is what he was doing as the day ended at midnight.

Some 31 separate activities were recorded, along with not only the duration but also the time each of these activities began and ended, and the codes describing the activity (for example, sleep = code 45; working = code 1; talking on the phone = code 96) and where it took place. Totaling activities across the day, we see that he spent 7.4 hours (445 = 345 + 100 minutes) sleeping, 6.8 hours (410 = 255 + 155 minutes) working, and 2.6 hours (155 minutes) eating meals. To calculate his free time during the day, the 15 minutes of exercise were added to the 60 minutes for the health club visit and the 140 minutes of telephone calls, to arrive at a total of 215 minutes, or 3.6 hours. While one might prefer to classify his health-related activities as personal care, or his shopping or meal out as free time, that is not consistent with the coding scheme described below. Nonetheless, any such recodings can be made subsequently within that coding scheme.

Time diaries and other methods of measuring time have to describe what people are doing, and the descriptions must be uniform enough that all human behavior can be collapsed into a manageable number of categories. This can be seen as artificial and arbitrary, because human behavior is potentially infinite in meaning and form. What you are doing is, ultimately, an existential question with endless political and ethical overtones.

The task of keeping the time diary, while presenting some recall difficulties, is fundamentally different from the task of making estimates. The diary keeper's task is to recall all of the day's activities in sequence in his or her own terms, not in the terms of the researcher. This procedure is similar to the way the day was structured chronologically for the respondent and to the way most people store their activities in and recall them from memory. Rather than having to consider a long time period, the respondent need only focus attention on a single day. Rather than working from some list of activities, the diary keeper simply describes the day's activities in his or her own words.

The diary procedure thus avoids most of the pitfalls of the estimate approach described above. There are still problems of memory, as when respondents have trouble piecing together a particular period during the day, but overall the task is rather clear both to the respondents and to the interviewers and proceeds with few structural problems once begun.

The diary technique presents respondents with a task that gives them a minimal opportunity to distort activities in order to present themselves in a particular light. Some respondents may want to portray themselves as hard workers or light television viewers, but in order to do so they must fabricate not only those activities but also the activities before and after them, making accounts of events later in the day more difficult. Besides, respondents can realize that this is only a one-day account and that on any given day they may work less or watch television more than usual. Moreover, respondents are not pressured to report an activity if they cannot recall it or do not want to report it.

Automatic procedures have now been built in to the diary recording procedures to ensure accurate reporting. Any time respondents report consecutive activities that involve different locations, they are reminded that some travel episode needs to be reported. Activity periods that last more than 2 hours automatically involve the probe "Were you doing anything else during that time, or were you (activity) for the entire time?" All periods across the day must be accounted for in order, so that the time-diary accounts total 1,440 minutes (see Figure 5).

In sum, the time diary is a micro-behavioral technique for collecting self-reports of an individual's daily behavior in an open-ended fashion on an activity-by-activity basis. Individual respondents keep or report these activity accounts for a short, manageable period, such as a day or a week—usually across the full 24 hours of a single day. In that way, the technique capitalizes on the most attractive measurement properties of the time variable, namely:

- All daily activity is potentially recorded (including activities that occur in the early morning hours, when most people may be asleep). Thus, the diary accounts are by definition complete across the 1,440 minutes of the day.
- All 1,440 minutes of the day are equally distributed across respondents, thereby preserving the "zero-sum" property of time that allows various "trade-offs" between activities to be examined—that is, if time on one activity increases, it must be zeroed out by decreases in some other activity.
- Respondents are allowed to use a time frame and an accounting variable that is maximally understandable to them and accessible to the way they probably store their daily events in memory.

The open-ended nature of activity reporting means that these activity reports are automatically geared to detecting new and unanticipated activities (for example, aerobic exercises; use of E-mail, VCRs, and new communications technologies), as well as capturing the full temporal context of how daily life is experienced (when did certain activities take place, what activities preceded or followed).

In these diary accounts, respondents report on each activity in which they engage across the full 24 hours of the day and record where they were and various other aspects of each activity. It is on the entries in the "primary activity" column of the diaries that attention in this book is largely focused.

## Earlier Diary Surveys

Before the 1985 national study, with 5,358 total respondents aged 12 and older, three national time-diary studies had been conducted using this general approach. These three studies and the organizations involved are:

- The Mutual Broadcasting Corporation 1954 study, in which more than 8,000 American adults aged 15 to 59 kept time diaries for a two-day period (more exact details are given in De Grazia, 1962). Unfortunately, only a few general data tables survive from this study for comparison with later studies, so we can review its results only briefly in this book. While most of these 1954 diary figures were surprisingly close to our 1965 results, the 1954 respondents reported less shopping and less away-from-home leisure time than the 1965 respondents—offset largely by more reading and more socializing in 1954; women reported less free time in our 1965 study, largely because of their increased paid work. (Robinson and Converse, 1972)
- The Survey Research Center, University of Michigan 1965 study, in which 1,244 adult respondents aged 18 to 64 kept a single-day diary of activities, mainly in the fall of that year. Respondents living in rural and nonemployed households were excluded (Robinson, 1977a). Supplementary data were collected from a community sample in Jackson, Michigan (n = 788). We make use only of the national part of the 1965–66 data, adjusting in later years for its focus on the urban and the employed.
- The 1975 Survey Research Center, University of Michigan, study, in which 1,519 adult respondents aged 18 and over kept diaries for a single day in the fall of that year (Robinson, 1976); in addition, diaries were obtained from 887 spouses of these designated respondents. These respondents became part of a panel, who were subsequently reinterviewed in the winter, spring, and summer months of 1976. About 1,500 of the original 2,406 respondents remained in this four-wave panel. Some 677 of these

respondents were reinterviewed in 1981, again across all four seasons of the year (Juster and Stafford, 1985). Because of the difference in activities between those who stayed or dropped out of the panel, we make use only of the original sample of 2,406 respondents and spouses interviewed in the fall of 1975.

## Methodology of the 1985 Americans' Use of Time Project

In the 1985 study conducted by the Survey Research Center at the University of Maryland, which is of major interest in this book, single-day diaries were collected from more than 5,300 respondents aged 12 and over. Unlike the 1965 and 1975 data reviewed in this book, these data were collected across the entire calendar year of 1985. This "Americans' Use of Time" study employed the same basic open-ended diary approach as the 1965 and 1975 national studies. An important innovation in the 1985 study was the explicit attempt made to spread the collection of diary days across the entire calendar year, from January through December 1985.

### The Mail-Back Sample

The data for the 1985 main (mail-back) study were collected from a sample of Americans who were first contacted by telephone using the random-digit-dial (RDD) method of selecting telephone numbers. All calls were made from the central telephone facility at the Survey Research Center of the University of Maryland at College Park.

Once a working telephone household was contacted, one respondent aged 18 or older in each household was selected at random. That person was given a brief (2- to 5-minute) orientation interview, followed by an invitation to participate in the diary/mail-out part of the study. If that respondent agreed, diaries were then mailed out for each member of the participating household aged 12 or over to complete for a particular day for the subsequent week.

Brief Call 2 and Call 3 interviews were made 4 to 6 days later to ensure that respondents had received the materials and understood how to complete them. After respondents had completed their time diaries, they then mailed all the completed forms back to the university for coding and analysis. Some 3,340 diaries from 997 households were returned using this mail-out procedure during the 12 months of 1985. It is the diaries obtained from adults aged 18 and over, however, that form the database for the analyses described in this book. Other 1985 data included parallel diary data from 808 additional respondents interviewed in a separate personal interview sample in the summer and fall of 1985, and from an additional 1,210 "yesterday" diaries obtained by telephone as part of the initial contact for the mail-back diaries.

## The Telephone Sample

The telephone sample consisted of the random sample of the population who were contacted in the first phase of the random-digit-dial sample. This consisted of the randomly selected adults (aged 18 or older) who responded to the first interview. Some 67 percent of respondents contacted by telephone, however, did complete a day-before diary over the telephone. This was the highest response rate for any of the three data collection modes.

## The Personal Sample

In addition to the 1985 mail-back and telephone diaries, a separate national sample of 808 diaries was collected by personal in-home interviews. Respondents in this sample followed much the same procedures for the initial telephone sample. One adult selected at random was to complete a retrospective diary from memory for the previous day. The interviewer then left diaries for all adult respondents in the household to complete for the following day.

The University of Maryland coders were extensively trained on the activity code category system and used the same complete set of coding conventions that had been developed by the Survey Research Center at the University of Michigan for its 1975 time-diary project. Each activity in the diary was coded descriptively as a separate block of 17 digits in length, which comprised the primary activity during the period (a three-digit code), the time the activity began and ended (each coded in 4-digit military time, for example, 8:00 A.M.. = 0800; 8:00 P.M. = 2000), location (1 digit), social partners (2 digits), and secondary activity (3 digits). The basic activity code categories are shown in Table 1, using the first two digits.

When this 17-digit entry for all activities in the diary was data-entered and computed, the totals were programmed into the machine to ensure that each day's diary entries added to exactly 1,440 minutes (24.0 hours). These "variable-field" data (that is, varying, depending on the number of activities

**Table 1.** Activity Codes for 1975 and 1985 National Studies (Based on Szalai et al., 1972)

| 00–49 Non-Free Time | 50–99 Free Time |
|---|---|

**00–49 Non-Free Time**

**00–09 Paid Work**
- 00 (not used)
- 01 Main job
- 02 Unemployment
- 03 (not used)
- 04 (not used)
- 05 Second job
- 06 Eating at work
- 07 Before/after work
- 08 Breaks
- 09 Travel to/from work

**10–19 Household Work**
- 10 Food preparation
- 11 Meal cleanup
- 12 Cleaning house
- 13 Outdoor cleaning
- 14 Clothes care
- 15 (not used)
- 16 Repairs (by R)
- 17 Plant, pet care
- 18 (not used)
- 19 Other household

**20–29 Child Care**
- 20 Baby care
- 21 Child care
- 22 Helping/teaching
- 23 Talking/reading
- 24 Indoor playing
- 25 Outdoor playing
- 26 Medical care—child
- 27 Other child care
- 28 (not used)
- 29 Travel/child care

**30–39 Obtaining Goods/Services**
- 30 Everyday shopping
- 31 Durable/house shop
- 32 Personal services
- 33 Medical appointments
- 34 Govt/financial services
- 35 Repair services
- 36 (not used)
- 37 Other services
- 38 Errands
- 39 Travel/goods and services

**40–49 Personal Needs and Care**
- 40 Washing, dressing, etc.
- 41 Medical care
- 42 Help and care
- 43 Meals at home
- 44 Meals out
- 45 Night sleep
- 46 Naps/day sleep
- 47 (not used)
- 48 NA activities
- 49 Travel/personal care

**50–99 Free Time**

**50–59 Educational**
- 50 Students' classes
- 51 Other classes
- 52 (not used)
- 53 (not used)
- 54 Homework
- 55 (not used)
- 56 Other education
- 57 (not used)
- 58 (not used)
- 59 Travel/education

**60–69 Organizational**
- 60 Professional/union
- 61 Special interest
- 62 Political/civic
- 63 Volunteer/helping
- 64 Religious groups
- 65 Religious practice
- 66 Fraternal
- 67 Child/youth/family
- 68 Other organizations
- 69 Travel/organizational

**70–70 Entertainment/Social**
- 70 Sports events
- 71 Entertainment
- 72 Movies
- 73 Theater
- 74 Museums
- 75 Visiting
- 76 Parties
- 77 Bars/lounges
- 78 Other social
- 79 Travel/social

**80–89 Recreation**
- 80 Active sports
- 81 Outdoor
- 82 Walking/hiking
- 83 Hobbies
- 84 Domestic crafts
- 85 Art
- 86 Music/drama/dance
- 87 Games
- 88 Other computer use
- 89 Travel/recreation

**90–99 Communications**
- 90 Radio
- 91 TV
- 92 Records/tapes
- 93 Read books
- 94 Magazines, etc.
- 95 Reading newspaper
- 96 Conversations
- 97 Writing
- 98 Think/relax
- 99 Travel/communication

Source: Americans' Use of Time Project, University of Maryland.

reported) were then processed by a special computer program that generated "fixed-field" compilations of diary time for each of the 94 activities across the day—that is, total daily minutes spent working, cooking, watching television, and so on, for that respondent for that day.

Further details on the 1985 study are given in Robinson and Bostrom (1994).

## Methodology of the 1975 Study

The 1975 study was based on data collected from a sample of Americans first interviewed in October–November 1975, as part of the 1975 fall omnibus study conducted by the University of Michigan's Institute for Social Research. It was designed to facilitate development of a fully articulated system of national economic and social accounts. Particular emphasis was placed on obtaining accurate estimates of yearly productive uses of time on a household basis for analysis using a microdata perspective (Juster and Stafford, 1985).

The respondents in the 1975 omnibus were chosen to form a representative sample of American adults 18 years of age and older living in the coterminous United States (excluding Alaska and Hawaii). As part of the time-use measurement effort, spouses of the respondents were interviewed too. The original respondents and their spouses were then reinterviewed three times during 1976 (in February, May, and September 1976), mainly by telephone. Only the first-wave personal-interview data (n = 2,406) are described in our analyses, because of the difference in activity patterns of those who stayed in this panel, compared with those who dropped out.

## Methodology of the 1965 Study

The 1965 study, also conducted by the University of Michigan, interviewed an urban, largely employed sample of more than 2,000 American adults aged 18–65 who kept complete diaries of their activities for a single day. Data were collected mainly between November 1 and December 15, 1965 (with the remainder collected in the spring of 1966). The sample was deliberately chosen to be an urban and employed group conforming to the guidelines of the multinational study of which it was a part (Szalai et al., 1972). Thus residents of non-SMSAs (areas with no city greater than 50,000 in population) were excluded, as well as residents of households in which no member

aged 18 to 65 was part of the labor force; full-time farmers were also excluded. Respondents were randomly assigned to fill out diaries on either a
weekday or a weekend.

Of the total sample, 1,244 adults were part of the national urban sample;
another 788 adults came from the city of Jackson, Michigan, and its suburbs.
Although showing basically the same patterns as the national study, the Jackson
data are not included in the national results reported here, in order to make
the trend comparisons more precise, but they are shown in Appendix A.

The field procedures involved the "tomorrow" approach—that is, the interviewer contacted the respondent and conducted a brief "warm-up" interview on the first day and left the diary for the respondent to enter the next
day's activities. The interviewer returned to the respondent's home on the
subsequent day (that is, the day after "tomorrow") to ensure that the diary
had been filled out correctly and to fill in any missing parts if it had not.

## Comparison of the Three Most Recent Studies

The 1965, 1975, and 1985 studies were all based on strict probability sampling methods across the nation. The major features of these national diary
studies are contrasted in Exhibit 1. Only the 1985 study was spread across

**Exhibit 1.**  Methodological Features of the National Time Diary Studies from the
Americans' Use of Time Project

|  | 1965 | 1975 | 1985 |
|---|---|---|---|
| Sponsor | Univ. of Mich. | Univ. of Mich. | Univ. of Md. |
| Sample size | 1,244 | 2,406 | 5,358 |
| Age range | 18–65 | 18+ | 12+ |
| Months | Oct.–Nov. | Oct.–Dec. | Jan.–Dec. |
| Mode/Response rate | Personal (72%) | Personal (72%) | Mail-back (3,340) (51%) |
|  |  |  | Telephone (1,210) (67%) Personal (808) (60%) |
| Diary type | Tomorrow (1,244); yesterday (130) | Yesterday (2,406) | Tomorrow (3,890); yesterday (1,468) |

SOURCE:  Americans' Use of Time Project.

the entire year. Moreover, the 1985 national data were mainly collected by prospective mail-back diaries, while the 1975 study employed the retrospective recall of activities done "yesterday." The 1965 and 1975 studies had somewhat higher overall response rates (72 percent and 72 percent), although not much higher than the telephone portion of the 1985 national study (67 percent). However, the 1985 study had more than twice the number of adult respondents over age 18 than the 1975 study (n = 4,939 vs. 2,406).

The 1985 national study had more spread across the year and across days of the week, while the 1975 study oversampled Sundays and undersampled Saturdays. All studies used open-end diary entries across the full 24 hours of a single day and the same basic code for diary activities—although the 1975 and 1985 studies employed more than twice as many activity codes, using an additional third digit appended to the code in Table 1.

In addition to these U.S. national studies and the studies from Jackson, Michigan (the overall results from which are in Appendix A), we also refer to two other recent diary studies from large representative samples. The first is the 1987–88 statewide study of California, in which 1,579 respondents aged 18 and older gave retrospective diary accounts of what they did "yesterday" (Wiley, Robinson, et al., 1991). The second was the 1986 national diary study conducted in Canada with 9,000 respondents (see Chapter 19). Like the 1985 University of Maryland study, both these studies were conducted by telephone and across the entire year. The comparative results are shown in Appendix B.

Three different modes of diary collection were used for methodological comparison in our 1985 U.S. national study: personal, mail-back, and telephone. As in earlier diary studies (for example, Robinson, 1977a, 1985b; Juster and Stafford, 1985) using the basic diary recording framework in Table 1, little difference in obtained time estimates was observed (see Appendix C). This is evidence of the basic reliability of the diary method, as described below. The telephone method did result in less "Not ascertained" time (code 48 in Table 1), and also less time reported in such shorter activities as radio-listening and meal cleanup.

As in earlier diary surveys, coding was done for the open-ended diary reports using the basic activity coding scheme developed for the 1965 Multi-national Time Budget Research Project (as described in Szalai et al., 1972). The Szalai et al. code (Table 1) first divides activities into non–free-time activities (codes 00–49) and free-time activities (codes 50–99). Non–free-time activities are further subdivided into paid work, family care, and personal care, with free-time activities being further subdivided under the five general headings of adult education, organizational activity, social life, recreation, and communication.

The more fine distinctions within these categories, captured in the over 250 categories developed in the 1985 study, reflect further distinctions under these broader headings. Nonetheless, the main value of the open-ended diary approach is that activities can be recorded or recombined, depending on the analyst's unique assumptions or purposes.

The Szalai et al. code has several attractive features. First, it has been tested and found to be reliable in several countries around the world. Second, and because of this, extensive prior national normative data are available for comparison purposes. Third, it can be easily adapted to include new code categories of interest to researchers who are looking into different scientific questions from various scientific disciplines.

Location, as described in the "where" category of the time diary, was coded into one of the basic location categories developed for the 1985 study (see Appendix D). The location coding can be aggregated to estimate time spent in travel, outdoors, or at home, which are all important parameters for analyzing trends in use of time. Unfortunately, these distinctions were not employed in earlier studies, so cross-time comparisons are not as exact as they are for activities.

When aggregated, then, activity-diary data have been used to provide generalizable national estimates of the full range of alternative daily activities in a society, from "contracted" time to "committed" time to personal care and all the types of activities that take place in free time. The multiple uses and perspectives afforded by time-diary data have led to a recent proliferation of research and literature in this field. Comparable national time-diary data have been collected in more than 25 countries over the last two decades, including virtually all Eastern and Western European countries.

## Methodological Support for the Accuracy of Time Diaries

Two important measurement properties of social-science measures are reliability and validity. Reliability refers to the ability of a measurement instrument to provide consistent results from study to study or under different conditions—that is, do we get similar results using the same method? Validity refers to the ability of an instrument to provide accurate or valid data, in the sense that it agrees with estimates provided by other methods (such as observation or beepers, as described above).

## Reliability

In the 1965 and 1975 studies, estimates from time diaries produced rather reliable and replicable results at the aggregate level. For example, Robinson (1977a) found a .95 correlation between time-use patterns found in the 1965–66 national time diaries (n = 1,244) and the aggregate figures for the single site of Jackson, Michigan (n = 788). Similar high correspondence was found for the American data and for time-diary data from Canada, both in 1971 and in 1982 (Harvey and Elliot, 1983).

Reliability was also noted using different diary approaches. Thus, a correlation of .85 was found between time expenditure patterns found in the U.S.-Jackson time study using the "tomorrow" approach, and time expenditures for a random one-tenth of the sample, who also filled out a "yesterday diary." In a smaller replication study in Jackson in 1973, an aggregate correlation of .88 was obtained (Robinson, 1977a).

Further support for the reliability of the diaries comes from the tables in Appendixes A, B, and C, which present data that show the rather convergent results that were obtained from the telephone, mail-back, and personal interviews in the 1985 national study; and from the overall national results and those obtained in 1986 in Jackson, Michigan, in 1987–88 in California, and in 1986 and 1992 in Canada.

## Validity

Almost all diary studies depend on the self-report method rather than on some form of observation. Like all verbal, and nonverbal, evidence, questions arise about the accuracy of the diaries. That can be seen as an unfortunate situation, because it leaves these self-report data open to basic questions of their being verifiable by some independent method of observation or report. But there are encouraging signs from the observational studies that have been conducted (for example, Kubey and Csikszentmihalyi, 1991).

Several studies bear directly on the validity of the time diary, in the sense of there being an independent source or quasi-observer of reported behavior. The first of these studies did not involve the time diary directly, but rather the low viewing figure from the time diaries relative to standard television rating-service figures that we found in our initial 1965 study. In this small-scale study (Bechtel, Achepohl, and Akers, 1972), the television-viewing behavior of a sample of 20 households was monitored over a week's time by means of a video camera. The camera was mounted on top of that set, thus allowing the video camera/microphone to record all the behavior that took place in front of the television screen.

The results of this study, as in the earlier camera-monitoring of television audiences by Allen (1968), indicated that both rating-service methods of television exposure (the Nielsen audimeters and the viewing diaries) produced estimates of viewing that were 20 to 50 percent higher than primary or secondary viewing activities reported in time diaries. In brief, the study provided considerable support for an explanation of the lower viewing times reported in time diaries than by commercial rating services. It also illustrated the need for a complete activity and open-end diary, rather than one focused only on a specific set of activities, such as television or housework.

Three more general validity studies published subsequent to Bechtel et al. provided further evidence of the validity of time-diary data. These examined the full range of activities, not just television viewing, and employed larger and more representative samples. However, none involved the independent observation of behavior as the Bechtel et al. (1972) study had.

In the first study (Robinson, 1985b), a 1973 random sample of 60 residents of Ann Arbor and Jackson, Michigan, kept beepers for a one-day period and reported their activity whenever the beeper was activated (some 30 to 40 times across the day). Averaged across all 60 respondents, the correlation of activity durations from the beeper and from the diaries was .81 for the Ann Arbor sample and .68 for the Jackson sample (across the nonsleep periods of the day).

In a second study, a telephone sample of 249 respondents interviewed as part of a 1973 national panel survey (Robinson, 1985b), respondents were asked to report their activities for a particular "random hour" during which they were awake that day—with no hint from the interviewer about what they had previously reported for that hour in their diary. An overall correlation of .81 was found between the two aggregate sets of data—that is, between the activities reported in the random hours and in the diary entries for those same random hours.

In a more recent study, Juster (1985) compared the "with whom" reports in the 1975–76 diaries of respondents with those of their spouses across the same day. Juster found that in more than 80 percent of these independently obtained husband and wife diaries agreed that their spouses were present or absent. In a separate analysis of these 1975 data, Daniel Hill (1985) found a

.92 correlation between time spent on various home energy-related activities and aggregate time-of-day patterns of energy use derived from utility meters.

More recently, some preliminary studies using the "shadow" technique described above have been conducted with student samples. The students shadow someone they know across a 12-hour period of the waking day, recording all the things each person does during that observation period. The next day, that student then asks the shadowed person for an unrehearsed account of the same activities. Although the samples so far have been very small and highly unrepresentative, with some highly variable individual reporting, agreement at the aggregate level on most activities across the day is ±10 percent.

The recent study of Presser and Stinson (1996) also bears on the validity of the diary, in that they found church attendance rates reported in time diaries were consistently lower than those reported on an estimate basis. That was also the result from observational studies of actual church attendance at the community level (Hadaway, Marler, and Chaves, 1993). While the observed rate in the community was still lower than that reported in the diaries, Presser and Stinson conclude: "The findings presented here confirm the conclusion . . . that there is a significant overreporting of religious attendance in traditional surveys. The overreport, however, is only half as large as they (Hadaway et al.) suggest (50 percent as opposed to 100 percent)."

In conjunction with the reliability studies, then, the data from these studies provide a considerable degree of assurance about the basic generalizability of time-diary data. This has been the case as well in methodological studies conducted in other countries (for example, Gershuny et al., 1986; Michelson, 1978). Nonetheless, a definitive well-controlled study needs to be conducted to update and extend these results.

## The Analytic Procedures Used in This Book

In the cross-time analyses that follow, several steps have been taken to ensure comparability of diary data across the three decades of study. First, analyses have been confined to the age 18–64 segment of the population—that is, the segment most likely to be in the labor force. That was also the only age segment examined in the 1965 study. The rural segment of the population, excluded in the 1965 data collection, has been examined to see whether it is different from the nonrural population in 1975 and 1985. Per se, they are not found to be different, as in the Chapter 12 evidence of how little difference there is between urban vs. rural people. Thus, rural respondents were combined with urban people in aggregating the 1975 and 1985 data.

More important, the technique of Multiple Classification Analysis (MCA) has been employed to control for this location difference and for other unwanted sources of differences in the data across years. In other words, when comparing housework across decades, adjustments need to be made for the fact that more women are employed and that fewer are married or have children. That is necessary to ensure comparing 1965 apples with 1985 apples in these analyses. Similarly, when comparing cross-decade data on child care, adjustment is needed for the lower percentage of respondents who have children and younger children in more recent years.

MCA was specifically designed by Andrews et al. (1973) to provide these types of statistical adjustments to survey data. What it does is effectively ensure that "other things are equal" in the analyses. An example of how the procedure works in practice is provided in Robinson, Triplett, et al. (1985). In effect, then, MCA acts as a corrective for the demographic characteristics that a "standard 1965 adult" would have had in 1985.

In more straightforward terms, the 1965 to 1985 results are shown in terms of four major subgroups: employed women, women not in the paid labor force, employed men and men not in the labor force. To simplify comparisons, these data are shown in terms of implicit hours per week, even though respondents generally kept diaries only for a single day. Here again, the MCA procedures have been useful in ensuring that day-of-the-week differences are taken into account in describing the trends that are identified.

# PART 2

# Work and Other Obligations

# 5

# The Overestimated Workweek and Trends in Hours at Work

Ask anyone how long they spend at work
and they can tell you exactly.
—Witold Rybczynski, 1991
*Waiting for the Weekend*

People think they know how many hours they work—that is, until they actually try to figure it out. This chapter looks at trends in time spent working since 1965 as revealed by time diaries. First, we document the problems with the traditional workweek estimate question used by the U.S. Census Bureau and the Bureau of Labor Statistics, as revealed by time diaries, then we compare the different trends indicated by the two data sources—the steady picture of work hours shown by the government data versus the decline in time spent working revealed by the time diary.

Data on hours spent at work are used for many basic economic calculations. They allow analysts to see whether changes in productivity can be attributed to changed production of outputs or to a change in the time required to produce those outputs. They also allow analysts to gauge whether workers remain as productive as previously, whether workers in one industry are working longer or shorter hours than workers in other industries, and whether unionized workers work shorter hours than nonunionized workers. As Mata-Greenwood (1992) described it, "The regulation of working time is an aspect which has a direct and measurable impact on workers' health, level of strength and fatigue, on the establishment's productivity and costs, and on the society's general quality of life."

---

### From an Actual "Think Aloud" Interview to Determine Time Spent Working

*"So, for last week, how many hours did you actually work at your main job?"*

*"I just figured this out for my time card. So, not including that one hour off and the nine hours off I think I worked, like, 41 and a half, including that time off. So, minus 9, is—32. I think I worked 32 and a half—something like that. OK. Oh, God, and for XXX, oh my God. My schedule goes from Thursday to Wednesday, I need to fall back on. Let me do it backwards. Did I work Saturday? Yes I worked Saturday? Sunday to Saturday or Saturday to Sunday? Sunday to Saturday. Saturday I worked from—6 to 10, and I worked Friday—no, Thursday—yes, I worked 12 to 4:30. Wednesday—yes, I worked—When did I work? I worked 5 to 11. And Tuesday, did I work? Nnnooo. Monday, did I work? Na, I volunteer worked that night. No, I didn't work. Sunday, did I work? Oh gosh, Sunday night, November— What day was that? November 24th. Gosh, did I work that day? I think I may have worked that day—What did I do? I watched the football game? That day I was with a friend all day. I watched the football game with XXX. We stayed over there until about—I don't think I did any work that day. So that's 4, 4 and a half, and 6, 10 and a half—I'll say 14 and a half hours."*

---

As central as these issues related to hours at work are, it is surprising that little effort has been made to establish statistically the basic validity of the work-hour data that government agencies collect regularly.

## Measuring Work Hours

Three different sources of national data on the workweek—data from work establishments, workweek estimates, and time-diary data—can be compared:

1. The oldest data series comes from work establishments and is based on the jobs available in firms. It comes from payroll accounts on employee work hours (or, more precisely the hours they are paid as part of contractual agreements). Those accounts show a steady decline in work hours over the last four decades as shown by the broken line in Figure 6. A major problem with these data is that they are calculated not on the basis of the individual worker but on the basis of the firm—thus making it impossible to translate these numbers to employees who work shorter versus longer hours, or who are of different ages or genders, and so forth. Nor do the data capture moonlighting on other jobs, overtime, paid days off, and the like. Moreover, the data do not cover self-employed workers, workers in very small firms, or workers in newer service jobs. Nor have the data been available from a probability sampling frame of work establishments.

2. Data obtained directly from workers in government surveys—usually the Current Population Survey (CPS) or the U.S. Bureau of the Census—are therefore usually relied on. The CPS asks respondents in a large (50,000 + per month) random sample of the general population with high response rates to estimate their hours at work. While these workweek-estimate questions vary from survey to survey, most agencies ask about hours at work in the preceding week, and others ask about normal, usual, average, or expected work hours.

If one were looking for upward movements in this surprisingly flat landscape of work hours since World War II, the trend data from these CPS numbers in Figure 6 do show a 1-hour increase since the early 1980s. At the same time, they show virtually no change since the early 1970s, and a 2–3 hour decrease since this series was initiated in the 1940s. Moreover, there has been virtually no change over the last decade, when concern about overworked Americans has peaked.

It is important to note that these relentlessly steady averages do not conceal significant increases in the proportion of the workforce putting in long hours. The 19 percent who reported working 50 + hours in 1995 is only 2 percentage points higher than the 17 percent of such workers in 1967. Furthermore, these CPS figures are already averaged across the year, so that there may be no need to weight them by weeks worked per year, as Schor (1991) did to produce her higher estimates of the work year.

There is an implicit assumption in these time-estimate questions that respondents are able to answer them accurately. The question assumes that in a few seconds respondents can recall, for each day of the preceding week, whether they worked, and then correctly add up the amounts for all seven

Figure 6.  Annual Averages of Hours Worked per Week, 1948–1995 (BLS data)

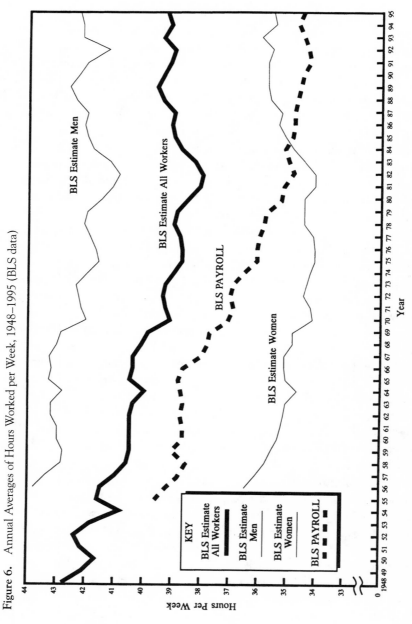

SOURCE: U.S. Census Bureau, Current Population Survey; Bureau of Labor Statistics, 1948–1995.

days of the week—a daunting task particularly for ordinary survey respondents, if they are involved in their first survey experience.

In her comprehensive review of work-time concepts, Mata-Greenwood (1992) distinguished at least eight distinct work- time concepts in the literature, such as "time worked," "time for work," "contractual time," and "time paid." Each of these are dependent on such fine-tuned distinctions as whether the time spent was "normal work time" or not, was devoted to actual work tasks or not, or was break time, rest time, or travel. That, moreover, may have little connection to working respondents who may define their "workweek" in terms of some broad contractual arrangement with their employer, rather than actual clock time. Hence, there is a tendency for answers to workweek-estimate questions to cluster at exactly 40 hours (Juster and Stafford, 1985), the most prevalent workweek norm in the United States. Yet, the "normal" 9-to-5 job adds up to 40 hours only if the respondent works straight through without lunch or other extended breaks.

The estimate-question approach therefore suffers from several questionable assumptions: the ability of respondents to understand the time frame of the question and the definitions of what is work and what is not, their ability to retrieve the information accurately from memory and to sum it properly, their willingness to disclose this information accurately to the interviewer— and independent of any temptation to portray themselves in a socially desirable or self-flattering light. On the face of it, then, the estimate approach appears to place great demands and expectations on the part of a typical respondent.

3. The third approach is the time-diary approach, the advantages and disadvantages of which were reviewed in Chapter 4. We next propose some hypotheses about how these diary and estimate questions should be related.

## Hypotheses About Work Time and the Total Time Diary

The more-detailed diary approach should provide lower estimates of work time, primarily as a result of several possible respondent reporting strategies and ambiguities. First, like most activities, work can be combined with other activities. For instance, during work hours, one can take care of personal business or pay bills, socialize (as in leaving work early with work colleagues to go to a restaurant or bar), or read the newspaper. While most workers may report this simply as work, other workers may report it for what it was (as encouraged by the time-diary format)—that is, not as work but as household work, social life, or reading.

Second, people who work long hours may be subject to distorted perception, particularly because those longer hours involve less-regular work schedules in relation to other workers. That makes the reporting task more difficult, because these respondents have fewer solid "anchor points" or time markers around which to base their estimates. They work during hours of the day and week when others do not, and they are therefore less able to include them accurately in their brief estimates. Moreover, they may feel deprived by having to work when others don't, so that work time seems longer because of their social isolation from the mainstream of society, which is not engaged in work at these points in time. Such work time is also likely to be subject to unscheduled interruptions and distractions, further adding to the sense of longer time. These conditions could easily lead not only to a distorted idea of where time goes, but also to the absence of convenient and solid anchor points from which to make accurate estimates.

Another factor that would lead to longer reported work hours involves the well-known statistical phenomenon of "regression to the mean," which arises when the estimating procedure asks respondents to estimate their hours worked "last week." To the extent that regression toward the mean is in operation, people who worked long hours in the previous week are likely to compensate by working fewer hours during the week or day being reported in the diary. That would also lead to estimates that are longer than diary workweeks of those estimating long workweeks.

The time-diary data we are using to test the relationship between diary and estimated work hours are far from ideal. First, the workweek-estimate questions often do not have the same time referent (that is, the last week) as the diary (the day before or the day after). Second, the estimate questions used in these time-diary studies differ from those used in government surveys and from survey to survey. Third, and related to these two points, the diary studies were simply not designed to match the estimate questions, or even to elicit precise data on time spent at work—but rather as general-purpose procedures to measure time spent on all different kinds of activities, including nonwork activities that might take place during scheduled work time.

This also means that these time-diary data cannot be expected to capture the fine distinctions in work time that are of interest to labor analysts, such as those outlined by Mata-Greenwood. Individual respondents who are sensitive to these distinctions may report various rest periods or travel during work in their diary accounts, but our time-diary instructions do not encourage respondents to report such periods at work on a systematic basis. The diary accounts reported here are no more sensitive to work than to any other daily activity, be it travel, household work, sleep, or TV viewing, which should be subject to the same reporting uncertainties on the part of the respondent.

A further problem in testing the validity of estimate data with these time-diary data is that the diary data are not available for the week, but for only a single day. This means we can only construct "synthetic weeks" for groups of respondents by adding together equal numbers of Monday diaries, Tuesday diaries (etc.), and weekend diaries to estimate work hours across the week.

In brief, there are many ways in which both the diary and the estimate questions fall well short of ideal for testing the relationship between the two measurement methods. The studies were simply not designed for that purpose. Nonetheless, we shall argue that the pattern of results is consistent enough across these diverse data sets to raise serious questions about the accuracy of the estimate data, and the conclusions reached from such data, not only by Schor (1991) but also by other analysts who saw no change across time in the same data (for example, Owen, 1989; Hedges, 1992).

In the analyses that follow, the data for the age 18–64 population for 1965, 1975, and 1985 are merged. That gives a total of more than 7,000 diary respondents across these three studies and allows a sufficient number of respondents for the following categories of estimated workweeks: 0 (not in the paid labor force), 1–19 hours a week (average 10 hours), 20–29 (average 25) hours, 30–34 (32) hours, 35–39 (37) hours, 40–44 (42) hours, 45–49 (47) hours, 50–54 (52) hours, 55–59 (57) hours, 60–64 (62) hours, 65–74 (70) hours, and 75+ hours.

These are the 12 categories of the prime independent variable (Est), which can be used to predict the hours of paid work reported in the time diary (Work). The dependent variable thus becomes the difference between the two, hereafter referred to as GAP, where:

$$GAP = Est - Work.$$

Thus, GAP takes on a value of 0 when the two measures of the workweek are identical, as when a respondent estimates a 35-hour workweek and a time diary contains 5 hours on the diary day—which is equivalent to 35 hours a week. Positive values of GAP occur when the estimated workweek—say, 55 hours a week—exceeds the amount of work reported in the diary, say, 5 daily hours (which translates to 35 hours over a week's time). Here the value of GAP is +20 hours (55–35 hours). Negative values of GAP indicate

**Figure 7.**   Differences Between Estimated and Diary Work Hours for Men and Women, 1985 data (in hours per week)

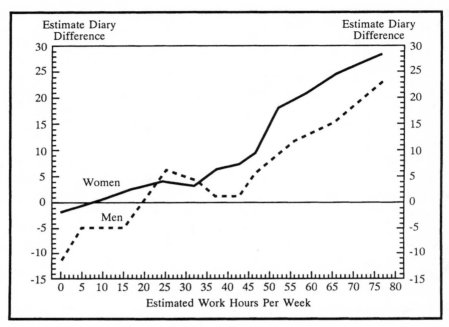

SOURCE: Robinson and Bostrom, 1994; Americans' Use of Time Project.

the opposite: more work in the diary than implied in the estimate response—say, 25 hours. Here the value of GAP is –10 hours (25–35 hours).

In addition to differences in GAP as a function of estimated work hours, the ways in which GAP differs between men and women are examined, because of the notable gender differences in work hours and reports of work hours that are found in virtually all surveys. Figure 7 shows these gender differences in the values of GAP for the 1985 data, as well as the overall pattern of increases in GAP among those with longer work hours, as discussed in more detail below.

## Diary-Estimate Comparisons

First, a comparison of the CPS distribution of work hours for people working 20 or more hours a week in 1985 with that for the 1985 University of Maryland Americans' Use of Time Project sample shows a similar distribution. In the CPS sample questions, for example, 25.5 percent estimated 50 or more work hours, compared with 25.4 percent in the University of Maryland national survey. This indicates that the 1985 Maryland time-diary sample report was similar to what the larger CPS sample reported in response to its work hours' question.

The calculations of Work (diary work hours) and GAP from the aggregated diaries of each level of Est (estimated work hours) are shown in Appendix E separately for 1965, 1975, and 1985. The first column shows the average values of Work across all three years combined and weighted equally. It can be seen that values of Work do rise steadily with Est, indicating that those who estimate longer work hours do report longer work hours in their diaries, as expected. Moreover, the relationship is close to monotonic, rising from 2.8 hours for those estimating no work, to 17.2 hours for those estimating 1–19 hour workweeks, up to 54.9 hours for those reporting 75 + hour workweeks. That last figure provides the only departure from overall monotonicity in this column, being slightly lower than the 55.2-hour figure for those estimating 65–74 hour workweeks.

The middle three columns of Appendix E show that the relationship essentially holds for each of the three survey years of study, although many more examples of nonmonotonicity are found *within* each year—such as the 46.2-hour figure for those estimating 75 + hours in 1965, and the 57.9-hour figure for those estimating 55–59 hours in 1975.

Column 5 of Appendix E shows the resulting values of GAP from these comparisons. Since GAP is based on actual hours and not on the ranges of estimated hours used in Appendix E, the values may be slightly different from what would be calculated from the table itself. Thus, the 14-hour value of GAP for the 60–64 hour category is larger than the 11-hour figure that would result from the 50.7-hour value of Work being subtracted from the midpoint of Est (62 hours).

Nonetheless, it is clear that values of GAP do rise as values of Est increase, being − 3 hours for the zero-hour category, + 2 hours for the 40–44 hour category, and + 25 hours for respondents estimating 75 + hours and over. There is a major departure for the 35–39 hour category, however, where the + 7-hour figure is larger than either + 2-hour figure for 30–34 or 40–44 hour groups. Otherwise, it is clear that GAP increases as Est increases, indicating greater overestimation among those working longer hours, as hypothesized.

A further pattern of interest in Appendix E is that values of GAP are lowest in 1965 and highest in 1985. That suggests that over the 20-year period respondents have been giving progressively higher overestimates in more-recent surveys. This shift, then, provides the basis for diary figures showing a net decrease since 1965, in contrast to the flat picture summarized in Figure 6 or the increase suggested by Schor (1991).

## Multivariate Analysis

In order to control for third variables that could account for these differences in the Figure 7 pattern, the data were entered into the MCA program described in Chapter 4 to provide adjustments in different work-hour categories, given the other predictors of the workweek. In the present analysis, we want to equalize the effects of survey year differences in days of the week, gender, and year on these different values of Est. That would ensure that the differences in Figure 7 are not due to disproportionate numbers of weekend, female, or 1985 diary days in the calculations. MCA can also act to smooth out irregularities in results due to such disproportions.

The MCA results in Appendix F do perform something of that corrective role. In these analyses, we have restricted the sample to people working 20 hours or more, the cutoff used in certain government analyses to define the respondent as employed. That is also the first group showing positive values of GAP in Figure 7. For this group of most active workers, it can be seen at the top of Appendix F that the value of GAP rises to about 5 hours a week (from 2 hours for the entire sample) before and after MCA. That is 5 hours lower than the estimated average 43-hour workweek for this sample and puts the overestimate closer to 12 percent for those working 20+ hours.

The final set of data in Appendix F indicate that the basic Figure 7 patterns not only hold up but also are slightly enhanced by the MCA adjustments for gender, day of the week, and survey year. Before adjustment, the difference in GAP between 20–29 hour work groups and those working 75+ hours is 29 hours (29–0), while after adjustment that figure is 31 hours (30 − (−1)). That is reflected in the rise of the correlation coefficient, Eta, from .17 to .19 after adjustment. It can also be seen that the After results have fewer irregularities in the progression from 20–75+ hour work groups than the Before results do. Thus MCA does provide slightly more consistent evidence to support the hypothesis.

Differences in the other variables are also of interest in this MCA. For example, the aforementioned increase in GAP between 1965 and 1985 is reflected not only in the 1-hour versus 7-hour gap between 1965 and 1986 but also in the slightly reduced 1-hour versus 6-hour difference after MCA adjustment. That statistically significant difference indicates that 1985 workers were more likely to overestimate their workweeks relative to the diary than were workers in 1965. Several potential reasons for this increased difference are suggested: the increase in service jobs with no fixed hourly schedule, more-flexible work schedules in general, increased pressures for family and personal business during work hours, and the increased blending of work and nonwork time.

Appendix F also indicates the presence of a significant gender gap in these workweek estimates. What makes these differences surprising is that it is women who are most likely to overestimate their workweeks, and women work shorter workweeks than men (and, as noted at the top of Appendix F, shorter workweeks are associated with lower values of GAP). Thus, the 2-hour gap between men and women doubles to 4 hours after MCA adjustment, again a difference that is statistically significant.

The final variable in Appendix F is day of the week, with the not surprising result that weekend diaries significantly underestimate the workweek, while weekday diaries overestimate it. Nonetheless, day of the week is a crucial variable to control and have adjusted in making comparisons across groups and survey years.

## Gender Differences

On almost any measure of work time (and in almost any country), women work fewer hours on their paid jobs than men do, except in the low-to-normal workweek categories (the 20–34 hour workweek categories and the 45–49 hour category) (see Figure 7; see also Appendix F). Among those reporting workweeks of less than 20 hours, including the zero-hour category of the unemployed, it is the men who underreport work hours; women report diary work hours that are rather consistent with their estimated hours. Above 35 hours a week, however, women's values of GAP become clearly and consistently higher than men's (with the exception of the 45–49 work hour category noted above), particularly past 50-hour workweeks, where women's GAP values are almost double those of men in each estimate category.

These results could be explained in terms of general traditional role expectations and experiences of men and women. Women have more experience in part-time jobs and are more familiar with the hourly requirements of fitting life around such schedules. When they take on jobs requiring longer work hours than normal for them, they have fewer anchor points with which to gauge how far from that norm their work hours really are.

Men, on the other hand, have much the same estimation problem, but they have more experience with long work hours, so their overestimation is not so severe as that for women. Men also have less life preparation for short-workweek jobs and for nonemployment than women, and that could explain their larger values for GAP under those conditions. It may also be the case that they feel that having less than a full-time job is the same as being not employed at all. In addition, they may define and see themselves as unemployed as far as receiving "unemployment" benefits is concerned. Whatever the reason, it would not seem appropriate to assign them to a zero-work category in calculations of work time for entire populations.

Finally, women, on average, feel more rushed than men, and such perceptions may contribute to women's overestimation of their hours.

## Implications of the GAP

There are systematic and significant deviations from the workweeks people estimate and the time devoted to work that the same people report in total time diaries they keep. We take these differences as reflecting the greater accuracy of the time diary (although more research is needed to verify that accuracy of the time diary, as noted in Chapter 4). Several explanations for why the estimated workweeks exaggerate actual time at work have been examined. The value of this deviation (GAP) remains rather large, particularly in 1975 and 1985, and thus does not seem to be a function of the way the estimate question was worded, the reference period of the question, the type of time-diary format (personal vs. telephone), or the day of the week the diary was kept. Values of GAP are larger in more recent years, possibly because of the increase in service occupations, with less predictable and less regular work hours.

Values of GAP vary systematically in almost linear fashion with the estimated length of the workweek—most clearly in the aggregate across surveys, but also rather systematically within each survey year. Values of GAP generally took on negative values among those claiming to be unemployed or doing less than 20 hours of work a week. They were slightly above average for those estimating 20–44 hour workweeks and became progressively higher among those claiming workweeks of 45 hours and higher. Among workers claiming to work more than 55 hours a week, values of GAP of more than 10 hours a week were common, indicating reports considerably above the actual hours worked.

Values of GAP were generally found to be higher among women workers than men workers. We attribute this to the departures from usual gender expectations regarding work, which also explains why men with low work hours underreported work hours far less than women. Such overestimation may also occur because of a greater likelihood of women's feeling rushed. It is interesting that estimated workweeks in the 35–45 hour "normal range" were associated with the most accurate workweek numbers, even though that is regarded as the least thoughtful and most stereotyped response.

The almost linear relation of GAP with estimated work hours generally rules out an explanation of the results in terms of simple regression toward the mean, because for that to occur we should find more curvilinearity in the data. That is, above-average values of GAP should also be found for those working shorter hours in the previous week, but in actuality, they have below-average values of GAP.

The higher values of GAP among those with longer estimated workweeks have important implications for estimating hours at work in a society, particularly with higher percentages of the work force in that category, such as the United States (Schor, 1991). It appears that simply taking these estimates at face value and averaging them would lead to serious overestimates of time spent working in American society.

The time-diary data suggest that only rare individuals put in more than a 55–60 hour workweek, with those estimating 60 or more hours on the job averaging closer to 53-hour weeks. In these high week categories, the ratio of GAP to actual hours worked is as high as 50 percent. Among those in normal 35–44 hour categories, the estimate is closer to 10 percent and is not as serious. Indeed, it is about at a level that could be explained by workers' including their lunch hours or work commutes as part of their workweek. Without specific prompting or monitoring by an interviewer, it would not be unreasonable for workers to consider this as part of the workweek, especially in a 9-to-5 job.

This research suggests that a careful measurement strategy, like the total time-diary method, is required in order to capture fully the complexity of people's daily work lives. Obviously, more attention needs to be paid to how to capture the specific work activities that take place on a work *day*, employing both observational and diary methods to understand respondent strategies in reporting their time at work. It is also possible to test the relationship between estimated and diary times for other activities besides work. For example, it has been hypothesized that differences in reported frequency of sexual activity of men and women results from much the same combination of overreporting and underreporting indicated by Figure 7 (Michael et al., 1994).

Finally, it should be noted that the results of this chapter are not peculiar to the United States. Robinson and Gershuny (1994) found much the same pattern in eight other countries for which diary and estimate data were available from the same respondents. These results are given in Appendix G.

## Overall Trends in Work Time

Table 2 summarizes these time-diary versus estimate differences in the simple format that will be used to describe cross-time changes in the other activities described in this book. It shows differences in diary paid work hours, excluding the work commute and lunch breaks but including coffee breaks and second jobs, for employed and nonemployed men and women aged 18 to 64 for 1965, 1975, and 1985. As in Figure 7, although classified as estimating zero hours of paid work time, nonemployed men average about 10 hours of paid work a week in their diaries, and nonemployed women average about 3 diary hours.

Regarding the economically active population, the diary work hours of employed women have declined from about 37 hours in 1965 to 36 hours in 1975 to 31 hours in 1985. Moreover, the percentage of employed women in these diary surveys has risen from about 45 percent in 1965 to 56 percent in 1975 to 60 percent in 1985, much as in Census Bureau data. The fact that the working women who report working fewer hours decreases the total number of work hours put in by women by almost 20 percent in large part accounts for the increased free time we find in Chapter 8 of this book. At the same time, women's hours of paid work are 38 percent of all work in 1985, compared with only 29 percent of all paid work in society in 1965. That is about the same ratio that emerges from CPS work-hour estimate calculations.

Moreover, a similar 7-hour decline is found in the work hours for employed men, from about 47 hours in 1965 to 43 hours in 1975 to under 40 hours in 1985. This is important because, as we shall see in the next chapter, these men are putting more time into housework—although hardly enough to offset their 7-hour decline in paid work (see Table 2).

**Table 2.** Trends in Average Hours Spent at Paid Work: Diary vs. Workweek Estimates (in hours per week)

|  | 1965 | | 1975 | | 1985 | |
|---|---|---|---|---|---|---|
| A. Diary Workweek Figures | | | | | | |
| *Women* | | | | | | |
| Employed | 36.8 | (306) | 35.8 | (489) | 30.8 | (1,234) |
| Nonemployed | 2.0 | (382) | 3.0 | (618) | 3.8 | (814) |
| Total women | 17.5 | | 17.8 | | 20.3 | |
| *Men* | | | | | | |
| Employed | 46.5 | (507) | 42.9 | (865) | 39.7 | (1,327) |
| Nonemployed | 10.5 | (54) | 8.7 | (124) | 10.6 | (354) |
| Total men | 43.0 | | 37.8 | | 33.6 | |
| Total diary paid work | 28.9 | | 26.8 | | 26.1 | |
| B. Workweek Estimate Questions | | | | | | |
| *Women* | | | | | | |
| Employed | 40.4 | | 40.2 | | 41.6 | |
| Nonemployed | 1.2 | | 1.9 | | 2.9 | |
| Total women | 18.4 | | 19.0 | | 22.7 | |
| *Men* | | | | | | |
| Employed | 47.1 | | 46.8 | | 46.4 | |
| Nonemployed | 3.9 | | 2.6 | | 3.1 | |
| Total men | 42.6 | | 40.3 | | 35.1 | |
| Total estimated paid work | 29.4 | | 28.5 | | 28.3 | |

SOURCE: Americans' Use of Time Project.

Such declines occurred during a period in which estimated work hours for these same respondents stayed at almost the same levels. These data (shown at the bottom of Table 2) are quite consistent with the rather flat CPS trend line (see Figure 6). In a nutshell, our time-diary data suggest a decline in work hours across time, in contrast to the basically constant numbers produced by the government workweek-estimate question. The analyses in this chapter provide several reasons why we have greater confidence in these diary data and the declines in paid work time that they indicate.

What the data in Table 2 do not show is the age shift that has accompanied these trend data—both in the time-diary data and in the CPS estimate data. There has been a shift from work done by older men (past age 55), reflecting earlier retirement and the anticipatory socialization that accompanies it, to the paid work done by younger women. Older women have also reduced their work hours and their work participation.

Age is not the only demographic factor that affects work hours. College-educated and higher-income people put in longer hours, as do the self-employed. The effects of marriage and children are different for men and women, both factors increasing the workweek for men but reducing it for women.

Geographic factors play little role in workweek length, and, except for vacation days, neither do seasonal factors. More work is done during the week, but Robinson (1989d) shows that since 1965 more work is done on weekends, especially on Sundays. The same spread of work time is found in when work is done during the day, as workers adopt new schedules to overcome worsening traffic conditions or to accommodate other circumstances or activities.

Whether it can be said that America is making "progress" if workers are working somewhat shorter hours but estimate they are working longer is left to the reader. The additional free time that may result represents opportunities for life outside of work that Americans have simply rushed past.

# 6

# Trends in Housework and Family Care

> Few tasks are more like the torture of Sisyphus than housework, with its endless repetition: the clean becomes soiled, the soiled is made clean, over and over, day after day.
>
> —Simone de Beauvoir

One major feature of time-diary data is that they shed light on the hitherto invisible and largely unappreciated world of unpaid work, recently referred to as the "informal economy." Diary data indicate that almost as much time is devoted to housework and family-care activities in that informal economy, as to activities in the formal economy (described in Chapter 5). The data on family-care activities provide several surprises and reveal complex trends.

Fenstermaker (1996) comments on the omission of housework in the sociological literature:

> And as for women's work—something quite different from "real work"—any mention of it was relegated to discussions of the family—the sole sociological province of women anyway. . . . Even among those sociologists interested in women's activities within the family, the unthinking exclusion of household work from the discipline meant that no one had taken a close look at the content, organization and structure of those activities. (P. 232)

But housework and family care have generally been ignored and misunderstood throughout history. While men and women often shared agricultural work more equitably in peasant life before industrialization, child-rearing and domestic life were still primarily the responsibility of the female. Yet, the notion of females as "homemakers" exclusively was foreign. In colonial America, wives worked alongside husbands in the fields as "yoke mates." They would hardly have been thought of as "dependents" (Coontz, 1992).

The process of industrialization sharpened the distinction between the sexes with regard to work and leisure. Money gradually replaced land as the basis of power, as factory work slowly replaced agricultural work. Men became the earners of money, which they parceled out to their wives and mates as they saw fit. While many male peasants at first sought to complete the dual tasks of working in the factory with farming after they returned from their first job, they gradually became defined solely as the labor force for owners of industry. Only about 15 percent of females were in that labor force at the beginning of the 1800s. Their time was more permeable and interruptible than men's, because they continually had to adjust their life schedules to the needs of husbands and children. Their mobility was generally less than men's, and even the forms of leisure expression open to them were frequently tied to their role as caretaker for husbands and children. Women, after all, were first and foremost the bearers of children. In 1800, females gave birth to an average of eight children during their life, five of whom survived until maturity (Hochschild, 1989).

While suburbanization strengthened the "cult of domesticity" that had gained prominence in Victorian England, twentieth-century women were temporarily pressed into the labor force during both world wars. It was not until the end of World War II, however, that women began to stay in the labor force or enter it in significant numbers. Gradually the percentage of women in the labor force has increased, and with these increases have come pressures for reducing the time women spend on homemaking chores and child care—pressures affecting both women and men.

Although women historically have been pressed into the labor force in times of crisis, there is good reason to believe that the changes during the last few decades represent far more than one more crisis response. In 1980, Masnick and Bane forecast long-term changes in women's roles that would occur in three stages: (1) entry into the labor force, (2) attachment to career, and (3) economic parity. American society currently appears to be somewhere between steps 2 and 3.

Changes in time use may therefore reflect concern for issues of equality, although in the future they may reflect issues of identity. That is, because women have been discriminated against based on their gender, the focus of attention has been on ending that discrimination, and that often leads to the desire for a unisex model of everyday life. Changes in time use clearly reflect progress toward that model, although parity has not been reached in several areas. The long-term direction, however, if parity in time use is reached, may be exploration of issues based on differences in identity between males and females.

## Measuring Time Spent in Household and Care

Time spent on household and family care is a critical indicator of such changes and has begun to capture the attention of social scientists. Perhaps belatedly, economists have come to acknowledge that activities that do not involve the exchange of money, such as housework and child care, do have important economic consequences (Becker, 1965; Juster and Stafford, 1985). Walker (1969) was a major pioneer in this development, providing some of the first solid behavioral data on the topic and examining the phenomenon in an appropriate historical context.

The results of three decades of subsequent time-diary research suggest the need for fundamental reconceptualizations of the psychological and societal ways in which household/family care time is organized and is changing. In other words, they suggest two irregular counterintuitive social trends. First, we found that household/family care time had not changed between the 1920s and the 1960s, despite the great changes in available household technology (Robinson and Converse, 1972; Vanek, 1974). More recently, however, that view has been revised, in light of the unprecedented declines since 1965.

The availability of time-diary data represents a great advance in the understanding of family care. Unlike the case for paid work, no time-estimate questions on housework had been devised, probably because of the low importance society placed on this activity. This may have been a blessing in disguise, because more-recent studies that have developed such questions indicate that household care questions are open to even more serious overestimates than the paid-work question (Marini and Shelton, 1993).

Marini and Shelton found that the multipart question developed for the 1987 National Survey of Families and Households (NSFH), when summed, gave a total of 31 hours a week of core housework for women and 16 hours for men. In contrast, our 1985 time-diary data for the same activities was 19 hours for women and 10 hours for men, indicating about a 50 percent overestimate in the NSFH data (if diary data are accepted as more accurate). The data from a 1981 time-diary study done by the University of Michigan (Juster and Stafford, 1985) gave similar totals of 19 hours for women and 8 hours for men. Surprisingly, the apparent overestimation in the NSFH questions was more evident for frequent activities like cooking and cleaning than for shopping and less frequent household maintenance. Marini and Shelton (1993, p. 379) concluded that: "Time diaries appear to provide the most valid and reliable measures."

The 1985 time diaries suggest that about 24 hours a week go into some form of total family care, which includes core housework and child care as well as shopping. Family care consumes about as much weekly time as paid work, which is about 20 percent of the waking time available to adults aged 18–64. Just over half of family care goes to housework, about one-third to shopping, and 10–15 percent to child care. A breakout of these various activities by gender and by employment status in percentage terms shows, first, that women put in about twice as many hours a week (30.9) as men (15.7) and, second, that nonemployed men and women put in about 50 percent more hours of family care than the employed (see Appendix H).

Figure 8 illustrates how that family care gets divided up differently between men and women. Women spend almost half of their family-care hours on the core housework activities of cooking, cleaning, and laundry, while men spend only about one-quarter of their family-care time doing housework. Men spend proportionately three times more of their family-care time (33 percent) on household repair, outdoor, and home-management activities than women (11 percent). Women also spend proportionately more time on child care than men, particularly in chauffeuring children various places. Men, on the other hand, spend more time traveling to stores and obtaining services, but somewhat less time proportionately shopping for groceries and durables.

**Figure 8.** Time Spent on Various Aspects of Family Care

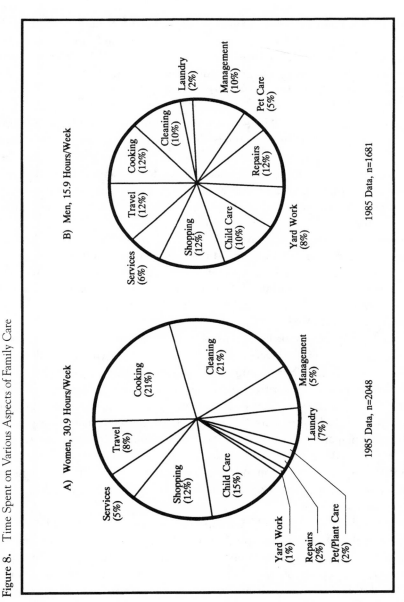

A) Women, 30.9 Hours/Week

Cooking (21%)
Cleaning (21%)
Management (5%)
Laundry (7%)
Child Care (15%)
Shopping (12%)
Travel (8%)
Services (5%)
Yard Work (1%)
Repairs (2%)
Pet/Plant Care (2%)

1985 Data, n=2048

B) Men, 15.9 Hours/Week

Laundry (2%)
Management (10%)
Pet Care (5%)
Cleaning (10%)
Cooking (12%)
Repairs (12%)
Travel (12%)
Yard Work (8%)
Shopping (12%)
Child Care (10%)
Services (6%)

1985 Data, n=1681

SOURCE: Americans' Use of Time Project.

When a woman takes on a paid job, she reduces her family-care time by about one-third, but overall she allocates that family care in much the same way the full-time housewife does. She does a little less cleaning and child care, but more shopping and pet/animal care. Put another way, almost all aspects of family care decline by about one-third for the employed woman (see Appendix H).

On the other hand, employed men differ from nonemployed men mainly in their greater child care, undoubtedly reflecting that these nonemployed men are older and less likely to have children under their care. It has been observed, of course, that as "work that is never done," time devoted to home-making has a built-in elasticity about it. To the extent that it is valued, or to the extent that other roles have been denied women, homemaking's impor-tance transcends mere time commitment.

In general, then, household/family care percentages vary little after em-ployment (Appendix H). Employment affects women's family care *time* more than what specific housework tasks get done during that time; however, it also affects *when* that housework is done, in the sense that employed women increase their housework on weekends while homemakers reduce it (Robin-son, Converse, and Szalai, 1972).

Social status factors play a role as well. In regard to male participation in child care, for example, level of formal education is a critical variable. In a nation which is rapidly splitting into haves and have-nots, the gender gap may close more quickly for those with higher levels of education and income than for those with lower levels, particularly those caught in the culture of poverty. Social class appears to have an important effect on the amount of time men spend in child-rearing and household maintenance activities. Numerous studies have found that men of higher social status are likely to spend significantly greater amounts of time in such activities compared to their counterparts of lower social status (Stone, 1972a; Juster and Stafford, 1985; Robinson, 1989a).

Technology is thought to be an important factor in family and household care, with the most common assumption about household technology that people have used this new arsenal of household appliances to save time. However, in Chapter 18 it is shown that parallel cross-time analysis of house-hold technologies, like washing machines, microwave ovens, and automo-biles, has suggested that their time-saving features seem to be effectively ignored by consumers. Rather than take full advantage of such time-saving features, there appear to be more consumers who opt instead for increased quality or increased output with the new technology (Robinson, 1980b).

# Changes Since 1965

The diaries from our Americans' Use of Time Project indicate some fundamental changes in the nature and extent of housework since 1965 in the direction suggested by the technology hypothesis. These changes have not been well understood nor appreciated, especially in light of recent popular writings on the topic that have used these data to argue essentially that Americans are either "running out of time" or shirking their parental responsibilities (Harris, 1987; Mattox, 1990).

An important factor here, of course, is the woman's employment status. The model implicit in what happens to a woman's (or man's) time when she becomes employed is shown in Figure 9.

In other words, the increased hours at work that a woman puts in as a result of becoming employed may reduce the hours of housework she does, but they do not eliminate them. Employed women still face the "second shift" of housework as soon as they return from work. These dual burdens of paid work and housework mean that a woman's free time is greatly decreased when she enters the paid labor market.

That supposition is supported in time-diary studies, but at the simple, onetime static level. Employed women are shown to have about 5 hours less free time than employed men, and 10 or more hours less free time than full-time housewives (see Chapter 8). However, the picture becomes more complicated across longer time periods. The scenario in Figure 9, in other words, does not apply in the dynamic context of aggregate diary data from the 1970s and 1980s. Instead, consistent and clear trends apparent in these data suggest the opposite—mainly that, like men, American women are now

**Figure 9.**   Presumed Impact of Becoming Employed on Time Use

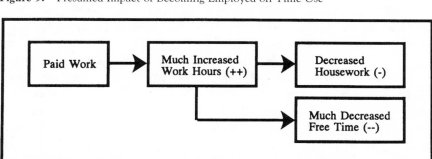

SOURCE: Americans' Use of Time Project.

enjoying more free time than they did in the 1960s, despite their greater participation in the paid labor force.

A pivotal factor here involves the complex dynamics of time spent on housework across time. Time spent by all women doing housework is on the decline. While some acceptance of this conclusion is based on the necessarily declining amount of housework done by the increased numbers of women who are now in the paid labor force, that is not the only explanation. Particularly between 1965 and 1975, less housework was being done both by women in the labor force and by full-time homemakers (Robinson, 1980b), as also shown in the MCA data (see Appendix I).

We noticed how the trends for men had moved in the opposite direction than the trends for women. Men were doing more housework—again independent of the demographic shifts of lower labor-force participation, lower marriage rates, and fewer children. While the rise in housework among men was also consistent, it was so much smaller than the decline among women that its presence became apparent only with the 1985 data. The result was that while men were doing roughly 15 percent of the housework in the 1960s, they were doing about 33 percent of it in the 1980s. Although this remains far short of a 50–50 split, it is clearly moving toward parity. These bottom-line summary numbers for housework are shown in Table 3, Part A.

## Child Care

The other two aspects of family care also measured in these time diaries do not show the trends toward gender equality found for core housework. In the United States, women still do almost 80 percent of the child care (Table 3, part B), much as in the 1960s. Moreover, most of the time men spend with the children is in the form of "interactive activities," such as play or helping with homework, rather than the "custodial" cleaning and feeding that is the mother's domain (Robinson, 1989a).

What has changed is that there are fewer children to raise and care for, and more of them are raised by single parents. Contrary to popular reports that parents are spending less time with their children (Mattox, 1990), the data in parentheses in Table 3 (for parents only) show that both employed and nonemployed women in 1985 spent just as much time in child care as those in the 1960s; moreover, the 1985 numbers are *higher* than those in the 1975 study. Indeed, as pointed out by Robinson (1989a), when Multiple Classification Analysis (MCA) is conducted to adjust for the smaller number

**Table 3.** Trends in Family Care, by Gender and Employment
(in hours per week, for those aged 18–64)

| | 1965 | | 1975 | | 1985 | |
|---|---|---|---|---|---|---|
| **A. Core Housework** | | | | | | |
| *Women* | | | | | | |
| Employed | 17.9 | (306) | 15.2 | (489) | 15.3 | (1,234) |
| Nonemployed | 34.2 | (382) | 27.5 | (618) | 23.8 | (814) |
| Total women | 26.9 | | 21.3 | | 18.7 | |
| *Men* | | | | | | |
| Employed | 4.4 | (507) | 5.8 | (865) | 8.4 | (1,327) |
| Nonemployed | 8.3 | (54) | 10.2 | (124) | 13.2 | (354) |
| Total men | 4.7 | | 6.5 | | 9.4 | |
| **B. Child Care (Parents only)** | | | | | | |
| *Women* | | | | | | |
| Employed | 2.7 | (6.3) | 3.2 | (5.6) | 3.6 | (6.7) |
| Nonemployed | 9.3 | (11.7) | 6.8 | (10.0) | 7.0 | (12.0) |
| Total women | 6.4 | (9.9) | 5.1 | (8.3) | 4.9 | (8.9) |
| *Men* | | | | | | |
| Employed | 1.8 | (2.6) | 1.7 | (2.6) | 1.6 | (2.6) |
| Nonemployed | 1.2 | (3.4) | 1.5 | (2.3) | 1.0 | (2.4) |
| Total men | 1.7 | (2.7) | 1.6 | (2.5) | 1.4 | (2.6) |
| **C. Shopping** | | | | | | |
| *Women* | | | | | | |
| Employed | 5.7 | | 5.3 | | 6.7 | |
| Nonemployed | 7.9 | | 7.7 | | 8.2 | |
| Total women | 7.0 | | 6.5 | | 7.3 | |
| *Men* | | | | | | |
| Employed | 4.9 | | 4.2 | | 4.5 | |
| Nonemployed | 5.7 | | 4.4 | | 6.1 | |
| Total men | 5.1 | | 4.2 | | 4.9 | |
| **D. Total Family Care (A + B + C)** | | | | | | |
| *Women* | | | | | | |
| Employed | 26.1 | | 23.7 | | 25.6 | |
| Nonemployed | 51.5 | | 42.0 | | 39.0 | |
| Total women | 40.2 | | 32.9 | | 30.9 | |
| *Men* | | | | | | |
| Employed | 11.1 | | 10.7 | | 14.5 | |
| Nonemployed | 15.2 | | 16.1 | | 20.3 | |
| Total men | 11.5 | | 12.2 | | 15.7 | |
| TOTAL (hrs/wk) | 27.3 | | 23.6 | | 24.0 | |

Source: Americans' Use of Time Project.

of these children and other household composition shifts (such as the absence of the father in a single parent home), mothers in the 1985 study are spending *more* time with their children than mothers in the 1960s.

Table 3 does show that less overall time in the adult population was spent raising children in the 1980s (particularly for nonemployed women), but that is simply because there were fewer children to raise. Per capita, in other words, 1980s children had slightly more parental time than children raised in the 1960s (Robinson, 1989a). Almost nothing in these data supports Mattox's uninformed calculations about any cross-time decline in parental child-care time in the United States.

That is not to say that there are no disturbing aspects regarding child care in the data at the static level. For example, single mothers spend about 3 hours a week less in child care than married mothers; they do not make up the time lost by the father being absent. The child in a fatherless family loses not only his 3 fewer hours of father-contact time each week but also 3 fewer hours of the mother's time.

It must be remembered, however, that the data in Table 3, part B, refer to child care only as a primary activity, when the child is the sole focus of the adult's attention. Secondary-activity child care, as when eating a meal and talking with the children, takes up almost half as much time as primary-activity time, effectively increasing the numbers in Table 3 by 50 percent or more. These secondary activities also show no decline. Moreover, total time spent in activities with the child being present—that is, total contact time with children—is almost four times greater than that shown in Table 3. (Unfortunately, comparable contact-time data are not yet available for the 1985 data.)

## Shopping

Women still do at least 40 percent more of the shopping in America than men, much as in 1965 (Table 3, part C). Indeed, the differential has increased some since 1965, as overall shopping time returned to its 1965 levels in 1985. As with housework and child care, employed women do notably less shopping than nonemployed women, but that gap has declined since 1965, with 1985 nonemployed women spending only about 20 percent more time shopping than employed women.

## Summary and Conclusions

Overall, then, the net reductions in child care and shopping since 1965, resulting from having fewer households with children and marital partners, have further contributed to the possibilities for more free time for women. These data are shown in Table 3, part D, as the sum of the data in the top part of Table 3. They show a decline of only one hour of total family care of employed women, but also a decline of more than 12 hours of family care among nonemployed women. In contrast, we find a 3-hour increase in the family-care time of employed men and a 5-hour increase among nonemployed men.

Counter to the trends in work time, men have shown an increase and women have shown a decrease in time spent in family-care and home-production activities. Together these activities consume almost as much time (24 hours a week) as paid work (27 hours a week) in America. The trends are a main impetus behind the more "androgynous" society described in Chapter 13 and were mainly the result of gender changes in core housework activities, not in child care or shopping. The latter two activities continued to be largely the province of women in the 1980s.

The declines in child-care time were almost entirely a function of fewer numbers of children in the population. As reported earlier (Robinson, 1989a), employed and nonemployed parents spent about as much time doing child care as in the 1960s. To some extent, fewer children also meant less core housework as well, but it was not accompanied by a decrease of shopping time in 1985.

The net results of the offsetting shifts of paid work and family care are summarized in Table 4. These totals lump all the paid work time in Chapter 5 with unpaid productive activity in this chapter, along with the work commute. When all productive activity is combined, the following trends emerge:

- Women show 6 hours a week less productive activity in 1985 than in 1965, particularly nonemployed women with a decline of more than 10 hours a week versus closer to a 7-hour decline for nonemployed women. Employed men also show a decline, but only 4 hours a week.
- When summed across the differential numbers of men and women who were employed in the three years, the data for men and women are almost indistinguishable, especially in 1965 and 1985. This suggests a remarkable

**Table 4.**  Trends in Total Productive Activity (in hours per week) (D in Table 3  +  Paid
Work in Table 2  +  Work Commute)

|                | 1965 | 1975 | 1985 |
|----------------|------|------|------|
| Women          |      |      |      |
| Employed       | 66.6 | 62.1 | 59.8 |
| Nonemployed    | 53.6 | 44.2 | 43.2 |
| Total women    | 59.4 | 52.3 | 53.2 |
| Men            |      |      |      |
| Employed       | 62.5 | 58.6 | 58.7 |
| Nonemployed    | 26.8 | 25.9 | 32.1 |
| Total men      | 59.1 | 53.7 | 53.1 |

SOURCE: Americans' Use of Time Project.

"invisible hand" that maintains a delicate balance between genders in
productive activity.
• The major changes in productive activity occurred between 1965 and
1975, in which a 6–7 hour decline in productive activity is observed. Since
1975, little net change can be observed. Nor has there been much sign of
an increase in productive activity, as suggested by Schor (1991), Hochschild (1989), and others.

The results suggest that a remarkable and largely unrecognized transformation of productive activity occurred in the 1960s and early 1970s, which
continues to characterize the way Americans use their time today. It has
continued despite the increased labor force and decreased family pressures
since the mid-1970s. It has also made possible the notable increase in free
time that we report in Part Three. There are, however, some changes in the
personal-care and travel time of the population that need to be taken into
account as well, which we do in Chapter 7.

As in the case of paid work time (Chapter 5), the results in Table 4 are
not peculiar to the American context. Figure 10 shows comparable data
on productive activity from 14 countries in which time-diary studies were
conducted with men and women aged 15 and older (Goldschmidt-Clermont
and Pagnossin-Aligisakis, 1995). The activity codes and age populations are
different from those in this chapter, so the numbers do not match exactly,
but it is clear that, with the exception of Austria, Bulgaria, and Italy, gender
equality in regard to total time in productive activity prevails in most Western countries. At the same time, that balance is achieved by averaging the

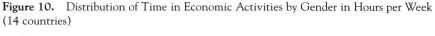

**Figure 10.**  Distribution of Time in Economic Activities by Gender in Hours per Week (14 countries)

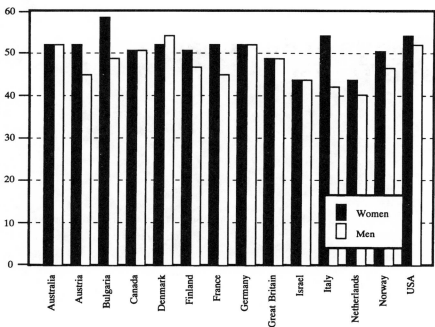

SOURCE: Adapted from Goldschmidt-Clermont and Pagnossin-Aligisakis, 1995.

much higher productive activity of employed women with the much lower productive activity of full-time homemakers.

The preponderance of the evidence presented in this chapter points to overall gender equality when all productive activity is taken into account. Moreover, this has remained much the case since 1965, even though the trends for the subcomponents of productive time have gone in different directions. Women are doing more paid work than in 1965, and they still do proportionately no less child care and shopping. Nonetheless, the data in Table 4 and Figure 8 indicate considerable pressures toward gender balance in productive activity—and in free time, as we see in Part Three.

# 7

# Trends in Personal Care and Travel

> All human troubles arise from an unwillingness to stay where we were born.
>
> —Pascal

Much of life is necessarily spent on activities that seem basic, ancillary, or necessary to complete other activities. Personal care and travel, which take up nearly half our lives, according to the data in this chapter, seem to fall mainly in that category. We need to sleep and eat, we need to wash our bodies, brush our teeth, and clothe ourselves, we need to get to places of work, to food suppliers, and to other markets and service providers.

There is, of course, considerable flexibility or elasticity in such basics of life. In some cultures, bathing is at least a daily ritual; in others, it is done minimally so as not to rob the body of its natural oils. French and Italian families may take 3 hours to eat a meal, while in an American suburb a household meal lasting more than 10 minutes may qualify as a family re-union. The differences between an instant shower and a leisurely bubble bath are pronounced in both function and meaning.

These personal-care activities are probably the least interesting time-diary categories because they ultimately refer to the simple maintenance required of all human beings and provide minimal opportunity for individuals to be productive or expressive. Everyone has to sleep, eat, and groom to function in society, and while some people can do those things in elaborate or elegant ways (as in REM sleep or gourmet meals), that detail is rarely evident in time-diary accounts.

## Personal Care

Data on the three categories of personal care—sleep, meals, and other per-sonal (grooming, personal, travel, and so on)—are presented in Table 5 by gender, employment status, and year. The numbers in Part D indicate the sum, or "bottom line," as far as variation in all three types of personal-care activities is concerned. They show:

- Minimal change across time for employed men and women and for nonem-ployed men, but an increase of more than 3 hours of total personal care a week for nonemployed women—the same group that showed maximum decrease in productive activity (Chapter 6).
- Personal-care data for nonemployed people that are between 1 and 8 hours a week higher, indicating again more ability to gain personal-care time when time pressures from productive activity are lower.
- Virtually no overall difference between men and women concerning the overall personal-care time needed to function in society.

If one were looking for a single critical indicator of the closing of the gender gap with regard to time use, it might be the equality of time spent in personal care.

For all the clichés about women spending hours in front of mirrors or men being oblivious to appearance or addicted to sleep, the time differences with regard to grooming and other personal-care activities are small. It should be remembered that, historically, in other times and cultures, males were the

**Table 5.** Trends in Personal Care and Travel (in hours per week)

|  | 1965 | | 1975 | | 1985 | |
|---|---|---|---|---|---|---|
| A. Sleeping | | | | | | |
| *Women* | | | | | | |
|   Employed | 55.5 | (306) | 56.9 | (489) | 55.3 | (1,234) |
|   Nonemployed | 56.0 | (382) | 60.3 | (618) | 57.6 | (814) |
| *Men* | | | | | | |
|   Employed | 54.2 | (507) | 55.6 | (865) | 54.7 | (1,327) |
|   Nonemployed | 60.6 | (54) | 60.0 | (124) | 59.5 | (354) |
| B. Eating (Meals at work) | | | | | | |
| *Women* | | | | | | |
|   Employed | 6.6 | (1.7) | 7.1 | (1.6) | 7.1 | (1.2) |
|   Nonemployed | 8.8 | (0.1) | 8.9 | (0.1) | 9.1 | (0.1) |
| *Men* | | | | | | |
|   Employed | 8.4 | (1.9) | 9.0 | (1.5) | 7.4 | (1.4) |
|   Nonemployed | 10.6 | (0.6) | 9.5 | (0.2) | 11.1 | (0.2) |
| C. Grooming, Personal, Travel, and Other | | | | | | |
| *Women* | | | | | | |
|   Employed | 10.2 | | 10.3 | | 10.5 | |
|   Nonemployed | 10.0 | | 8.9 | | 11.5 | |
| *Men* | | | | | | |
|   Employed | 7.9 | | 7.9 | | 9.2 | |
|   Nonemployed | 7.9 | | 10.9 | | 10.4 | |
| D. Total Personal Care (A + B + C) | | | | | | |
| *Women* | | | | | | |
|   Employed | 74.2 | | 75.9 | | 74.1 | |
|   Nonemployed | 74.9 | | 78.2 | | 78.3 | |
|   Total women | 74.6 | | 77.2 | | 75.8 | |
| *Men* | | | | | | |
|   Employed | 72.4 | | 74.0 | | 72.9 | |
|   Nonemployed | 79.7 | | 79.9 | | 80.4 | |
|   Total men | 73.2 | | 75.0 | | 74.5 | |
| E. Total Travel | | | | | | |
| *Women* | | | | | | |
|   Employed | 8.5 | | 9.0 | | 10.9 | |
|   Nonemployed | 7.5 | | 7.4 | | 7.9 | |
|   Total women | 8.0 | | 8.2 | | 9.7 | |
| *Men* | | | | | | |
|   Employed | 10.6 | | 10.3 | | 9.5 | |
|   Nonemployed | 12.5 | | 11.0 | | 11.0 | |
|   Total men | 10.8 | | 10.4 | | 11.0 | |

SOURCE: Americans' Use of Time Project.

flashy dressers, sporting silk, lace, long hair, jewelry, bright colors, perfume, and otherwise representing the more highly decorated sex.

Other interesting differences are revealed in the subcomponents of personal care.

## Sleeping

For example, sleep data (which include naps during the day) show the least variance across time. While many people claim they are so busy that they forgo hours of sleep, little evidence of decreased sleep appears in Table 5. Nonetheless, the data also show an increase in sleep in 1975 (particularly for unemployed women), but a return to 1965 levels after that. The exact reasons for this increase in sleep time are not clear, but it did occur in the same period as an initial drop in productive activity (see Table 4). Although the differences amount to less than 2 hours a week, employed women get a little more sleep than employed men. If anything, the opposite pattern is found for nonemployed men, who sleep more than nonemployed women.

Analyses of other factors related to sleep (which over the study years averages remarkably close to the stereotyped 8-hour-a-day number) similarly reveal minimal differences by demographic predictors. This is also true with regard to age: older people sleep more, but only if they are not employed. Few differences are found by status factor (such as education and income), by marriage or parental status (if anything, mothers of young children get more sleep than average, perhaps because of fatigue), by geographic factors, or by seasonal factors. The two temporal factors that make a difference are time of day (Robinson [1993d] notes how bedtimes have generally gotten earlier since 1965) and by day of the week—with increased sleep being obtained on the weekends.

## Eating

Meal times were higher among men than women in all three years, but the gap dropped to less than one hour in 1985, as employed men's total meal times declined from 10.3 hours in 1975 to 8.8 hours in 1985, and women's meal times remained virtually unchanged. The nonemployed take more time for meals, but the overall difference is less than an hour a week. About an hour and a half of the meal times of workers occur at the workplace rather than at home or in restaurants.

Three types of meals are included in this category: meals eaten at home, meals eaten at restaurants, and meals eaten at work. Since 1965, meal times both at home and at work have decreased, as meals at fast-food places and other restaurants have increased. By 1985, about 25 percent of meal times were spent at restaurants, about 10 percent at work, and about two-thirds at home. Most of the increase in meals out occurred between 1965 and 1975, and the restaurant meal numbers were down slightly in 1985, suggesting that the trend in increased meals out had peaked, perhaps as people chose to spend more time at home and could order pizza and other food delivered to their homes.

As with sleep, minimal differences in meal times are found by age, status factors, geographic factors, or seasonal factors. Married people have longer meal times than people who are not married, and parents have longer meal times than nonparents, but again the differences are less than an hour a week.

## Other Personal Care

In general, there have been minor increases, of about an hour a week, in other aspects of personal care since the 1960s, particularly for men. However, women still report about an hour more time than men for such activity in 1985, with nonemployed people also reporting an hour more grooming care as well.

This "other" category comprises mainly washing and dressing (about 55 percent), but it also includes unreported diary time (about 20 percent of "other time," which is about 15 minutes a day) in which respondents refused, forgot, or otherwise failed to report what they were doing; about 15 percent goes to trips related to personal care, mainly for meals out. The remaining 10 percent of time here includes caring for and assisting other people (both residents at home and not) or personal medical care. Those were mainly female activities in 1965, but they became equal by gender in 1985 and have remained stable over time, with the exception of a small increase in meal trips, mainly for employed men.

As with other personal-care activities, differences in this set of diverse activities otherwise remained minimal across age, education, income, marital, parental, geographic, and seasonal factors.

## Implications of Trends in Personal Care

Overall, then, the roughly 75 weekly hours devoted to all these personal-care activities remained generally unvarying across the years and across social categories. That means they have had little impact on the differences in time allocation found for productive activities, or for the related conclusions discussed earlier. The one exception is for the 3 hours of increased personal-care time for nonemployed women, which goes along with their decreased family care and other productive time (Chapter 6). To the extent that life-style changes have produced pressures on personal lives, it is found in the decreased meal times of employed men. Even that has been offset by an increase in grooming and meal travel times.

Subtracting the personal-care time of 74 hours a week from the total of 168 hours leaves about 94 hours a week as a basis for comparing the balance between productive and free-time activities. Because we know not all of that time is absolutely required for personal maintenance, a base figure of 100 hours a week, for time to be split as either productive or free, could be used as a simple and convenient benchmark to assess how the social or nonpersonal part of the week is spent. That would add about 6 weekly hours of nonessential sleeping, eating, and personal-care time to the base of free time. If we also subtracted the hours of work breaks, play with children, or discretionary shopping (all of which are higher among the nonemployed) from productive activity, that would imply further increases in the amount of free time people have available.

## Sexual Activity

A major limitation of our time-diary studies is the obvious underreporting of socially undesirable, embarrassing, and sensitive behaviors (see Chapter 1). Since the most prominent of these is sexual activity, it makes more sense to estimate frequency and time on these sensitive behaviors using special surveys or observation studies that are specially geared to handle respondents' uneasiness about discussing these activities.

The University of Chicago's recent survey, published under the title *Sex in America*, provides just such data (Michael et al., 1994). On a topic long considered too taboo to obtain honest answers, the Chicago team was able to complete interviews with nearly 80 percent of a randomly chosen national sample of 3,432 adults aged 18 to 60. They employed several consistency checks to ensure that they were getting frank and consistent replies to their questions. Responses generally matched those from other surveys and in other countries. Frequency reports of heterosexual sex by men and women matched relatively well, as they should, and the differences by age, education, marital status, and other factors also seemed plausible.

One of the more surprising results in the survey, however, was the relatively low frequency and time devoted to sexual activity across the entire adult population. The numbers of sexual partners were far lower than expected, and so was the frequency of sex. While almost 10 percent of American adults engaged in intercourse four or more times a week, more than 10 percent had engaged in no sex at all in the previous year. The overall average was about once a week.

Multiplying by the average estimated length of each episode gives an average of about half an hour a week of sexual activity missing from our time diaries. That amount could easily get subsumed in the 74 hours of general personal care reported in Table 4, or in the free-time hours (discussed in Part Three).

This effectively removes a major challenge to the overall accuracy or completeness of the diaries. For readers concerned about this gap in the diaries, Michael et al.'s data can be effectively used in combination with diaries to identify more-or-less active segments of the population. Furthermore, many of Michael et al.'s findings dovetail with our own findings, such as the "more-more" pattern we describe in Chapter 18, which is found across several types of sexual behavior in the Michael study. As with different types of leisure behavior, people active in one type of sexual behavior are active in other types as well—rather than in the compensatory pattern in which people's sexual energies go in one direction if they don't go in another. For example, masturbation is reported more among people who are also more active in sexual intercourse.

## Travel

In modern societies, traveling is a part of everyday life—travel not only to work but also to a wide variety of leisure venues: to dinner or the theater, to the beach, theme park, or campsite. It is difficult to imagine how much change has occurred over time in the attitudes of people toward traveling long distances for pleasure. Sociologist Eric Cohen (1972) commented on this change:

> Whereas primitive and traditional man will leave his native habitat only when forced to by extreme circumstances, modern man is more

loosely attached to his environment, much more willing to change it, especially temporarily, and is remarkably able to adapt to new environments. He is interested in things, sights, customs, and cultures different from his own, precisely because they are different. Gradually, a new value has evolved: the appreciation of the experience of change, strangeness, or novelty. This experience now excites, titillates, and gratifies whereas before it only frightened. (P. 1)

Not only is there a flexibility or elasticity about travel, but it can also run the gamut from absolutely compelled behavior (out-of-work coal miners who cannot sell their modest homes and thus must drive 200 miles early every Monday morning to work in an oil refinery, sleep in a rented room, and then drive home Friday evening) to totally voluntary activities (an elderly couple on a drive with no fixed destination, perhaps stopping for ice cream or inspecting a new house being built in another part of town). Travel may also be a necessary part of a leisure experience, such as driving a car to the airport, boarding a plane, landing in Miami, and driving a rented car to Key Largo.

Americans spend just over 10 hours a week in travel. Of that, a little less than 30 percent is associated with the commute to work, 30 percent is associated with child care and shopping, 30 percent with free-time activities, and the rest with meals out and other personal care. These travel data have been added in with the appropriate productive activities (Chapters 5 and 6) and the 3 hours of weekly free-time travel are included in that free-time category in the next section as well.

These components of travel have shifted slightly over time, with increased recreation and restaurant travel to accompany the 1965–85 increases in recreation and restaurant meals. Since the 1960s, there has also been an increase in travel related to child care and organizational activities among women. The commute to work has remained virtually identical across time (consistent with Census Bureau data on commuting time), as has travel associated with shopping and social activities.

Total travel time does not vary much by year, gender, or employment status. There was a small decrease in 1975, associated with the first OPEC oil crisis, during which Americans saw gasoline prices double and then double again. Since then, however, the public seems to have adjusted to these prices to the point that the increased travel time in 1985 put travel at a higher level than in 1965.

More of that gain was registered by women than men, and particularly by employed women. Their 1985 travel was equal to that for employed men. In earlier decades, women traveled about 2 hours less than men—yet another example of increasing gender convergence (see Chapter 13).

At the same time, the differences by employment status are different for men and women, with nonemployed women traveling less than employed women, while nonemployed men travel more than employed men. This probably reflects the more homebound nature of the housewife and more of the environmental searching in which nonemployed men engage.

Travel declines about 30 percent across the life cycle from ages 18–24 to 55–64. It is likewise about 30 percent higher among college graduates, compared with people who had not finished high school. In general, travel activity otherwise varies little by role factors, such as marriage or parenthood, geography, or season. The components of travel do vary by role factors, however, as in the case of greater child chauffeuring by parents and the greater shopping activity of married people. Travel goes up slightly on the weekends and has shifted somewhat across time as commuters appear to be rising earlier to beat rush-hour traffic.

One important aspect of our diary data is that they show more travel and more trips than reported in the 1992 National Transportation Survey conducted for the U.S. Department of Transportation (1994). In that survey, respondents keep a simpler travel diary for a single day, which is not unlike our approach to measuring time, except that respondents need not report all their activities, only the trips they took. Yet the 2–3 trips reported in these transportation diaries are far below the average of 5–6 trips in our complete time diary. This is a surprising finding, given the greater demands of our complete diary on respondents. In other words, the more information asked of respondents, the more they will give. These Department of Transportation data show much the same distribution across trip purpose and correlates of travel time as time diaries, despite the overall lower numbers.

## In Retrospect and Prospect

The obligatory or nonfree activities (Chapters 5, 6, and 7) take up more than 75 percent of our time and more than 60 percent of our waking time.

The sum of the 30 hours of paid work time (and its commute), 24 hours of household/family care, and 74 hours of personal care accounts for 128 hours of the 168 hours in the week. What remains is the approximately 40

Figure 11. Cross-Time Differences in Types of Time for Men and Women

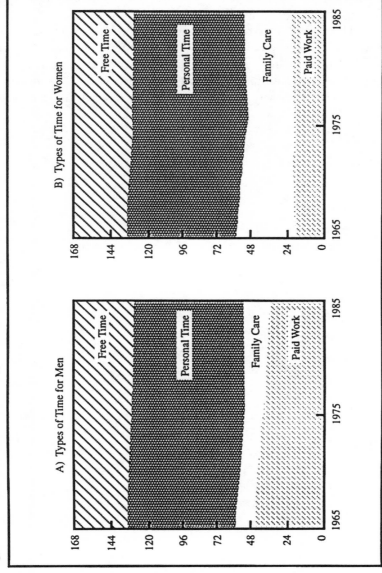

SOURCE: Americans' Use of Time Project.

hours a week that we can define as free time. These hours are examined in Part Three, as summarized in Chapter 8.

Figure 11 provides a summary of how these four basic types of time are spent and how that time has changed since 1965 for both men and women. Both graphs show the increases in free time and how they result largely from decreases in paid work for men and decreased hours of household/family care for women. Time spent with personal care remains basically unchanged since 1965.

# PART 3

# Free Time

# 8

# Trends in Free Time, 1965–1985

Half our life is spent trying to find something to do with the time we have rushed
through life trying to save.

—Will Rogers

It is important to distinguish free time from "leisure." While it has various meanings, "leisure" addresses the question "Given a minimum of obligations and constraints, what is worth doing?" For the ancient Athenians, leisure was a way of life for males that ideally was devoted to contemplation, learn-ing, and self-perfection, but in the modern world "leisure" has been watered down to imply a period of time or cluster of activities that are voluntary and/ or pleasurable (De Grazia, 1962).

In contrast, "free time" consists of all activities considered less essential to daily survival. Generally, people have to work, care for their families, and care for themselves. In free time, they can engage in activities that allow them maximum opportunities for choice, pleasure, and personal expression. For our time-diary studies, free time includes time spent with voluntary organizations, socializing, recreation, hobbies, and communication activities. Thus, "free time" is a concept that reflects the influence of industrialization, in which work was scheduled first and everything before and after it was "free time."

Leisure may be thought of as being reinvented by each culture. Modern leisure was a social invention that accompanied industrialization. In Britain, for instance, it was during the 1840s that "a discrete area of human activity called 'leisure' became recognizable."

> But, . . . it did not develop in any simple linear fashion, as an aspect of industrialized progress. It was enforced from above as a form of social control, by magistrates, clergymen, policemen, milliners, poor law commissioners. Its rationale was, in the end, despite religious and moral camouflage, that of the economic system. It concerned, most simply, the taming of a workforce. (Clarke and Critcher, 1985, p. 59)

While "leisure" is a concept that encapsulates many obvious ironies, most Americans can still easily distinguish when they are at work and when they are not. The goal of our free time, however, has become "recreation," activity that refreshes, diverts, and otherwise "re-creates" us for work again. As Margaret Mead (1958) observed, recreation is a reward that must be earned and re-earned by one's work.

Many social commentators continue to claim that Americans have little free time. As measured in our time diaries, however, free time in 1985 averaged almost 40 hours a week for all people aged 18–64; that compares with less than 35 hours in 1965. This part examines in detail the time spent in free-time activity. How the 40 hours of free time gets distributed, and the average number of weekly hours associated with each for adults aged 18–64, is illustrated in Figure 12.

The domination of Americans' free time by the media, and especially by television, is illustrated clearly by the left half of the pie chart. When "secondary" activities on the diary form are included (activities reported in the separate column "Doing anything else?" in Figure 1), these media activities would surpass half of free time. Secondary media activity data in the 1965–85 studies totaled between 3 and 4 hours of weekly time, much of it

**Figure 12.**   Free Time: Total Hours for 1985 = 39.6

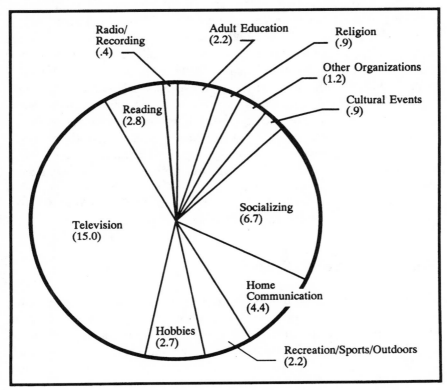

SOURCE: Americans' Use of Time Project.

in the form of television viewing accompanying other free-time activities, such as reading and socializing. The radio/recording slice in the above chart is also small, for the same reason; more than 90 percent of such listening is done as a secondary activity. On the other hand, most reading is done as a primary activity, so that the 5-to-1 ratio of television to reading (almost 3 hours a week) would become closer to 7 to 1 if both secondary and primary activities were added together.

Of the remaining right half of free-time activities in Figure 12, the most prominent is socializing, in the form of visits, meals, parties, receptions, and other informal activities that take place in a home, restaurant, or bar (unless the respondent describes it as a meal or eating out, in which case it is coded as a meal—part of "personal care" in Chapter 7). Many family and telephone conversations are included here as well. Altogether, these social activities comprise almost 30 percent of free time—often a forgotten but still prominent free-time activity in an age dominated by television and the media.

Sports and hobbies take up about 5 hours a week or 12 percent of free time, and a little more goes to hobbies (especially needlecraft activities) than to sports and recreation—mainly in the form of walking. Of the remaining away-from-home activities, adult education takes up the most time, followed by religion, other organizational activities, and cultural events (which includes mainly attending sports events, fairs, and movies).

In other words, the allocation of free time to such "worthwhile" leisure activities as reading serious literature, engaging in community activities, or attending cultural events is a blip on the free-time radar screen. The remainder of this chapter concentrates on the variations in who has more or less amounts of this free time and how that has been changing. Chapters 9, 10, and 11 examine specific free-time activities.

## Trends in Overall Free Time

Table 6 shows the trends in this important summary statistic on the quality of American life since 1965, with differences by gender and employment status. Nonemployed people have more free time, but the employment differential is greater for men (19 hours) than for women (12 hours). That gap between nonemployed women and men has closed across time, with nonem-

**Table 6.**   Trends in Free Time (in hours per week, for those aged 18–64)

|  | 1965 | | 1975 | | 1985 | | 1985 Minus 1965 |
| --- | --- | --- | --- | --- | --- | --- | --- |
| Women |  |  |  |  |  |  |  |
| Employed | 27.2 | (306) | 30.0 | (489) | 34.0 | (1,234) | +6.8 |
| Nonemployed | 39.2 | (382) | 45.4 | (618) | 46.4 | (814) | +7.0 |
| Total women | 34.0 |  | 38.4 |  | 38.9 |  | +4.9 |
| Men |  |  |  |  |  |  |  |
| Employed | 33.0 | (507) | 35.3 | (865) | 36.3 | (1,327) | +3.3 |
| Nonemployed | 61.1 | (54) | 61.6 | (124) | 55.6 | (354) | −5.5 |
| Total men | 35.7 |  | 39.2 |  | 40.4 |  | +4.7 |
| Total Sample (hrs/wk) | 34.8 |  | 38.7 |  | 39.6 |  | +4.8 |

SOURCE: Americans' Use of Time Project.

ployed men having 9 hours more weekly free time than nonemployed women in 1985, compared with 21 more hours in 1965 and 16 more hours in 1975.

The free-time differences between men and women have generally been minimal across the years, from 1.4 weekly hours in 1965 to 1.2 hours in 1985. As with time spent in productive activities, some invisible hand seems to have been keeping the genders roughly equivalent on this important statistic.

The data of greatest interest in Table 6 are those showing the 5-hour increase in free time since 1965—the main gain occurring between 1965 and 1975. Although the gain since 1975 has been only one hour a week, indicating little difference over the last decade, this 5-hour average gain per week is of considerable significance. It translates to a gain of more than six 40-hour workweeks of additional free time per year, or an additional month and a half of vacation. As we shall see, that may not have been its impact or value, but that is its magnitude. This gain in free time was shared by virtually all segments of the population.

## Background Differences in Available Free Time

### Biological Factors

In general, the largest differences in free time are found by role factors; differences by age, gender, and race are less significant. Table 7 shows how free time varies by the various demographic and background factors in Figure 4. Men have about one hour more free time a week than women in Table 6, but after MCA adjustment women have closer to 4 hours less free time than men—reflecting, first, the 2 hours more free time of employed men over employed women and, second, the 9 hours more free time of nonemployed men than nonemployed women.

The relationship of age to free time is U-shaped, with highest free time reported by those aged 18–24 and 55–64, who have 10–12 more hours of free time than those aged 25–54. Middle age is associated with minimal free time, given that these are the peak years of career and family obligations. Once these role factors are adjusted by MCA, age differences are much smaller.

African Americans have a little more free time than whites, but most of that difference is canceled out once other factors are taken into account.

**Table 7.** Differences in Free Time by Background Factors (in hours per week, for those aged 18–64)

| | 1985 | 1985 minus 1965 |
|---|---|---|
| Total | 39.4 | + 4.8 |
| **A. Biological Factors** | | |
| *Gender-Employment* | | |
| Employed women | 34.0 | + 6.8 |
| Nonemployed women | 46.4 | + 7.0 |
| Employed men | 36.3 | + 3.3 |
| Nonemployed men | 55.6 | − 5.5 |
| *Age* | | |
| 18–24 | 48.5 | + 8.3 |
| 25–34 | 37.1 | + 0.6 |
| 35–44 | 35.2 | + 2.8 |
| 45–54 | 36.2 | + 4.4 |
| 55–64 | 45.6 | +11.6 |
| *Race* | | |
| White | 39.2 | + 5.9 |
| African American | 42.3 | + 6.4 |
| Hispanic | 39.4 | NA |
| **B. Status Factors** | | |
| *Education* | | |
| High school incomplete | 41.0 | + 1.8 |
| High school grad | 39.8 | + 6.5 |
| Some college | 40.0 | + 3.6 |
| College grad | 37.6 | + 1.1 |
| Grad school | 40.0 | + 0.0 |
| *Income* | | |
| Lowest quintile | 38.7 | + 0.0 |
| Second quintile | 46.5 | +11.2 |
| Third quintile | 39.0 | + 2.5 |
| Fourth quintile | 39.2 | + 6.5 |
| Fifth quintile | 37.0 | + 2.6 |
| Not reported | 35.5 | + 2.3 |
| **C. Role Factors** | | |
| *Estimated Workweek* | | |
| 0 Hours | 48.8 | + 6.7 |
| 1–9 hrs | 41.0 | + 8.9 |
| 10–19 hrs | 44.6 | − 0.4 |
| 20–29 hrs | 38.8 | + 9.2 |
| 30–39 hrs | 37.5 | + 3.3 |

|                             | 1985        | 1985 minus 1965 |
|-----------------------------|-------------|-----------------|
| 40–49 hrs                   | 34.1        | + 3.7           |
| 50–59 hrs                   | 32.4        | + 2.5           |
| 60 + hrs                    | 28.0        | + 2.5           |
| *Marital Status*            |             |                 |
| Married                     | 34.4        | + 2.1           |
| Divorced/separated/widowed  | 38.2        | + 5.1           |
| Never married               | 47.5        | + 7.9           |
| *Children Under 18*         |             |                 |
| None                        | 41.6        | + 5.1           |
| One                         | 37.7        | + 4.9           |
| Two                         | 36.4        | + 0.8           |
| Three                       | 35.7        | + 1.7           |
| Four +                      | 30.3        | − 0.6           |
| *Children Under 5*          |             |                 |
| None                        | 40.5        | + 5.6           |
| One                         | 32.4        | + 0.6           |
| Two +                       | 34.4        | − 2.2           |
| *Children*                  |             |                 |
| None                        | 41.6        | + 5.5           |
| All older                   | 38.1        | + 4.6           |
| Preschooler                 | 33.0        | − 0.5           |
| D. Other Factors            |             |                 |
| *Urban*                     |             |                 |
| Yes                         | 39.7        | + 5.1           |
| No, rural                   | 39.0        | NA              |
| *Day*                       |             |                 |
| Monday–Friday               | 5.1 hrs/day | + .9 hrs/day    |
| Saturday                    | 6.3 hrs/day | + .7 hrs/day    |
| Sunday                      | 7.4 hrs/day | − .3 hrs/day    |

SOURCE: Americans' Use of Time Project.

## Status Factors

Differences by education are irregular and minimal, varying only one hour between those highest and lowest in years of education. Income differences are somewhat larger, especially for those with the lowest income (the lowest quintile in Table 7), probably because they put in fewer hours of paid work. Those highest in income have about 4 hours a week less free time than those in the second quintile of income.

## Role Factors

Estimated hours of work clearly have a strong direct effect on free time, being highest, at 49 hours of free time per week for those not employed, declining to 45 hours for those estimating a 10–19 hour workweek, 39 hours for 20–29 hour workweeks, 34 hours for 40–49 hour workweeks, 32 hours for 50–59 hour workweeks, and 28 hours for estimated workweeks of 60 hours or more.

In other words, while free time does vary with workweek length, it is not on a 1-to-1 basis. For estimated workweeks of 50 hours or less, there are declines of about 5 hours a week for every increment of 10 hours of work; past that workweek length, the declines are between 1 and 3 hours for each 10 hours worked. Some of these differences (or lack of differences) are due to the discrepancies between estimated and diary work data discussed in Chapter 5, but it appears that every hour of added work time translates closer to a half–hour decline in free time.

Marriage is also associated with free time in important ways. Married people in 1985 reported more than 10 hours more free time per week than people who were not married. Children too are associated with less free time, particularly if the children are younger than five years of age. Parents of these preschool children have about 9 hours less free time per week than those without children, while parents of older children have about 4 hours less free time each week. Each additional child decreases free time by about an hour a week.

## Location Factors

People in rural areas have about one hour less free time each week than people in urban or suburban areas. Differences by region of the country are similarly negligible. People living in apartments have more free time, but mainly because they are less likely to be married or to have children.

## Temporal Factors

Free time increases from 5 hours a day on weekdays to 6 hours on Saturdays to 7.4 hours on Sundays. Across the week, then, 25 of the 40 weekly hours of free time occur on weekdays, which may have more limited value in terms of their possibility for leisure—that is, with a whole day of free time, a broader range of activities is possible, such as taking a trip, sailing a boat, or perusing books in the local library. These activities would be very difficult to squeeze into 45-minute-a-day gains during workdays.

Perhaps that is one reason TV viewing increased in an almost 1-for-1 ratio with increases in free time. Television is ideally designed to accommodate additional small increments of time during weekdays. Had such time gains been repackaged into days or weeks of "free time," the changes in free time described below might have been fundamentally different. Television is readily available in the home, immediately accessible and at low cost, and may be meaningfully consumed in increments of one hour, a half hour, or less. It can be used by people who are tired, illiterate, have a disability, or want to do something else at the same time. It is usable across almost the entire life cycle.

Overall then, the groups in Table 7 that have most weekly free time in America today are nonemployed men (56 hours), those aged 18–24 (49 hours), and the never married (48 hours). (However, it may not make sense to talk of unemployed people as having "free time" if that free time is forced on them, as Schor [1991] suggests.) In contrast, the groups with the least free time are those estimating 60+ hour workweeks (28 hours), employed women (34 hours), those aged 35–44 (35 hours), and parents of four or more children (30 hours) or preschoolers (33 hours).

Somewhat clearer distinctions emerge when the population is disaggregated separately by the three main role factors: employment, marriage, and parenthood. The highest free-time numbers are found among men (63 hours) and women (57 hours) who have none of these role obligations. The lowest numbers are found for employed women with children—surprisingly lower (29 hours) for mothers who are married (and thus have a spouse who could help) than for employed single mothers (31 hours). Employed married men with children (33 hours) and employed married women with children (32 hours) also have much below-average amounts of free time. Nonetheless, these are nontrivial amounts of free time overall, with 28 hours a week translating to more than 4 hours a day. Aggregates of people with no free time, or even less than 20 hours a week, seem difficult to find using our time-diary method. Yet most Americans estimate that they have only about 18 hours of free time a week (see Chapter 16). Individuals with such low amounts of free time undoubtedly exist, but they seem relatively rare in the population, and the only way to locate them more precisely would probably be with a weekly diary.

## Changes Since 1965

The second column in Table 7 shows the changes in free time from 1965 to 1985 across the same background variables. The overall 5-hour gain in free time was far higher in some categories than in others.

In the case of gender differences, for example, both men and women registered this same 5-hour increase. When examined separately by employment, however, there is closer to a 7-hour increase for both employed and nonemployed women. In contrast, there is a 3.3-hour gain for employed men, and a 5.5-hour decrease for nonemployed men. In other words, the increased labor force participation by women and the decreased participation by men serves to mask the differential gains in free time achieved by men and women. Women actually gained more free time than men, once their employment status was taken into account.

The same U-shaped distribution by age is found for gains in free time as for free time in the static 1985 data. The indication is that middle-aged people gained less free time than youngest or oldest adults. Especially remarkable was the nearly 12-hour gain in free time by those in the "preretirement" ages of 55–64, particularly in contrast to the 3-hour gain among those aged 35–44 and a less than one-hour gain among those aged 25–34. In contrast, race differentials across time were minimal.

Turning to the status factors of education and income, there are greater gains among high school graduates and people with some college education. In contrast, both college graduates and those with graduate training show less than a one-hour gain in free time. The gains by income are similarly concentrated in lower income categories, especially the 11-hour gain among those in the second lowest income quintile. Those in the top income bracket registered less than a 3-hour increase.

Gains in free time were higher among those not in the labor force or with shorter estimated workweeks. Those with estimated workweeks of 60 hours or more showed less than a 3-hour increase in free time. Married people showed only a 2-hour gain in free time, compared with a 6-hour increase among the nonmarried. Those without children showed a 5-hour gain, compared with less than a one-hour gain among those with preschoolers and a 5-hour gain among those with older children. In general, then, more gains are found among those with fewer role obligations.

No differences were found in the gain by rural-urban residence or by region.

There were interesting differences by day of the week, with weekdays registering almost a one-hour-a-day increase, Saturdays registering a 0.7-hour-a-day increase, and Sundays registering a half-hour-a-day decrease. In other words, Sunday began to lose its place as a day of rest, while other days gained in the free time they contained. This is another example of "time blending," or lack of distinction in time use across categories, here by day of the week.

What stands out most in these cross-time comparisons, however, is the increasing gap between "haves" and "have-nots" as far as free time is concerned. It can be seen in the greater increases in free time among two age-groups (18–24 and 55–64) with most free time in 1965. But the increasing free-time gap is seen more dramatically for the three role factors—the 7-hour gain among the nonemployed, the 6-hour gain among the nonmarried, and the 6-hour gain among those without children—in contrast to the 3-hour gain among those estimating 40 + hour workweeks, the 2-hour gain among the married, and the less than one hour gain among those with preschool children. In other words, taking on each of these roles in the 1980s meant even less opportunity to gain in free time.

These results suggest a "rich get richer" trend as far as free time is concerned, and that the groups that chose to forgo or relinquish work and family responsibilities have been the major beneficiaries of the gain in free time shown in Table 7. However, even most of the groups that have such greater role responsibilities still do show gains in free time (of 2 to 3 hours). An MCA controlling for these role factors still shows almost a 4-hour overall gain after these role factors have been controlled.

The road has been complex and circuitous, but the end result is that most Americans have more free time than they did in the 1960s, America's cultural revolution. Perhaps that has been one of the unrecognized and enduring legacies of the "liberation" movements of the 1960s.

# Changes Since 1985

It has been more than a decade since our 1985 study, and it might be asked whether free time has changed significantly in the interim, given the reported expanded economic pressures on American workers, the reported downsizing of work organizations, and increased marriage and birth rates in the late 1980s and early 1990s. Several sets of data have been examined to determine whether this is a possibility.

1. Bureau of Labor Statistics data on the length of the workweek have shown virtually no change in estimated hours of work per week (see Figure 6).
2. Television rating service data show declining hours of network TV viewing, as cable television and VCRs have cut into prime-time audiences. However, there is no evidence of declining hours with regard to TV viewing, the major way in which Americans spend free time, as we shall see.

Television is an important indicator of time, being the first activity Americans say they would give up if they needed more time (see Chapter 16).

3. Free-time numbers for Canada in 1992 were about the same as they were in 1986 (see Appendix B). Canadian data mirror the U.S. data closely.

4. Free-time data gathered in 1991–93 by Spring (1993), using another form of diary recording, show roughly the same 40 hours of free time shown in Table 7.

5. Diary activity estimates collected by the NPD market research firm from 3,000 of their respondents between 1992 and 1994 suggest no decline in free time. Even though the methods used are different from ours, comparisons with our free-time data for the population aged 18–90 show for 1992–94 NPD 154 minutes of TV viewing per day (versus 137 minutes in the 1985 Maryland University national study); 43 minutes reading time (versus 29 minutes for the Maryland study); 18 minutes for hobby category (versus 21 minutes); 15 minutes for exercise category (versus 20 minutes); 37 minutes visiting time (versus 41 minutes in the Maryland study). While not providing an overall estimate of free time, NPD did calculate that hours of "entertainment" totaled about 263 minutes a day, compared with 238 minutes for our 1985 study. If anything, then, the 1994 NPD data suggest that Americans have even more free time than our 1985 numbers showed.

6. Finally, calculations from some preliminary estimates from 1993–96 time-diary studies show that the amount of free time is close to the 1985 figures (Robinson and Blair, 1995).

Thus, our 1985 numbers on free time still appear to be generally applicable to the American public.

## A Comparison with Estimate Questions

There are significant disparities between the diary data in Table 6 and those produced by estimate questions. These estimate questions essentially ask respondents: "How many hours of free time do you have a week?" There are many problems with such estimate questions (as in Harris and Associates, 1988).

First and foremost, what do respondents consider "free time"? Will respondents think to include all the free-time activities described at the outset of this chapter (Figure 12)? Even if given examples, will they be able to sort out each of these activities in their minds and sum them separately? What days of the week will they have in mind in summing their day-by-day answers? At the most basic level, will they remember that there are five weekdays and two weekend days and that they probably have more free time on Sundays than Saturdays or other days of the week?

It is therefore not surprising that respondent estimates of free time are again highly inconsistent with diary data. The overall discrepancies between time-diary and estimate questions are even greater than those found for work and housework; they are off by 100 percent or more. The most widely publicized estimate response was produced by the Louis Harris organization in 1988. Harris reported that his respondents estimated they had only 17 hours of free time a week, compared with 26 hours in the 1960s. Closer inspection revealed that Harris had changed his estimate question in the interim (Hamilton, 1991), making true comparison impossible (see Chapter 3).

But estimate questions have been included in other national surveys, and the results are generally in line with Harris's recent estimate numbers. One survey was the Hilton Organization's Time Values Survey of 1991, described in Chapter 16. Here, the estimated amount of free time was about 19 hours a week. The question is not exactly the same one Harris used, but it produced roughly the same number.

What is most paradoxical in these 17–19 hour respondent estimates of total free time is that they are generally lower than the hours per day survey respondents estimate they devote to the single activity of television. As noted in the next chapter, people have consistently estimated that they watch 3 hours of television a day—which translates to 21 hours a week (Robinson, Triplett, et al., 1985; Robinson, 1993e). That is 2 to 3 hours higher than the total amount of free time they estimate. Somehow, television viewing time does not appear to be an activity that survey respondents include when they estimate how much free time they have.

Analyses of these free-time estimates indicates that respondent responses *are* sensitive to the various predictors of free time found in Table 7. People with longer workweeks or more children estimate that they have less free time, and younger and older people say they have more than average free time. For obvious reasons, however, those estimate data cannot otherwise be taken seriously at face value as measures of how much free time Americans have, given that they are less than half that reported in time diaries.

# 9

# Trends in Television Time and Other Media

> Entertainer, painkiller, vast wasteland, companion to the lonely, white noise, thief of time. . . . What is this thing, this network of social relations, called television?
>
> —Todd Gitlin

Time-diary studies make clear how television has truly revolutionized the time structure of daily life. Television not only took over time spent on "functionally equivalent" media activities (radio, movies, reading fiction), but also made inroads on other free-time and non–free-time activities. There is every indication that television will continue to supplant other activities as new technologies interface with the home television screen.

Television is of special interest to time-use researchers because it is the one technology that is so clearly linked to time. It is accessed almost instantly, provides regular programming geared to the hours on the clock, and provides anchor points in time around which other activities can be regulated.

According to many social commentators, television became the pivotal use of free time based around both escapism and consumption. Cultural historian Christopher Lasch describes how "the appearance in history of an escapist conception of 'leisure' coincides with the organization of leisure as an extension of commodity production." Thus, he sees "the same forces that have organized the factory and the office have organized leisure as well, reducing it to an appendage of industry" (Lasch, 1979, p. 217). From the beginning, television has been a sales medium showcasing new kinds of life and leisure experiences for millions of Americans.

Television programming not only rejected the tragic view of life but also promoted the notion of the "quick fix," in which problems were overcome within half an hour. Things happened quickly on television because commercial sponsors wanted the widest possible audiences with short attention spans and little complexity. These quick fixes often included the use of violence and sexuality, and it was usually an individual, rather than a group or organization, who solved problems.

Television brought an endless variety of attractive material goods to the attention of viewers through advertising, and success and happiness were equated with the use of these products. Although television treated viewers as observers rather than participants, it quickly became the most time-consuming form of leisure for Americans, as it does today.

In many ways, television worked against the traditional middle-class values of deferred gratification and the work ethic. Both television commercials and programming taught Americans that they could have what they wanted, now. Television is believed to have affected the Baby Boom generation in three distinct ways. First, it separated the Baby Boomers from traditional social elders, teaching them lessons without the intervention of parents or teachers. Second, it presented a world that was remarkably similar from channel to channel, referred to as a "vast wasteland" by Federal Communications Commission Chairman Newton Minnow. Finally, television violence, which was so much more prevalent than the violence in real life, created a sense of fear about the world (Light, 1988). Television may have led to Americans "amusing ourselves to death," to use Postman's (1985) words.

To the extent that these negative assessments are correct, it may be argued that:

> Television is not vulgar because people are vulgar; it is vulgar because people are similar in their prurient interests and sharply differentiated in their civilized concerns. All of world history is moving increasingly toward more segmented markets. But in a broadcast medium, such a move would be a commercial disaster. In a broadcast medium, artists and writers cannot appeal to the highest aspirations and sensibilities of individuals, manipulative masters rule over huge masses of people. (Gilder, 1994, p. 49)

While cable and VCR use has allowed more individual levels of participation, most of television remains a "top down" managed medium, providing noninteractive entertainment and other programming on a few channels. It reflects a mass culture that is quickly decentralizing into segments.

The impact of increased time spent viewing television is reflected in domestic architecture. Consider the savage assessment of architecture scholar James Howard Kunstler (1993):

> The American house has been TV-centered for three generations. It is the focus of family life, and the life of the house correspondingly turns inward, away from whatever occurs beyond its four walls. (TV rooms are called "family rooms" in builders' lingo. A friend who is an architect explained to me: "People don't want to admit that what the family *does* together is watch TV.") At the same time, the television is the family's chief connection with the outside world. The physical envelope of the house itself no longer connects their lives to the outside in any active way; rather, it seals them off from it. The outside world has become an abstraction filtered through television, just as the weather is an abstraction filtered through air conditioning. (P. 167)

Such elite criticism of television has been a popular sport for decades, and as a mass medium television is an easy and obvious scapegoat for almost any problem in society. Harder evidence from the social sciences has become available, from Gerbner, Gross, et al.'s (1980) "scary world" hypothesis, to Kubey and Csikszentmihalyi's (1990) evidence that television fosters viewer passivity and grumpy moods after viewing, to Putnam's (1995b) evidence that television has played a role in reducing America's stock of "social capital" (see Chapter 11).

Television has become an important way in which people experience the world, much as McLuhan (1964) hypothesized. Television coverage boosted public support for the space program and the civil rights movement, reshaped public opinion about Vietnam, and made celebrities of many ordinary people. Neuman (1982) documented how viewers of popular prime-time programs do become actively involved in the plots of programs and do subject them to critical thinking.

Thus, although television has been widely criticized, it remains immensely popular and does engage its audiences. It is ideally suited to taking up small gains in free time. This, then, is where most of the action in time-use dynamics has occurred—and where we can expect it to occur in the future.

## Early Changes in Daily Life Associated with Television

When the daily activities of television owners and nonowners in the 1965 multinational time-diary study (of which the U.S. data were a part) were compared, remarkable similarities were found in the post-TV behaviors of set owners across the 15 survey sites in the study (Robinson, 1972b; Robinson, Converse, and Szalai, 1972; Robinson, 1969). These European countries were in earlier stages of television diffusion than the 95 percent saturation levels in the United States at the time, so they provided almost ideal opportunities to study the impact of television in terms contrasting how owners and nonowners were now spending their time. Ideally, it would have been better to compare the same people before and after television acquisition, as Coffin (1955) did, but the 1965 rates of set ownership did vary between 25 percent in Bulgaria and 80 percent in Germany, providing a broad range of respondents in societies at various stages of the television adoption process.

Table 8 shows results from this owner-nonowner comparison using the international time-diary data. In brief, it shows that television owners in almost all societies were spending less time than nonowners in "functionally equivalent" activities: 8 minutes less listening to the radio, 6 minutes less reading books, 3 minutes less going to the movies, and 3 minutes less watching television in other people's homes. But they were also spending less time in the nonmedia free-time activities of socializing (12 minutes less), hobbies and other leisure activities (6 minutes less), and conversation (5 minutes less).

More interesting were the changes in non–free-time activities, because changes from the functional equivalence argument were not expected. In-

**Table 8.** Differences in Activities of TV Owners vs. Nonowners, 1965 (in minutes per day, international data)

|  | TV Owners | Nonowners | Difference |
|---|---|---|---|
| 1. Main job | 254.2 | 253.2 | + 1.0 |
| 2. Second job | 3.7 | 4.1 | − 0.4 |
| 3. At work other | 10.6 | 10.8 | − 0.2 |
| 4. Travel to job | 28.2 | 28.4 | − 0.2 |
| Total work | | | + 0.2 |
| 5. Cooking | 55.0 | 56.7 | − 1.7 |
| 6. Home chores | 57.9 | 58.1 | − 0.2 |
| 7. Laundry | 27.9 | 32.9 | − 5.0 |
| 8. Marketing | 18.1 | 18.1 | 0.0 |
| Total housework | | | − 6.9 |
| 9. Animal, garden | 11.5 | 17.6 | − 6.1 |
| 10. Shopping | 7.7 | 6.4 | + 1.3 |
| 11. Other house | 19.1 | 20.8 | − 1.7 |
| Total household care | | | − 6.5 |
| 12. Child care | 17.9 | 16.8 | + 1.1 |
| 13. Other child | 11.5 | 10.1 | + 1.4 |
| Total child care | | | + 2.5 |
| 14. Personal care | 55.0 | 59.5 | − 4.5 |
| 15. Eating | 84.7 | 84.6 | + 0.1 |
| 16. Sleep | 479.3 | 491.8 | −12.5 |
| Total personal needs | | | −16.9 |
| 17. Personal travel | 18.4 | 19.0 | − 0.6 |
| 18. Leisure travel | 16.4 | 20.5 | − 4.1 |
| Total nonwork travel | | | − 4.7 |
| 19. Study | 15.7 | 18.1 | − 2.4 |
| 20. Religion | 3.5 | 6.2 | − 2.7 |
| 21. Organizations | 5.3 | 3.6 | + 1.7 |
| Total study and participation | | | − 3.4 |
| 22. Radio | 5.2 | 13.2 | − 8.0 |
| 23. TV (home) | 86.5 | 7.3 | +79.2 |
| 24. TV (away) | 1.1 | 4.0 | − 2.9 |
| 25. Read paper | 15.2 | 15.3 | − 0.1 |
| 26. Read magazine | 3.9 | 5.4 | − 1.5 |
| 27. Read books | 8.3 | 14.1 | − 5.8 |
| 28. Movies | 3.1 | 6.5 | − 3.4 |
| Total mass media | | | +57.5 |

|  | TV Owners | Nonowners | Difference |
|---|---|---|---|
| 29. Social (home) | 14.6 | 11.7 | + 2.9 |
| 30. Social (away) | 22.4 | 33.9 | − 11.5 |
| 31. Conversation | 14.5 | 19.5 | − 5.0 |
| 32. Active sports | 2.4 | 2.6 | − 0.2 |
| 33. Outdoors | 15.8 | 17.5 | − 1.7 |
| 34. Entertainment | 3.9 | 3.9 | 0.0 |
| 35. Cultural events | 1.0 | 1.1 | − 0.1 |
| 36. Resting | 23.8 | 24.8 | − 1.0 |
| 37. Other leisure | 16.7 | 21.9 | − 5.2 |
| Total leisure |  |  | − 21.8 |
| Total minutes per day | 1,440.0 | 1,440.0 | 0.0 |

SOURCE: Robinson, 1972b.

NOTE: Data are weighted to ensure equality of days of the week and respondents per household across 13 countries.

stead, television owners spent 13 minutes less time sleeping, 6 minutes less gardening, and 5 minutes less on laundry and personal grooming. Such differences were not found in all societies or social groups, but they are not the types of activities one might have predicted would have resulted from television's arrival.

Even larger differences were found for secondary activities: there was a 22-minute decline in radio listening, offset by an almost equivalent rise in secondary TV viewing (see Appendix J). Television owners also spent 10–30 minutes less time alone, and 20 minutes more time with their spouses and children (thus perhaps inadvertently promoting a new form of family life, as described in Robinson, 1990). In line with the declines in socializing with friends and relatives, contact time with friends and neighbors was also lower for TV owners. Equally impressive differences were found by location, with TV owners spending more than half an hour more time at home indoors than nonowners, mainly at the expense of spending time in the yard, in other people's homes, and on the streets. Television did bring people home, but indoors rather than outdoors.

When similar comparisons with other household technologies were made, these television differences became even more impressive. For example, no systematic or important differences were found in the time spent traveling by people who owned cars and those who did not, nor were there—lower (or higher) travel times in societies with more cars. In much the same way, there was little difference in the housework activities of societies that had greater or lower access to household technology. These appliances may have reduced labor, but not the time doing housework, much as Morgan et al. (1966) found. More discussion on this topic is in Chapter 18.

Having a TV set in the home, then, was associated with a virtual doubling of time spent with the media as a primary activity, from 1.1 hours a day to 2.1 hours a day. Differences of a similar magnitude were found in the Coffin (1955) pre-post television study conducted over a six-month period of peak television diffusion in Fort Wayne, Indiana. Coffin found that the 160-minute daily gain in viewing time (as a primary or secondary activity) was accompanied by a 70-minute loss in daily radio-listening and a 14-minute loss in reading magazines and newspapers.

This suggests that television's impact can be dramatically captured directly in terms of how people spend time. The impact of other technologies is reflected in other ways, such as the way the automobile, the high-rise elevator, and the telephone affected how we used space. With the car, people could move farther from the city or the place of work; with the telephone, that move became even easier, also making it possible to keep in touch with relatives and friends across the country. Earlier, with the elevator, we could concentrate workplaces in more central locations. None of these spatial technologies, however, are associated with significant rearrangements of time, at least not as dramatically as with television.

## 1975 Differences in Viewing

The 1965 multinational data provided the basis for another conclusion about television time—that American television viewing had reached its peak in the 1960s (Robinson, 1969). It was apparent that, while Americans watched more television than residents of other countries, that was mainly a function of the higher ownership of sets in the United States. On a per-owner basis, viewers in other countries watched virtually as much as Americans did. Moreover, when we asked Americans if they wanted to watch more television, or would have watched more if there had been better programs available on the diary day, only about 10 percent said they did. Thus, there seemed to be little reason to expect that Americans would increase their 10 hours of weekly television viewing, and with only 4 percent of homes not having a set.

Our 1975 diary data provided us with a rude shock. They showed that TV viewing had increased to nearly 15 hours a week, about the same 5-hour gain that was found for free time. At first, this was believed to be simply a coding error, so a separate set of new coders recoded both the 1975 and the 1965 diaries. Yet, the recoded results matched the original results almost identically. People were simply now reporting 50 percent more television viewing in their 1975 diaries (Robinson, 1981a).

Other explanations were sought: longer broadcast days allowing fringe viewing, more independent stations that were now broadcasting, and the early availability of cable television. While these accounted for some of the difference, the major factor associated with more viewing was the availability of color sets, something that was still a rarity in 1965. Whether it was a side effect of color television per se, or the characteristics of those who bought color sets, is not clear. But it was clear that television had made dramatic new inroads on people's use of time, beyond its original significant impact (Robinson, 1981a).

This time, moreover, television's gain did not come mainly at the expense of other free-time activities. As noted in earlier chapters, the main activities to show a decline between 1965 and 1975 were paid work and housework. How much of a direct trade-off was involved is again not clear, to the extent that people were cutting corners on these two productive activities to satisfy their appetites for what was on television. Nevertheless, the two trends in decreased productivity and increased television did occur in the same decade.

One free-time activity—newspaper reading—did decline dramatically between 1965 and 1975, and that decline did seem to be television induced. And the decline seemed to be a direct byproduct of the increased popularity of local news programs over the same time (Robinson and Jeffres, 1981). (These local news broadcasts did have the advantage over local newspapers, in terms of a trained new army of "news consultants," who relied extensively on audience surveys to put newscasters in touch with potential viewers in ways that traditional newspaper journalists could never imagine.) The loss in newspaper-reading time was almost directly mirrored in the increased diary time spent watching local news programs. It is interesting that the losses were greater among older newspaper readers than among younger readers reared on television.

The panel component of the 1975 study made it possible to examine some longer-run implications of television viewing—in particular, to identify the other free-time activities with which it was associated. As viewing went up, what activities showed decline? There were few positive correlations between most activities and television viewing (Robinson, 1981a). Of course, people who watched television more worked less, but they also did less housework, did less shopping, and ate out less—and participated less in almost all away-from-home free-time activities: adult education, religion, cultural events, socializing, and recreation. Ironically, television time did correlate positively with activities that had been identified as earlier victims of the set: sleeping, resting, and newspaper reading.

In other words, the more people stayed home to watch, the more they did other home-based activities. Conversely, the more people watched, the less they interacted with others outside the home, particularly in the form of "social capital" activities like socializing and organizational participation, which are examined in Chapter 11.

## 1985 Differences in Viewing

The 1985 data, on the other hand, followed our initial 1965 predictions of viewing constancy rather well. Television viewing was up by less than one hour from 1975 levels (although mainly among women). In other words, the 1975–85 decade seems to have been a consolidation period for television, one in which it attracted somewhat more of the female audience—which is further evidence of a larger trend of increased gender similarity across activities.

Table 9 shows much greater growth of viewing in the 1965–75 decade, and the greater growth of women's viewing since 1965, to the point that women were watching 92 percent as much as men in 1985 (compared with 82 percent as much in 1965). The 7-hour gain among nonemployed women was particularly pronounced, since their gain in free time was also 7 hours.

Table 10 shows above-average gains by those aged 55–64 (+7 hours), African Americans (+9 hours), the grade-school educated (+7 hours), those with 0-hour workweeks (+7 hours), and the divorced-widowed (+7 hours). The lowest gains were reported by the lowest income group (+2 hours) and by those with larger numbers of children (+1–2 hours). The gains were slightly lower on Sunday but otherwise equally distributed across the week. Not one group showed a decrease or constancy in viewing levels, despite several such entries for free time. Some groups may not have gained free time across the study period, but all groups had experienced an increase in television viewing.

**Table 9.** Trends in TV and Other Media Time (in avg. hours per week)

| | 1965 | | 1975 | | 1985 | |
|---|---|---|---|---|---|---|
| A. Television | | | | | | |
| *Women* | | | | | | |
| Employed | 7.3 | (306) | 11.0 | (489) | 12.1 | (1,234) |
| Nonemployed | 10.9 | (382) | 16.7 | (618) | 18.1 | (814) |
| Total women | 9.3 | | 14.1 | | 14.5 | |
| *Men* | | | | | | |
| Employed | 11.5 | (507) | 15.1 | (865) | 14.6 | (1,327) |
| Nonemployed | 15.5 | (27) | 20.0 | (124) | 20.2 | (354) |
| Total men | 11.9 | | 15.8 | | 15.8 | |
| Total | 10.4 | | 14.9 | | 15.1 | |
| B. Reading | | | | | | |
| *Women* | | | | | | |
| Employed | 2.7 | | 3.0 | | 2.6 | |
| Nonemployed | 3.7 | | 3.4 | | 3.5 | |
| Total women | 3.3 | | 3.2 | | 3.0 | |
| *Men* | | | | | | |
| Employed | 4.1 | | 2.8 | | 2.5 | |
| Nonemployed | 4.2 | | 3.6 | | 3.2 | |
| Total men | 4.1 | | 2.9 | | 2.7 | |
| Total | 3.6 | | 3.1 | | 2.8 | |
| C. Radio/Recordings | | | | | | |
| *Women* | | | | | | |
| Employed | 0.6 | | 0.4 | | 0.2 | |
| Nonemployed | 0.3 | | 0.6 | | 0.5 | |
| Total women | 0.5 | | 0.6 | | 0.3 | |
| *Men* | | | | | | |
| Employed | 0.7 | | 0.5 | | 0.4 | |
| Nonemployed | 0.8 | | 2.0 | | 1.0 | |
| Total men | 0.7 | | 0.7 | | 0.5 | |
| Total | 0.6 | | 0.7 | | 0.4 | |

SOURCE: Americans' Use of Time Project.

**Table 10.** Differences in TV Time by Background Factors

| | 1985 (in hours) | Change Since 1965 (in hours) | % Free Time |
|---|---|---|---|
| Total | 15.1 | +4.8 | 40 |
| **A. Biological Factors** | | | |
| *Gender-Employment* | | | |
| Employed women | 12.1 | +4.8 | 40 |
| Nonemployed women | 18.1 | +7.2 | 40 |
| Employed men | 14.6 | +3.0 | 45 |
| Nonemployed men | 20.2 | +4.7 | 40 |
| *Age* | | | |
| 18–24 | 14.6 | +4.8 | 35 |
| 25–34 | 14.6 | +3.1 | 43 |
| 35–44 | 13.8 | +4.3 | 43 |
| 45–54 | 14.7 | +4.2 | 43 |
| 55–64 | 18.5 | +7.3 | 43 |
| *Race* | | | |
| White | 14.4 | +4.1 | 37 |
| African American | 19.4 | +6.9 | 47 |
| Hispanic | 14.8 | NA | 37 |
| **B. Status Factors** | | | |
| *Education* | | | |
| Grade school | 21.3 | +6.6 | 53 |
| High school incomplete | 18.8 | +5.7 | 50 |
| High school grad | 16.6 | +6.2 | 45 |
| Some college | 12.6 | +4.6 | 37 |
| College grad | 11.3 | +4.6 | 35 |
| Grad school | 11.8 | +5.0 | 35 |
| *Income* | | | |
| Lowest quintile | 15.5 | +2.0 | 44 |
| Second quintile | 19.5 | +5.2 | 45 |
| Third quintile | 15.1 | +4.1 | 42 |
| Fourth quintile | 14.3 | +4.1 | 41 |
| Fifth quintile | 12.9 | +4.2 | 39 |
| Not reported | 14.1 | +6.8 | 43 |
| **C. Role Factors** | | | |
| *Estimated Workweek* | | | |
| 0 hours | 18.6 | +6.7 | 40 |
| 1–9 hours | 13.5 | +3.9 | 38 |
| 10–19 hours | 14.0 | +6.5 | 38 |
| 20–29 hours | 13.5 | +4.1 | 39 |

|  | 1985 (in hours) | Change Since 1965 (in hours) | % Free Time |
|---|---|---|---|
| 30–39 hours | 13.9 | + 3.3 | 43 |
| 40–49 hours | 12.0 | + 1.7 | 43 |
| 50–59 hours | 12.1 | + 3.6 | 44 |
| 60+ hours | 9.1 | + 1.7 | 43 |
| *Marital Status* |  |  |  |
| Married | 14.8 | + 3.9 | 44 |
| Divorced/separated/widowed | 16.7 | + 7.4 | 43 |
| Never married | 14.7 | + 6.0 | 35 |
| *Children Under 18* |  |  |  |
| None | 15.6 | + 5.6 | 41 |
| One | 14.8 | + 4.8 | 44 |
| Two | 13.7 | + 2.0 | 41 |
| Three | 14.5 | + 4.3 | 45 |
| Four + | 13.7 | + 2.3 | 45 |
| *Children Under 5* |  |  |  |
| None | 15.2 | + 4.9 | 41 |
| One | 14.2 | + 3.8 | 47 |
| Two + | 13.9 | + 1.4 | 42 |
| *Children* |  |  |  |
| None | 15.6 | + 5.7 | 41 |
| All older | 14.4 | + 3.8 | 42 |
| Preschooler | 14.1 | + 2.9 | 46 |
| D. Other Factors |  |  |  |
| *Urban* |  |  |  |
| Yes | 14.3 | + 4.9 | 41 |
| No, rural | 15.4 | NA | 42 |
| *Day* |  |  |  |
| Monday–Friday | 2.1 | + 0.7 hrs/day | 44 |
| Saturday | 2.2 | + 0.6 hrs/day | 35 |
| Sunday | 2.6 | + 0.4 hrs/day | 38 |

SOURCE: Americans' Use of Time Project.

# Differences Across Background Factors

## Biological Factors

Many background differences exist in terms of hours of television viewing. Nonemployed men and women watch more than their employed counterparts by about 6 hours a week, but their proportionate viewing as a function of free time is slightly lower. The greater gains among women since 1965 are again evident.

Viewing hours are rather steady across age-groups, until the preretirement segment of age 55–64, who watch about 4 hours a week more than those 18–54. However, on a percentage basis, it is the 18–24 age-group that stands out as well below average. African Americans watch 5 hours more television a week than whites, representing 47 percent of their free time—notably higher than the viewing levels for whites.

## Status Factors

The major demographic predictor of television viewing is the status factor of education, with those having only a grade-school education watching almost *twice* as much as college graduates. That is reflected in percentage terms as well; the 21 hours of grade-school respondents represent more than half of their free time (53 percent) compared with just over one-third for college graduates. Income is another important predictor of viewing levels, but its predictive power is mainly a function of education; lowest income groups spend 44 percent of their free time viewing, compared with 39 percent among those with highest income.

## Role Factors

Respondents with 60 + hour workweeks report half as much viewing in their diaries (9.1 hours) as those not employed (18.6 hours), but in proportion to their free time they watch slightly more: 43 percent, compared with 40 percent for those not employed. Divorced/widowed people spend 2 more hours a week watching than those who are married or who have never married, but that is only 35 percent of the free time of the latter group. People with children watch 1–2 hours more a week than those without children, but that is a higher percentage of the fewer hours of free time they have available. The same is true for parents of very young children.

## Temporal Factors

Viewing increases somewhat on weekends, but so does free time. Proportionately, Sunday viewing consumes 38 percent of free time and Saturday viewing 35 percent, compared with the 44 percent of free time television takes up on the weekday. Given days with more free time to organize, then, people spend less of it in front of their TV sets. But even on weekend days with larger amounts of free time to spend, television manages to capture almost 37 percent of free time.

Thus, television remains the dominant feature of Americans' free time. Even TV-averse groups, such as the college educated and the more affluent, devote more than one-third of their free time to television. Moreover, their viewing levels moved up generally in line with the gains of less-educated groups. In addition, Nielsen ratings and audiences surveys indicate that the program-taste levels of the college educated do not appear to be notably different from those of their less-educated counterparts (for example, Bower, 1973).

Much of television's attraction is that it is ubiquitous and undemanding. And it has become even more attractive now that there are more channels, better picture quality, and remote controls. As an activity, television viewing requires no advance planning, costs next to nothing, requires no physical effort, seldom shocks or surprises, and can be done in the comfort of one's own home—with pizza only a telephone call away. But is it the best use of free time? This question is examined in subsequent chapters—particularly in Chapter 17, which considers the psychological benefits of viewing in relation to other activities.

## Trends in Reading

There has been an overall decline in reading time (see Table 9), which is mainly a result of the decline in newspaper reading time described earlier in this chapter. Time spent reading books, magazines, and other materials has actually risen slightly to offset somewhat the decline in reading newspapers. Newspaper reading accounted for 62 percent of all reading in 1965, but by 1985 it was down to 34 percent.

Almost 3 hours a week are devoted to reading (which does not include reading done as part of paid work); the weekly number becomes exactly 3 hours if reading as a secondary activity is included.

### Biological Factors

Women read a little more than men—the reverse of the pattern found in 1965, yet another indicator of growing gender equivalence with time. The decline in men's reading time is a result of less time spent reading the newspapers, although men still read newspapers more than women. The decline in women's overall reading time, however, is directly tied to women's increased participation in the labor force. Both employed and nonemployed women spend about the same time reading as they did in 1965.

Reading time is almost three times higher among those aged 55–64 than among 18–24-year-olds. But a cohort perspective indicates that this does not portend declining readership for the future. Almost all age-groups have increased their reading time as they aged between 1965 and 1985. For example, those 18–24 read 2.0 hours in 1965, 2.5 hours when they were 25–34 in 1975, and 2.9 hours as 35–44-year-olds in 1985; those aged 18–24 in 1975 read 1.8 hours then and 2.4 hours in 1985. Newspapers may be headed for more tough times, but the overall "death of print" seems to be an exaggerated prediction (Robinson and Jeffres, 1981).

## Status Factors

College graduates spend more than twice as much time reading than those with a grade school education, and that is not surprising. Consistent with the "increasing knowledge gap hypothesis," reading times declined less for the college educated than for those with less education. In other words, the reading time gap across education levels is greater than it used to be. Those of higher income also read somewhat more, but here the gap is decreasing with time as the less affluent have increased their reading time.

## Role and Time Factors

Respondents with longer workweeks read somewhat less, as do married people and people who have children at home. Rural-urban differences again are minimal. Reading does increase by about 50 percent on Sunday, somewhat the result of the larger Sunday newspaper.

Reading has thus remained a resilient free-time activity. While one could lament the fact that only one-sixth as much total time is devoted to reading as to television, people do seem to increase their reading time as they age. In particular, women continue to be particularly supportive of or reliant on this "obsolete" form of leisure activity.

## Radio/Recordings

The radio/recording data (see Table 9) are a gross underestimate of the prevalence of such activities. Moreover, the decline in radio use as a primary activity may be misleading; almost an hour and a half of secondary-activity radio listening was found in 1985, up markedly from the 60 minutes of such listening in 1965. Radio thus remains another robust mass medium. In general, radio listening is reported more by the less educated, by the nonmarried, and on the weekend.

## Television Data from Estimates and Alternative Sources

There are other estimates of television viewing times from media rating services, as well as usage data for the other media. Indeed, advertisers and stations spend millions of dollars each year to keep track of what television and radio programs people tune in to or what magazines or newspapers they read. However, our time-diary data raise serious questions about the accuracy of these rating service data.

The problems begin with sampling of respondents. The rating services are rarely able to achieve response rates of more than 40 percent of the public. Worse, those who respond are probably the more avid viewers or readers. Worse still are the measures used to track the amount of viewing or reading that takes place. For example, TV audience sizes are determined in terms of whether the respondents watched a fraction of a particular television program, not according to how much of the program they actually watched.

That is why the estimates of average TV viewing time in the time-diary data are far lower than the estimates from rating service data. This conclusion was reinforced when actual family viewing was observed on videotape in a 1970 in-home study of actual viewing (Bechtel et al., 1972) and compared with usual rating service data. Even though family members knew that their viewing was being recorded on videotape, they still reported overestimated viewing in terms of the Nielsen-type diaries they kept.

The greater validity of the time-diary numbers, which were lower, was captured directly on the videotapes. Like the Nielsen audimeter, the tapes recorded the audience whenever the TV set was turned on. Unlike the Nielsen meter, the tapes showed large periods of time (about 20 percent ) when the set was on but no one was watching. They also recorded periods (another 20 percent) when someone in the room was reading, conversing, or engaged in some other activity that detracted from viewing. When that nonviewing activity time was subtracted, the Nielsen meter ratings did provide estimates that were rather close to what people reported in their time diaries.

That the Nielsen viewing figures declined dramatically when the audimeters were replaced by "people meters" (which required viewers in the late 1980s to *actively* report when they were viewing) thus came as little surprise. Again, the complete time-diary method gave more-accurate estimates, in the sense that they did match television use when viewed as a *primary* activity.

The difficult question of what television viewing really is remains. The videotapes from the Bechtel et al. study provided several ambiguous episodes when it was not clear whether viewing was taking place or not—even when someone was looking directly at the screen but seemed totally oblivious to what was on it. Such ambiguities were covered in the diary with the secondary activity probe "Were you doing anything else?" and that probe is also able to pick up a considerable amount of additional viewing—about 30 minutes in 1965, 36 minutes in 1975, and 47 minutes in 1985. More of such secondary viewing is reported by women than by men, and particularly by nonemployed women who are at home during the day. Overall, 40 percent of secondary-activity viewing was done to the accompaniment of household care activities (15 percent with meals, 10 percent with reading, and 20 percent with socializing).

In 1985 an even more inclusive measure in the diary was added—a column labeled "Was the television on?"—to see what viewing might be escaping our primary + secondary measure. Additional possible viewing showed little gain with the new measure—only about 20 minutes more per day. When added together, the 123 minutes of primary viewing, plus the 47 minutes of secondary viewing, plus the 18 minutes of "tertiary" viewing added up to 188 minutes—just over 3 hours a day.

Ironically, that 3-hour-a-day number is the average generated by the simple estimate question "How many hours of television do you watch on an average day?" Television viewing, then, is one activity for which there are reassuring results with an estimate question. It is a question that originated with the Roper Organization but that has more recently been adopted by the General Social Survey of the University of Chicago and by the Survey of Public Participation in the Arts (SPPA) conducted by the Census Bureau. In the most recent SPPA national survey (Robinson, 1993e) with nearly 6,000 respondents, the average estimate of 3 hours a day was again close to our most recent time-diary data.

The definition of what television viewing is or is not will become more ambiguous as the TV set is used for new functions: videocassettes, pay-for-view channels, video games, even computer use. The home viewing environment will become even more multifaceted in the future, as computers and "information superhighways" begin to interface with the home television. Will time-diary respondents report these television variants for what they are, or simply as television viewing? Clearly, more sensitive probing for these new types of viewing variants will be called for, not only in future time-diary studies but in estimate questions as well.

On this issue, a further important technological breakthrough in audience measurement methodology may be near. Compared with complete time diaries until now, all the techniques used by ratings services—media diaries, audimeters, people meters, and telephone coincidental procedures—seem flawed. Recently, however, some ratings firms have developed a small device that people can attach to their clothing and that will automatically record the channel frequency of any TV or radio station signal the person comes in contact with during the day. Such a device offers clear and unambiguous measures about the likely exposure time to these media.

It is unfortunate that other daily activities do not generate similar electronic traces that would allow researchers to track all activities in such an unobtrusive manner. Several electronic devices have been proposed, including those described in Chapter 4, but none offers the completeness or accuracy of activity coverage that is offered by the old-fashioned time diary. In other words, a "technological fix" to replace the diary does not appear to be on the horizon.

These new electronic technologies would represent a clear improvement over today's people meters, which require that viewers enter their presence continually in order to be counted as viewers. When finally developed for field audience measurement, that less obtrusive technology should allow for increased response rates in ratings surveys, as well as for superior measurement. That should offer an ideal opportunity to validate the accuracy of our time-diary measures of media exposure. Nonetheless, no badge can distinguish primary activity viewing from secondary activity viewing.

Even the lower figures from diary research, however, point to television's having become the dominant free-time activity in America. The VCR did not seem to make much of a dent in regular viewing habits, although cable and remote controls may have turned channel surfing into the most exercise many Americans now get. It may become more dominant in the future, as it is linked to computers and other technologies of the information superhighway. The aging of the population may further contribute to increased television viewing.

# 10

# Home Computers and Use of Time

Will the future see an increasing gap between the information-rich and the infor-
mation-poor? Access to the Net and
access to college are going to be the gate-
ways, everywhere, to a world of communications and information access far
beyond what is accessible by traditional
means.

—Howard Rheingold, author of
*The Virtual Community*

The major factor expected to change everyday life in the twenty-first century is the personal computer, and the rapidity of that change is reflected in the recent spurt in the number of homes that have computers. In the mid 1980s, less than 10 percent of American homes had a home computer, but by the end of 1995 the figure was approaching 35 percent. One major factor behind that growth has been the increased popularity and diffusion of on-line infor-mation services, which more than doubled from 1994 to 1995 to include almost one in 10 Americans, according to a 1995 *Times-Mirror* national survey (Kohut, 1995).

## The *Times-Mirror* Survey

This survey was detailed enough to provide an unusual in-depth opportunity to examine how the use of such new technology was affecting the use of more traditional media, media that serve many of the same information and entertainment functions. If one could obtain information on almost any topic instantly from direct sources in whatever detail one wanted, would that not reduce reliance on traditional news media (which contain only a fraction of what the news consumer was really interested in)? Would a new technology that gave people access to entertainment geared toward their particular interests, or made it possible for people to discuss favorite programs or topics with members of like-minded "chat groups," take time away from mass entertainment programs of lesser appeal or interest? Many media experts clearly believe so. According to George Gilder (1994),

> The computer industry is converging with the television industry in the same sense that the automobile converged with the horse, the television converged with the nickelodeon, the word-processing program converged with the typewriter, the CAD program converged with the drafting board, and digital desktop publishing converged with the linotype machine and the letterpress. (P. 189)

The *Times-Mirror* survey was able to address questions concerning the relationship of home computer use to other media use more directly than other surveys that have investigated this new phenomenon, particularly in regard to the most publicized and exciting of new technologies: on-line services such as the Internet.

The significance of the home computer relative to traditional media is its interactivity. Rather than being a passive recipient or consumer of information or entertainment, the computer user is directly involved in a two-way or multi-way network of communication. Users of the Internet and the World Wide Web can become involved in sharing with fellow enthusiasts the latest information and gossip on a topic in as much detail as they want. No longer does sought-after information require time-consuming "snail mail" or frustrating voice-mail telephone tag. Users can not only develop their own newspapers or news magazines, but also design their own entertainment programs. It is anticipated that future developments will make it possible for television users to access their favorite programs over the Internet as well.

Much the same is anticipated for personal communication. E-mail has become one of the most-used features of the Internet, making it possible to maintain almost instant contact with close friends and relatives. Indeed, renewed contact with long-lost acquaintances has reached notable proportions of the population, and it is assumed that the amount of personal contact and caring between those already in contact made possible by the Internet has mushroomed as well. In the 1995 *Times-Mirror* survey, two-thirds of e-mail users said they also used it for work purposes, and almost 70 percent said e-mail had increased communication between higher and lower levels of management. Similar benefits are said to be available to telecommuters, who can now tend to matters of the home while continuing to hold a full-time job without the hassle of the daily commute.

Not all the projected impacts of the Internet and home computers have been so positive, however. In particular, decreased reliance on print media may eventually deal a death blow to a medium still adjusting to the impact of television. Much of what used to be the function of libraries already has been turned over to the computer, and it has been projected that books and magazines could become as obsolete as the library card catalog. Certain government organizations have already replaced their printed reports with data on diskette or CD-ROMs.

## Changes in Activities

The feature of the *Times-Mirror* survey that makes it so valuable and insightful is its focus on a single day's activities. Like the time diary, the single-day focus moves respondents from the almost impossible task of trying to estimate the complex effects of a new technology on their lives to the simpler role of merely reporting what they did "yesterday." Unlike the diary, however, the estimate questions in this survey could cover only a few aspects of daily life, mainly the media. As noted above, however, these media activities are seen as the activities most "at risk" from the new information technology, so it is particularly appropriate to examine them in the close detail that the "yesterday" approach used in this survey makes possible.

Basically, the *Times-Mirror* survey allows us to examine whether the people who use the home computer and on-line services more than others also report lower levels of traditional media use on a particular day. It also allows us to examine whether the effects are direct and "monotonic"—that is, whether there is proportionately less media use as new electronic media are used progressively more. The one-day reporting period means that the respondents are only minimally in the position of trying to make connections between the technology and their use of time. They simply have to report their time and do not have to try to connect their time estimates to the presence of the technology. Indeed, the traditional-media-use questions in the survey were asked before these technology issues were raised.

Many previous surveys had examined these issues, but with biased samples. This is particularly true for surveys conducted over the Internet itself, rather than by a more traditional and global survey approach, such as the telephone or personal survey. A 1995 Nielsen survey, for example, found that estimated use of the Internet is about twice as high in a survey conducted via the Internet than in one done by random-digit-dial telephone. At the same time, the Nielsen survey reported a far higher extent of use than the *Times-Mirror* and other telephone surveys, and its apparent oversampling of more affluent respondents (and hence Internet users) has been cited as a reason for questioning its results. Moreover, the *Times-Mirror* survey examined a comprehensive range of home computer uses, not simply the Internet, making it possible to relate the results to a fuller range of computer-related behaviors.

## *Times-Mirror* Survey Methodology

The 1995 *Times-Mirror* technology survey was conducted by telephone with a national probability sample of 3,603 respondents aged 18 and older during May and June 1995. Households were selected using the random-digit-dial method to avoid the myriad problems associated with lists of telephone numbers, as compiled in a local telephone directory. The first eight digits of the number were randomly selected from lists of working exchanges that were first stratified by state, county, and exchange within county, so that the number of numbers was proportional to that exchange's share of working banks of telephone households.

At least six attempts were made to complete an interview at every selected telephone number, with calls staggered across different times of day and days of the week. While not all days of the week are equally represented, at least

10 percent of the interviews were conducted on each day of the week, and those day-of-the-week differences are adjusted for in the analyses that follow. In order to adjust for the somewhat lower percentages of males, African Americans, younger people, and less-educated respondents, the data were weighted to 1993 Census Bureau characteristics on these factors.

The survey questionnaire was developed in consultation with a wide range of specialists in new technology, consumer behavior, and survey design. It underwent an extensive set of pretests to improve the flow and comprehensibility of the questions. Many of the questions were exact replicates of a parallel 1994 survey, allowing certain trend comparisons, as described below.

The questionnaire began with questions on usual and yesterday use of the media of television, newspapers, magazines, books, radio, and movies, then moved on to news information topics and certain general political and social attitudes, and then to an extensive set of questions on various uses of the home computer, followed by aspects of on-line use for those who had access to on-line services. The questionnaire ended with the usual background factors of gender, education, age, and the like. For nonowners of computers, the survey usually took less than 15 minutes; for on-line users, 30 or more minutes were needed to complete the survey.

For the five traditional news media questions on yesterday usage, the following eight categories of extent of use were provided for respondents, and these were assigned the implicit mean values shown on the right to produce average daily minutes of exposure in the analyses presented below:

| | |
|---|---|
| Did not use the medium | 0 minutes a day |
| Used 1–5 minutes | 2 minutes |
| 6–9 minutes | 7 minutes |
| 10–14 minutes | 12 minutes |
| 15–19 minutes | 17 minutes |
| 20–29 minutes | 25 minutes |
| 30–59 minutes | 45 minutes |
| 1 hour or more | 75 minutes |

Somewhat broader respondent categories were used to report extent of general television use and movie attendance, with similar allocations of estimated mean values; to translate monthly movie attendance into minutes per day, each estimated monthly attendance was multiplied by 120 minutes (for estimated length of the movie) and divided by 30 (for number of days per month); that translates to an estimate of about 4 minutes a day for each attendance.

In the case of frequency or extent of various types of home computer use (general, word processing, and so on) over longer time periods, the six scale categories read to respondents were as follows, along with the implicit average value shown at the right:

| Every day | 7 days a week |
| 3–5 days/week | 4 days |
| 1–2 days/week | 1.5 days |
| Once/few weeks | 0.5 days |
| Less often | 0.1 days |
| Never or don't have | 0 days |

These were the values used in the correlational analyses that follow. Questions about extent of use of home computers and on-line services for "yesterday" employed categories similar to those for traditional media.

## Results

In general, the 1995 survey found lower average amounts of "yesterday" media time than in 1994, suggesting that these new technologies had something to do with that decline, as expected. Overall, there was a decline of about half an hour in reported yesterday time with traditional media between 1994 and 1995, most of which was for entertainment television (18 minutes) and television news (7 minutes).

How were these declines associated with the use of new technologies at the individual level rather than the aggregate level? First, the amount of daily time spent with the home computer was estimated at only 13 minutes a day (closer to 55 minutes for the 14 percent using a computer yesterday and to 40 minutes for the 34 percent having a computer). Second, the amount of time on-line was only 3.5 minutes (but 86 minutes for users). Neither time estimate was available for the 1994 survey, so this 15–17 minutes of total computer use is clearly not all an increase from 1994. Indeed, daily home computer use was the same in both years—14 percent of respondents; however, questions on the amount of daily use were not included in the 1994 survey for comparison with 1995.

Thus, there was ample time to accommodate all of these as increases within the 30-minute decline in traditional media use calculated above. But is that the case in terms of aggregate estimates of usage at the individual level? That is, are there decreases in media use among the users of home computers and on-line services? That is the issue in Table 11, which shows the extent of traditional media use (in minutes of yesterday usage) as related to the extent of use of home computers for general and for specialized functions. Table 12 shows these differences by longer-range use of the computer, first in general and then by use for special purposes, such as word processing or game playing.

The overall relationships in Tables 11 and 12 are summarized with the Pearson correlation coefficients shown at the end of each row, with the statistical significance of the coefficient denoted by "a" if significant at the .05 level and "b" if significant at the .01 level. A positive coefficient signifies that media use goes up with more new technology use, while a negative sign means media use goes down.

## Relationships with Other Media Use

One trend immediately apparent from Tables 11 and 12 is that there are more positive relationships than negative ones. This indicates that new technologies are associated with increased use of other media, not decreasing use. The pattern is particularly evident for the print media of newspapers, magazines, and books. In other words, the more one uses new computer technologies on a given day or in general, the more one uses the old print media. Moreover, the data in Tables 11 and 12 show that this holds not only for overall home computer use but also for the specialized uses of word processing, finances, games, and CD-ROM use.

Many of these correlations are not significant, however, and even the ones that are significant have coefficients that are about .10 or below, which means they explain less than 1 percent of the variance in use of the other media. One reason for the low values is the nonmonotonic nature of the relationships. In the case of newspaper use and general computer use, for example, the 51 respondents reporting more than 4 hours of computer use estimate about 27 minutes of reading, compared with 32 minutes for those who used personal computers for 3–4 hours, and with 28 minutes for 1–2 or 2–3 hours.

Nonetheless, this 27-minute-per-day number is still above the 20-minute figures for the respondents reporting no home computer use, and that is what

**Table 11.** Mass Media Use and Use of Home Computers "Yesterday" (in minutes per day)

| Used home computer yesterday for: | 4+ Hrs | 3–4 Hrs | 2–3 Hrs | 1–2 Hrs | 1 Hr | ½–1 Hr | <½ Hr | Not Used "Yesterday" | No Computer | = | Correlation |
|---|---|---|---|---|---|---|---|---|---|---|---|
| Personal Computer | (51) | (38) | (77) | (55) | (117) | (108) | (108) | (541) | (2,672) | = | (3,603) |
| TV | 88 | 112 | 66 | 57 | 90 | 77 | 79 | 74 | 90 | | -.02 |
| TV news | 23 | 33 | 31 | 36 | 39 | 30 | 29 | 32 | 34 | | -.03 |
| Radio news | 21 | 10 | 17 | 16 | 14 | 18 | 18 | 15 | 15 | | .04 |
| Newspaper | 27 | 32 | 28 | 28 | 23 | 21 | 24 | 26 | 20 | | .05[a] No |
| Magazine | 23 | 20 | 20 | 17 | 14 | 16 | 13 | 17 | 12 | | .10[b] No |
| Book | 21 | 25 | 19 | 17 | 25 | 32 | 19 | 24 | 16 | | .05[a] Yes |
| Movies | 4 | 4 | 4 | 4 | 4 | 4 | 3 | 3 | 3 | | .02 |
| On-Line Services | (17) | (9) | (13) | (12) | (31) | (23) | (69) | (410) | (3,019) | = | (3,603) |
| TV | 31 | 19 | 98 | 122 | 63 | 89 | 68 | 82 | 92 | | -.04 |
| TV news | 30 | 18 | 34 | 30 | 34 | 35 | 31 | 32 | 34 | | .02 |
| Radio news | 32 | 13 | 25 | 7 | 24 | 22 | 14 | 19 | 15 | | .04 |
| Newspaper | 17 | 15 | 18 | 37 | 25 | 27 | 28 | 25 | 20 | | .01 |
| Magazine | 15 | 24 | 15 | 27 | 16 | 17 | 22 | 19 | 12 | | .03 |
| Book | 28 | 30 | 16 | 25 | 22 | 11 | 22 | 20 | 17 | | .03 |
| Movies | 5 | 2 | 6 | 3 | 4 | 4 | 5 | 3 | 3 | | .06 |

SOURCE: Based on Kohut, 1995; *Times-Mirror* Survey.

[a]Correlation significant at .05 level.
[b]Correlation significant at .01 level.

Yes—Significant also after MCA adjustment.
No—Not significant after MCA adjustment.

**Table 12.** Mass Media Use and Longer-Term Use of Home Computers, 1995 (in minutes per day)

| Use: | Every Day | 3–5 Week | 1–2 Week | Once, Few | Less Often | Never | Don't Have | | Correlation |
|---|---|---|---|---|---|---|---|---|---|
| Use PC | (281) | (395) | (352) | (171) | (83) | (147) | (2,672) | = | (3,603) |
| TV time | 76 | 79 | 74 | 79 | 61 | 87 | 95 | | −.06[a] No |
| TV news | 33 | 30 | 33 | 33 | 29 | 34 | 35 | | −.04 |
| Radio news | 18 | 17 | 19 | 15 | 14 | 14 | 15 | | .05 |
| Newspapers | 27 | 22 | 22 | 21 | 18 | 20 | 19 | | .07[b] Yes |
| Magazines | 19 | 16 | 15 | 12 | 14 | 13 | 11 | | .10[b] Yes |
| Books | 25 | 24 | 24 | 19 | 16 | 16 | 14 | | .13[b] Yes |
| Movies | 4 | 4 | 3 | 3 | 4 | 2 | 2 | | .13[b] Yes |
| Word Process | (72) | (230) | (393) | (286) | (114) | (182) | (2,321) | | |
| TV time | 64 | 79 | 71 | 81 | 75 | 77 | 94 | | −.06[a] No |
| TV news | 29 | 34 | 31 | 31 | 34 | 31 | 35 | | −.03 |
| Radio news | 17 | 20 | 13 | 17 | 16 | 17 | 15 | | .05 |
| Newspapers | 28 | 27 | 22 | 22 | 19 | 29 | 19 | | .08[b] Yes |
| Magazines | 20 | 18 | 15 | 15 | 13 | 13 | 11 | | .09[b] No |
| Books | 26 | 28 | 28 | 19 | 19 | 16 | 15 | | .13[b] Yes |
| Movies | 4 | 4 | 4 | 4 | 4 | 3 | 2 | | .10[b] No |
| Financial | (65) | (115) | (266) | (213) | (63) | (559) | (2,321) | | |
| TV time | 97 | 70 | 74 | 77 | 63 | 77 | 94 | | −.02 |
| TV news | 44 | 33 | 31 | 35 | 32 | 29 | 35 | | .01 |
| Radio news | 18 | 19 | 20 | 20 | 19 | 15 | 15 | | .02 |
| Newspapers | 32 | 23 | 22 | 25 | 16 | 21 | 19 | | .06[a] Yes |
| Magazines | 17 | 15 | 16 | 17 | 17 | 15 | 11 | | .05 |
| Books | 16 | 22 | 22 | 21 | 27 | 24 | 15 | | .03 |
| Movies | 4 | 4 | 4 | 4 | 3 | 4 | 2 | | .07[a] No |
| Games | (85) | (146) | (286) | (245) | (156) | (363) | (2,321) | | |
| TV time | 101 | 84 | 75 | 78 | 65 | 69 | 94 | | .00 |
| TV news | 31 | 34 | 30 | 34 | 28 | 33 | 35 | | −.02 |
| Radio news | 21 | 18 | 18 | 18 | 17 | 16 | 15 | | .04 |
| Newspapers | 25 | 22 | 23 | 22 | 19 | 24 | 19 | | .04 |
| Magazines | 17 | 15 | 17 | 16 | 13 | 16 | 11 | | .05 |
| Books | 31 | 25 | 23 | 19 | 17 | 26 | 15 | | .10[b] Yes |
| Movies | 5 | 4 | 4 | 4 | 4 | 4 | 2 | | .09[b] No |
| CD-ROMS | (53) | (110) | (148) | (124) | (73) | (99) | (2,993) | | |
| TV time | 58 | 84 | 78 | 71 | 62 | 68 | 91 | | −.04 |
| TV news | 35 | 29 | 35 | 31 | 31 | 33 | 34 | | −.02 |
| Radio news | 16 | 19 | 17 | 16 | 15 | 17 | 15 | | .02 |
| Newspapers | 24 | 25 | 23 | 21 | 25 | 25 | 20 | | .04 |
| Magazines | 16 | 18 | 15 | 18 | 14 | 17 | 12 | | .05 |
| Books | 21 | 25 | 23 | 22 | 11 | 21 | 16 | | .05 |
| Movies | 5 | 5 | 4 | 3 | 4 | 3 | 3 | | .01 |

SOURCE: Based on Kohut, 1995; *Times-Mirror* Survey.

[a]Correlation significant at .05 level.
[b]Correlation significant at .01 level.

Yes—Significant after MCA.
No—Not significant after MCA.

accounts for the overall positive correlation. In Table 12, the correlation with newspaper reading is also stronger for the more "literate" use of the computer (that is, for word processing) than for finances, games, or CD-ROMs, as one might expect.

The expected negative relations—more computer use going along with decreased media use—are more apparent for the broadcast medium of television (but not for radio news), and again they are statistically significant for general PC use and word processing. For movies, the relationship is more positive.

## Control for Other Factors

This pattern of results suggests an alternative explanation for these correlations—namely, one in terms of respondents' social class. People of higher social class have repeatedly been found to use print media sources more and television less (Robinson, 1967, 1980), and they are more likely to be purchasers and users of new computer products. How much, then, can the Table 11 and 12 findings be explained by these social class variables? To answer that question, the data in Tables 11 and 12 were subjected to Multiple Classification Analysis (MCA) so that differences in media and computer use by gender, age, and day of the week were also controlled.

The MCA results (see the final column of Appendix K) suggest that about half of the original correlations can be explained by these background factors. This is particularly the case for the negative correlations with television use, indicating that the higher television use of nonowners can be explained by their lower levels of income and education. Many of the positive relationships with print media and movie-going are effectively explained by these factors as well.

The patterns for the 10 correlations that do emerge as significant after MCA adjustment are indicated by a "yes" in the final columns of Appendix K. Many of these relationships also contain notable departures from regular and steady patterns of increases, and that significance is maintained primarily because of the lower print-media usage of people who do not own computers. That is generally the case for the significant correlations between general computer use and the reading of newspapers and magazines. Even the significant pattern for book reading shows an irregular decline of 25–24–23–20–15–18–16 minutes (from highest to nonuse of a home computer yesterday), although it is still clear that book reading is higher among more frequent home computer users.

The important point, however, is that this reading is not lower but generally above average among more frequent computer and on-line users. Indeed, it suggests a more symbiotic or supplemental relationship between old print and new electronic media—either being used to reinforce information picked up from either medium (as in looking for verification of a computer fact in a print source) or obtaining content in one medium not found readily in the other (as in finding obscure sports information on the Internet to contrast with today's scores).

## The On-Line User

As noted above, much of the basis for the correlations found in Tables 11 and 12 lies in the simple differences between computer owners and nonowners. In order to free the analyses from this restraint, separate analyses were conducted only among the 595 on-line users identified in the survey. In addition, a separate oversample of 402 on-line users in the survey was added to the analyses to give a total sample of 997 on-line users for these analyses.

The results for this restricted sample were similar to the results in Tables 11 and 12 (as shown in Appendix L), although fewer significant results were obtained (somewhat because of the smaller sample size involved). In other words, we still generally find that computer and on-line users tend to be heavier consumers of print media and that their television and radio use is not much different from the rest of the population.

## Conclusions

In contrast to the expected lower usage of traditional media by users of new computer technologies, data from the 1995 *Times-Mirror* survey suggest a more reinforcing or supplemental relationship. In general, new technology users are more likely to use more traditional media as well, particularly books. That is not an unfamiliar finding among media researchers, in that they generally find that information-seeking follows a "the more, the more" pattern, through which those already well informed become better informed through new information sources (Robinson, 1968; Tichenor et al., 1970).

Consistent with this pattern and with original expectations, new users are also more likely to estimate lower use of the broadcast media of television and radio. However, these relationships could be explained by their common relationship with social class and other background factors, rather than any intrusion from new information technologies.

To the extent that the use of traditional media declines, then, one cannot directly blame it on new technologies. Many other uses of time that could account for these declines can be identified, as total time-diary studies examining the impact of new technologies show (for example, Table 8). In examining the activities affected by television's initial impact using this method, for example (Chapter 9), we found that less than one-third of television's time displacement could be accounted for by the media that were considered its "functional equivalent."

While significant declines in use of radio, movies, and fiction reading did occur, that combined loss was matched by declines in social life and in sleep and personal hygiene; laundry and yard/garden work was also lower. In other words, the effects of new communications technologies usually extend beyond the activities one might expect would be most affected. While the notion of "functional equivalence" did explain many of the changes, there were many other activities for which that argument would have to be greatly stretched to account for the activities that were affected.

The *Times-Mirror* survey did include two questions related to such nonmedia behaviors—in particular, social life—and again the results are not as expected or easy to explain. Consistent with expectations of e-mail and other computer functions serving to replace more traditional forms of communication, there was a 7-point drop (from 63 percent in 1994 to 56 percent in 1995) in the percentage of the public saying they had "called a friend or relative just to talk" on the preceding day. At the same time, this was more than offset by a 12-point increase in the percentage saying they had visited with family or friends (from 57 percent to 69 percent).

Similar to the pattern for most of the media, there was no relationship between computer use and telephoning for a social chat, so that decline does not seem to be associated with presence of a home computer. The increase in visiting, on the other hand, was associated with greater use of the home computer. That was particularly true for respondents reporting heavier playing of games on the computer. In this case, then, we are left with the particularly counterintuitive finding that computer use is associated with increased personal interaction.

This finding can be explained in that certain computer games require another player to be enjoyed maximally or that computer users get together to share information and strategies. But this is not the most intuitive hypothesis from which to start.

Such a complex and counterintuitive set of findings, then, suggests that it will be some time before any simple explanation of the effects of new computers on everyday behavior will emerge. They also make it clear that full time-diaries of current users will be needed in order to fully appreciate the range of daily behaviors affected by these new information technologies and to verify that the aggregate declines in daily media usage in the present survey are found using different methodologies.

Finally, these findings are one more piece of evidence of the have–have-not society that has clearly emerged in American culture. The haves are busy, information-rich, more rushed, and exhibit greater "more-more" behavior, being more likely to participate in most forms of leisure activities than their less-privileged counterparts, even if they work longer hours. The have-nots are less likely to use home computers or print media, are usually less rushed (with the notable exception of women who are single parents), and show a less diverse pattern of leisure activity.

# 11

# Social Capital
# and the Rest of Free Time

Visitors to the Avenue of the Giants can
experience the world's tallest trees without leaving their cars.
—*Vacation the North Coast,* May 20, 1994

While television and the media may have become the dominant use of free
time in American society, they still account for only half of free-time activities. This chapter focuses on the final and most varied category of time-diary
activities: social, recreational, athletic, and arts activities, among others.
Such activities also tend to be among the most enjoyable (see Chapter 17).

These types of activities reflect the artistic or humanitarian aspects of a
culture that are ultimately and disproportionately used to characterize that
culture. Even in contemporary societies, with their technological preoccupa-

tions and economic imperatives, the arts and humanities describe the acme of culture, the aspects that elevate life beyond the repetition of drab functions and indistinguishable products. So too is a culture evaluated more on the vitality of its community life than on its consumer artifacts.

Social critics have recently lamented the loss of community in America (Bellah et al., 1985; Etzioni, 1993; Putnam, 1995a). Most of these activities tie individuals more closely to friends, neighbors, and fellow citizens—or at least involve levels of physical, moral, and mental interaction and engagement that one's work, family care, and media use do not offer.

## The Decline of Social Capital

Recent research by Robert Putnam documents the decline of "social capital," which he defines as "features of social life—networks, norms and trust—that enable participants to act together more effectively to pursue shared objectives" (Putnam, 1995a). Documentation of the decline in social capital includes greatly decreased membership in voluntary organizations, such as the Boy Scouts, the League of Women Voters, Parent-Teacher Associations, and the Red Cross, as well as decreased participation in many other organized activities, such as league bowling. Because Putnam believes that a democracy is dependent on social capital—that is, on voluntary participation—such declines are ominous. Moreover, democracies are not the only societies that depend on social capital: it has been argued that the inability of Russia to move from a communist state to a capitalist state has to do with its lack of social capital (Putnam, 1995b).

Putnam uses time-diary data to strengthen his case, citing a roughly 25 percent decline in time spent in informal socializing and visiting since 1965, and the nearly 50 percent decline in the time Americans spend in club and organizational activities. While the reasons for this decline are not completely understood, Putnam believes that the increased time spent in television viewing has been a critical factor. When many other explanations, such as longer work hours, are examined, they do not fit well as an answer. For example, workers with longer workweeks do not spend less time in civic activities; they spend more. Their time spent watching television, however, is almost 30 percent less.

Putnam examined a long list of explanations for the decline of social capital, including business and time pressure, economic hard times, residential mobility, suburbanization, the stress of two-worker families as women move into the labor force, disruption of marriage and family ties, changes in the structure of the economy, the events of the 1960s, the welfare state, and the civil rights revolution. After eliminating each of them as suspects, he is left with television as the culprit:

> Television flashed into American society like lightning in the 1950s. In 1950 barely 10 percent of American homes had television sets, but by 1959 90 percent did, probably the fastest diffusion of a technological innovation ever recorded. The reverberations from this lightning bolt continued for decades, as viewing hours per capita grew by 17–20 percent during the 1960s and by an additional 7–8 percent during the 1970s. In the early years, television watching was concentrated among the less educated sectors of the population, but during the 1970s the viewing time of the more educated sectors of the population began to converge upward. Television viewing increases with age, particularly upon retirement, but each generation since the introduction of television has begun its life cycle at a higher starting point. By 1995 viewing per television household was more than 50 percent higher than it had been in the 1950s. (Putnam, 1995b, p. 18)

Television thus emerges as a prime suspect in the decline of social capital.

## Eight Nonmedia Free-Time Activities

Trends in social capital and other nonmedia uses of free time since 1965 are shown in Table 13. These "other" free-time activities can be categorized into formal and informal activities. Informal activities are those that individuals usually engage in on their own to satisfy various leisure needs. The most time-intensive of these is visiting and interacting with other people, which usually take place in homes, at parties, in bars, and in restaurants. Informal activities provide the opportunity for opening up and exchanging personal feelings and opinions with other people. That is the basis of the "social fabric" of society. Included as a separate category here are telephone and other home conversations, through which family members can voice their needs, opinions, and wishes. Two separate types of recreational activity— sports/exercise and hobbies/avocations—are included in this informal cate-

**Table 13.**   Trends in Social Capital and Other Free-Time Activities
(in hours per week, for those aged 18–64)

|  | 1965 | 1975 | 1985 | 1985 minus 1965 |
|---|---|---|---|---|
| A. Informal |  |  |  |  |
|   Socializing | 8.2 | 7.1 | 6.7 | − 1.5 |
|   Communication | 3.6 | 3.4 | 4.4 | + 0.8 |
|   Sports/exercise | 1.0 | 1.6 | 2.2 | + 1.2 |
|   Hobbies | 2.2 | 2.8 | 2.8 | + 0.6 |
| B. Formal |  |  |  |  |
|   Religion | 0.9 | 0.9 | 0.9 | 0 |
|   Other organizations | 1.3 | 1.5 | 1.2 | − 0.1 |
|   Sports/cultural events | 1.2 | 0.6 | 0.9 | − 0.3 |
|   Adult education | 1.8 | 2.3 | 2.2 | + 0.4 |
| Total | 20.2 | 20.2 | 21.3 | + 1.1 |

SOURCE: Americans' Use of Time Project.

gory as well. These provide opportunities to improve or restore health, or to maximize personal talents or self-expression.

The other four sets of activities involve interacting with more formal organizations: schools, churches, cultural organizations, and voluntary associations. Such activities usually involve prescheduling, and often with some sort of agenda. Adult education allows intellectual growth and development. Religious services offer spiritual inspiration and sociospiritual bonding with others who share like beliefs. Cultural events offer diversion, insights, and reflection on the larger meanings of life. Voluntary organizations allow individuals to join others in pursuit of common goals not otherwise attainable in society (Lappe and DuBois, 1994).

While the above description presents these activities in terms of their loftiest ideals (and perhaps not in the way most people experience them), they still offer participants an opportunity to assert themselves or to transcend the more routine aspects of daily life. They at least offer the maximum *potential* for individual growth and expression, compared with the one-way process of television.

It is therefore reassuring to find that about half of free time is still devoted to these eight diverse types of nonmedia activity in the bottom summary number in Table 13. Moreover, nonmedia types of activities have managed to gain one hour a week of time commitment since 1965. Not all activities in this category have shared in this increase, and it is unfortunate that social life has declined by more than one hour a week since 1965—perhaps as a casualty of television. Adult education, hobbies, and sports/exercise, on the other hand, are up—particularly in relation to the low base times reported in 1965. Participation in sports and exercise more than doubled between 1965 and 1985. And across an era when many observers have doubted America's commitment to moral and family values, attendance at religious services (and organizations) has remained fairly constant.

## Informal Activities

### Social Life

More than three-quarters of social life consists of visiting friends, neighbors, or relatives in their homes or in the respondent's home; the remainder of the time is spent, for example, at parties/receptions or at bars and lounges, the former having showed the major decline since 1965. Part of the decline may simply have to do with increased suburbanization—people live farther from one another, perhaps making more use of telephone communication.

The major decline in socializing occurred for nonemployed women, with some decline occurring as well because more women in 1985 were employed. Neither employed men nor employed women showed much decline in visiting. Men and women in 1985 are equally likely to participate in social activities, which are far more likely to be reported by 18–24-year-olds than by respondents over 25.

Socializing is found about equally in all education and income groups. Less social time is found for married people, and among parents of younger and more children. Rural-urban differences are minimal. Socializing nearly doubles on weekends, being especially high on Saturdays.

### Conversation

Of the various activities in the "conversation" category, about one-third consisted of home conversations, one-third consisted of telephone conversations, and one-third was spent on correspondence and intrapersonal conversation (resting and relaxation).

The only increase in telephone and other home communication was found for employed men. Women engaged in such communication activities at the same levels as they had in 1965, and they engaged in these activities about 25 percent more than men. No notable differences by age were found.

Conversation was slightly higher among the better educated, but not among the more affluent.

Time spent in conversation was lower among those with longer work-weeks, among married people, and among people with more and younger children. Rural-urban differences were minimal, as were day-of-the-week differences, once the other factors are taken into account.

## Sports/Exercise

About half of sports/exercise activity in 1985 was in the form of active sports (especially exercises/aerobics, bowling, golf, and tennis), about 30 percent were in the form of hunting/fishing/excursions, and about 20 percent were walking and hiking activities. Participation in sports and exercise activities more than doubled between 1965 and 1985—the major increase found among these activities. This doubling of participation time was found across all four sex-employment categories, but the gain was somewhat higher for women. By 1985, women were doing more than half as much fitness and outdoor activity as men in 1985, a higher rate than in 1965.

People aged 18–24 were about 30 percent more likely to spend time engaged in sports and exercise activities than older people, but no declines for people in their forties and fifties were found. Participation was slightly higher among the college educated but no higher among higher-income groups.

Sports/exercise was not much lower among those having longer estimated workweeks, except for those working 60 + hours. Participation was highest among the never married, but mainly because of their younger age. Having older children was not associated with lower participation, nor having a pre-school child. Rural-urban differences were again minimal, while participation rose 50 percent on weekend days in line with the greater amount of free time available.

## Hobbies

About one-third of the hobby activities in the time diaries consisted of needlework activities, one-third involved board-card-computer games. The rest of hobby time included computer use, collections, art work, and making music.

Participation in hobby activities also increased since 1965, more so for employed men than for women. That was because time on (mainly female) needlework activities declined, while (mainly male) computer use increased.

Women continued to do slightly more of all this activity in the 1985 data, and those aged 55–64 did almost twice as much as younger age-groups. Participation was a little lower among the more educated and the most affluent.

Time spent with hobbies is higher among those who do not work or who work less than 20 hours (mainly women), but it declines irregularly as one's workweek length increases. Hobby activities are higher among those who are married and among those without children, especially preschool children. Participation is slightly higher among rural residents. It is more prevalent on Saturdays than other days of the week.

## Formal Activities

### Religious Activities

Among more formal uses of free time, religious observance (including reading the Bible) has remained steady across time and across gender-employment categories across time. A further 20 percent of time could be added to this category if we were to consider participation in religious organizations as a religious/social activity rather than an organizational activity.

Women take part in religious activities almost twice as much as men. Participation increases with age, with those aged 55–64 reporting twice as much time in religious activities as those aged 18–34. Blacks participate in religious activities twice as much as whites. Participation is rather equivalent across education categories, but it is well below average among more affluent individuals.

Time spent with religious activities tends to be shorter for people who work longer hours, but not on a regular or systematic basis. It is slightly lower among the never married, among nonparents, and among parents of preschool children. It is higher in rural than urban areas, and, not surprisingly, about eight times more prevalent on Sundays as on other days of the week. Unfortunately, no questions were asked about religious affiliation or strength of affiliation in the 1985 study, to make it possible to examine attendance differences by these important correlates of participation.

### Other Organizations

This category contains time on all other forms of associational activity, such as for Scouts, political groups, and social groups (like the VFW or PTA). Religious organizations emerge as the largest single category here, in terms of time expenditure. This category also includes the travel associated with all religious and organizational activity, but unfortunately this travel cannot be broken out further to relate it to type of organizational activity.

When this travel time is parceled out of the Table 13 entry of 1.2 hours in 1985, time spent on all these voluntary associations is less than an hour of time a week, about the same time Americans spent on religious activity. A brief glimpse at respondent descriptions of organization activity indicates that most of it serves a social function, rather than helping, altruistic, or political-action purposes. Far more altruistic activity appears in the form of *personal* help than altruistic activities done through a formal organization, reflecting the presence of those "thousand points of light" we keep hearing about.

Across time, the rather similar figure for organization activity across time in Table 13 conceals an important shift among women: employed women are now spending about 50 percent *more* time on these voluntary activities, while nonemployed women are spending about 20 percent *less*. However, nonemployed women still do about 30 percent more organizational activities than employed women, which is about 30 percent more than men do. This organizational activity increases rather steadily with age, with 55–64-year-olds doing about twice as much as those aged 18–24. College graduates report twice as much time as those who had not completed high school, and the more affluent are slightly more active as well.

Those with longest and shortest workweeks report most voluntary activity—about half again as much as those working 30–40 hours. Married people are also more active, but the presence of children is not associated with notably different levels of voluntary activity. Voluntary organization activity is about 50 percent higher in rural areas, and occurs more on weekends, especially Sunday.

## Cultural Events

The nearly one hour a week spent on activities in this category consists of about 40 percent attendance at sporting events (mainly at the high school level), 33 percent movie attendance, 15 percent fairs and amusement parks, and 12 percent attendance at museums, concerts, and other cultural events; the latter number translates to an average of 5 minutes a week or just over 4 hours a year of arts participation per capita. About 25 percent less time was spent on these entertainment activities in the 1980s than in the 1960s.

Much the same levels are found across gender and employment groups.

Cultural participation in 1985 was almost the same among men and women, and it declined with age to the point that 45–64-year-olds spent only 60 percent as much time on it as 18–34-year-olds. College graduates spend two to three times as much time as those with less than a high school degree; the more affluent are also above average in participation.

Length of the workweek is not associated with levels of participation, nor is marriage or parenthood—except for those with preschool children, whose participation is at half the levels of other parents or nonparents. Rural participation is only slightly lower. Attendance more than doubles on weekends, being twice as high on Saturdays as on Sundays or Fridays.

## Adult Education

Because most of the 2.2 hours spent on educational activities appears to be degree-related school work for students rather than for personal enlightenment, education is the most questionable activity we include under free time. Of educational activities, a little more is in the form of attending classroom instruction or lectures rather than on subsequent homework. That roughly 1:1 ratio is well below the 3:1 ratio of homework to class time assumed by many college professors of their students. That 1:1 ratio is what we found as well in diary surveys of college students.

While men report a little less educational activity than in 1965, women have almost doubled the time spent on education, to the point in 1985 that they spend 80 percent as much time as men. Educational activity declines markedly with age, being more than 20 times higher among 18–24-year-olds than those 55–64. It is also, of course, generally higher among those with more education, particularly those who have not finished their college education. It does not vary by level of income, however, perhaps because of the low income of most college students.

Lower levels of education activity are found the longer the estimated workweek, among married people and those without children (particularly parents of preschoolers). Educational activity is slightly lower in rural areas, and about twice as prevalent during the week as on weekends.

## Overall Trends Since 1965

The rather steady total figures of half of free time for the diverse set of more self-expressive types of activities (see Table 13) conceal a great deal of variation across various activities and social backgrounds. Across time, there are increases in sports/exercise and hobby activities, which largely offset the decreases found in socializing and entertainment. Such a combination of trends cannot be described by a simple set or pattern of trade-offs, as those found for the media or productive activities—although in general it may be that individual activities (like fitness and exercise) have gained as social activities (such as visiting and attending social events) have declined. Overall, however, this set of activities has managed more or less to hold its own in an era of free time increasingly dominated by television.

The time-diary data indicate trends that are consistent with Putnam's hypothesis about declining social capital, but not unambiguously or uniformly. Only three of the eight activities in Table 13—socializing, religion, and other organizations—seem to be direct indicators of social capital, and even these need further refinement to capture the essential facets of social capital. For example, to the extent that people attend organizations or religious services simply to be seen by others or to enjoy a free meal or other perks from the organization, they are not taking action toward social goals.

Part of the problem as well is that there are notable and not well understood differences in matching the 1965 sample with later surveys for this set of social capital activities. When related travel times are subtracted and the 1965 sample is matched on a location-to-location basis (using a University of Michigan matching program), a different picture emerges from that in Table 13. As shown in Table 14, this matching procedure results in 1965–85 declines in religious and organizational activities that are more consistent with the Putnam hypothesis.

As in Table 13, the downward trend for socializing is more dramatic. The marked decline in dinner and other social parties (code 76 in Table 1) is a major reason for this decline, which is highly consistent with the Putnam

**Table 14.**    Trends in Social Capital Activities for Matched Samples (in average hours per week, for those aged 18–64)

|  | 1965 | 1975 | 1985 | Difference |
|---|---|---|---|---|
| Socializing | 6.8 | 6.2 | 5.7 | − 1.1 |
| Religion | 1.0 | 1.0 | 0.9 | − 0.1 |
| Organizations | 1.3 | 1.1 | 0.8 | − 0.5 |
| TOTAL | 9.1 | 8.3 | 7.4 | − 1.7 hrs per week |

SOURCE: Americans' Use of Time Project.

NOTE: Excludes associated travel.

hypothesis. At the same time, the infrequency of these activities and their varied character in the diaries limits our ability to test Putnam's hypothesis as precisely as we would like.

## 1990s Trend Data on Participation in Arts and Fitness Activities

In order to track whether there have been any important changes in two of the important expressive and personal activities described in this chapter, we examine two quite-recent national surveys that covered those activities in considerable detail and accuracy. The first survey focused on participation in the arts; the second survey was on fitness activities.

Both surveys shared several methodological features that make them exceptional examples of behavior surveys that do not use the time-diary method. The first attractive feature is the size and quality of the samples interviewed. The Survey of Public Participation in the Arts (SPPA) interviewed 13,675 adults in 1992 (to replicate a 1982 survey with a sample of 17,254); the Health Promotion and Disease Prevention Survey (HPDP) interviewed more than 30,000 adults in both 1985 and 1990. Both surveys were conducted by the U.S. Bureau of the Census, and response rates were 80 percent or higher—levels we have yet to attain in time-diary surveys, or in almost any other national survey conducted by a nongovernment agency. Census Bureau surveys are renowned for their precision and standardization. Such large samples make it possible to examine important minority groups (in terms of age or education as well as ethnicity) in sufficient numbers to detect fine differences in participation. Thus, both samples contain national samples of 1,000–4,000 African Americans, of people past age 65, or of college graduates.

Both surveys were also spread equally across all 12 months of the year, meaning that they were not subject to seasonal biases. More important, exceptional care was given to constructing the activity questions to ensure that there was minimal ambiguity about the behavior in question. Moreover, both surveys covered a broad array of relevant activity—more than 20 different types of arts participation (both as spectator and performer) and more than 20 different types of fitness activity. That makes it possible to get a clearer sense of the relative popularity and frequency of specific forms of arts or fitness activities. What is the ratio of opera attendees to those who attend performances of musicals or the ballet, or those who visit an art museum?

What percentage of the population are joggers, compared with basketball or soccer players or bowlers?

Even more interesting is that it means that we can examine the extent of overlap or competition across these activities. Are opera attendees more or less likely to attend ballet or other arts performances? Do people who jog show higher or lower levels of participation in basketball, yoga, or racquetball? What are the age, gender, or education group correlates of participation that differ across activities or that appear to facilitate participation?

In terms of the time frame used for activity participation, the HPDP fitness survey has the advantage, because of its shorter and more recent time frame: the preceding two weeks. In contrast, the SPPA survey asked about arts participation over the last year—necessitated by the lower rates of arts participation over a two-week period. Both surveys then followed up with frequency questions that made it possible to separate frequent participators from infrequent participators and to use open-end categories so that responses would not be confined to pre-set categories of time

Both surveys were also longitudinal surveys that repeated the same questions across time, in this case making it possible for us to measure exact changes in two important uses of free time since our 1985 survey. The cross-time trends are discussed below.

## Arts Participation

At first glance, various economic and cultural trends in the late 1980s and 1990s did not bode well for the arts. Artists became embroiled in well-publicized political controversies, and countless economic uncertainties and stagnant household incomes cut the amount many Americans could spend for tickets; in addition, ticket prices for many arts events became out of reach.

Despite these omens, participation in the arts remained relatively steady across the decade. The number of adults who went to an art museum or gallery at least once in the previous year increased from 22 percent in 1982 to 27 percent in 1992—an increase of more than 12 million visitors a year (see Table 15). Adults who attended an arts and crafts fair at least once a year increased from 39 to 41 percent, or 7 million more attendees. The percentage who attended theater and other nonmusical plays increased from 12 percent to 14 percent, or 5.6 million new seats occupied.

Many of the gains were offset by losses in other types of arts activities, however. The percentage of adults who went to historic sites at least once a year declined from 39 percent to 35 percent, and the number who attended musicals and operettas declined from 19 percent to 17 percent. There was

**Table 15.**    Trends in Arts Participation (in percentage of respondents participating in last year)

| | 1982 | 1985 | 1992 | % Point Change: 1982–92 |
|---|---|---|---|---|
| Percentage Attending | | | | |
| Art museums | 22.1% | 21.9% | 26.7% | +4.6% |
| Art/craft fairs | 39.0 | 40.0 | 40.7 | 1.7 |
| Stage plays | 11.9 | 11.6 | 13.5 | 1.6 |
| Jazz | 9.6 | 9.5 | 10.6 | 1.0 |
| Ballet | 4.2 | 4.3 | 4.7 | 0.5 |
| Opera | 3.0 | 2.8 | 3.3 | 0.3 |
| Classical | 13.0 | 12.7 | 12.5 | −0.5 |
| Musicals | 18.6 | 16.6 | 17.4 | −1.2 |
| Historic/design parks | 39.0 | 38.0 | 34.5 | −4.5 |
| Percentage Personally Doing Public Performance of | | | | |
| Play jazz | 0.7 | 0.7 | 0.8 | +0.1 |
| Play classical | 0.9 | 0.9 | 0.9 | 0 |
| Sing opera | 0.2 | 0.1 | 0.1 | −0.1 |
| Sing musicals | 0.7 | 0.8 | 0.9 | +0.2 |
| Acting | NA | 0.8 | 0.8 | NA |
| Public and Nonpublic Participation | | | | |
| Pottery | 8.4 | 11.0 | 12.0 | +3.6 |
| Needlework | 24.8 | 28.0 | 32.0 | +7.2 |
| Photography | 11.6 | 10.0 | 11.0 | −0.6 |
| Painting | 9.6 | 9.0 | 10.0 | +0.4 |
| Creative writing | 7.4 | 6.0 | 7.0 | −0.4 |
| Music composition | 2.1 | NA | NA | NA |

SOURCE: Robinson, 1993e; Survey of Public Participation in the Arts, National Endowment for the Arts.

also a 3 percent decline in people who read novels, short stories, poetry, and plays.

Overall, more than 41 percent of American adults said they attended an arts event in 1992 (defined as a performance of jazz or classical music, operas, musicals, plays, or ballets, plus art museums and galleries). In surveys conducted in 1982 and 1985, that portion was 39 percent, so some overall slight increase was observed.

## Who Attends?

The most avid long-term audience for the arts comes from the college educated. Education remains the best predictor of a person's participation in the arts. Some 77 percent of adults with postgraduate degrees attend at least one arts event a year, compared with less than 10 percent of those with no high school education. Income also predicts arts participation, but most of these differences are explained by educational level.

Other demographic factors play a lesser role in attending arts events. Women participate in the arts slightly more than men do, and the elderly participate less than do younger adults. Whites participated more than African Americans or members of other races, but this difference disappeared after statistical adjustment for education and income.

Some demographic groups had gained in arts participation. African Americans showed greater gains in attendance at live performances than whites, perhaps reflecting a growth in the number of middle-class blacks during the 1980s. And empty-nesters (adults aged 45 to 75) showed faster gains than Baby Boomers (aged 25–44), particularly in attendance at classical music performances, musicals, and plays. Again, this may be due to the faster income gains in free time that older adults enjoyed during the 1980s.

Generation X respondents, on the other hand, did not share in this gain. Attendance at jazz performances among young adults (aged 18–24) declined sharply between 1982 and 1992, and so did their reading of literature. But a bigger problem may be an erosion of the education-arts connection. Arts participation declined slightly between 1982 and 1992 at most levels of educational attainment, and the decline was greater for adults who had at least some college education. In other words, college-educated people in 1992 were not as active in the arts as their counterparts in 1982.

## Personal Participation

Personal participation in the arts is of course much lower than attendance at arts events, but several million adults describe themselves as artists by avocation—far more than the number who describe art as their main occupation. About 25 percent of adults say they do some needlework at least once a year, and about 4.5 million had their handiwork displayed for the public. About 8 percent of adults took part in modern, folk, or tap dancing, with an estimated 2.2 million adults reporting that they danced in a public performance.

In general, the percentage of amateur artists also held steady between 1982 and 1992, but there were downturns. The portion doing needlework declined from 32 percent to 25 percent, and those who did pottery, metal, leather, or other crafts declined from 12 percent to 8 percent. Only 40 percent of Americans said they had taken music lessons, down from 47 percent in 1982. Only 18 percent had taken classes in the visual arts, down from 24 percent. But the percentage who had taken an art-appreciation class showed an increase, from 20 percent to 23 percent.

Arts appreciation continues to follow "the more, the more" principle: people who attend one event tend to go to others, and even sports fans and gardeners are also more likely to be arts attendees. As a result, the arts do not really compete with one another, and the success of one branch of the arts tends to help others. The real adversary of the arts, however, is television.

As with the more direct measures of social capital, the general rule is that the more television people watch, the fewer arts events they attend. But the relatively few people who watch arts events on television are more likely than average to attend a live performance. In other words, watching a lot of television doesn't necessarily dull your taste for the arts, but it might unless you watch "Great Performances."

## Fitness Activity Participation

Fitness was a major theme of the 1980s. Exercise addicts were visible on jogging paths, in health clubs, and in health-food stores. The "no pain, no gain" lifestyle seemed destined to continue, as medical studies confirmed the benefits of an active lifestyle. And when President Bill Clinton continued the practice of jogging on the White House grounds, he took the torch from George Bush.

In the 1990s, however, the love affair Americans have with fitness may be on the decline. Many weekend athletes have hung up their shoes, according to the National Center for Health Statistics data. Its National Health Interview Survey (NHIS) shows that overall participation declined 10 percent between 1985 and 1990. The National Center for Health Statistics included the topic of health promotion and disease prevention as part of the 1985 and 1990 NHIS. The NHIS is a continuous cross-sectional nationwide survey conducted through personal interviews in a representative sample of U.S. households. The 1985 sample consisted of 36,399 eligible households, 90 percent of which completed the Health Promotion and Disease Prevention portion of the questionnaire. The questionnaire collected baseline data on general health (including nutrition), injury control, blood pressure, stress, exercise, smoking, alcohol use, dental care, and occupational safety and health. The 1990 sample was 41,104, with a response rate of 83 percent.

The 1985 and 1990 NHIS surveys thus interviewed more than 75,000 adults and covered 22 specific activities, ranging from aerobics to gardening, from tennis to yoga. Respondents reported whether they had participated in each activity during the two weeks preceding the survey, how many times they had participated, and how much time they spent participating. To capture seasonal fluctuations in activities, they were surveyed throughout the year. While the NHIS does not show that more Americans have turned into couch potatoes, it clearly indicates that something in Americans' fitness habits has changed (Robinson and Godbey, 1993b).

## Popularity

Table 16 gives participation rates and frequencies for sports/exercise activities in the National Center for Health Statistics 1990 studies. Next to walking, yard work and gardening are Americans' most popular physical activities. In 1990, some 26 percent of Americans did yard work or gardening in the preceding two weeks. Calisthenics or general exercise was reported by 18 percent. The next most popular set of activities included aerobics, bicycling, jogging, swimming, and weight lifting. Some 7 to 11 percent of respondents said they had done at least one of these activities in the two weeks preceding the survey.

Lower in the list are more traditional and team-oriented sports, such as baseball, softball, basketball, bowling, golf, and tennis. Only 3 to 5 percent of adults had participated in these activities for the two-week period. Hiking also falls into this range, at 4 percent. The least popular activities included team sports like football, soccer, and volleyball, and some individual activities, such as handball, skating, skiing, and yoga.

The data show that the most traditional sports in America—baseball, basketball, football, golf, and tennis—each engaged less than 6 percent of the adult population in the preceding two weeks. The number of people who bicycled was almost four times those who played basketball.

One reason for the relative popularity of individual sports is easy to understand: doing sit-ups in the living room is simpler than getting a team together at the park. But even working out to an aerobic videotape takes more effort than sitting on the couch.

The share of adults who did any formal exercise in a two-week period (Table 16) declined from 22 percent in 1985 to 18 percent in 1990. The share who did gardening or yard work fell from 29 percent to 26 percent. The participation rate for 19 of the 22 activities declined, with the exceptions of walking, bicycling, and basketball.

**Table 16.**    Trends in Fitness and Exercise Activities

Question: "In the past two weeks (outlined on the calendar), beginning Monday (date), and ending this past Sunday (date), have you done any (of the following exercises, sports, or physically active hobbies):"

| | % Participating | | No. of Times | |
|---|---|---|---|---|
| | 1985 | 1990 | 1985 | 1990 |
| Walk for exercise? | 36 | 45 | 16 | 4.1 |
| Jogging? | 10 | 8 | 0.5 | 0.4 |
| Hiking? | 4 | 4 | 9 | 9 |
| Gardening or yard work? | 29 | 26 | 11 | 9 |
| Aerobics or aerobic dancing? | 8 | 7 | 39 | 36 |
| Other dancing? | 10 | 8 | 29 | 24 |
| Calisthenics or general exercise? | 22 | 18 | 163 | 127 |
| Golf? | 4 | 4 | 10 | 12 |
| Tennis? | 4 | 3 | 7 | 8 |
| Bowling? | 5 | 4 | 11 | 9 |
| Biking? | 10 | 11 | 53 | 57 |
| Swimming or water exercise? | 9 | 8 | 35 | 31 |
| Yoga? | 0.7 | 0.8 | 5 | 5 |
| Weight lifting or training? | 9 | 9 | 47 | 47 |
| Basketball? | 4 | 5 | 14 | 15 |
| Baseball or softball? | 4 | 3 | 10 | 8 |
| Football? | 1 | 1 | 4 | 3 |
| Soccer? | 0.8 | 0.8 | 0.02 | 0.02 |
| Volleyball? | 2 | 2 | 0.05 | 0.05 |
| Handball, raquetball, or squash? | 2 | 2 | 0.05 | 0.04 |
| Skating? | 1 | 1 | 0.02 | 0.02 |
| Skiing? | 1 | 1 | 0.03 | 0.03 |
| TOTAL | | | 6.16 | 5.51 |

SOURCE: Robinson and Godbey, 1993b, National Center for Health Statistics, National Health Interview Survey.

The few people who were active were not active as frequently. The active minority participated in fitness activities an average of 6.8 times over the two-week period in 1990, compared with 7.6 times in 1985. The biggest losers in terms of frequency were jogging, exercising, nonaerobic dancing, and gardening.

## Demographic Differences

It might appear that the decline in fitness activity has a simple demographic explanation. The U.S. population is aging, and the elderly are not as physically active as younger people. But this explanation does not hold, because the data show a declining pattern of activity for all age-groups, not just the middle-aged and the elderly. In fact, the decreases are sharpest among younger adults and women (see Appendix M). The same declines were found over other demographic categories as well, such as income, gender, marital status, race, and presence of children. Even college-educated adults, the heaviest participants in regular exercise, reported a decline since 1985.

Why are people in all walks of life less active in the 1990s? There are many explanations. Historically, Americans have had a boom-and-bust pattern of participation in sports and exercise. "One day in 1926," lamented F. Scott Fitzgerald "we looked down and found that we had flabby arms and a fat pot" (Boyle, 1962, p. 62). Rational recreation movements of the 1920s led to the doctrine of "muscular Christianity," in which the promotion of exercise, from gymnastics to folk dancing, was combined with character-building and religious instruction. Long before the advent of the couch potato, social critics were warning about the dire consequences of "spectatoritis."

Such sports as bicycling have gone through boom and bust cycles for the past one hundred years. While sports and exercise participation has definitely increased since the 1960s, specific activities remain cyclic or even fadlike in nature, like isometric exercises.

Another reason for the recent decline in exercise and sports participation may have to do with logistics. Single and working parents who must rush around to buy food and get children to baseball games may find it too difficult to get up a game themselves, and concerns about crime may also inhibit people from using public facilities.

A third reason may be cutbacks in funding for sports and exercise. Budgets have been cut for government recreation and parks departments across the country; it is more difficult to find money to repair municipal gyms, tennis courts, and swimming pools. The gutting of the Land and Water Conservation Fund Act during the Reagan administration put an end to matching funds for cities to develop recreation facilities, and some legislators now refer to federal funding for swimming pools and parks as "pork-barrel" spending.

Finally, Americans are getting mixed signals from the media about the benefits of exercise and a good diet. Studies show that regular exercise adds less than one year to a person's life. Other studies identify the risks of injury in sporting activities, including joint strain from jogging and long-term muscle damage from weight lifting. Americans who pay attention to these studies, as well as those who have ruined their knees, may have decided that the gain was not worth the pain.

This attitude shift can be particularly harmful to the kinds of exercise people do just for their health, rather than for fun. For example, people who join health clubs solely for their health often become inactive within six months, just as 9 in 10 dieters gain back the weight they lose. Lifting weights and walking on treadmills are not fun for most people, and if they begin to doubt the benefits they will stop doing it.

One fitness activity may have become significantly more popular in recent years—walking. Walking is one of the most common activities, but it is difficult to measure because the NHIS did not ask about walking as exercise in the same way in the two surveys; as a result, the apparent increase in participation from 36 percent in 1985 to 45 percent in 1990 cannot be interpreted clearly. Some increase makes sense, however, given evidence from the medical community that walking benefits the cardiovascular system almost as much as jogging does, and with less risk of injury.

## Overall Trend Directions

In contrast to the slightly increased levels of arts participation between 1982 and 1992, fitness participation suffered about a 10 percent decline between 1985 and 1990 (see Appendix M). Some of that may have been offset by an increase in walking, which is not trendable. It was about that time that fitness experts were touting the benefits of walking; the "no pain, no gain" philosophy was increasingly being called into question.

One important way in which the two surveys did agree was on the decreased participation of "Generation X," those aged 18 to 24. These young adults showed decreased participation in many arts activities, especially in reading literature, as well as the major declines in fitness participation. Whether this signals future declines in these more-demanding of free-time activities is too early to tell, but the signs cannot be regarded as positive.

The greater declines in fitness participation among women than men is also contrary to the general trend toward gender equality since 1965 that we noted in this activity. It may be an isolated trend in an isolated period, but it also is counter to the general trend toward increased "gender blending," which we have already noted often in the preceding chapters.

The time-diary numbers do remind us of the relatively small amounts of free time devoted to these activities in 1985. Just 5 minutes a week (about 4 hours a year) are spent attending arts events, which is less than one-half percent of free time and less than 1 percent of the time devoted to television viewing, some of which is arts-relevant, with SPPA data indicating that television and radio audiences are two to three times as large as for live arts events (Robinson, 1994). On the other hand, almost twice that amount (7 minutes a day) is spent in practice or rehearsal of arts content at the personal level, such as playing the piano or writing poetry. That works out to more like 3 percent of free time.

Close to 10 percent of free time goes into sports and exercise activities. While a substantial amount of that time may be devoted to the more seden-tary forms of sport (fishing or bowling), it is clear that such activities have become mainstays in the lifestyles of large numbers of Americans. Again, comparisons with data in other countries make Americans appear to be working harder toward keeping up their health in this way.

# PART 4

# The Demographics of Time Use

# 12

# Background Predictors of Time Use

The problem with being unemployed is that you never get a day off.

—P. Corrigal

There are many popular stereotypes about how different Americans use time. Wealthy people make poor people do most of the work. Older people sleep more. African Americans spend more time playing sports than whites. Things move slower in the South, faster in the Northeast. Issues like these are examined in this part, along with larger questions about whether different population groups are becoming more similar or more different with regard to time use. In order to facilitate the discussion, 15 major background variables associated with time use are arrayed in Table 17.

**Table 17.** Summary Correlations of Background Factors and Activities (1985 Data)

| BACKGROUND FACTOR → | Biological | | | Status | | | Role | | | | Temporal | | Ecological | | |
|---|---|---|---|---|---|---|---|---|---|---|---|---|---|---|---|
| | Sex | Age | Race | Education | Income | Occupation | Work Hours | Marital Status | Parenthood | | Season of Year | Day of Week | Urban or Rural | Reg | Hsg |
| (+ + for) | Women | Older | Black | College ed. | High | Profession | High | Married | P18 Yes | P5 Yes | Summer | SS | Rural | Sth | Hse |
| **Contracted Time** | | | | | | | | | | | | | | | |
| Work | – – | –,+ | o | + | + | | + + + + | o | o | – | o | – – – – | o | + | o |
| Commute | – – | –,+ | o | + | + | + o | + + + + | + | o | – | o | – – – | – | + | o |
| **Committed Time** | | | | | | | | | | | | | | | |
| Housework | + + + + | + + + | – | – – | o | o | – – | + + + | + + | + + | o | + | + | o | + + |
| Child care | + + + | – – | o | o + | o | o | – – | + + + | + + | + + | o | – | o | o | + + |
| Shopping | + + | o | – | + | o | o | – – | + + + | + o | + o | o | o | o | – | + + |
| **Personal Time** | | | | | | | | | | | | | | | |
| Sleep | o | o | o | – | o | – | – | o | o | o | o | + | o | o | – |
| Meals | – | + + | – | o | o | o | o | o | o | – | o | + + | o | o | o |
| Groom | + | o | + | – | o | o | o | – | o | – | + | + + | o | + | o |
| **Free Time** | | | | | | | | | | | | | | | |
| Education | o | – – | o | + o | o | o | – | – | o | o | – | + | o | – | o |
| Religion | + | + + + | + | o | – | o | o | o | o | o | o | + + + | + | + | o |
| Organization | o | + + | o | + + | o | o | o | + | o | o | + | + + + | o | o | o |
| Cultural event | o | – | o | + | + | o | o | o | o | o | o | + | o | o | o |
| Visiting | o | – | o | o | o | o | o | – | o | o | + | + + | o | o | o |
| Sports | – | o | o | o | – | o | – | – | o | o | o | + + | + | o | o |
| Hobbies | o | o | o | o | o | o | – | – | o | o | o | + | o | o | o |
| Communicate | + | o + | o | – | – | o | o | o | – | – | o | + + | o | + | + |
| TV | – | + o | – | – | – | o | – | o | – | o | – | + + | o | – | – |
| Read | o | + | + | – | o | o | o | o | o | o | – | + + | o | o | o |
| Stereo | o | o | o | + | – | o | – | o | o | – | – | + + | o | – | o |
| **Total free** | o | + – | o | o | – | – | – | – | – | – | o | o + | o | – | – |
| Travel | – | – | o | + + | + + | + | + | o | + | – | o | o | o | – | o |

SOURCE: Americans' Use of Time Project.

NOTE: See also Appendix S: "How to Read Table 17."

At first glance, Table 17 may seem daunting, and it does require a few minutes of study (see also Appendix S). A few comments about general patterns in the table may help orient the reader to its contents. First, it is perhaps surprising that the greatest numbers of + or − values are generally associated with the three role factors, particularly with hours at work but also with marriage or with the presence of children. Second, several large differences are also noted for the biological factors of gender and age (less so for race). Third, there are some notable differences by the status factor of education (but less so by occupation or income). Fourth, some large differences are also found, of course, for day of the week, although some of these differences in terms of number of hours spent at work and free time are less than commonly assumed. Many seasonal and locational differences are also less than might be expected.

In terms of examining these differences in more detail on an activity-by-activity basis for our four classes of predictors, the following major differences seem most prominent.

## Biological Factors

### Gender

Gender differences are concentrated mainly in productive activities and in the traditional direction of men doing more paid work and women doing more family care, especially child care and laundry. These two facets of productive activity tend to cancel each other out, so that amounts of overall free time are about equal (see Tables 4 and 6). Within free time, the major differences appear for women's greater participation in religious activities and men's greater participation in sports activities. In addition, women spend slightly more of their free time participating in organization activity, hobbies, and home communication, while men spend slightly more free time on adult education, television viewing, and radio/recordings.

### Age and Life-Stage

Table 17 also highlights certain age differences (within those aged 18–64) that appear for a number of activities. Within paid work and its commute, the contradictory − + sign is used to indicate that the inverted U-shaped distribution of work time by age, with lowest work hours for 18–24-year-olds and for the 55–64 age-group. Older people, of course, do far less child care, but that is offset in large part by the greater time they spend doing housework. Older people also spend somewhat more time eating meals.

The greater free time of these 18–24 and 55–64-year-olds again reflects their shorter workweeks. But despite their greater free time, older people spend much less of their free time on adult education, attending cultural events, socializing, and sports. While their television viewing and hobby time are only a little above average, older adults read much more and participate more in religious and organizational activities than younger adults.

These findings thus generally confirm what is described in other places in this book—namely, that it is the middle third of adult life that is the busiest. The fact that the leading edge of this current Baby Boom segment of the U.S. population is approaching the final one-third of their life span will bring about profound changes in time use, perhaps even slowing the overall pace of everyday life.

## Race

Racial differences are less prominent. African Americans do slightly less housework and slightly less shopping. They spend somewhat more time on personal grooming and spend slightly less time eating meals. African Americans have slightly more free time, which they use more to watch television and attend religious services. They also read less, but they listen more to radio/recordings. These racial differences are discussed in more detail in Chapter 15.

## Status Factors

### Education

Education differences are larger than income or occupation differences, as noted above. College-educated people spend slightly more time working and commuting to work, and more time shopping and caring for children (even though they have fewer children) than the less educated. In contrast, they do less housework. They also sleep less and spend less time on grooming activities than those with a high school degree or less. While overall meal and eating times are the same by education level, college graduates spend more time eating out.

Overall, then, college graduates have less free time, but they still spend more of their free time reading, going to cultural events, being involved in organizational/educational activities and doing sports/exercise activities. On the other hand, college graduates spend far less time watching television or listening to radio/recordings as a primary activity than do the less educated. However, they still spend more than one-third of their free time watching television.

## Income

Many of these activity differences are shared by higher-income people, but not to as great an extent. Thus, people with higher incomes spent more time working and commuting to work and slightly less time sleeping or grooming. Despite their lower amounts of free time, they spend more time attending cultural events and less free time watching television, although television still takes up about 40 percent of the free time of those whose incomes are in the highest 20 percent of the sample.

## Occupation

Even fewer differences have been found by occupation, independent of education and income. The longer work hours of managers and the higher TV hours of blue-collar workers are largely a function of education differences. Nonetheless, this is not a variable that has been well measured in recent diary surveys, and some important time use differences by occupational status have been described by Robinson, Athanasiou, and Head (1969). More discussion of these status factors, and the lack of many important differences by the factor of status, is provided in Chapter 15.

## Role Factors

### Work Hours

While they may exaggerate their work hours (see Chapter 5), there is no question that people who estimate that they work long hours actually do put in more hours on the job. They also put in more hours commuting to work, which means they have considerably less time for all three types of family care: core housework, child care, and shopping. While they sleep considerably less, they spend no less time on grooming, and they make up for their shorter meal times at home with more meals at work and in restaurants.

The relationship between work hours and free time is far from being one to one, however (see Chapter 8). For every additional hour of work, closer to half an hour of free time is given up, even less as the estimated workweek goes beyond 50 hours. The free-time activity that is most associated with lower work hours is adult education (which could also be stated in terms of students having more free time), although television, reading, home communication, hobbies, and religious activities are also lower among those having longer workweeks. Attending cultural events, socializing, and sports are less tied to workweek length, however, and participation in organizations seems hardly affected at all.

## Marital Status

It is not surprising that marital status affects mainly time spent on family care, especially for raising children. Being married is also associated with more at-home meals and less eating out, and also with less sleep and less personal grooming time.

Married people have less free time than the nonmarried, especially for such activities as adult education, socializing, and listening to radio/recordings. Married people also spend less time with hobbies, playing sports, and in home communication. However, they spend more free time in organizational activities.

## Parenthood

Having more and younger children at home is also associated with having less free time, mainly because of increased child-care time, but also because of more associated household chores. Having infants or preschool children is also related to less work time, meal time, and personal grooming time.

Adult education is the main free-time activity that is lowest among those with infants to care for, but attending cultural events, playing sports, television viewing, and reading are also lower. Those who have only older children show lower television use as well and lower socializing.

## **Locational and Temporal Factors**

### Location

Differences by region of the country are minimal, and the differences that are found seem mainly a function of education or age differences among people of the various regions. While it might be assumed that Californians lead laid-back lifestyles, in contrast to New Englanders' spending their time working or going to church, few such differences are apparent in the diary data. For although they have less free time, residents of the South spend more time going to church and watching television.

Living in a rural area is related to less time working and commuting to work but also to somewhat more housework. Some free-time activities, such as religious and organizational activities and sports/exercise, are engaged in more by rural residents; other activities, such as reading, are engaged in less. Overall, residents of rural areas have about as much free time as city or suburb residents and spend the same amount of time in travel. One must keep in mind that few current residents of these rural areas still live on farms.

Differences between those who live in single family homes rather than apartments revolve mainly around the greater home and family care associated with these larger spaces, and the greater numbers of family members who inhabit them. Much the same is reflected in the greater attention to home care among those who own rather than rent. House owners sleep less and have less free time, particularly for socializing, home communication, television, and stereo use; they do spend more time on hobby activities.

## Temporal Factors

Differences by season or time of year are surprisingly small, particularly once the greater vacation days in the summer months are taken into account. Gardening and outdoor sports are of course more prevalent in warmer weather, but other than the increase in attending cultural events (such as fairs and festivals) and the slight decline in television viewing (probably not the case in southern and other states, where hot summer weather chases people indoors), seasonal differences are not noteworthy. This may indicate the extent to which nature has been neutralized by modern living conditions as a factor in the way Americans spend their everyday lives.

The large day-of-week differences are not unexpected, particularly the decline in paid work time and its related commutes that take place on weekends. It is important to keep in mind that these weekend differences have recently become less pronounced. Weekends are associated with more housework and shopping, especially on Saturdays, but with lower child care time as well. Sundays are associated with increased time spent on all forms of personal care, not only for sleep but also for meals and grooming. Even though free time increases markedly on the weekends, not all free-time activities share in that increase. Adult education, including homework, is actually lower. Social, cultural, and sports activities show the most increase over weekday participation levels, but the largest increase is for religious activities on Sundays—which is more than eight times as high than on other days of the week.

Even larger differences are found by time of day, but most of these are so obvious that they need little comment here.

## Some General Patterns

Overall, then, the differences in Table 17 by the three role factors—work hours, marriage, and parenthood—are associated with the largest differences in how Americans spend time. Education differences are important for many of the ways people use their free time, and they are largely responsible for the differences found by income and occupation. Differences by geography and season are minimal.

In previous chapters, we noted how some of these correlations in Table 17 have changed since 1965. For example, we cited several instances of lower correlations with gender, as women work longer hours, do less housework, or watch more television relative to men. Larger correlations with age have been observed, as people aged 55 and older do less paid work. It has also been noted how differences by the role factors of work, marriage, and parenthood have increased over the last few decades.

The next chapter turns to more detailed discussion of differences by gender.

# 13

# Gender Differences and Trends: Toward an Androgynous Society

> The practice of seizing women from the enemy as trophies gave rise to a form of ownership—marriage, resulting in a household with a male head.
>
> —Thorstein Veblen

Perhaps the most important ongoing social revolution in the United States is the change in women's roles. While such changes may be realized more among young women than among older women, and among better-educated women than less-educated ones, they are pervasive. They receive new vitality from prominent events that highlight continual sexual harassment, such as the Clarence Thomas hearings or the O.J. Simpson trials.

We have already remarked on the large number of gender differences in how Americans spend time. In addition to the marked gender shifts in productive activities (see Chapters 5 and 6), women spend less time eating meals and traveling but more time grooming. Within the nearly equal free time men and women have, women use less of it for sports/exercise activities and television as primary (not secondary) activities; in contrast, they spend more of their free time for communication and religious activities.

But none of these activity differences is as dramatic as the activities for work and family care by women. Men still do 70 percent more paid work (or 62 percent of all paid work in society), while women do twice as much of the family care (or 68 percent). This continues to be the principal source of much of the dismay about women's inequality in literature and in politics.

This chapter examines how gender ratios in activity have changed across time. In particular, the data are probed for evidence of a trend toward greater "androgyny" in society. An androgenoid individual is one who has a balance of characteristics that are culturally defined as male and female. As Bem (1974) described it: "The concept of androgyny suggests that it is possible for an individual to be both assertive and compassionate, instrumental and expressive, stereotypically masculine and feminine, depending on the situational appropriateness of these various modalities."

It is interesting that the issue of gender inequality did not arise in earlier studies that calculated the free time of men and women using common definitions of free time. In one of the earliest studies of time use in the affluent suburb of Westchester County, New York, Lundberg et al. (1934) found men averaging 7.4 hours of free time a day, versus 8.2 hours for women; housewives had the most free time, 9.2 hours. In the national 1954 study of the Mutual Broadcasting Company, women had 34 hours of free time per week, versus 28 hours for men. In that context, the present time-diary results suggest that women have actually lost advantages in free time relative to men. These earlier studies, however, were conducted in times when women were not in the paid labor force in large numbers and when they had less access to leisure resources, such as an automobile or discretionary income, and less freedom to use them.

## Trends Since 1965

Nonetheless, there is not enough detailed information remaining in these earlier diary studies to detect general trends toward time androgyny, as can be done with the 1965–85 data set. All the gender correlates of activity are shown in Table 18. Each entry in the table shows the gender ratio in 1965,

**Table 18.**    Ratio of Men's to Women's Time on Various Activities Across Time

| | 1965 | 1975 | 1985 | Toward Gender Homogeneity |
|---|---|---|---|---|
| Contracted Time | | | | |
| Work | 2.50 | 2.10 | 1.70 | More |
| Commute | 2.60 | 2.30 | 1.70 | More |
| Committed Time | | | | |
| Housework | 0.18 | 0.31 | 0.50 | More |
| Child care | 0.27 | 0.31 | 0.29 | Same |
| Shopping | 0.73 | 0.65 | 0.67 | Less |
| Personal Time | | | | |
| Sleep | 0.98 | 0.96 | 0.99 | Same |
| Meals | 1.21 | 1.18 | 1.08 | More |
| Groom | 0.78 | 0.88 | 0.87 | More |
| Free Time | | | | |
| Education | 2.70 | 1.50 | 1.30 | More |
| Religion | 0.67 | 0.63 | 0.57 | Less |
| Organizations | 0.79 | 0.66 | 0.75 | Same |
| Events | 1.50 | 1.00 | 1.00 | More |
| Visiting | 0.82 | 0.96 | 1.06 | More |
| Sports | 2.60 | 2.90 | 1.90 | More |
| Hobbies | 0.58 | 0.57 | 0.85 | More |
| Communication | 0.56 | 0.78 | 0.78 | More |
| TV | 1.28 | 1.12 | 1.09 | More |
| Read | 1.24 | 0.91 | 0.90 | More |
| Stereo | 1.45 | 1.19 | 1.66 | Less |
| Total Free | 1.04 | 1.01 | 1.03 | Same |
| Travel | 1.36 | 1.27 | 1.13 | More |

SOURCE: Americans' Use of Time Project.

NOTE: Values above 1.0 represent greater male participation; values below 1.0 represent greater female participation.

1975, and 1985, with numbers above 1.0 indicating *men* do that much more of the activity, and numbers below 1.0 indicating *women* do that much more of the activity.

Of the 21 activities in Table 18, greater gender homogeneity or androgyny occurred for 14, or two-thirds of the activities (see the far-right column of the table). No effective change was found for 4 of the activities, and *greater* gender differences were found for 3 of them: shopping, religious activities, and listening to radio/recordings. The first two showed increasingly high female participation across time, while for stereo use men listened increasingly more (although such listening took up less than one hour a week and does not include secondary listening).

The most prominent movements toward gender homogeneity occurred for productive activities: the greater paid work (and related commute) of women relative to the decline for men, coupled with the greater core housework time for men relative to the large decline for women. No such trends toward equality were found for child care or for shopping, however.

Nor was much of the slightly greater sleep and nap time of women changed across time, although the gap did close from 10 minutes in 1965 to 4 minutes in 1985, after reaching 22 minutes in 1975. However, women did close the gap in men's greater meal times, and men closed the gap in women's greater grooming times.

Turning to obligatory activities, gender gaps were also found to narrow for 8 of the 11 types of free-time activities described in Table 18, even though the slightly higher free time of men remained rather intact. Women spend relatively more free time in adult education, reading, watching television, playing sports, and attending cultural events; men spent relatively more free time socializing, doing hobbies, and in home communication. No change was found in women's greater participation in organizational activities.

The final row in Table 18, "Travel," perhaps best illustrates the greater "liberation" of women across the recent decades. Time spent traveling was no longer 36 percent more prevalent among men as it was in 1965, but only 13 percent more prevalent. While nonemployed women spent more time getting away from home in 1985, travel for employed women increased more, to the point that they had reached parity with men in their time on the road.

## Interpretation

Androgyny in time use appears to be increasing across each of our four time-use categories: contracted, committed, personal, and free time. Greater androgyny of time use has occurred not only because females have changed their time-use patterns in ways that more closely resemble traditional male patterns, but also because males have changed their time use in ways that more closely resemble traditional female patterns. This is not to argue that gender is no longer relevant in explaining differences in time use; it continues to be of pivotal importance. It does appear, however, as though the dramatic changes in women's roles that have been documented over the last three decades are also reflected in how they describe their use of time in our time diaries.

Women's roles have changed remarkably over the last few decades. According to Howe and Strauss (1993, p. 73), today's young women differ in that they

> probably represent the largest one-generation advance in de facto sexual equality in American history. The 13th (born between 1961 and 1981) is the first generation of women who exceed men in average educational attainment. They're the first to pursue competitive athletics in significant numbers. They're the first to attend military academies, the first to enter the legal, medical, and business professions in double-digit percentages, and the first to approach male salaries in a wide variety of occupations. Knowingly or not, they're the front line shock troops in America's feminist campaign to achieve on-the-job economic equality. For all full-time U.S. workers, the median earnings of women may linger at only 70 percent of the median for men, but that ratio varies from a low of roughly 60 percent among the 50ish Silent Generation to a high of over 80 percent among 20ish 13ers.

Women's historical plight may have been forgotten. Almost all leisure activity used to be sex-segregated—for example, women rode tricycles rather than bicycles during the early bicycle craze; they visited each other only in sex-segregated areas on most social occasions, or in separate rooms in taverns; during the Civil War, women whose husbands had been killed were often required to wear mourning attire for seven years; and women achieved full voting rights only in 1920.

As "leisure" came to mean "free time"—the time left over after paid work (and as society was gradually reorganized to accommodate the leisure needs of the factory worker during his free time), leisure increasingly applied to the lives of men but not to those of women. The public house or bar, for example, replaced many rural forms of recreation for the male factory worker, but such places were almost exclusively for men and no equivalent facilities were available for females (although for some the church may have fulfilled a similar role in terms of socialization).

Even the "rational recreation" movements that sprang up in Europe and then in North America, seeking to reform the leisure habits of the working class, concentrated mainly on men. For women, the emphasis was on teaching working-class women to be better homemakers and mothers. The activities in which women engaged that might be considered leisure activities continued to have a decidedly domestic flavor. In almost all leisure contexts, women were subservient to men and could abandon their role of supporter and caregiver only rarely. This is not to imply that women had no free time, but rather that their generally inferior social status denied them access to most of the free-time opportunities available to men.

Certainly, much of this change has to do with the different life situations of men and women rather than with attitudinal or behavioral changes. The percentage of the households in the United States that contain traditional families—that is, a mother, a father, and children—has declined to about 26 percent. And more than ever, women are deferring marriage, getting increasing amounts of formal education, and living alone.

Not all of the more androgynous time-use patterns reflect changes in the attitudes of males or females, although certainly such changes are occurring. More similar hours of work may be occurring because many females no longer believe that marriage will last a lifetime. Much of the feminist movement has been a response to changing conditions, such as being pressed into the labor force, rather than an initiator of such change.

Be that as it may, the change in time-use patterns between males and females in Table 18 is occurring with extraordinary rapidity. Thus, in only a 20-year period the ratio of hours of paid work by males compared with females has dropped from 2.5 to 1.7, the educational use of free time has dropped from 2.7 to 1.3, and participation in sports/exercise from 2.6 to 1.9. In contrast, housework has risen from .18 to .50.

It may be that gender is becoming the same kind of "false" variable often attributed to age in the 1960s and 1970s. That is, age was often referred to as a variable that masked other more-important variables in predicting behavior, such as income, education, or health status. As older people have become more diverse in terms of level of formal education, income, and health, age probably predicts less about many behavioral and attitudinal issues. As the life situations of females become more diverse, gender too should become less predictive of numerous characteristics—time use among them.

We are not making the argument that movement toward gender equity in time use constitutes "progress." Women continue to suffer from many forms of discrimination. To assume progress is also to assume that other ascribed statuses—such as age, ethnic status, or other conditions into which people are born—should play no role in differentiating between people. The principal dilemma in discussing differences in time use (as with anything else) from the standpoint of gender, or of age or ethnic status, is that there is no way to examine such differences in human behavior and attitude without inferring inferior-superior relationships. Thus, for example, if males spend more time watching television than females, it must mean something either positive or negative for females.

It has been argued that males and females who are comparatively androgynous may be better able to cope with various life situations or experience fewer constraints on their leisure behavior:

> Androgyny is a valuable concept because it allows us, if only artificially, to separate socio-culturally constructed gender roles from biological sex. Much of the research to date has shown that women who were high in both masculine and feminine traits (i.e., who were androgynous) were highest in self esteem (Whitley, 1984). Females and males who were low on both aspects were lower in self-esteem. (Henderson et al., 1989, p. 127)

This does not mean that a unisex model with regard to time use is optimal. Indeed, many feminists would argue against women's leisure becoming more like men's, if men's free time does not also become more leisurely:

> There is certainly no future in advocating that women's leisure should become more like men's, if this means women become involved in activities which are selfish, hierarchically organized, overly-commercialized, aggressive, competitive and focused on rivalry rather than companionship. (Deem, 1986, p. 149)

Progress toward gender equity with regard to leisure instead means that there is a wide range of options with regard to people's roles in life, as well as options in terms of time use. It also means that equality of opportunity is enforced by laws that make no *a priori* assumptions. And one cannot safely infer that women have adequate access to other resources besides time. When women cannot go outside the home for entertainment because they fear for their safety, or cannot afford higher costs for enrichment activities, we are still a long way from parity.

Moreover, there are the invisible rules that prevent women from taking risks or make them feel their "work is never done." How can they have "free time" when they are always expected to be on call or to act as primary caregivers? Time-diary data tell an optimistic story about gender equality with regard to clock time, but they need to be supplemented with richer information about the constraints on or expectations about how time is spent.

# 14

# Widening Age Gaps in Time Use

It is difficult to imagine that once upon a time the person you are now was a wiggling, conservative molecule. In that world the passage of time made little sense. As the zygote grew into an embryo, fetus, infant, toddler, and young man or woman, the reality of time changed its character.

—J. T. Fraser

In terms of time use, age matters. In particular, the reduced working hours of those aged 55–64 have led to larger age differences in time use than in earlier eras. In this chapter, we examine not only these age differences, but the time-use patterns of two groups that have been excluded in the analyses thus far: children aged 0–17 and senior citizens in the full retirement years after age 65. Data are also presented on how the time use of younger children differs from that of children over the age of 12.

In order to examine and review all these age correlates of activity more comprehensively, they are arrayed systematically in Table 19, separately for men and for women. Each entry shows the hours per week for five age-groups: 12–17, 18–24, 25–54, 55–64, and 65 +. This makes it possible to trace differences in time use across almost the entire life cycle. It also makes it possible to see the possible trade-offs and substitutions people seem to make as they progress through the life cycle. They provide insights about the natural "experiments" that take place as various life-stages introduce either more constraints on free time or more liberated amounts of free time.

## The Free Time of Older People

For example, people aged 55–64 now find themselves with much more free time as they take early retirement or reduce their work hours. In 1965, they reported longer work hours than any younger age-group, while in 1985 they were well below average. Adding in the nearly 2 hours less of commuting time gave the 55–64 age-group about 18 hours of decreased work time, which they could spend on other activities in 1985.

While most of that reduced work went to free-time activities, not all of it did. About 2.5 hours went into increased work around the home, and nearly another hour was now spent on shopping. Personal care also rose about 2 hours a week, but rather than being used for increased sleep time or meal time (meals were now consumed at home and in restaurants), it went instead to increased grooming activity—an activity usually associated with increased work or activity outside the home. Nor did the travel activity of those aged 55–64 increase; it was slightly lower than in 1965.

Rather than having 18 hours of increased free time, then, those aged 55–64 had closer to 12 hours more. Once again, the major recipient of that increased free time was television. Reading and stereo use also increased slightly. Other more participative activities grew as well, particularly hobby and craft activities, and sports and outdoor activities and home communication also increased. However, time on other more participative free-time activities was basically unaffected. No increase was found in socializing, in adult education, in religious and organizational activities, or in attending cultural/sports events.

Despite having gained an additional 12 hours of free time, the only non-media activities showing an appreciable gain among the 55–64 age-group were hobby activities and, to a lesser extent, sports and exercise. Like the

**Table 19.** Age Differences in Time Use (1985 data, in hours per week)

| | Men | | | | | Women | | | | |
|---|---|---|---|---|---|---|---|---|---|---|
| | 12–17 | 18–24 | 25–54 | 55–64 | 65+ | 12–17 | 18–24 | 25–54 | 55–64 | 65+ |
| **Contracted Time** | | | | | | | | | | |
| Work | 2.5 | 24.1 | 36.0 | 21.5 | 7.2 | 2.4 | 19.6 | 21.0 | 12.5 | 4.7 |
| Commute | 0.3 | 3.2 | 4.1 | 2.2 | 0.8 | 0.2 | 2.1 | 2.4 | 1.3 | 0.4 |
| **Committed Time** | | | | | | | | | | |
| Housework | 5.9 | 7.0 | 9.2 | 13.5 | 16.7 | 6.5 | 11.1 | 19.3 | 22.9 | 22.8 |
| Child care | 0.5 | 0.4 | 1.7 | 0.7 | 0.3 | 1.9 | 4.7 | 5.3 | 1.8 | 1.0 |
| Shopping | 3.3 | 4.9 | 4.7 | 5.4 | 5.6 | 5.5 | 6.8 | 7.2 | 7.4 | 6.6 |
| **Personal Time** | | | | | | | | | | |
| Sleep | 62.9 | 58.5 | 54.9 | 57.5 | 58.7 | 65.0 | 58.8 | 56.2 | 55.3 | 60.3 |
| Meals | 7.9 | 8.4 | 9.5 | 11.2 | 12.1 | 8.6 | 7.5 | 8.7 | 10.4 | 10.9 |
| Groom | 9.9 | 10.1 | 9.2 | 9.5 | 12.0 | 12.6 | 11.6 | 10.4 | 11.6 | 11.4 |
| **Free Time** | | | | | | | | | | |
| Education | 25.6 | 10.9 | 1.5 | 0.6 | 0.4 | 22.1 | 7.1 | 1.6 | 0.1 | 0.1 |
| Religion | 1.1 | 0.5 | 0.6 | 1.4 | 2.0 | 1.0 | 0.9 | 1.1 | 1.4 | 2.0 |
| Organizations | 1.8 | 0.7 | 0.9 | 2.2 | 1.1 | 1.3 | 1.1 | 1.2 | 1.8 | 1.4 |
| Events | 1.7 | 1.1 | 0.9 | 0.6 | 0.1 | 1.8 | 1.1 | 0.8 | 0.6 | 0.2 |
| Visiting | 7.3 | 11.2 | 6.6 | 6.7 | 6.0 | 5.5 | 9.4 | 6.4 | 5.7 | 5.5 |
| Sports | 6.9 | 4.2 | 2.9 | 2.8 | 3.0 | 3.5 | 1.8 | 1.5 | 1.5 | 1.8 |
| Hobbies | 6.7 | 2.0 | 2.5 | 3.5 | 3.5 | 5.1 | 2.3 | 2.7 | 4.8 | 4.9 |
| Communication | 2.8 | 3.7 | 2.8 | 3.1 | 4.5 | 2.7 | 3.0 | 3.3 | 3.7 | 3.9 |
| TV | 17.5 | 14.7 | 16.1 | 18.2 | 24.9 | 17.9 | 14.6 | 14.3 | 18.7 | 22.1 |
| Read | 1.3 | 0.8 | 2.6 | 4.7 | 6.7 | 1.3 | 2.2 | 2.9 | 4.4 | 5.5 |
| Stereo | 0.7 | 0.6 | 0.5 | 0.9 | 1.3 | 1.1 | 0.7 | 0.3 | 0.3 | 0.6 |
| Total Free | 73.4 | 50.5 | 37.8 | 44.7 | 53.2 | 63.3 | 44.0 | 36.0 | 43.0 | 47.9 |
| Travel | 9.3 | 11.9 | 11.0 | 9.2 | 7.2 | 9.2 | 10.0 | 9.8 | 7.7 | 6.1 |

SOURCE: Americans' Use of Time Project.

rest of the population, then, the media became the major beneficiaries of this increased free time for people in preretirement years.

That is much the same pattern of change seen in Table 19, which compares the activities of people who actually reached retirement age (aged 65 + ) with those in younger age-groups. Compared with their counterparts aged 55–64, male senior citizens have more than 8 hours more free time, and women have almost 5 hours additional. But men aged 65 + spend nearly 7 more hours watching television, and senior women spend almost 4 more hours viewing. There are increased hours spent reading, and for men there is increased home communication as well, but virtually no gain in more participative nonmedia activities. Indeed, attending cultural events becomes all but nonexistent among these senior citizens, and time for social and organizational activities is notably lower as well, despite increased free time. Travel is down nearly 20 percent compared with people aged 55–64. In contrast, sleep time is higher by 5 hours for senior women, and grooming time is up 2.5 hours for senior men.

Both of these "quasi experiments" with the time use of older citizens thus suggest that rather than engaging in more participative (and, we shall see in Chapter 17, more enjoyable) free-time activities, their time largely gravitates toward television. To some extent, that is the same situation for the younger population, but gains in free time have been so much greater among older people that one might have hoped for more spread among more participative activities as well as the media. Reading and home communication/conversation are also higher among the elderly, but gains relative to television must be considered disappointing.

Free time among the elderly is not infinite. It amounts to 53 hours a week for men and 48 hours for women, and this represents a gender gap that seems to appear as people enter their retirement years. While the division of housework and shopping does become more equitable in retirement years, women still do most of it. That gender gap in productive activity is again offset to some extent by the slightly higher paid work time of eldest men and the higher sleep time of eldest women (see Table 19).

The groups with highest amounts of free time are adolescents, but that is an artifact of their "work"—going to school—being counted as a free-time activity. When school time is subtracted, the amount of free time among adolescents comes closer to that of 18–24-year-olds than senior citizens. However, adolescents do less housework, child care, and shopping than 18–24-year-olds—and they are able to obtain 4–6 hours more sleep. In terms of free time, adolescents spend more time at religious, organization, and cultural events, and more time on television, sports, and hobby activities as well. Where 18–24-year-olds do spend *more* time relative to adolescents is on socializing and visiting.

A more detailed examination of these differences among adolescents and young adults that follows draws on data from a supplemental sample from a 1987 California statewide survey of time use to increase the sample of adolescents in the 1985 national survey.

## Time Use Among Adolescents

Parents feel their teenagers watch too much television. Teachers complain that they don't do enough schoolwork. Child advocates worry that they spend too much of their formative years working for money. And health professionals say they don't get enough physical exercise.

How teenagers really use time is contained in time-use diaries obtained from 418 respondents aged 12–17. We compared the results with a similar sample of unmarried adults aged 18–24. Only results that were replicated in a similar 1987–88 time-diary study in California, with 160 additional teenagers, are reported.

The major contrasts between the time use of teenagers (aged 12–17) and young adults (aged 18–24) grow out of the transition from school to work. Teenagers average less than 3 hours a week in work-related activity (including travel to and from work), compared with young adults who work 23 hours a week. But teens spent about 24 hours a week in school-related activities, compared with only about 9 hours for young adults. Thus, paid work appears to take up all the time a teenager once spent in school activities, plus an additional 5 hours a week.

What happens during teens' extra hours? Teenagers spend 4–6 hours more time sleeping and napping each week than do their 18–24-year-old counterparts. Teens watch television more than 17 hours a week, compared with about 14 hours for unmarried young adults. But teenagers also spend time in more active pursuits. They spend more time on sports, both as participants and as spectators, than young adults. Teens also play more board games and cards.

In contrast, young adults spend more time than teens on less-active, less-formal types of socializing, such as visiting, going to parties, going to bars, and talking on the phone. Time spent with formal organizations and religious activities declines as one enters the years past adolescence.

The time teenagers and unmarried young adults spend doing family chores differs by less than 5 hours a week. However, teens spend less time preparing meals, cleaning, and doing laundry than young adults do, while teenagers spend more time on yard and garden work, repairs, and pet care. These differences reflect a major lifestyle change for teens: from living with parents in larger homes, to apartment life with roommates their own age. Contrary to popular belief, teenagers don't spend more time in the kitchen or bathroom. Young adults and teens take about the same amount of time to wash, dress, and eat meals. Reading books, magazines, and particularly newspapers shows an increase among young adults. Many of these time-use differences happen gradually through the teenage years.

There are, moreover, differences between teens. Adolescents aged 12–15 spend more time sleeping, watching television, and playing games than do those aged 16–18. In contrast, older teens spend more time doing paid work, visiting friends, going to the movies, engaging in hobbies, and doing homework.

Gender differences among teenagers tend to follow traditional patterns. Teenage girls spend more time than boys preparing food, shopping for groceries, caring for young children, doing indoor cleaning, and being involved with plant/pet activities. However, the time that either boys or girls contribute to housework is not likely to affect the free time of their mothers much. It averages less than one hour a day. Stereotypically, girls spend slightly more time than boys on grooming and personal hygiene. Girls also spend more time doing homework, while boys spend more time participating in sports and pursuing hobbies. Boys and girls spend the same amount of time reading, however.

This brief overview of how teenagers spend time shows a group that is in transition to adult life. They still have the benefits of more free time and sleep time, but they are also taking on more adult responsibilities.

## Time Use Among Younger Children

Recent data on how children under the age of 12 spend their time are now available from cross-sectional samples. Two sources of such data are examined in Table 20, one at the national level from a sample of 229 children aged 3–11 interviewed by researchers at the University of Michigan in 1980 and 1981, the other from a 1989–90 sample of 894 California children aged 3–11 interviewed by the University of California. The latter sample has the advantage of being more recent, and also more representative (a response rate of over 80 percent, versus about 30 percent for the Michigan survey), more comprehensive (data was collected across the whole year rather than over two periods during the year), and covering activities more fully.

While the two studies generally produce similar results, lifestyles and activities that are peculiarly Californian are in evidence in Table 20. For example, children in California reported 8 hours in weekly outdoor activity and 7 hours of sports, compared with less than 2 hours and 3 hours in the national sample; conversely, indoor play is only about 10 hours in California versus 18 hours nationally. Arts activities are nearly 2 hours a week among California children versus about half an hour in the national sample, but hobbies are higher in the national sample. The national sample also reported more hours in school (21 hours a week versus 17 hours in California), although study

**Table 20.** Time Use of Children Aged 3–11: Comparisons of 1989–1990 California Children's Data with Data from the 1980–1981 University of Michigan National Study of Time Use (in hours per week)

| Children Aged 3–11 | 1980–81 National (n = 229) | 1989–90 California (n = 894) |
|---|---|---|
| Paid work | 0.8 | 0.2 |
| Housework | 2.8 | 3.4 |
| Eating | 9.4 | 9.2 |
| Sleeping | 69.6 | 72.2 |
| Other personal care | 5.1 | 4.5 |
| School | 21.3 | 13.2 |
| Studying | 1.4 | 1.5 |
| Church | 2.3 | 0.4 |
| Visiting | 2.1 | 0.9 |
| Sports | 2.5 | 7.0 |
| Outdoors | 1.6 | 8.2 |
| Hobbies | 0.4 | 0.1 |
| Arts activities | 0.5 | 1.9 |
| Playing indoors | 17.9 | 9.6 |
| TV | 16.9 | 19.2 |
| Reading | 1.1 | 1.4 |
| Conversation | 1.3 | 1.1 |
| Rest/relaxation | 1.4 | 0.7 |
| Other activities | 6.9 | 12.9 |
| Not ascertained | 2.8 | 0.2 |
| TOTAL | 168 | 168 hrs/wk |

Source: Wiley et al., 1991.

Note: Coding and further details are provided in Appendix N.

time was about the same; that may be because only the fall and spring seasons were covered in the national survey.

Nonetheless, on most other activities the two surveys produce remarkably convergent time data, similar enough to support the following conclusions about differences among younger children (in comparison with older adolescents):

- Paid work time among young children averages about 2 hours a week.
- Housework among young children is about 3 hours less, which translates to less than half that of teenagers (3 versus 6 hours a week).
- Sleep time is 5 hours a week higher, and meal time is one hour a week higher.
- Visiting/social life is less than 20 percent of that among adolescents (1 versus 6 hours), and conversation is one-third.
- Total play and sports time is more than double that of adolescents (22–25 versus 10 hours a week).
- Weekly television hours (17) are about the same as adolescents, as is time spent reading (1.3 hours).

In general, then, as children grow into adolescence, their personal care and play time decline as they take on more social, housework, and paid work responsibilities. Further age breakdowns for children from the two studies are in Appendix N.

## Time Use Among Senior Citizens

There is life after work. Even though a person's lifestyle changes significantly after age 65, older Americans remain active in many ways. In the 1985 nationwide time-diary studies, about 600 respondents in the study, and just over 400 in 1975, were 65 years of age and older. Because of the small sample sizes, the data in this analysis have been amplified using responses from the 1987–88 time-diary study of 250 Californians aged 65 and older. We again highlight only the findings that are consistent in both the national survey and the California study.

Most of the differences in time use between older Americans and other adults result from the decrease in time spent working, not from any clear physical effects of aging. Those who continue to work after age 65 have time-use patterns similar to those of younger working adults. But among older Americans in general, work time drops to less than 25 percent of what it is for those aged 18 to 64. Retirement age thus frees up 25 hours a week for men and 18 hours for women, on average.

Some of this spare time goes into increased housework—about 7 more hours each week for men and 4 or 5 more hours for women. Time spent in personal care also increases. As a result, men aged 65 and older have about 15 more hours of free time than younger men, while older women enjoy about 12 more hours of free time than younger women.

The large increase in housework time by retired men seems surprising. After all, most 65-year-old American men acquired their social attitudes in the years before women's liberation. Yet older men do almost double the household work of men in their thirties and forties; in contrast, women aged 65 and older spend only one-third more time doing housework than younger women. On average, then, men aged 65 and older do more than 40 percent of the housework, compared with only 33 percent among younger men aged 18 to 64.

This increase has not affected all aspects of housework equally. Activities that are traditionally the man's role, such as yard work, repairs, and gardening, show the greatest increases for men after age 65. Men also increase time spent on traditionally female tasks, such as cooking and cleaning. But when it comes to laundry, traditional boundaries still hold. Men aged 65 and older do less than 20 percent of it. They also get involved in far less child care than do older women.

The amount of time spent shopping remains relatively unaffected by retirement age. Men's shopping time increases slightly after age 65, while women's shopping time drops slightly. The same pattern applies to time spent on personal hygiene.

Time spent eating out remains about the same, but older Americans do spend significantly more time eating at home. Overall, meal times increase by almost 50 percent. Older men spend 10 hours each week at the dinner table; women spend about 9 hours.

Older Americans also sleep more, but much of this increase is due to an increase in daytime naps. Nap time nearly doubles after a person reaches age 65. Unreported activity increases as well. It is difficult to say whether this increase is due to memory failure, sensitivity to divulging personal information, or other reasons.

## Free-Time Activities

Although older Americans do have more free time, some free-time activities seem to decline in importance as people age. Older Americans spend less time than other adults pursuing adult education and organizational activities; they go to fewer movies, sports events, and other entertainment events; and they are less likely to spend time at parties, bars, or cafés.

The media—television, radio, and newspapers—claim most of the gain in an older person's free time. Television gets the largest share of this increase, picking up more than 50 percent of it. The 25 hours that older men spend watching television each week (22 hours for older women) approaches half of their total free time and more than 20 percent of their total awake time. And television time is not fully reflected in these numbers. If someone is reading a newspaper while watching television, half of this would count as reading time. While reading time totals only 6 to 7 hours each week among the elderly, that is significantly more than the 2.8 hours a week spent by Americans aged 18–64.

Older Americans may generally lead more sedentary lives, but they are only a little less active than younger people in many ways. They spend more time walking than younger people, and there is no significant decrease in outdoor sports, recreation, and hobby times. The amount of time spent playing cards and other games increases. And older women spend nearly twice as much time doing needlework. Visiting and socializing take up about the same amount of time for people of all ages. Older adults spend somewhat more time writing letters and notably more time participating in religious activities.

When diary data on the elderly from the 1985 study are compared with a study conducted in 1975, relatively few differences emerge. The number of hours older Americans spent on paid employment was higher in 1985 than in 1975, but the increase was only about 2 hours a week. There was also an increase of 1 to 2 hours a week in time spent on housework. In general, then, the trends among the elderly mirror those found among younger adults.

## Time Use Among the Newly Retired and Very Old

To examine how the aging process itself may affect time use, we divided the elderly into two groups: the newly retired (aged 65–74) and the very old (aged 75 and older). Again, we find paid employment accounting for the major difference between these two groups. Men aged 75 and older work only 5 hours each week, on average; women work less than 3 hours. But many of the differences in time use between the youngest and the oldest elderly remain surprisingly small.

The time someone aged 75 and older spends caring for children declines significantly, but time spent doing housework falls only slightly. Shopping times are somewhat lower for women, but not for men. Eating out decreases, while grooming time increases. Women increase the amount of time they spend sleeping, but men do not.

The oldest Americans spend more time watching television, listening to the radio, and reading newspapers than do 65–74-year-olds. The amount of time they spend playing sports and traveling declines, along with the time spent on most hobbies. But the differences in time use between the "new old" and the "old old" are not as great as the differences between the preretirement and postretirement populations. Employment, not age, is the major influence on an older person's time use.

## Lifestyle Contrasts of Adolescents and Senior Citizens

The two groups at the opposite ends of the age spectrum show some interesting if occasionally disheartening patterns of time use under conditions of minimal attachment to the paid labor force. While both enjoy 10–15 hours a week more free time than those caught up in the middle of their work careers, the most visible share of that free time is devoted to television. In that way, they mirror the main shifts in free-time allocation of the working population during the same period (see Chapters 7 and 8).

These two groups also get 5–10 more hours of sleep a week than those in the working-age population, which may be beyond what is biologically necessary. Meal times are also higher among older people, while teenagers report lowest amounts of time for food consumption. Unlike teens, older people also spend increased time doing housework and reading, in contrast to the decreased time spent traveling and in educational activity.

Also unlike older people, adolescents spend higher amounts of time playing sports and going to cultural events, part of the general trend in society to spend less time in such activities as one ages. In both groups, then, we find activities that ought to be more prevalent among those at the opposite ends of the age continuum. Thus, it would be encouraging to see increased sports, educational activity, cultural participation, and travel generally, among the elderly, and more reading and home communication among those who are about to enter adult life. Perhaps increased contact across the two age-groups could accomplish that.

# 15

# Status and Racial Differences in Time Use

The future orientation of the middle class person presumes . . . a "surplus" of resources to be invested in the future and a belief that the future will be sufficiently stable both to justify his investment (money in a bank, time and effort in a job, investment of himself in marriage and a family, etc.) to permit the consumption of his investment at a time, place, and manner of his own choosing and to his greater satisfaction.

—Elliot Liebow

To the extent that society has different expectations of individuals, based on their social and ethnic statuses, it is not surprising that these statuses become predictors of how an individual's time will be used. This chapter looks at a few of the more important and enduring personal statuses that shape everyday life.

Sociologists have identified many important differences in the daily lives of individuals of different social status or class. Most of these relate to access to various important resources in society, particularly income and wealth.

More recently, they have noted parallels in noneconomic resources and forms of capital. Terms such as "social capital" and "cultural capital" have been coined to identify other resources and ways in which people wield power and influence in society as a function of their social status (Bourdieu, 1977; Coleman, 1982).

Historically, it has been assumed in the writings of thinkers as diverse as Marx and Veblen that people with higher levels of education and income enjoy more leisure than poor or working-class people. In Thorstein Veblen's classic treatise (1899) on the "leisure class" almost a century ago, leisure was seen as: "non-productive consumption of time. Time is consumed non-productively from a sense of the unworthiness of productive work, and as evidence of pecuniary ability to afford a life of idleness" (p. 90).

Veblen saw history as a process by which humans, through an ethic of workmanship, created the surplus wealth that was to give them some sense of security on earth. The same surplus, however, permitted a new group of motives to be created. Wealthy people found their pleasure in "invidious distinctions" at the expense of others, mainly in the form of "conspicuous consumption," flaunting their wealth to others. These behaviors, combined with the ability to avoid productive work and to use the time of others in unproductive ways, were the hallmarks of the wealthy leisure class of the 1890s. Movie-goers were recently shown glimpses of this lifestyle in the feature film "The Age of Innocence."

In modern American society, however, the privileged get the better jobs rather than more leisure. While college-educated people may live in better homes, drive fancier cars, or wear designer clothes, they do not have more free time; indeed, having abundant free time is not a badge of honor. Even the issue of what social class is most given to conspicuous consumption is subject to question. As Riesman (1958) observed, "The working class has fallen heir to conspicuous consumption, which the leisure class is giving up" (p. 186).

It is not surprising, then, that Americans with a college education work longer hours than people with less-formal education (see Table 17). Education differences are larger than income or occupation differences, and college-educated people spend not only more time working but also more time commuting to work, as well as more time shopping and caring for children (even though they have fewer children) than the less educated. They also sleep less and spend less time on grooming activities than those with a high school degree or less, but they spend more time eating out. Part of this may be because they also feel more rushed and more stressed than people with lower levels of education (see Chapter 16). Overall, then, today's privileged class of college graduates does not have the privilege of more free time.

One positive finding about college graduates is that they are more likely to spend their free time in ways that can be thought of as "worthwhile" (see Table 17). They spend more time reading, going to cultural events, being involved in organizational/educational activities, and participating in fitness activities than those with lower levels of education. Moreover, college graduates also spend far less time watching television or listening to radio/recordings as a primary activity than do the less educated.

Many of these activity differences are shared by higher-income people, but not to as great an extent. Thus, higher-income people also spend more time commuting to work and less time sleeping. They also have less free time and spend less of that free time watching television. Even that supremely inexpensive way of spending free time in front of the set still takes up almost 40 percent of their free time.

These time differences across social status are notable and consistent, but they fail to reveal several crucial aspects of the ways that more affluent/ educated individuals live their lives differently from those who are less privileged. The insensitivity of simple time-expenditure data to social class factors is evident in earlier sociological research. For example, there are few consistent differences between the time expenditures of executives and blue-collar workers in Lundberg et al.'s (1934) diaries from the most affluent suburb of Westchester County; exceptions were the slightly higher radio listening by blue-collar workers and slightly higher club activity of executives. Reiss (1959) failed to confirm several straightforward hypotheses about the social contact times of people of different social classes, or differences by rural-urban location.

Thus, more-subtle and detailed ancillary information is required to capture the real lifestyle differences between the more and less privileged. Do not the more affluent work more hours because they can enjoy that work by influencing others or because the work has elements of play? Do not their more lavish home surroundings make their housework less onerous? Do they not dote on their children more, investing more time in chauffeuring them to private lessons and computer camps and pampering them with the latest technology? Don't they control them more with guilt rather than with physical punishment? Are their movie choices not more informed by Siskel and Ebert? Is not their conversation more cosmopolitan and less tied to family matters? When they play sports, aren't tennis and golf preferred to bowling? Don't they listen to classical and show-tune music rather than country-western or soul music? Even within the same genre of music, don't their favorite melodies involve more chord changes? Isn't more of their hobby time spent on the computer rather than on needlework or cars?

Ample studies in the sociological literature illustrate these important status distinctions implicit in the same activity category. For example, Gottlieb (1957) documented vastly different behaviors exhibited in neighborhood bars and in cocktail lounges, and Blum (1964) noted subtle and unexpected cultural differences in the TV viewing by working-class African Americans. However, these require insights that are probably possible only with in-depth observation or anthropological training.

Only in this way may we also be able to address and answer questions about whether the lifestyles of the more affluent are of measurably higher "quality" than those of lower social class. Thus far, the answers from quality-of-life studies that have asked respondents to rate these features of their lives on standardized rating scales do not show much difference by social status (Campbell, Converse, and Rodgers, 1976; Andrews and Robinson, 1991). But these hardly can be taken as the final answer on this pervasive age-old question.

# Racial Differences*

The preceding two chapters have described differences in activities related to biological factors of gender and age. Differences by the biological factor of race, which often reflect differences in social status, have their own origins and sociological literature.

Debates about the progress African Americans have made in the United States persist as different authors reach different conclusions from the same data. How much closer are African Americans to taking part in the same activities as their white American counterparts? How much difference in activity patterns can be attributed to being African American in the United States, a country in which race continues to influence or determine differential levels of education, occupational achievement, and income?

The first study that examined the concept of African American convergence was Gunnar Myrdal's *An American Dilemma* (1944). Almost twenty

---

*Co-author of this section is Ronica Rooks. A far more detailed analysis of racial differences is provided in her thesis "Racial Differences in the Use of Time: Convergence vs. Divergence" (University of Maryland, 1995).

years after Myrdal's first edition was published, he added a postscript: "There could be no doubt that the races were moving rapidly toward equality and desegregation by 1962. . . . The dynamic social forces creating inequality will, I predict, be practically eliminated in these decades" (Myrdal, 1962, pp. xliii–xliv).

Myrdal believed these changes were "most complete in the economic sphere, next in the legal and political spheres, and least in the sphere of social relationship(s)" (p. xxvii). In contrast, only six years later, the *Report of the National Advisory Commission on Civil Disorders* (1968), also known as the Kerner Commission report concluded: "Our nation is moving toward two societies, one African American, one white—separate and unequal" (Kerner et al., 1968, p. 1).

Both studies have since generated a vast amount of literature concerning the economic improvement of living conditions of African Americans. The literature on economic issues—individual earnings, occupation, education, family income, and employment—provides important lifestyle indicators about purchasing power in American society. Education is important because higher education not only gives people access to greater earnings, but also gives them access to skills that enable them to enjoy different activities than those with lower education.

## Are Differences in Time Use Converging?

Certain scholars support the notion of *convergence* in different realms since the 1960s: Farley (1984) in the areas of individual earnings, occupations, and education; R. B. Hill (1978, 1981), with individual earnings and occupations; Freeman (1976), with income, occupations, and education; Fisher (1992), with individual earnings and family income; Smith and Welch (1986), with individual earnings and education; Moynihan (1972) and Glazer (1978), with family income; and Sowell (1981) and Wattenberg and Scammon (1973), with occupation, family income, and higher education.

On the *divergence* side of the debate are authors who believe that despite gains made in the 1960s, many of those gains had been undone by the 1990s. In particular, the Milton B. Eisenhower Foundation concluded that "the famous prophecy of the Kerner Commission—of two societies, one black one white, separate and unequal—is more relevant today than in 1968, and more complex, with the emergence of multiracial disparities and growing income segregation" (Ostrow, 1993, p. A23).

Furthermore, in accordance with this perspective are the findings of R. B.

Hill (1978, 1981), Cotton (1989), Swinton (1988), Bryce (1973), Branch and Williams (1988), and Felder (1984) on family income; Smith and Welch (1986) and Farley (1984), with family income and employment; Bates (1988), with unemployment; Fisher (1992), with occupations; Pinckney (1984), with unemployment, family income, and occupations; and Jaynes and Williams (1981), with fluctuating gains and losses of African Americans in the areas of employment, occupation, and education.

African Americans are hypothesized to show convergence in "contracted time," which includes work and commuting time, because they have had greater access to education and training since the 1960s, enabling them at least to be employed and to work hours similar to those of whites. The Equal Employment Opportunity Commission and affirmative action laws have helped to lower the barriers of discrimination that have historically prevented some African Americans from finding jobs. The economy's expanding white-collar and service sectors, which tend to employ a large percentage of African Americans (Pinkney, 1984, pp. 90–92), have contributed to the convergence of work and commuting time between the two groups.

African Americans should also show convergence in "committed time," including housework, child care, and shopping. The movement of labor from a manufacturing to an information/technological workforce should limit the time spent in committed activities for both African American and white workers. Similarly, African Americans should show convergence in "personal time"—sleeping, eating meals, or grooming. In contrast, African Americans are likely to spend more time grooming than whites, possibly because blacks struggle with having the proper image for acceptance in the white-dominated business and social world (Tyler, 1992, p. 235). They may also spend more time grooming because looking good produces a "feeling good" sensation that helps them cope with the pressures of racism.

Regarding free-time activities, African Americans are expected to spend more time going to church and participating in religion-affiliated activities, as a result of the legacies of slavery. Attending church services was for slaves a way to temporarily escape oppression and to reinforce their belief that God would provide a better life in heaven. Today the church represents a place of security and independence where African Americans have gained self-definition and self-determination (Harding, 1981, p. 44). Of particular importance are the leaders the churches have provided for African Americans, leaders who are trusted, listened to, and understood.

Another free-time activity that is apparently diverging is television viewing. Based on a study by the BBDO Worldwide advertising agency, viewing patterns appear to be growing further apart. In 1992 a survey found almost 50 percent more TV viewing in African American households, an average of 73 hours a week, compared with 50 hours a week for nonblack households (Kolbert, 1993).

## Bivariate Differences

Differences by race are arrayed systematically in Table 21. Differences in other basic racial/ethnic groups are not shown because of the small samples involved. Even the samples of African Americans included only 130–285 respondents per survey.

Of the 21 activities in Table 21, differences by race are consistently in the same direction for most of them. With regard to paid work, for example, African Americans spend more time commuting to work, even though racial differences in time spent working are neither large nor consistent. This may be because blacks live farther from their place of work or because they rely more on public transportation. All three household production activities show consistent racial differences, with African Americans spending more time in child care but less time doing core housework or shopping.

With regard to personal-care time, African Americans spend half again as much time as whites on personal grooming, but a little less time on eating meals. Sleep differences are neither large nor significant.

The result is that African Americans have 2–3 more hours of free time each week than whites—which is not significant, given the small sample sizes involved. However, within that free time there are two activities that blacks do spend much more time on than whites: religious activities and television viewing. In each survey, African Americans spent almost twice as much time going to church as whites did, and 5 more hours a week watching television; they also listen more to radio and recordings.

In contrast, African Americans spend less time reading and going to cultural events, such as fairs and museums, although these do not represent as large amounts of free time as the 5 hours more of television they watch. Differences in free time spent for education, sports, and home communication are neither significant nor consistent; African Americans spent more time visiting in 1965 and 1975, but less time in 1985.

Although many of these activities on which African Americans spend less time are done away from home, and TV viewing is done mainly at home, this does not mean blacks spend more time at home. Travel times are roughly equivalent for whites and blacks.

**Table 21.** Trends in Various Activities by Race (White and African American), (in hours per week)

| (n =) | 1965 White (1,755) | 1965 AfrAm (131) | 1975 White (1,817) | 1975 AfrAm (197) | 1985 White (2,768) | 1985 AfrAm (285) | Higher By |
|---|---|---|---|---|---|---|---|
| Contracted Time | | | | | | | |
| Work | 29.6 | 32.2 | 26.6 | 25.8 | 26.3 | 23.4 | Same |
| Commute | 2.6 | 3.3 | 2.5 | 3.0 | 3.0 | 3.5 | AfrAm |
| Committed Time | | | | | | | |
| Housework | 17.3 | 15.5 | 14.9 | 11.9 | 14.7 | 11.9 | Whites |
| Child care | 4.2 | 4.8 | 3.3 | 4.8 | 3.0 | 3.1 | AfrAm |
| Shopping | 6.3 | 3.8 | 5.3 | 5.3 | 6.4 | 5.0 | Whites |
| Personal Time | | | | | | | |
| Sleep | 55.0 | 53.8 | 57.4 | 59.7 | 56.1 | 55.1 | Same |
| Meals | 9.3 | 8.2 | 10.0 | 6.1 | 9.1 | 7.5 | Whites |
| Groom | 8.8 | 9.3 | 8.9 | 10.7 | 9.8 | 14.4 | AfrAm |
| Free Time | | | | | | | |
| Education/Travel | 1.0 | 1.0 | 2.3 | 1.7 | 2.3 | 2.3 | Same |
| Religion | 0.8 | 1.7 | 0.8 | 1.5 | 0.8 | 1.7 | AfrAm |
| Organizations/ Travel | 1.4 | 0.9 | 1.1 | 0.7 | 1.2 | 1.2 | Whites |
| Events | 0.9 | 1.7 | 0.6 | 0.3 | 1.0 | 0.5 | Whites |
| Visiting/Travel | 8.2 | 9.8 | 7.0 | 8.5 | 6.7 | 6.3 | Same |
| Sports | 1.0 | 1.2 | 1.7 | 0.9 | 2.4 | 2.4 | Same |
| Hobbies/Travel | 1.8 | 0.6 | 2.8 | 2.0 | 2.8 | 2.3 | Whites |
| Communication | 3.2 | 2.7 | 3.2 | 5.1 | 4.3 | 4.5 | Same |
| TV | 10.5 | 12.7 | 14.8 | 16.7 | 14.6 | 19.6 | AfrAm |
| Read | 4.0 | 3.0 | 3.5 | 0.9 | 3.0 | 1.6 | Whites |
| Stereo | 0.5 | 0.7 | 0.6 | 1.5 | 0.3 | 0.8 | AfrAm |
| Total Free | 33.3 | 35.9 | 38.4 | 40.0 | 39.2 | 42.3 | AfrAm |
| Travel | 9.4 | 9.8 | 9.2 | 9.5 | 10.4 | 10.3 | Same |

SOURCE: Americans' Use of Time Project.

How much are these differences simply a function of the different education levels, ages, occupations, family structures, and so on, of African Americans compared with whites? To answer this question, an MCA was performed on the 1985 data for the six major differences described above. Except for the insignificance of the greater free time African Americans have, all of the above differences remained statistically significant, and virtually unchanged, after MCA adjustment. Thus, even after taking into account the lower levels of education and employment, and different genders and ages, African

Americans still watched more television, attended church more, did less housework, spent more time grooming, and so on. These seem to be factors that distinguish the lifestyles of African Americans and whites.

## Converging Lifestyles?

There is the question of whether the lifestyles of African Americans and whites are becoming more similar, in light of various affirmative action programs and antidiscriminatory measures taken since the 1960s. That closing of gaps is what we found for the gender differences in Chapter 13. Does it hold for race as well?

The evidence from Table 21 is much more mixed. On the one hand, the greater amount of time African Americans spend on child care, travel, and visiting has diminished considerably, as have the lower amounts of time they spend participating in organization activity and working with hobbies. Racial differences in these activities have come closer to parity since 1965.

On the other hand, there are an equal number of activities for which the racial gaps have increased, particularly in regard to the media. The greater television and stereo times for African Americans over whites have widened, as have blacks' lower reading times. The same is true for African Americans' spending more time grooming and less time eating meals. The paid work time for African Americans, however, is lower than for whites—the reverse of the pattern found in 1965.

## Multivariate Results

A multiple regression model was performed for all the diary activities, using race, year, and an interaction term between race and year. In this model, the interaction term between race and year was statistically significant for only four activities: personal time, grooming, attending events, and television watching. In 1965, whites started out with more personal time, but after 1975 African Americans spent more time in these activities. For grooming activities, the gap between African Americans and whites continued to grow larger from 1965 to 1985, with blacks spending more time grooming. For attending social events the analysis indicates that before 1975, African Americans were spending more time than whites going to social events, but afterward the trend reversed in favor of whites. The last activity for which the race and year interaction was significant—watching television—also indicates a steady trend toward divergence between African Americans and whites from 1965 to 1985.

When education and income were added as control variables, however, for three out of these four activities—personal time, attending events, and television viewing—the interaction term was no longer significant. In the case of grooming, however, the interaction term between race and year remained statistically significant.

In sum, race was found to be an important explanatory factor for the activities of religion and watching television. The multiple regression results supported expectations that religion and television viewing were activities African Americans spent more time participating in than white Americans. Out of the 21 activities in Table 21, cross-time regression results revealed that only time spent grooming was statistically significant, and that was in the direction of divergence. For most activities, then, cross-time differences between African Americans and white Americans have not become significantly similar over time.

# PART 5

# Subjective Time

# 16

# Perceptions of Time Pressure

The American is always in a hurry.

—Alexis de Tocqueville

Hurrying was, in a sense, a consequence of democracy. If people were free to do what they wished, their wishes might multiply. Alexis de Tocqueville recognized that, for Americans, the problem with time might not be so much how they used time or how many hours they spent working or at leisure, but what they might ultimately want from time.

By themselves, minutes-per-day data in the time diary almost defy interpretation. There must be an understanding of the respondent's perception of time. How a person feels about time or what someone hopes to accomplish may ultimately be more important than how one actually spends the time. After completing a one-week time diary that showed about 50 hours of "free time" activity a week, one student told us, "I still feel rushed." Similarly, after reviewing both our time-diary data on declining hours of work and our attitudinal data showing that many Americans believe they are becoming even more rushed, a marketing expert Leonard Berry (1990) nonetheless recommended "marketing to the perception" rather than the reality: "Time diaries may be the most accurate way to measure how people actually spend their time, but it is perception that shapes behavior. People who *believe* they are pressed for time will respond accordingly."

Until this point, this book has concentrated on the number of minutes people spend on various activities. This part, Part Five, deals with three separate aspects of the subjective nature of time. This chapter focuses on feelings about time pressure or stress, the subjective aspect of time that has most captured the attention of societal observers. People's relative enjoyment of or satisfaction with time spent in various activities is described in Chapter 17. In Chapter 18, we examine relationships between the inputs of time expenditures and the "outputs" from that activity—the clean home, which is presumably the purpose of housework, or the higher marks in school, which are indicators of successful study.

In examining the matter of time pressure in the present chapter, several disparate measures related to the notion of "time famine" are described. Of primary concern are perceptions people have that their lives are "rushed," that they do not have enough time to fit in everything they want to or should do. Some of these questions were first asked in our 1965 study. Second, more recent data on self-perceptions of general "stress" from time constraints and other sources are reviewed. Third, data from a 1991 Hilton survey on indicators of "time crunch" are examined, including perceptions people have that they have less free time than in the past. The estimates of free time that respondents give in these surveys are markedly lower than the amounts time-diary studies show they have. Finally, questions related to time "elasticity," the ways in which daily time could be stretched or compressed by altering time spent on those activities, are reviewed. What daily activities do respondents say are most expendable or most easily given up?

## Feeling Rushed

The oldest and most complete benchmark on time pressure is based on the two questions developed for the first 1965 national study of time: one on feelings of being rushed, the other on feelings of having time on one's hands. The questions are presented in Table 22, along with the frequency response to the questions in 1965 and in eight subsequent national surveys, through 1995, for the rushed question and in five surveys on the time-on-hands question, also through 1995.

The "always feel rushed" response has shown a gradual increase since the 1965 study, in which 24 percent of the 18–64 group described themselves as always rushed. By 1975, some 28 percent of the aged 18–64 sample reported being always rushed, and the number rose again to 35 percent in 1985 and to its peak of 38 percent in 1992; the two most recent national surveys show a slight decline, as discussed at the end of this chapter. Much the same is found for the total population of all people aged 18 and older, rising from 22 percent in 1971 to 27 percent in 1982 to 35 percent in 1992.

Parallel decreases are found at the other end of the scale item, with the 27 percent saying "almost never feel rushed" in 1971 decreasing to 20 percent in 1985 and to 17 percent in 1995. Further, the percentage of the samples aged 18 and over saying on the second question that they "almost never" had time on their hands rose from 47 percent in 1971 to 56 percent in 1995; in contrast, those saying "quite often" dropped from 13 percent to 9 percent over the 24-year period.

Across time, then, both questions show that people today feel more harried than 25–30 years ago. This is clearly counter to what might be inferred from the Chapter 8 diary trends in increased free time.

The diary and subjective measures do seem to reflect the same phenomenon, in that the groups in these surveys that experience greater feelings of being rushed tend to be those with less free time noted in their time diaries: women, the middle aged, and whites; the college educated and the more affluent; the employed, married people, and parents. In general, this is also the same pattern of predictors as in 1965, with one main exception: the lack of increase in feeling rushed among those 55–64, the group gaining most free time since 1965.

Thus, although the correlates and determinants of feeling rushed have stayed much the same, the trends have not. Counter to the increase in their free time, significantly more respondents feel time pressure today than 30 years ago.

## Perceived Stress

Since 1985, the federal government's National Center for Health Statistics near Washington, D.C., has been collecting trend data on Americans' per-

**Table 22.** Perceptions of Feeling Rushed

A. "Would you say you always feel rushed, even to do the things you have to do, only sometimes feel rushed, or almost never feel rushed?"

| National (age 18+) | Mich 1965 | Mich 1971 | Mich 1975 | Mich 1978 | GSS 1982 | MD 1985 | PSU 1992 | MD 1994 | MD 1995 |
|---|---|---|---|---|---|---|---|---|---|
| (n =) | (1,130) | (9,519) | (1,513) | (3,665) | (1,852) | (2,976) | (1,208) | (503) | (1,208) |
| % Always rushed, age 18–64 | NA (24%) | 22% (25%) | 25% (28%) | 18% (23%) | 24% (28%) | 32% (35%) | 35% (38%) | NA (35%) | 29% (33%) |
| % Sometimes rushed | (53%) | 51 | 49 | 57 | 52 | 48 | 48 | (50) | 54 |
| % Almost never | (23%) | 27 | 26 | 25 | 24 | 20 | 18 | (15) | 17 |
|  | 100% | 100% | 100% | 100% | 100% | 100% | 100% | 100% | 100% |

B. (If sometimes/never rushed): "How often would you say that you have time on your hands that you don't know what to do with—quite often, only now and then, or almost never?"

| | Mich 1965 | Mich 1971 | Mich 1975 | Mich 1978 | GSS 1982 | MD 1985 | PSU 1992 | MD 1994 | MD 1995 |
|---|---|---|---|---|---|---|---|---|---|
| (n =) | (2,261) | (2,411) | — | (2,993) | (1,404) | — | NA | (329) | (849) |
| % Quite often | 15[a] | 13 | — | 9 | 18 | — | NA | 7[b] | 9 |
| % Only now and then | 37[a] | 40 | — | 43 | 41 | — | NA | 32[b] | 35 |
| % Almost never | 48[a] | 47 | — | 48 | 41 | — | NA | 61[b] | 56 |
|  | 100% | 100% | | 100% | 100% | | | 100% | 100% |

Source: Americans' Use of Time Project.

[a]Asked only if "never rushed."
[b]18–64 only.

ceptions of stress in their lives. The questions used are quite straightforward, asking respondents to describe the extent to which they have experienced stress in their lives over the previous two weeks and in the previous year, using a four-category response scale from "a lot" to "a moderate amount" to "a little" to "almost none." Interviews are conducted across the entire year with the same large samples described at the end of Chapter 11—more than 30,000 in 1985 and 1990 and more than 20,000 in 1993—so that the total column in Table 23 is based on more than 90,000 respondents. Table 23 shows the percentage reporting either "a lot" or "moderate" stress in the previous two weeks for 1985, 1990, and 1993 (the yearly stress question was not asked in 1985).

The percentage reporting these levels of stress did increase 6 points between 1985 and 1993 (versus the 13-point increase in feeling rushed over the previous 30 years and the 8-point increase since 1985). Again, the increase is counter to the increase in diary free time, and it is found in virtually all segments of society.

Nonetheless, the correlates of stress were much the same in the 1990s as they were in 1985—and as they were for feeling rushed. Women felt more stress than men, and increasingly so since 1985. Highest stress was reported by the middle-aged, peaking in the 35–44 age-group and dropping notably after age 54. Whites felt more stress than African Americans or Asian Americans.

Among the status factors, there was again higher stress among the college educated and the more affluent. With its large sample size, the NCHS study also provides detailed breakouts by occupational level that verify not only that middle-class and white-collar occupations are higher in stress, but also that, among them, administrators, managers, and higher-level salespeople are more likely to feel stress than other executives and office workers. While blue-collar and service workers report below-average stress levels, that is not true for police and fire workers, who are also significantly above average in the stress they report. In contrast, household and cleaning workers, along with the retired, report the least stress in this very large national sample.

## The Time Crunch

Another recent approach to the question of felt time pressure in the American public was provided in a 1991 national survey conducted for the Hilton Time Values Project (Robinson, 1991b). The sample size was far smaller

**Table 23.** Differences in Stress by Background Factors and Year (percentages reporting "a lot" or "moderate" stress in the previous two weeks)

|  | Total: | 1985 | 1990 | 1993 |
|---|---|---|---|---|
| Total Sample | 54% | 50% | 56% | 56% |
| **A. Biological Factors** | | | | |
| *Gender* | | | | |
| Male | 52 | 50 | 54 | 53 |
| Female | 57 | 52 | 59 | 58 |
| *Age* | | | | |
| 18–24 | 58 | 55 | 61 | 60 |
| 25–34 | 62 | 59 | 65 | 62 |
| 35–44 | 66 | 61 | 68 | 67 |
| 45–54 | 60 | 54 | 63 | 61 |
| 55–64 | 48 | 44 | 51 | 50 |
| 65–74 | 34 | 31 | 36 | 36 |
| 75 + | 30 | 28 | 30 | 33 |
| *Race* | | | | |
| Asian | 44 | 41 | 43 | 47 |
| African American | 45 | 40 | 48 | 46 |
| White | 57 | 53 | 59 | 58 |
| **B. Role Factors** | | | | |
| *Marital Status* | | | | |
| Married | 56 | 52 | 58 | 57 |
| Widowed | 37 | 34 | 39 | 38 |
| Divorced | 61 | 58 | 64 | 62 |
| Separated | 62 | 56 | 68 | 62 |
| Never married | 57 | 54 | 60 | 58 |
| *Employment Status* | | | | |
| Work | 61 | 57 | 64 | 62 |
| Housewife | 46 | 43 | 48 | 48 |
| School | 63 | 61 | 66 | 44 |
| Other (retired, etc.) | 38 | 33 | 39 | 40 |
| **C. Status Factors** | | | | |
| *Education* | | | | |
| Grammar | 34 | 32 | 36 | 36 |
| Some high school | 46 | 42 | 48 | 48 |
| High school grad | 54 | 50 | 56 | 55 |
| Some college | 63 | 60 | 65 | 62 |
| College graduate | 65 | 63 | 67 | 64 |
| Graduate school | 67 | 67 | 68 | 64 |

|  | Total: | 1985 | 1990 | 1993 |
|---|---|---|---|---|
| *Income* (in thousands) | | | | |
| <$5K | 55 | 49 | 58 | 62 |
| 5– 6.9K | 48 | 42 | 50 | 52 |
| 7– 9.9K | 47 | 44 | 49 | 49 |
| 10–14.9K | 50 | 46 | 53 | 51 |
| 15–19.9K | 51 | 48 | 54 | 52 |
| 20–24.9K | 54 | 52 | 55 | 54 |
| 25–34.9K | 57 | 55 | 59 | 56 |
| 35–49.9K | 61 | 60 | 63 | 60 |
| $50K> | 65 | 62 | 67 | 64 |
| D.  Geographic Factors | | | | |
| *Region* | | | | |
| East | 54 | 49 | 57 | 55 |
| Central | 57 | 55 | 59 | 59 |
| South | 52 | 49 | 55 | 53 |
| West | 57 | 53 | 56 | 58 |
| *City* | | | | |
| 1 million | 56 | 53 | 58 | 56 |
| 200–999 | 56 | 51 | 59 | 57 |
| 100–250 | 52 | 47 | 54 | 54 |
| *Metro Area* | | | | |
| City | 54 | 51 | 56 | 55 |
| Suburbs | 57 | 53 | 60 | 58 |
| Rural | 52 | 47 | 54 | 54 |
| E.  Lifestyle Factors | | | | |
| *Health* | | | | |
| Excellent | 55 | 57 | 58 | 54 |
| Very good | 56 | 53 | 58 | 57 |
| Good | 53 | 48 | 54 | 55 |
| Fair | 55 | 49 | 56 | 62 |
| Poor | 64 | 61 | 66 | 66 |

SOURCE:  Robinson and Godbey, 1996; National Center for Health Statistics, National Health Interview Survey.

(n = 1,008), and the data collection was less elegant, than the NCHS effort, but the questions were far more detailed and informative. Perhaps the most provocative result from the study was the finding that almost half the survey respondents said they would be "willing" to give up a day's pay to have an extra day off from work.

This could be taken as a dramatic reflection of the burdens of work that Americans felt, but it should be treated more as a momentary opinion than as a firm action-oriented policy stand. Earlier surveys (BLS, 1987; Juster and Stafford, 1985) demonstrated that, when given the choice of working more or fewer paid hours, higher proportions of American workers preferred *more* work hours to fewer hours—although most respondents said their current balance was acceptable.

Indeed, a 1993 statewide survey conducted only in Maryland included both questions and found almost as high a percentage of Marylanders (45 percent) saying they wanted the day off without pay, as in the 1991 Hilton national survey. In contrast, when asked the work-hours question, only 12 percent said they wanted to work fewer hours (versus 32 percent saying they wanted more hours, 52 percent the same hours, and 4 percent unsure). The two questions do seem to tap the same sentiment: 75 percent of those saying they wanted more hours said they wanted their day off, compared with only 33 percent of those saying fewer hours. However, the day's-pay-for-days-off question does not appear to reflect as serious a sense of time commitment on this issue.

Therefore, the 10 items that were used to form a "time crunch scale" proved to be a more insightful and reliable gauge of the time pressure the Hilton respondents felt. These items are shown in Table 24, along with the percentage of respondents who agreed with each statement. It is interesting that the average 32 percent agreement across the 10 items is very close to the 35 percent who felt always rushed in the 1992 survey (see Table 22), even though the items cover a different and wider variety of content than the single "feeling rushed" item.

What is more interesting is that the demographic correlates of the crunch scale (Table 24, Part B) are largely the same as those for feeling rushed and for those reporting stress in Table 23. Women, particularly working women, were significantly higher than men on the scale. The peak crunch years again were ages 35–44, falling off markedly after age 45. Having children was associated with higher time crunch scores, as were higher levels of education and income. The results for marital status were not as consistent, with married and never married people being lower on the scale than divorced people, particularly for women. In this way, the time crunch scale resembles the stress item more than the "feeling rushed" item.

Moreover, the correlates of the crunch scale were much the same for the question on wanting the extra day off from work. More women (55 percent) wanted the day off than men (44 percent); those aged 35–44 were more

**Table 24.** Items on the Time Crunch Scale and Scale Correlates

| A. Items | % Agreeing |
|---|---|
| 1. I often feel under stress when I don't have enough time. | 43 |
| 2. When I need more time, I tend to cut back on my sleep. | 40 |
| 3. At the end of the day, I often feel that I haven't accomplished what I set out to do. | 33 |
| 4. I worry that I don't spend enough time with my family or friends. | 33 |
| 5. I feel that I'm constantly under stress—trying to accomplish more than I can handle. | 31 |
| 6. I feel trapped in a daily routine. | 28 |
| 7. When I'm working long hours, I often feel guilty that I'm not at home. | 27 |
| 8. I consider myself a workaholic. | 26 |
| 9. I just don't have time for fun anymore. | 22 |
| 10. Sometimes I feel that my spouse doesn't know who I am anymore. | 21 |
| Average across the ten items | 32% |

B. Demographic Differences (Mean number of agreements with the above 10 statements in the Hilton Time Values Survey, by selected demographic groups, 1991)

| | Women | Men |
|---|---|---|
| Total | 3.5 | 2.9 |
| *Age* | | |
| 18–29 | 3.6 | 2.8 |
| 30–49 | 3.8 | 2.9 |
| 50–59 | 2.4 | 2.8 |
| 60 and older | 2.7 | 2.8 |
| *Employment* | | |
| Full-time | 3.7 | 2.8 |
| Part-time | 3.3 | 4.1 |
| Not employed | 3.1 | 2.7 |
| *Children at Home* | | |
| Under age 6 | 4.0 | 2.8 |
| Aged 6–11 | 4.1 | 2.7 |
| Aged 12–17 | 4.1 | 3.2 |
| No children under 18 | 3.3 | 2.8 |
| *Race/Ethnic Origin* | | |
| White | 3.3 | 2.8 |
| African American, Hispanic | 4.4 | 2.8 |
| *Marital Status* | | |
| Single | 3.2 | 2.9 |
| Married | 3.3 | 2.9 |
| Divorced/widowed | 4.3 | 2.5 |

SOURCE: Robinson, 1991b; 1991 Hilton Time Values Survey.

interested (55 percent), as were parents (52 percent) and those with graduate school education (58 percent). Results for marital status were again unpredictable, with the never married (58 percent) expressing most interest. Perhaps it is their lower need for increased income, or the options of doing more things with their increased time than are available to married or divorced people, that drives their higher interest in having that day off.

Finally, there are the survey questions asking respondents whether they have more or less free time than they did 5 or 10 years previously. Both Roper and Penn State surveys find that the perception that there is less free time was shared by about 47 percent of Americans in the early 1990s, compared with only 22 percent who say they now have more free time. To some extent, that response reflects reality, in that the time-diary studies do show that people aged 25–34 clearly have less free time than when they were aged 15–24 (see Chapter 14), and that is the group most likely to feel that they have been time-deprived. But for the older segments of the population, the time-diary numbers indicate that more "same" or "more" responses should have been given in order for the question to reflect what our diaries have been showing.

## Time Elasticity

Another subjective measure considered is not as clearly linked to time pressure as those discussed above, but its results are clearly germane to the issue of how time pressured Americans really feel. The question is asked in the time-diary context and asks the respondent to ponder the following question:

*"Suppose that early on the (time-diary day) you discovered that something had come up suddenly. You could tend to it any part of the day or night, but somehow you simply had to find one hour to take care of it before you went to bed again. In a day like the one you had yesterday on (diary day), what things would you have given up to make room for that hour?"*

The question was repeated for a 3-hour activity that had to be done. By far the most frequent response to this question when it was asked in 1965 was "television." The lack of importance or attachment to this most pervasive of free-time activities could not have been more persuasively demonstrated than by the nearly 90 percent of viewers who nominated television as the first activity they would forgo. This was true whether measured in terms of hours given up or in terms of the amount of time to be given up.

What this measure reflects, then, is the casual investment viewers make when they decide to watch television. Watching television is the activity they feel is least necessary in their lives. While above average in the enjoyment levels television provides people, television viewing scores notably below the ratings more active forms of free time get (see Chapter 17). Yet in several contexts (for example: retirement; increased free time since 1965), television is the activity that people choose behaviorally when they do in fact get more free time. As noted earlier, that increase is hardly consistent with the picture of a time-harried society that the other measures of a time-stressed society convey. We discuss this issue more in subsequent chapters that examine further subjective aspects of television as a free-time activity in the lives of Americans.

## Is a Slowdown Beginning?

The evidence in this chapter points mainly to an increase in the pace of life in America across the decades, but data from a 1994–95 national survey point to a slowing down, if not a turnaround, in the process. The data were collected from national samples of 1,200 respondents aged 18 and over interviewed by telephone by the University of Maryland's Survey Research Center between June 1994 and June 1995, and 504 additional respondents interviewed in Fall 1994 (Robinson and Godbey, 1996).

The surveys contained four questions related to the pace of life that have been discussed in this chapter. They show the following:

- The percentage of the 1995 sample saying they "always feel rushed" was down 6 percentage points from the 1992 number (see Table 22).
- The percentage saying they had experienced moderate or a great deal of stress in the previous two weeks was 54 percent, down 2 points from the 56 percent in the 1993 NCHS study (see Table 23).
- The percentage saying they would give up a day's pay for a day off dropped from 49 percent in 1991 to 45 percent in 1994–95 (in Maryland, a state with higher levels of education than the United States as a whole).
- The percentage saying they had less free time than five years previously fell from 54 percent in 1991 to 45 percent in 1994–95.

On each of these questions, then, there was a small if statistically insignificant movement away from the more time-pressured response.

We also included a related question that had been asked in the 1975 University of Michigan national diary survey concerning how tired employed respondents usually felt after a day at work. To the extent that the pace of life is affecting people, feeling more tired after work should be a prime indicator. In fact, there was a small decline from 1975 to 1995 in the percentage of respondents who felt "very tired," from 24 percent to 23 percent, and a slight increase in those who were "not very tired," from 22 percent to 23 percent. In other words, virtually no change can be detected in this crucial consequence of whatever increased pace of life has occurred in the public.

Similar indications are evident in cross-time questions asked by the Roper Organization. They found an 11 percentage point increase (from 34 percent to 45 percent) in the proportion of 1995 respondents saying "quiet relaxation at home" was a major reason for enjoying the weekend, along with a 5-point increase in "time with family and friends." No other reason changed by more than 2 percentage points (Roper Reports, 1995). The proportion saying they had about the right amount of free time increased from 35 percent in 1993 to 42 percent in 1995.

Taken together, then, these results suggest that some slowdown in the pace of American life has taken place since the early 1990s. It is difficult to say how serious or durable this change is, but it is important to note that it has occurred. At the same time, it is important to remember that the 1995 feelings of being rushed and of not having excessive time (Table 22) are still significantly higher than in 1965, and that the 1995 levels of perceived stress are higher than in 1985. However, these most recent surveys indicate that that may not translate to other plausible consequences of feeling rushed—or that Americans may be adapting to the faster pace of life.

# 17

# How People Feel
# About Their Daily Activities

The unexamined life is not worth living.
—Socrates

The overexamined life ain't so hot either.
—Unknown

Given the greater concern over America's time famine, people's feelings about how much they like what they do with their time—the affective aspects of time—have received comparatively little research attention. However, they could provide greater insights into why people spend their time the way they do. Indeed, there is evidence that how people feel about certain activities makes it possible to predict how they will actually spend their time.

Measurement of this subjective or feeling aspect of time has been approached in many ways, usually involving some numerical rating scale on which people rate activities from most favored to least favored. Some scales define the dimension in terms of the amount of satisfaction people derive from an activity, others define it in terms of liking or enjoyment. Researchers who examined these two concepts of satisfaction versus liking in relation to how a person perceives the quality of his or her life find that they can refer to different ways in which people evaluate aspects of their lives (Andrews and Withey, 1976; Andrews and Robinson, 1991). The other main difference in the measurements taken to date is that some are obtained about activities in general, or in the abstract (that is, without reference to a specific time period in a diary), while others are obtained from ratings of activities reported in time diaries—that is, "in real time," as they are being experienced by respondents on the spot.

In general, the various approaches give rather convergent results, but there are interesting discrepancies as well. Unfortunately, few of the measurements have been repeated across time, so that trends in satisfaction or enjoyment associated with different activities could be tracked, although we again report more recent updates at the end of this chapter.

Five sets of satisfaction/enjoyment data for different activities are presented in Table 25. All but one involve national data sets, and they cover both diary-based and general measures. The first three sets of data, collected before 1975, are less complete and employ smaller sample sizes. Nonetheless, these first three studies agree on the following differences across activities:

- Work is average to above average in terms of rated satisfaction or enjoyment, with the commute to work a little below average in one study.
- Housework activities are below average in enjoyment, especially cleaning, maintenance, and repair activities.
- Interactional activities with children are rated above average—particularly playing with children, which is rated well above average.
- Shopping is rated below average, especially shopping for groceries.
- All three personal-care activities—sleep, meals, and grooming—are rated above average.
- Among free-time activities, socializing is generally rated highest, followed by sports, hobbies, cultural events, and entertainment.
- Television rates as average to below average in enjoyment, especially in relation to other more active uses of free time.

Thus, television viewing was not only the first activity that cross-section samples of the American public would give up in the 1960s; it was well down their list of favorite ways to spend free time.

**Table 25.** Differences in Activity Enjoyment Ratings

| Year: | 1965 | 1973 | 1975 | 1975 | 1985 |
|---|---|---|---|---|---|
| Label: | Satisfied | Satisfied | Like | Enjoy | Like |
| Scale: | 1–5 | 1–5 | 1–7 | 0–10 | 0–10 |
| Context: | General | General/Diary | Diary | General | Diary |
| Sample: | National/Jackson | Jackson | National | National | National |
| (n =) | (1,800) | (140) | (133) | (2,000) | (2,500) |
| **Activity** | | | | | |
| Work | 3.7 | 4.0 | 5.8 | 8.0 | 7.0 |
| Work commute | NA | 3.9 | 4.8 | NA | 6.3 |
| Cooking | 3.2 | NA | 5.2 | 6.2 | 6.6 |
| Cleaning | NA | 3.9 | 4.6 | 4.2 | 4.9 |
| Maintenance | 3.6 | 3.9 | 4.5 | 5.1 | 5.5 |
| Paperwork | NA | NA | 4.2 | NA | 5.2 |
| Child care | 4.7 | 4.2 | 5.4 | 8.9 | 6.4 |
| Child play | 4.5 | 6.3 | 6.3 | 8.6 | 8.8 |
| Grocery shop | NA | 3.8 | 4.1 | 4.6 | 5.5 |
| Other shop | 3.2 | 3.9 | 4.3 | 4.3 | 6.6/5.1 |
| Sleep | NA | 4.4 | 5.6 | 7.5 | 8.5 |
| Eating | NA | 4.3 | 5.7 | 7.4 | 7.9 |
| Grooming | NA | 4.2 | 5.9 | 7.4 | 6.5 |
| Education | NA | 4.1 | 5.0 | NA | 6.0 |
| Religion | 3.8 | 4.3 | 5.3 | 7.3 | 8.5 |
| Organizations | 2.7 | 4.1 | 4.3 | 5.0 | 7.2 |
| Culture events | NA | 4.6 | 5.5 | 6.5 | 8.5 |
| Socializing | 4.0 | 4.6 | 5.5 | 7.7 | 8.2 |
| Sports | 3.4 | 4.5 | 5.0 | 6.5 | 9.2 |
| Hobbies | 3.6 | | 5.8 | 6.8 | 7.5 |
| TV | 3.4 | 4.1 | 5.0 | 5.9 | 7.8 |
| Read paper | 3.7 | 3.9 | 5.6 | 7.1 | 7.8 |
| Read book, mag. | 3.7 | 4.2 | 5.7 | 7.0 | 8.3 |
| Stereo | NA | NA | NA | NA | 8.0 |
| Conversations | NA | NA | NA | 8.3 | 7.2 |
| Relaxing | 3.5 | 4.3 | 5.5 | NA | 8.2 |
| Travel | NA | NA | 4.8 | NA | 7.3 |
| Average | 3.6 | 4.2 | 5.2 | 6.8 | 7.0 |

SOURCE: Americans' Use of Time Project.

## The 1975 Data

In large part, the findings from the early activity rankings were replicated with the general ratings data from the 1975 study (column 4 of Table 25). That study had the advantage of a larger sample (over 1,500 respondents) and a more activity-focused set of ratings. Once again, social activities and conversation, especially with children, were at the top of the list, and housework activities were near the bottom. Personal-care activity rated well above average. However, no ratings were obtained for relaxing, travel, and many free-time activities that show up in other ratings as being above average. More detailed analysis can be found in Juster (1985), who found surprisingly small differences across socioeconomic groups in engaging in activities that brought them more enjoyment.

Again, these ratings were for the activities in general, not as they were being experienced. This leads to some interesting rating contrasts with the 1985 data set.

## The 1985 Data

Because the 1985 study was diary-based, it covered all activities (the ratings appear in Appendix O) and surveyed the degree to which respondents enjoyed or disliked some 200 different activities, based on more than 60,000 ratings.

The first important conclusion in the 1985 data, as in the earlier studies, is that the things Americans like to do far outweigh the things they do not like to do. Thus, on a scale of 0 to 10, few daily activities average below the midpoint of 5. The average rating of 7.0 across all activities in Table 25 indicates that Americans view most of their daily tasks in a positive light. Moreover, it is close to the 6.8 rating found for all the general 1975 activities.

No single activity in Appendix O rated a perfect 10 in the survey, but sex came closest, with an average rating of 9.3. Less-intense expressions of affection, such as hugging and kissing, rate an 8.8. People also like their sleep, which averages 8.5; no doubt this includes some new parents who may value sleep over sex. Eating is also highly rated, but Americans enjoy eating away from home more than eating at home (8.2 versus 7.8). This is probably because eating out does not involve food preparation and cleanup, both of which rate far lower than eating on the scale.

Some leisure activities are more enjoyable than these personal-care activities. Americans who enjoy active sports, such as softball and tennis, rank them almost as high as sex, at 9.2. Fishing, excursions, and other outdoor ventures average 9.1; painting, other art projects, and playing music average 9.0. Most other leisure activities score between 8 and 9 on the 10-point scale, including going to the movies, attending sports events and concerts, reading books and magazines, and watching videos. People who go to bars or nightclubs give this activity an 8.9, while attending social events and playing games rates an 8.6. Spending time with children provides almost as much enjoyment as grown-up leisure. Playing with children rates an 8.8, and talking with or reading to them rates an 8.6.

Americans like to schmooze almost as much as they like to nosh. Socializing and visiting rates an 8.2. They also like to talk with family members: conversations with household members rate an 8.0. Work and lunch breaks combine socializing and eating, so they score 8.2 and 7.9, respectively. In contrast, even in the electronic age, face-to-face meetings are rated more favorably than remote communication. Talking on the telephone rates only 7.2, and writing letters is at 7.1.

People enjoy mass communication less than face-to-face personal communication but more than telephone or mail contacts. Americans spend more free time watching television than doing anything else, but they rate it only 7.8, lower than most other free-time activities. Watching television is less enjoyable than watching videos, which ranks 8.3. Americans also rate newspaper reading at the same level as television (7.8), which is lower than they rate reading magazines (8.2). This could indicate that some read newspapers out of a sense of obligation, or that what they read in the paper is not as enjoyable. They also rate listening to the radio lower than other media activities, at 7.3.

## Work and Family Care

It is natural for people to enjoy free-time activities. But American diary respondents also enjoyed many of the things they have to do. While some people dislike working, others enjoy it. On average, Americans give work outside the home a 7.0 rating, about as high as gardening (7.1). Work rates a little higher than the two related activities of commuting to work (6.3) and, for those who have them, second jobs (6.7). People who work at home rate their work as slightly less enjoyable (6.6) than those who work outside the home.

Many aspects of household and family care also fall in the mid-range. In particular, Americans are mildly positive about routine child care (6.4), cooking (6.6), shopping for clothes (6.6), pet care (6.0), getting dressed (6.1), and providing help to other adults (6.4). Taking care of babies is about as enjoyable as talking on the phone (7.2) and as helping children with homework (7.0).

How much people enjoy traveling depends on where they are going. Commuting to work (6.3) actually rates higher than getting to the mall or other shopping destinations (6.2). Students (aged 18 or older) rate their trip to school at only 5.6, but the trip home is a more positive 6.9. Trips to more enjoyable activities, such as visiting, eating out, and going to church rate higher than commuting to work or school. Overall, then, travel is most enjoyable when it involves free time or children.

Perhaps it is inherent optimism, or perhaps it is because we were taught to keep quiet if we couldn't say something nice. Whatever the reason, Americans tend to rate even the things they most dislike in the middle of the 10-point scale. Most of these least-enjoyed activities involve household chores, including laundry (4.8), routine housecleaning (4.9), doing dishes (4.9), and yard work (5.0). Paying bills and ironing don't fare much better, at 5.2. Shopping for necessities like food and stamps rates just above 5.0, the same as a trip to the bank or the garbage dump.

Americans are not quite so negative about serving meals to others (5.5) and doing miscellaneous housework, such as moving furniture or packing clothes (5.7). They dislike doing work brought home, doing the same tasks at work or in school. At the absolute bottom of the scale are health-related activities—going to the doctor or dentist, self-treatment, and taking care of sick children. All rank below a 5.0, as does taking care of sick cars. Root canals and transmission overhauls seem to define the lower depths of daily life in America.

Thus, most people tend to give unpleasant but necessary household tasks a neutral score of 5. To be sure, some rate laundry and dishwashing at the very bottom of the scale, but they are balanced out by those who claim to enjoy scrubbing toilets. In fact, about as many people say they enjoy housework a great deal as hate it, although the majority are lukewarm about it.

## Differences in General and Diary-Based Ratings

In general, then, the overall high-low rating activities in the 1985 study were much the same as in the first three studies in Table 25. There are some interesting differences between the 1975 general ratings and the 1985 diary ratings, particularly since they have about the same overall average value of about 7.0. In the case of paid work, for example, the general rating is above average (8.0), while the diary rating is only average (7.0). That suggests that paid work as experienced has many more "down" periods than respondents care to admit in their overall ratings. Much the same is found for basic (custodial) child-care activities and for conversations.

On the other hand, the pattern for most free-time activities is the reverse; higher ratings in the diary than overall. That pattern is easily explainable, because many of the respondents rating sports, religion, organizations, or cultural events low on the scale are simply not "into" them. Thus, those who choose to do them are people who really appreciate the activities.

That also seems to be the case for the most prevalent of free-time activities: television viewing. While below average as a general activity, television viewing is above average in "real time" in the diary. This suggests that the programs Americans choose to view are not as bad as they generally assume. Nonetheless, the enjoyment levels for television are still below the average of most other free-time activities as in Kubey and Csikszentmihalyi (1990).

## Demographic Differences

In earlier studies, time-diary data showed significant gender differences, particularly for the housework activities that women rated higher than men. In the 1985 data, however, women (who continued to do more housework than men) did not like it more than men. Both women and men rated cooking, housecleaning, laundry, yard work, and grocery shopping at the same mediocre level. From the earlier ratings in Table 25, one might expect women to enjoy activities that involve the home, family, and socializing more than men do, but they don't. The only noticeable differences between the sexes is that women like paid work more than men do, possibly because they are more likely to have more choice between working and not working.

Why do demographics make so little difference in what Americans do and do not like? Choice is the key reason. Women may not be as involved as men in sports, but those who are enjoy sports just as much. College graduates may watch less television than others, but they enjoy what they do watch just as much as less-educated people. Older people may value life more than younger people, but their average enjoyment of all daily activities is just slightly higher: 0.2 points on a 10-point scale. Single and married adults seem to enjoy basically the same things, as do working and nonworking people. Nor do people like their activities more on weekends than on weekdays, even with the greater amounts of free time on weekends. Day-of-the-week differences thus belie the popular assumptions in the saying "Thank God, it's Friday."

## The Relationship of Attitudes and Behavior

These attitudinal data have interesting correlations with the time spent in those activities, as recorded in the time diaries. This was done first with the satisfaction ratings in the original 1965 study, and the results showed a remarkable correspondence between these attitudes and independently reported behavior—for the 10 activities for which a correlation could be reasonably constructed. Comparing the diary times for those who said they got a "great deal" of satisfaction from an activity with those who said they got "none," ratios of the order of magnitude 1.5 to 8.0 were obtained in terms of the greater diary time spent on that activity by those who derived more satisfaction from that activity.

The differences in this ratio were greatest for television and for religious activities. Respondents who said they derived "a great deal" of satisfaction from television watched an average of 131 minutes a day, as recorded in their time diaries, compared with only 17 minutes for those who said they got no satisfaction from watching television, a ratio of almost 8 to 1. For religion, the differences were 21 minutes a day for time-diary religious activity among those deriving great satisfaction from religion to only 3 minutes among those saying none (or some or little satisfaction). The comparable minutes-per-day numbers for sports were 15 to 3, for reading 51 to 9, and for organizations/ clubs 22 to 4. The ratio dropped to about 2 to 1 for shopping and relaxing, and to below that for cooking, work, and caring for children. This latter group of activities, of course, is one over which individuals have less control and are non–free-time activities. Nevertheless, the finding that people who derive great satisfaction from work or cooking spend half again as much time on these necessary activities as those who say they get no satisfaction from them says a great deal about the degree to which diary times reflect levels of enjoyment of these activities.

These might be considered unwarranted causal conclusions from simple survey data, but they are based on the ratings being obtained well after the time-diary data were collected. In addition, the findings held up after controls were put on the data for several important demographic predictors of time spent on these activities, such as gender, age, and education.

## The 1975 Data

With the availability of panel data from the 1975 study, however, it was possible to gain a better handle on these temporal factors. The activity enjoyment data were collected in the second wave of this four-wave panel study, and it was again possible to show the same levels of correlation between the ratings and the time-diary figures for the same Wave 2 data.

It was also possible to show that the relationship to diary times was at virtually the same levels in Wave 3 and 4 data collections. In other words, the Wave 2 enjoyment ratings remained very powerful predictors of time-diary data collected 3–6 months after they were given. This all but eliminated the possibility that respondents were simply giving ratings that matched what they were reporting in their diaries.

This, then, provides striking evidence for the long-disputed assumption that there *is* a relationship between people's attitudes and their behavior. In the course of daily life, respondents *do* engage in activities that bring them greater enjoyment. In line with hedonistic explanations of daily life, people do what they say they like to do.

This "hedonistic model" further explains some but not all of the major shifts in time use described in earlier chapters. Major time-diary declines were found for household activities, which are clearly at or near the bottom of all the ratings in Table 25. Declines were also found for work as an activity, which while generating about-average enjoyment is rated lower than most of the free-time activities. The decline of newspaper reading is interesting, in light of the higher ratings given to reading books and magazines. The increase in sports time is also consistent with its high rating.

The hedonistic model does less well in explaining why television captured so much of the newly available free time after 1965. Television is rated above average across all activities but considerably lower than many free-time activities—and below sleep and eating out as well. In particular, it is rated lower than socializing activities that have shown some decline across time. Thus, while Americans may prefer the time they spend getting together with other people, the ease and lower costs associated with TV viewing apparently outweigh the costs involved in more social forms of interaction and communication.

Finally, it may be that the way in which increases in free time were realized from 1965 to 1985, coming mainly in small time increases on weekdays, made TV viewing an easy way to "absorb" such small daily increases.

## A 1995 Update

Recent updated ratings on six of the activities in Table 25 come from a national sample of 1,000 respondents interviewed in December 1995 by the

University of Maryland Survey Research Center. One of the biggest changes in terms of enjoyment had to do with television, and it was in a negative direction. Television showed a significant decline of more than one full point on the 0–10 rating scale, from 6.0 in 1975 to 4.8 in 1995. The drop was about the same for men and women and for different age-groups. A similar drop of more than one point was found for reading the newspaper, again regardless of gender or age-group. Reading books and magazines dropped, but by a much smaller margin.

In contrast, there were no notable declines for the three productive activities for which ratings were repeated in the 1995 study: paid work, housecleaning, and cooking. In fact, housecleaning, the activity at the bottom of the 1975 ratings, showed a slight *increase*; the increase was found for both women (from 5.2 to 5.6) and men (from 3.1 to 3.8). The other household activity, cooking, also showed different trends by gender, going down for women (from 7.1 to 6.5) but up for men (from 4.7 to 5.5). Both these trends thus reflect changes in activities, with men reporting more cooking and cleaning since 1975. In other words, in line with our hedonistic model, parallel trends are found for attitudes and behavior. Perhaps this will form the basis for further increases in such core housework activities in the future.

Against these consistencies and increases, then, the declines in enjoyment of television are particularly striking. For women in the 1995 survey, it means they rate television watching (4.8) below cleaning the house (5.6) as an enjoyable activity; for men, it means they rate television below cooking. Again, there has been no decrease in viewing to match the declines in attitudes, but if these ratings are to be believed, a decrease in viewing could follow. The result would be an unprecedented decline in the favorite way Americans like to spend their free time.

Television is not the only free-time activity to suffer a decline in the public's enjoyment. The greater declines in ratings for newspapers than books/magazines mirror the greater decline in time spent reading newspapers—which is in line with our hedonistic model, described above. It may foretell further declines in newspaper reading, an activity that has been eroding steadily since 1965. In this case, however, that decline may not have been engendered by television, which has also declined in popularity, but rather by the fact that the public sees it as a less enjoyable activity—particularly now in relation to other types of reading material.

On the general ratings scales, then, Americans seem to be rating free-time media activities lower and productive activities like housecleaning and paid work higher. Whether this would hold for diary ratings, or whether it portends changes for Americans' choice of activities, are interesting topics for future research. It may be that the low levels of satisfaction with the chief way Americans use free time—television—is a signal of general dissatisfaction with our culture. Whether Americans will do something about such dissatisfaction remains to be seen.

# 18

# The Results from Inputs of Time

More effort, more productivity.

—Euripides

No actions remain sincere, simple explosions of spontaneous impulse; all are instrumental.

—Kenneth J. Gergen

More than 30 years ago an astute British observer of the human condition, C. Northcote Parkinson, stated his famous law of organizational behavior: "Work expands to fill the time available for its completion." As seasoned procrastinators know in their hearts, Parkinson's adage explains why term papers are never begun until the day before they're due, why there are long lines on April 15 or on the day car registrations expire, and why we always seem to be running late for something.

Parkinson saw the "law" as a way to describe the foibles of bureaucracy—

for example, why the size of the British Admiralty expanded during a period in which the number of naval vessels decreased. A major reason for the law's success in predicting bureaucratic behavior was that there were more important factors at work than time or cost management—mainly bureaucrats who expanded their staffs or work time as a way to promote their own self-importance in the organization. That perhaps explains why we see the lack of correspondence between time expenditure and the other "rational behavior" we shall describe—time considerations are simply not consciously factored into the decision-making process.

Parkinson saw amusing corollaries, such as finance committees that spent only a few minutes on major budget items involving thousands of dollars but invested hours of heated debate over the coffee fund or other budget items involving trivial amounts of money. The law seems as much in evidence today as when it was first conceived. Many students can describe how the principle has worked in their own lives once it is explained to them—not only in getting their term papers done, but also in their home and work lives. They remember when their work staff was cut in half and more work got done by the skeleton staff that was left, or the way some assignment was completed under an impossible deadline. That is not to say that time is always or usually irrelevant—some time is always needed to complete any task—but that we should not be surprised when we find a marginal correlation between time expenditures (inputs) and related results (outputs).

In this chapter we attempt to relate inputs of time to certain outcomes. None of these examples is an ideal data set in the sense of having measures of productivity as clearly defined as in a factory or laboratory setting, but they generally affirm Parkinson's conclusion.

## Study Time

The most compelling evidence comes from Schuman et al.'s study of the relationship between time spent studying and course grades. They first noted:

> The measurement of effort is very difficult and we do not know of any sociological investigation that attempts to attack the problem directly. . . . Whether the homilies our culture—for example, Genius is one percent inspiration and ninety-nine percent perspiration—have in fact much truth remains not only unsubstantiated, but largely uninvestigated. (P. 946)

Schuman et al. (1985) reported the results of several studies in which they found the same result: no significant correlation between grades and time spent studying. Laudably, Schuman and his colleagues were skeptical of this early insignificant relationship between the two, and they subsequently replicated these early results with more elaborate studies utilizing a broader variety of measures and observers to help explain the lack of correlation. Throughout their analyses, they were able to control for academic ability measures that could have accounted for the result. In other words, it was not simply a consequence of smarter students organizing their study time better than less-adept students. Study time per se made little difference in grades. Time spent attending classes did make a difference, but not hours spent studying.

## Household Care Time

The results of Schuman et al. largely dovetail with various results from the time-diary studies in which we attempted to relate outputs from time expenditures to time inputs. Thus, in the 1975 study, we devised several measures related to the outputs from household care time: (a) interviewer observations and ratings of the cleanliness of the respondent's home, (b) the respondent's own ratings of the cleanliness of the home, and (c) similar cleanliness ratings that the respondent estimated would be made by a "picky person" they knew. While these three ratings were slightly lower if the woman was employed, no significant correlation was obtained for any of these three output measures (Robinson, 1982). In other words, employed women, who in Chapter 6 were found to spend 40 percent less time doing housework than full-time homemakers, did not live in homes that were rated as significantly less tidy, either by interviewers or by respondents themselves. Much the same result was found when we repeated these analyses in 1995 studies.

## Survey Participation

A similar lack of significant correlation between inputs of time and related outputs emerges from a different output measure in the time-diary studies—the willingness of respondents to participate in and complete our time-diary survey itself. Here, the panel-type features of the 1975 and 1985 studies were used to note the activity differences between respondents who participated at Time 1 and those who also continued to participate at Time 2.

In 1975 that involved examining the Time 1 diary activities of those who agreed both to the first personal interview and to the second telephone reinterview, compared with those who did not agree to the second interview. In several respects, the time diaries of those who agreed to complete the second interview indicated they were busier people. They worked longer hours and did more family care; they slept and ate less. More important, they watched significantly less television and got less rest.

In 1985, the initial contact was by telephone, and the telephone diaries were examined for differences in activities between those who mailed their Stage 2 diaries back to us and those who did not. The results were quite consistent with those found in 1975 and are not explained by education or other background factors; mail diary respondents who returned them worked more and watched television less. As mentioned earlier, this finding directly counters the proposition that time findings were suspect because busy people were systematically less likely to participate in our diary research (Hochschild, 1989). Perhaps people participate in our surveys because they are proud of how much they do in a day. Thus, people who are less busy may have lower self-esteem and don't want to embarrass themselves in a survey. Whatever the reason, it does not appear that time demands keep people from participation in our diary surveys, or perhaps surveys in general.

## Arts Participation

The survey results on arts participation are insightful because perhaps the main reason stated by most people who do not participate in surveys is that they "don't have time."

Lack of time does not appear to be the main reason for survey nonparticipation, nor does it explain certain patterns of arts participation based on the SPPA survey described in Chapter 11. In that survey, respondents were asked about the main reasons they did not attend various arts events more often. For each type of artistic event examined, the main reason offered by respondents for not attending more was that they did not "have enough time" (Robinson, Triplett, et al., 1985). In the case of visiting art galleries and museums, more than four times as many respondents cited lack of time rather than lack of money as the reason for not going more, and in the case of attending jazz or classical music performances the ratio was almost 2 to 1 in favor of lack of time being the main barrier.

That was the reason respondents offered, but it did not square with other data from the survey. For example, people who reported longer work hours (and hence less free time) did not report less arts participation. Indeed, they reported more participation than average, much as Putnam (1995a) found in his study of organization activity. Part of that correlation was explained by the more-educated and affluent both working longer hours and attending more arts events. After these and other factors were adjusted using Multiple Classification Analysis, it turned out that people working longer than 50 hours were about average in terms of arts participation. Thus, long work hours per se turned out to be no barrier to participation. And while marriage and children were associated with lower attendance, after MCA adjustment the decrease was about 10 percent for marriage and at most 20 percent for having children.

Thus, these results indicate that if people care enough about something they will find a way to fit it into their schedules. *Time can be found.* This also reinforces the Parkinsonian adage that if you want something done—give it to a busy person.

Being busy has become an important status symbol. The excuse "I don't have time" has become a polite way of saying "I'd rather do something else." From the time-diary data, that something else is most likely to be TV viewing, not an activity of great importance or satisfaction.

## Not How Much Time, But How We Think About Time

If the amount of time expended is irrelevant to output, what does matter? Social psychologist Philip Zimbardo may have developed a better measure—one that does involve time—but in terms of how people *think* about time rather than how they use it. That approach involves asking people questions about whether their thinking about time is oriented toward the past, the present, or the future.

The items in Zimbardo's scale are shown in Appendix P. His research has demonstrated that people with a future orientation are more able to achieve success, as measured by a variety of tasks involving group and individual problem solving. Again, he has controlled for academic ability factors that may explain the results. It is not how well students do in school that predicts task success, then, but whether they think in the future tense.

What Zimbardo's measure gets at probably has less to do with time per se than with mental organization. People who are future oriented have an ability to visualize some form of output and then to take the steps that are required to achieve that output. Time is the medium through which this visualization takes place, but means-end thinking and future orientation are required to achieve these goals over a period of time.

## Technology, Another Factor Irrelevant to Time

The major trends described in this book—the decline of household care time and the growth of free time—appear to be an outcome of technology in the daily lives of Americans. The profound and growing role of television was described in terms of one technology that has revolutionized people's lives temporally (Chapter 9). When it comes to other household technologies, however, the time-diary evidence is far less convincing. It is much more difficult to find differences in time use between those who are owners of other household technologies and those who do not own these technologies.

This result first appeared in Morgan et al.'s (1966) national survey of "productive Americans." They found that respondents with more items of household technology spent no less time doing household work than people with less technology. However, the measure of housework was a crude general-estimate question not tailored closely to relevant household tasks that could be done with each appliance; thus, there was no way to relate washing machines or dryers to time doing laundry. Nonetheless, even among families with preschool children, the *more* appliances there were in the home, the *more* housework time respondents estimated they did.

The result was suggested as well by aggregate data that came from our first 1965 national data, when the U.S. results were compared with results for societies having far less technology. While Americans did less housework than respondents from Eastern European countries (very few of whom had washing machines and many of whom did not even have running water in the home), the times spent doing housework were not much lower (Robinson, Converse, and Szalai, 1972). Housewives in America spent 324 minutes a day doing housework, compared with 352 minutes for housewives in Bulgaria and 364 minutes in Yugoslavia. Housewives in Belgium, France, and Germany, also with high levels of technology, spent closer to 400 minutes a day on housework, about the same as in Poland, Czechoslovakia, and Peru. Thus, simply the presence of technology was largely unrelated to time spent doing housework.

Much the same conclusion was reached when we compared the 1965 results on housework time with those from the 1920s and 1930s in America, when few such appliances were available (Robinson with Converse, 1972; Vanek, 1974). Indeed, some of these comparisons showed women in the 1960s doing even more housework (Walker, 1969).

In the 1975 national study, a more direct comparison was made by including separate questions on individual pieces of technology and performing multivariate analyses to control for the effects of other predictors of time spent on household care, such as employment status and number of children (Robinson, 1980b). People with dishwashers spent 1 minute *more* time doing housework, those with washing machines spent 4 minutes *more,* and those with vacuum cleaners spent 1 minute less, after MCA controls. Similar insignificant results were found when the appliances were matched to the housework task—for example, dishwashers with meal cleanup.

The one exception in the 1975 study was for microwave ovens, a new technology at that time. Owners of microwave ovens were found to spend 10 minutes less time doing housework. The problem was that less than 5 percent of the sample owned these ovens, so the decline was based on a sample of less than 50 women. Nonetheless, the result was plausible. Here, perhaps, was the technology that could reduce housework time. If all that had to be done was to take prepared food out of the refrigerator and heat it, food preparation time was obviously being saved.

We anticipated extending these results with 1985 data, when the ownership rate had moved past 50 percent and the public had time to become familiar with and capitalize on its time-saving features, but these expectations did not materialize. Respondents who owned microwave ovens in 1985 spent only 5 minutes less time a day preparing meals (and doing housework in general) than nonowners did. After MCA adjustment for other factors, that difference was cut in half and was not statistically different. Thus, not even the microwave oven, with all its time-saving potentials, was associated with significantly reduced housework time.

## Why Time-Saving Appliances May Not Save Time

How is it possible to get these results when these appliances have the clear potential to save time? The answer may again have to do with the fact that time-saving is not the major reason that people use the technology. These machines clearly *can* make things simpler and save drudgery. They are true *labor*-saving devices that have *time*-saving features, and these are features that are attractive to and probably used by millions of Americans who have discovered that they can reduce housework time with them. The problem is that the saving of time is offset by the millions of other Americans who disregard or subvert the time-saving features of the technology—the people who scour the dishes before loading them into the dishwasher or who use the dishwasher but put the dishes away after every meal. The same may be true for those who take the time to add special seasonings to microwave food or who prepare several dishes separately and then find themselves scrambling to keep them all equally warm.

The microwave oven also provides a good illustration of how easy it is to confuse different facets of time use. The oven obviously reduces the time required to cook food—that is, the elapsed time between putting the food into the oven and having the food hot enough to eat. That does not necessarily translate into reduced time for the human operator to prepare the meal for cooking and serving, as when more ambitious meals are prepared. Indeed, the oven is so efficient that many meals prepared using it may be heated so quickly that our respondents do not bother reporting them in their diaries. Heating the meal, however, is only part of the task; to the extent that the table must be set, beverages poured, and side dishes prepared, the potential time savings get lost in the process. Thus, what likely occurred with other technology is happening with the microwave oven: potential time savings are turned into increased output or improved quality.

The time data related to automobile use may be instructive, in that the travel times of people with cars (both in the United States and across countries in the multinational data) are again not much different from those without cars. For almost any given trip, it is clear that the car will get people to a destination faster than walking, bicycling, or taking public transportation. Instead of investing these time savings in other activities, however, car owners seem to choose instead to go more places or longer distances in the time they (and others in society) have already allotted for travel, probably according to some Parkinson-like scheme they have developed for allocating their daily time.

Similarly, in the case of home appliances parallel increases in output can be achieved. For example, there is anecdotal evidence that with home washers and dryers in the 1960s people took advantage of them in conjunction with new wash-and-wear fabrics to change their clothes more often. In effect, they may have allowed Americans to have cleaner and more diverse wardrobes. In the case of dishwashers, the dishes are probably cleaner and are more hygienic than if they were done by hand. In all these ways, people seem to choose increases in output or quality over savings in time. Much the same may apply to the more recent shift to gas-fired grills from charcoal grills (*New*

*York Times*, May 26, 1996). Put in Parkinsonian terms, there is some norm or "mental image" of the amount of time that should be devoted to certain activities. Whatever can be accomplished within that time is what determines the time spent on the activity.

## An Indirect Effect of Technology?

Since 1965, however, there has been a significant reduction in the time spent preparing meals and doing housework. And since 1965 there has also been a remarkable increase in the availability of household appliances. Are the two completely unrelated? Or has the availability of the technology affected expectations about the amount of time one should spend on certain activities? If one can reduce time with the technology, does that not devalue the time that is devoted to household care tasks and make them even less appealing as things to do? Does the example of those forerunner Americans who do save time with the appliances provide a model for the rest of us without the technology to follow? Perhaps it is in these more subtle ways that technology and time use are related.

The results present Americans with a further paradox. One of the main reasons people presumably work as hard as they do is to have the latest technology at their disposal as part of "the good life." But if they buy the technology to save time and it doesn't save time, are the hours they work to purchase the technology a good investment of their time? The machines are probably used to save labor, and that may justify their purchase, but saving time does not seem to be one of their virtues.

In this chapter we once again confront the fundamental irrelevance of time. Whatever time is devoted to an activity, or to a certain technology at our disposal, the allocations of time seem the same. If people want something badly enough, time is unlikely to be the confining resource—particularly in nonwork settings, where efficiency is not a dominant criterion. By their own admission, Americans need to look no further than the 15–20 hours they devote to the technology of television each week to find the time to do the things they want to do.

# 19

# Comparisons with Other Countries

In the rich countries all slacks in the use of time have been eliminated, so far as is humanly possible. The attitude to time is dictated entirely by the commodity's extreme scarcity. The day of the sluggard is over.

—Staffan Linder

Time use has varied markedly by country. In the pioneering study by Szalai et al. (1972) comparing time use in 12 countries, American respondents reported spending about average amounts of time on most productive activities, with the exception of the larger amounts of time spent shopping (see Table 26). Sleeping and eating times were below average, particularly in comparison with Germany, Belgium, and France.

This chapter was co-authored with Vladimir Andreyenkov, Stephen McHale, Anna Andreyenkova, and Ilona Andreyenkova.

**Table 26.** Cross-National Differences in Time Use, 1965 (in hours per day)

| | U.S. Cities (50,000) | U.S. (Jackson, Mich.) | France (6 cities) | Belgium (425 cities) | West Germany (100 districts) | West Germany (Osnabruck) | Hungary (Gyor) | Poland (Torun) | Yugoslavia (Maribor) | Yugoslavia (Kragujevac) | Bulgaria (Kazantik) | Russia (Pskov) | Czechoslovakia (Olomouc) |
|---|---|---|---|---|---|---|---|---|---|---|---|---|---|
| 1. Regular work | 3.8 | 4.1 | 4.2 | 4.3 | 3.7 | 3.7 | 5.4 | 4.9 | 4.3 | 4.0 | 5.6 | 5.4 | 4.9 |
| 2. Second job | 0.1 | * | 0.1 | 0.1 | * | * | * | * | 0.2 | * | * | * | * |
| 3. Nonwork | 0.4 | 0.4 | 0.2 | 0.1 | 0.3 | 0.2 | 0.5 | 0.3 | 0.3 | 0.4 | 0.6 | 0.6 | 0.1 |
| 4. Trip to/from work | 0.4 | 0.3 | 0.4 | 0.4 | 0.3 | 0.3 | 0.7 | 0.6 | 0.5 | 0.5 | 0.7 | 0.5 | 0.5 |
| 5. Prepare food | 0.7 | 0.7 | 0.7 | 0.8 | 1.0 | 0.8 | 1.0 | 1.0 | 1.3 | 1.1 | 0.8 | 0.9 | 1.1 |
| 6. Clean house | 1.0 | 0.8 | 1.2 | 1.1 | 1.2 | 1.2 | 0.9 | 0.8 | 0.9 | 0.8 | 0.7 | 0.6 | 0.9 |
| 7. Laundry/mending | 0.4 | 0.4 | 0.5 | 0.3 | 0.4 | 0.4 | 0.6 | 0.6 | 0.7 | 0.5 | 0.3 | 0.4 | 0.6 |
| 8. Other upkeep | 0.3 | 0.3 | 0.3 | 0.2 | 0.3 | 0.3 | 0.3 | 0.3 | 0.4 | 0.4 | 0.2 | 0.3 | 0.4 |
| 9. Pets/garden | 0.1 | * | 0.2 | 0.1 | 0.5 | 0.3 | 0.6 | * | 0.8 | 0.1 | 0.4 | 0.1 | 0.1 |
| 10. Sleep | 7.8 | 7.9 | 8.2 | 8.3 | 8.3 | 8.1 | 7.7 | 7.5 | 7.8 | 7.6 | 7.8 | 7.7 | 7.8 |
| 11. Personal care | 1.1 | 1.0 | 0.9 | 0.7 | 0.9 | 1.0 | 0.9 | 0.9 | 0.8 | 1.0 | 0.8 | 0.8 | 1.2 |
| 12. Eating | 1.2 | 1.1 | 1.7 | 1.6 | 1.5 | 1.6 | 1.0 | 1.1 | 1.1 | 1.1 | 1.2 | 1.0 | 1.0 |
| 13. Resting | 0.3 | 0.4 | 0.6 | 0.5 | 0.5 | 0.6 | 0.4 | 0.6 | 0.4 | 0.7 | 0.7 | 0.3 | 0.4 |
| 14. Child care | 0.4 | 0.4 | 0.6 | 0.3 | 0.4 | 0.3 | 0.4 | 0.4 | 0.4 | 0.3 | 0.3 | 0.5 | 0.4 |
| 15. Shopping | 0.5 | 0.6 | 0.4 | 0.3 | 0.4 | 0.5 | 0.3 | 0.5 | 0.3 | 0.4 | 0.4 | 0.4 | 0.6 |
| 16. Nonwork trips | 0.8 | 0.9 | 0.5 | 0.5 | 0.3 | 0.4 | 0.5 | 0.6 | 0.6 | 0.8 | 0.6 | 0.9 | 0.4 |
| 17. Education | 0.2 | 0.1 | 0.2 | 0.3 | 0.1 | 0.2 | 0.3 | 0.3 | 0.3 | 0.3 | 0.2 | 0.6 | 0.2 |
| 18. Organizations | 0.3 | 0.3 | 0.1 | 0.2 | 0.1 | 0.1 | 0.1 | 0.2 | 0.1 | 0.1 | 0.1 | 0.1 | 0.1 |
| 19. Radio | 0.1 | 0.1 | 0.1 | 0.1 | 0.1 | 0.1 | 0.2 | 0.2 | 0.1 | 0.3 | 0.3 | 0.1 | 0.2 |
| 20. Television | 1.5 | 1.7 | 0.9 | 1.4 | 1.0 | 1.2 | 0.7 | 1.2 | 0.7 | 0.6 | 0.3 | 0.7 | 1.1 |
| 21. Reading | 0.6 | 0.6 | 0.4 | 0.6 | 0.4 | 0.5 | 0.4 | 0.6 | 0.5 | 0.5 | 0.5 | 0.8 | 0.6 |
| 22. Social life | 1.2 | 1.2 | 0.6 | 0.7 | 0.8 | 0.9 | 0.4 | 0.6 | 0.6 | 1.1 | 0.2 | 0.3 | 0.4 |
| 23. Conversation | 0.3 | 0.3 | 0.3 | 0.2 | 0.3 | 0.3 | 0.2 | 0.2 | 0.2 | 0.5 | 0.2 | 0.2 | 0.2 |
| 24. Walking | * | * | 0.2 | 0.2 | 0.6 | 0.5 | 0.2 | 0.2 | 0.3 | 0.2 | 0.4 | 0.2 | 0.3 |
| 25. Sports | 0.1 | 0.1 | * | * | 0.2 | 0.1 | 0.1 | * | 0.1 | * | 0.1 | 0.1 | * |
| 26. Various leisure | 0.3 | 0.3 | 0.4 | 0.5 | 0.2 | 0.3 | 0.1 | 0.2 | 0.2 | 0.6 | 0.3 | 0.2 | 0.3 |
| 27. Amusements | 0.1 | 0.1 | 0.1 | 0.2 | 0.1 | 0.1 | 0.1 | 0.1 | 0.1 | 0.2 | 0.3 | 0.3 | 0.1 |
| Total[a] | 24.0 | 24.0 | 24.0 | 24.0 | 24.0 | 24.0 | 24.0 | 24.0 | 24.0 | 24.0 | 24.0 | 24.0 | 24.0 |
| Free time (13, 17–27) | 5.0 | 5.1 | 3.9 | 5.0 | 4.4 | 4.9 | 3.2 | 4.4 | 3.6 | 5.1 | 3.6 | 4.1 | 3.9 |

SOURCE: Robinson and Converse, 1972, based on data in Szalai et al., 1972.

*Average time less than 3 minutes.

[a]Entries do not always add to 24 hours because of rounding.

Overall, Americans in 1965 reported above-average amounts of free time, compared with the Western and Eastern European countries in the Szalai study. However, Americans devoted more of that free time to three distinct activities—television, socializing, and religion—and that was particularly true in relation to Eastern European countries. However, Americans spent less time walking and resting than people in the other countries.

As noted in Chapter 8, the television difference could be explained by the greater diffusion of television sets in the United States at the time. However, Americans significantly increased their viewing since 1965, so one interesting question is whether Americans are still notably different in terms of this use of free time. More generally, as the world becomes smaller and more time-coordinated as a result of satellites and computer systems, will Americans continue to find ways of spending time as distinctive as they were in 1965?

In this chapter, diary and subjective data from other countries, particularly Japan, Russia, and Canada, are reviewed, shedding light on this issue.

## Japan

Many observers see Japan as the world's leading time-famine country, based on economist Staffan Linder's (1970) scale from time-rich to time-poor countries. Japan now has a term that denotes death from overwork (*karoshi*), and the Japanese have also devised legendary time-saving innovations, such as renting fake colleagues and relatives in order to save people from spending time at ceremonial occasions. In spite of this, many of the ways the Japanese organize their work time and their work lives (for example, with "quality circles," team management, and long-term organizational commitment to employees) have been promoted as models of more productive living for Americans.

How do these different ways of organizing life affect the lives of ordinary Japanese citizens? How do the Japanese differ from Americans in how they feel about their time? These questions are addressed with two distinct data sets: time-diary studies and opinion surveys.

### Time-Diary Studies in Japan

The Japanese are well ahead of the Americans in the size, frequency, and magnitude of their time-diary studies. The main broadcast company in Japan, NHK, has been conducting massive diary studies with the Japanese public since 1960. These studies involve samples of at least 50,000 respondents, compared with our largest study of about 5,000 Americans. These surveys have been conducted every 5 years, not every 10 years, as in the United States.

There are, however, methodological problems with the NHK studies that limit our ability to compare their data with our data, and more so than for comparisons with other countries. First, it is not clear what the sampling frame for these studies is, and particularly whether it is a full national probability survey, in which all Japanese citizens have an equal chance of being selected. Second, it is not clear what response rates are achieved within that sampling frame. Third, the survey period is very short, 1–2 weeks, so it is not clear what results would be obtained for other times of the year. Fourth, the coding categories are very restricted and are concerned mainly with television-radio usage (obviously the main area of daily life of interest to NHK). That means that use of broadcast media may be overestimated by respondents (if they are like respondents in other countries). Fifth and related, respondents are allowed to report more than 24 hours of activity, and although that makes sense for audience research purposes, it makes strict comparability to our 24-hour time diaries problematic.

For these reasons, we turn instead to more recent diary data collected by the Japanese Central Statistical Office, which seem more compatible with our diaries. Again, the sample sizes of more than 250,000 respondents are astronomical by our standards, and it does appear that common time-diary instruments were used in these 1976 and 1991 studies. They have the added advantage over the NHK data of using a 24-hour diary, and the organizational affiliation of the interviewers should not affect the activities reported.

One most unfortunate feature of these Japanese raw data is that they cannot be shared with researchers from other countries, so that the refined tabulations necessary to match the data with the U.S. data cannot be made. Instead, we are forced to make the best match possible with the data tables in their reports. The Japanese data in Table 27 for men and women aged 15 and older are for the 1976 and 1991 data, thus denoting 15-year trends in the Japanese public; the numbers in parentheses contrast the Japanese and 1985 U.S. data (for people aged 18 and older) to note larger cross-national differences.

## Trends Across Time in Japan

The most important trend in the Japanese 1976–91 comparisons is the reduction of work time and the increase in free time for both men and women.

**Table 27.** Differences in Time Use: Japan and the United States (in hours per week, for those aged 15 + )

| Age: | Men Japan 15 + | Men Japan 15 + | Men (U.S.) 18 + | Women Japan 15 + | Women Japan 15 + | Women (U.S.) 18 + |
|---|---|---|---|---|---|---|
| | 1976 | 1991 | 1985 | 1976 | 199 | 1985 |
| **Contracted Time:** | | | | | | |
| Work | 42.3 | 40.4 | (30.0) | 23.4 | 20.8 | (17.7) |
| Commute | 5.0 | 5.5 | ( 3.4) | 2.4 | 2.9 | ( 2.0) |
| | 47.3 | 45.9 | (33.4) | 25.8 | 23.7 | (19.7) |
| **Committed Time:** | | | | | | |
| Housework | ⎰ 0.9 | 1.4 | (10.3) | ⎰23.0 | 20.0 | (19.3) |
| Child care | ⎱ — | 0.3 | ( 1.3) | ⎱ — | 3.2 | ( 4.3) |
| Shopping | 0.5 | 1.0 | ( 4.9) | 4.0 | 3.8 | ( 7.1) |
| | 1.4 | 2.7 | (16.5) | 27.0 | 27.0 | (30.7) |
| **Personal Time:** | | | | | | |
| Sleep | 57.8 | 54.8 | (56.0) | 55.5 | 53.0 | (56.9) |
| Meals | 11.0 | 10.8 | ( 9.8) | 11.7 | 11.8 | ( 9.0) |
| Groom | 6.1 | 6.5 | ( 9.6) | 7.8 | 8.7 | (10.7) |
| Medical | 1.4 | 0.9 | ( 0.1) | 1.5 | 1.1 | ( 0.1) |
| | 76.3 | 73.0 | (75.3) | 76.5 | 74.6 | (76.7) |
| **Free Time:** | | | | | | |
| Education* | 5.8 | 5.7 | ( 2.2) | 4.5 | 4.8 | ( 1.6) |
| Religion | NA | NA | ( 0.8) | NA | NA | ( 1.2) |
| Organizations | 0.6 | 0.6 | ( 0.7) | 0.5 | 0.6 | ( 0.8) |
| Events | NA | NA | ( 0.8) | NA | NA | ( 0.8) |
| Visiting | 3.4 | 3.6 | ( 5.1) | 3.1 | 3.1 | ( 4.8) |
| Sports | 1.4 | 1.6 | ( 3.0) | 0.6 | 0.9 | ( 1.6) |
| Hobbies | 4.1 | 4.7 | ( 2.2) | 2.9 | 3.6 | ( 2.8) |
| Communication/rest | 6.5 | 9.3 | ( 3.9) | 6.8 | 9.7 | ( 5.0) |
| TV | ⎰17.0 | 17.2 | (17.0) | ⎰16.6 | 16.1 | (15.8) |
| Read | — | — | ( 3.0) | — | — | ( 3.3) |
| Stereo | — | — | ( 0.6) | — | — | ( 0.4) |
| Travel | 2.1 | 2.5 | ( 3.2) | 1.6 | 2.6 | ( 2.8) |
| Other | 2.0 | 1.0 | ( 0.3) | 2.2 | 1.3 | ( *) |
| | 37.2 | 40.7 | (40.6) | 34.2 | 37.9 | (39.3) |
| TOTAL | 168 | 168 | (168) | 168 | 168 | (168) |
| Total Travel: | 7.1 | 7.9 | (10.5) | 4.0 | 5.5 | (9.1) |

SOURCE: Yanai, 1995; Americans' Use of Time Project.

NOTE: Numbers in parentheses are for comparison purposes.

*Education not included in free-time calculation.

The nearly 4-hour gain in free time thus parallels the increase in free time in the United States. While there was a 2–3 hour decline in the workweek of Japanese men and women, one half-hour of that gain was lost to greater commuting time over this period.

Perhaps the most striking figures in Table 27 concern the minute amounts of time Japanese men put in on family-care activities: less than 3 hours a week in the 1991 survey. But that number still represents a doubling of the time men spent doing household work over the 15-year period, and it is found for both core housework and shopping activities. While this may be seen as a significant change in the lifestyles of Japanese men, Japanese women continue to do more than 90 percent of the housework (versus about 95 percent in 1976). Unlike women in America and other Western countries (Gershuny and Robinson, 1988), however, there was no decrease in the total family-care activities of Japanese women.

In terms of personal-care activities, virtually no change is found in the eating times of Japanese men and women since 1976, although sleep time decreased 2–3 hours per week. However, personal grooming time increased, particularly for women. There was a corresponding decrease in time for medical care though, suggesting some sort of trade-off in personal-care matters. Travel time also increased, again more for women than for men.

As noted above, the result was that Japanese men and women had almost 4 more hours of free time than in 1976. Unlike the United States, that increase did not go to television, nor did much of the increase go into more active forms of leisure. The increase instead went into conversation and relaxation; whether that involves family or relatives or co-workers—or rest—is not clear from the data. The other gains were scattered across the other uses of free time, with a bit more going to hobbies than to other activities.

In comparison with American trends, then, the Japanese also reduced their work hours. Japanese men used some of that time for more family care, although the women did not decrease their family-care activities. Instead of devoting their increased free time to television, however, the Japanese spread the increase across a number of activities. The biggest gainer was communication and relaxation, as sleep time declined.

## Comparisons with the United States

While comparisons may not be exact because of the different activity codes and age-groups in Table 27, the 1991 data for Japanese men show more than

30 percent additional time at paid work in their time diaries than American men; adding in their longer commute times meant that their work-related activities totaled almost 12 hours more per week. The paid work gap was lower for Japanese women, about 3–4 hours a week, but we do not know what percentage of these Japanese women were in the paid labor force, in order to make direct comparisons with American women.

In contrast, Japanese men reported almost 14 hours less per week on family-care activities than American men, virtually offsetting their excess paid work hours. The family-care times of women in the two countries are close, although American women spend much more time shopping.

Japanese men spend about 1 hour less time each week sleeping than American men, but 1 hour more eating meals; however, American men (and women) spend about 2 more hours a week grooming, with some of that difference made up by the greater amount of time devoted to medical care by the Japanese. In contrast, Japanese women get about 4 hours a week less sleep, while spending 3 more hours eating meals. The end result is that Japanese men and women spend about 2 hours less overall for personal care each week than American men and women.

While Japanese women travel less than American women, and Japanese men travel less than American men, the gap is greater for women. This again indicates that the men have a greater independence from the home.

The gains Japanese men and women have made in free time since 1976 means that they have virtually the same free time as their American counterparts. Americans spend about 3 more hours of their free time with the media—probably watching television—but that cannot be compared directly because the Japanese diary data lump television with reading and other media. Americans also spent more free time visiting and socializing with others, playing sports and participating in outdoor activities and attending religious services. The three activities that dominate the nonmedia free time of Japanese men and women are conversation/relaxation, taking adult education classes, and hobbies. Compared with Americans, the Japanese spend about twice as much nonmedia free time in conversation and relaxation, and up to three times as much time pursuing hobbies and education.

In general, then, compared with American men, Japanese men differ from American men in that they do far more of their productive activities in the workplace than at home (see Table 27), perhaps partially because of the much smaller size of Japanese homes. They sleep and groom less but spend more time at meals. Less of their free time is spent with the media or with social life, but more goes to conversation, education, relaxation, and hobbies.

In contrast, Japanese women show about the same amounts of time spent in productive activities as American women (although probably fewer Japanese women are employed). The personal-care time of Japanese women is also somewhat lower because they have less sleep time and grooming time. As with Japanese men, media use and visiting time are lower than for American women, but conversation, education, relaxation, and hobby times are higher.

Despite their longer work hours, then, the Japanese have found ways to introduce more leisure activities, such as conversation, hobbies, and education, into their lives. Informal conversations with observers of Japan and with Japanese colleagues suggest that the pace of life in Japan may generally be as fast as in the United States, but that the pace of life at the Japanese workplace is more relaxed. We were recently able to examine these issues using many of the subjective survey questions described in Chapter 16.

## Subjective Time Responses in Japan

Data on the issues of time pressure and time perception that were asked respondents in American national surveys were collected in a 1993 national survey in Japan by the Japan Public Opinion Institute, an affiliate of the Gallup Organization. This household survey was conducted with a national cross-section of 1,475 Japanese adults aged 18 and older in January 1993, with an estimated response rate of more than 70 percent. The questions were exact translations of time-related questions asked in a 1991 Time Values Survey of American adults and by the National Center for Health Statistics.

Considerable methodological care went into translating the American items into Japanese, particularly because the concepts of time and the pace of life are so different in this cultural setting. Subsequent factor analyses and item analyses indicate that we were successful in conveying the gist of each item's meaning in this cross-cultural context after several stages of back translation.

Various time-pressure and stress questions are presented in Table 28, along with time-estimate and time-diary data on hours of free time available in each country. The first set of 8 items (lettered 1a to 1h) were used to create a "time crunch" scale that reflects the cumulative extent to which respondents feel these forms of time pressure across the several life-issue areas raised in the items. Item 2 is the single question about whether workers would trade a day's pay to get a day off from work, and item 3 is on calling in sick to get

**Table 28.**  Comparison of Japanese and U.S. Time Pressure Responses (in percentage giving designated response)

|  | Age 18+ | | Under Age 55 | |
|---|---|---|---|---|
|  | U.S. | Japan | U.S. | Japan |
| *Americans More Time Crunched* | | | | |
| *1a. I plan to slow down in the '90s. | 41% | 30% | 40% | 27% |
| *1b. I'd rather be kept busy. | 79 | 65 | 79 | 62 |
| *1e. Not enough time with family, friends. | 43 | 27 | 45 | 29 |
| *1f. I feel constantly under stress. | 41 | 24 | 42 | 27 |
| 4. Experienced great/moderate stress. | 65 | 40 | 68 | 44 |
| 5. I feel always rushed to do things. | 35 | 17 | 39 | 19 |
| 9. I enjoy myself more at work. | 15 | 8 | 17 | 6 |
| 10. I have less free time than 5 years ago. | 47 | 30 | 55 | 37 |
| *Japanese More Time Crunched* | | | | |
| *1d. At end of the day, I haven't accomplished what I set out to do. | 44% | 54% | 43% | 56% |
| 2. I would give up a day's pay for a day off. | 49 | 64 | 51 | 66 |
| 3. I call in to work sick just to relax. | 22 | 39 | 24 | 38 |
| 3a. More than five days. | 2 | 7 | 2 | 7 |
| Average *number* of days. | 3.0 | 4.5 | 3.0 | 4.4 |
| 6. I often have free time on my hands. | 41 | 65 | 41 | 64 |
| *Japanese and Americans Equal in Time Crunch* | | | | |
| *1c. When I need time, I cut back sleep. | 49% | 54% | 51% | 59% |
| *1g. When I work long hours, I feel guilty. | 33 | 29 | 34 | 31 |
| *1h. I feel under stress when time short. | 55 | 51 | 57 | 57 |
| 7. Estimated weekly *hours* of free time. | 19.0 | 19.5 | 18.4 | 18.8 |
| 8. Ideal weekly *hours* of free time. | 26.1 | 28.0 | 26.2 | 28.2 |

SOURCE: Americans' Use of Time Project; Robinson, 1991b.

*Time crunch scale.

a day off; both items are from the 1991 Hilton Time Values survey (see Chapter 16). Item 4 comes from the National Center for Health Statistics large-scale assessment of general stress in the American population in its National Health Interview Surveys. Items 5 to 10 come from various time studies conducted since 1965 at the University of Michigan and by the Roper Organization.

The responses have been arrayed in three groups, those where Japanese report being *less* time pressured, those where they are *more* time pressured, and those that show about *equal levels* of pressure in the United States and Japan. Generally, the Japanese report themselves as less time crunched than Americans on most of the survey items. This includes reporting "great" or "moderate" stress in the past year, "almost always being rushed to do things," preferring to be kept busy, spending too little time with family and friends, and having less free time than five years previously.

## Time Crunch

Thus, Japanese respondents emerged as generally feeling *less* time pressured than Americans in Table 28 in that:

- Only 40 percent reported "great" or "moderate" stress in the past year, compared with 65 percent of Americans. Only 24 percent reported feeling constantly stressed, compared with 41 percent of Americans.
- Only 17 percent reported "almost always being rushed to do things," compared with 35 percent of Americans.
- Some 27 percent felt they spent too little time with family and friends, compared with 43 percent of Americans.
- Some 30 percent said they had less free time than five years previously, compared with 47 percent of Americans.
- Some 65 percent said they would rather be kept busy than have time on their hands, compared with 79 percent of Americans.

On the other hand, 54 percent reported being unable to accomplish their daily goals, compared with 44 percent of Americans.

## Time Off

Far more Japanese workers (64 percent) said they would be willing to give up a day's pay to get a day off than American workers did in 1991 (49 percent). And U.S. surveys since 1991 still indicate that less than half of American workers would choose that day off in response to this question. Moreover, almost twice as many Japanese workers (39 percent) as American workers (22 percent) said they had called in sick to work simply because they needed time to relax, and those who did took almost five days off that way in the previous year, compared with three days for American workers.

## Estimated Free Time

When it comes to the amount of free time they actually have, workers and nonworkers in both countries estimate that they have roughly the same amount of free time each week: about 19 hours. As in the United States, men in Japan report having more free time than Japanese women do, but that gender gap is wider in Japan; Japanese working women estimated that they have only 16.5 hours of free time per week.

With regard to the free time they would like to have, Japanese respondents, like Americans, say they would like about 50 percent more free time than they now have—or about 28 hours a week. Men say they want more free time than women do, even though they report having more free time already.

## Time Structure

Despite generally feeling less time pressure, there are hints that time in Japan may be just as constrained. Nearly two-thirds of Japanese respondents (65 percent) say they almost never have time on their hands that they don't know what to do with, compared with 68 percent of Americans. Moreover, almost equal percentages of Japanese and Americans say they feel stress when pressed for time, feel guilty about neglecting family duties when working long hours, and look to cutting sleep time as a way of making more time available.

## Demographic Correlates of Time Attitudes in Japan

Lack of free time and feelings of stress are experienced by the same categories of people in Japan and in the United States. Differences on the time crunch scale (average score in Japan = 2.4, versus 3.2 in the United States) and five other stress and time-pressure items across demographic groups (see Appendix Q) reveal that women feel more time crunch than men and that employed women score particularly high on the scale. In addition, Japanese women who are not in the labor force report almost as much time crunch as employed men.

In terms of age, time crunch mainly affects those aged 25–34, and to a lesser extent those aged 35–44, namely those who are in the peak years of career and family obligations. The peak crunch years for Japanese men is 25–34 and for women ages 35–44. Yet feelings of stress and being rushed are found among single people more than married people, even though singles report having almost 50 percent more free time. Women in larger households also reported more of such feelings, to some extent probably reflecting the tensions involved in raising children.

As in the United States, college-educated people reported more time crunch and stress generally than those with less education. That was true for the related factor of income as well, but the differences were smaller and less consistent than for education. Also as in the United States, geographic factors made surprisingly little difference in how stressed or rushed people in Japan felt. Rural dwellers and home owners reported about the same time crunch and stress as big-city dwellers and renters.

### Are the Japanese the Real Workaholics?

Are the Japanese more attached to their work than American workers? According to this survey, only 8 percent of Japanese workers said they enjoyed themselves more in their work, and 40 percent enjoyed their work and their free time equally. In the United States, 15 percent of American workers said they enjoyed their work more, and 61 percent said they enjoyed work and free time equally. In Japan, then, almost half (49 percent) said they enjoyed themselves more in their free time, but in the United States that number was only 24 percent.

This greater enjoyment of free time is particularly high among younger Japanese adults under 30, 65 percent of whom choose the free-time option. This is also the group that most feels it has lost free time in the last five years. Greater enjoyment of free time, in contrast, drops to only 30 percent for the older generation over age 60, which suggests a very different work orientation among the new generation of Japanese workers.

Japan is often portrayed as a society that does not know how to slow down and enjoy free time. Coupled with the finding that they report seldom having unwanted time on their hands, the results here suggest that Japanese workers are already able to take off work to enjoy more free time. That promises to become more true in the Japanese work force of the future, if the results of the present survey are any indication.

## Russia

Unlike Japan, Russia has recently undergone a most dramatic change in the structure of daily life. Indeed, it is one of the most dramatic and fundamental rates of change in human history. In American terms, it has been described as simultaneously experiencing the American Constitutional crisis of the 1780s, the American Civil War of the 1860s, and the Great Depression of the 1930s. The revolution of the 1990s may have changed the structure of life in Russia more than its revolution of 1918—and in a much shorter period of time, without any overall guiding ideology or overarching political structure in what has often been described as an emerging gangland culture.

How have these changes affected the time allocations and perceptions of Russian citizens? Similar time-diary and subjective data on time as spent in the contrasting culture of Russia are available. As with Japan, we examine two separate data collections: one for time, the other for subjective data. The diary data on time use come mainly from the single city of Pskov, located about 300 miles northwest of Moscow near the borders with Latvia and Estonia.

Pskov was chosen originally as the representative city for the 1965 multinational study of Szalai et al. (1972), so it provides a valuable benchmark community against which to assess changes over the last 30 years. Recent national time-diary studies indicate that the type of activities in Pskov are similar to those elsewhere in Russia, as was the case of its 1965 "sister city" of Jackson, Michigan, in the United States (see Appendix A).

## Time-Diary Changes in Pskov

A January 1995 time-diary study in Pskov involving a probability sample of 506 respondents aged 18–59 was designed as an exact replication of a January 1986 study in Pskov with 2,181 respondents. This in turn was a replication of the 1965 study in which almost 3,000 respondents aged 18–64 kept time diaries (Szalai et al., 1972). Before describing the 1986–95 changes in Pskov (Table 29), it is interesting to note some of the longer-term changes that were found in the 1965–86 replication (as reported in Robinson, Andreyenkov, and Patrushev, 1988). These were changes that had occurred while Pskov was still a city in the former Soviet Union, and therefore they reflect changes that occurred during socialism between 1965 and 1986.

Thus, it should come as no surprise that virtually no changes were found in the *paid* work hours of workers between 1965 and 1986 (although fewer women were employed in 1986). Much as the fact that the price of bread was the same as in 1948, this can be taken as an indicator of the constancy of Russian daily life in Soviet times. There was, however, a decline of 6–8 hours a week in family-care activities among women, particularly in cooking, cleaning, and household upkeep. In contrast, men were doing slightly more family care, particularly cooking, shopping, and child care. Thus, notable changes had occurred in family-care time, much as in the United States.

Because sleeping, eating, and personal care also showed virtually no change since 1965, Russian men showed no change in their free time; in contrast, Russian women increased their free time by 4–6 hours a week. As in other countries, the major beneficiary of that free time was television, which grew by a factor of 3 over that period. Television-viewing hours in 1986 now totaled almost 13 hours a week, or more than 40 percent of free time. Most of that gain was due to the increase in television sets, as TV ownership was at only about 50 percent in 1965 but had grown to 98 percent (73 percent color) by 1986. Nonetheless, as in the United States, that level of growth in viewing was not simply explained by more homes with television sets. Pskov residents were watching more hours per set.

What was displaced as a result of this growth in television viewing? The casualties were the same as in other countries: radio, reading, and movies. Another activity that declined was also communications-related, originally coded as "adult education." This was mainly in the form of "cultural and literary instruction," usually provided at the factory for Soviet workers. Whatever its content or reason for demise, the 5-plus hours devoted to such instruction in 1965 had dwindled to less than one hour by 1986. Among men, there was nearly a 2-hour decline in walking as well.

Not all activities declined in the wake of television's intrusion on free time in Pskov. Social life and hobbies actually increased, particularly among women. There was a one-hour increase in rest as well.

In all, then, Pskov residents reported much the same trends toward a "post-industrious" society in their time diaries as Americans had since 1965. Housework for women was down significantly, and both Russian women and Russian men were using more of their increased free time for television and for rest. What was remarkable about these results was that two societies, each of which had defined the other as an "evil empire" and each of which had minimal cultural or social contact with the other across this Cold War period, showed the same shifts in daily living patterns. These trends were noted in other countries as well, but the finding that these two antithetical societies shared common social trends was remarkable nonetheless.

## Changes Since 1986

The dramatic shift from autocratic socialism to fledgling capitalism appears to have resulted in some changes in daily life in Russia, but the similarities in time use since 1986 are particularly notable, given the turmoil during this period. Work hours are down only slightly for employed men and women, and no increase in second jobs is reported.

What has changed is household production, particularly in the form of increased gardening and shopping, and this affects men more than women. On the other hand, travel time is down. Sleeping and personal care time are also up slightly, and there is more than a 40 percent increase in meal times.

Greater sociability is also suggested by the increase in the free-time activity of visiting, but that is one of the few free-time activities to show an increase. The activities that were earlier "casualties of television" continued to decline, as movie-going, radio, adult education, organizational activity, walking, and sports now take up less than an hour a week. Reading time has been cut almost in half among men and is also down for women. Television use itself, however, did not suffer much recent decline, nor did resting, both of which increased for women.

Overall, then, with the increases in household production and meals, employed men in Pskov suffered a 5-hour drop in free time while employed women lost closer to 1 hour a week. Some of that decrease may be offset by the sociability undoubtedly associated with the longer meal times, and there is no indication that all the economic and political uncertainties afflicting Russian households caused Pskov residents to get less sleep.

The changes in general do not seem as large as might be expected, but only if one remained employed and differences may be masked by the winter season in which the data were collected. In the 1993 national diary survey conducted in early summer, the amount of gardening time totaled more than 5 hours a week, reflecting how many Russians had become dependent on their private farming to make ends meet. Otherwise, the national data were very similar to those for Pskov (Table 29).

## Comparisons with the United States

For these data, the most appropriate comparison is with the 1985 data from Jackson, Michigan (Appendix A), because common time-diary and coding procedures were designed into that U.S. study. Comparison reveals surprisingly close hours of paid work. In general, working men and women in Pskov continue to report 1–2 more hours of work per week in their diaries than their Jackson counterparts.

Men in Jackson in 1985 reported more time spent in household work and travel than men currently in Pskov, but the gardening times in Pskov are 10 times higher than they were in Jackson. While the family-care times among

**Table 29.** Pskov (Russia) Time-Use Data by Sex and Employment Status, 1986–1995 (in hours per week)

| | Men | | | | | | Women | | | | | | Total Sample | |
| | Not Employed (78) (60) | | Employed (797) (115) | | Total (875) (175) | | Not Employed (250) (144) | | Employed (1,056) (168) | | Total (1,306) (312) | | (2,181) (487) | |
| Activities | 1986 | 1995 | 1986 | 1995 | 1986 | 1995 | 1986 | 1995 | 1986 | 1995 | 1986 | 1995 | 1986 | 1995 |
|---|---|---|---|---|---|---|---|---|---|---|---|---|---|---|
| 1. Regular work | 5.0 | 8.2 | 43.4 | 41.7 | 39.8 | 30.0 | 0.4 | 4.0 | 39.9 | 34.4 | 32.2 | 19.8 | 35.5 | 23.7 |
| 2. Second job | 0 | 0.1 | 0.1 | 0.1 | 0.1 | 1.0 | 0.1 | 0 | 0.2 | 0 | 0.2 | 0 | 0.1 | * |
| 3. Non-work | 0.9 | 1.3 | 4.8 | 4.1 | 4.4 | 4.0 | 0.4 | 0.5 | 3.9 | 4.0 | 3.2 | 3.2 | 3.7 | 2.5 |
| 4. Trip to work | 1.0 | 1.5 | 5.2 | 5.0 | 4.8 | 3.5 | 0.1 | 0.4 | 4.2 | 4.0 | 3.4 | 2.3 | 4.0 | 3.0 |
| *Work Related* | 7.0 | 11.0 | 53.5 | 51.0 | 49.2 | 38.5 | 1.0 | 4.9 | 48.0 | 42.5 | 39.1 | 25.4 | 43.3 | 29.2 |
| 5. Preparing food | 3.9 | 3.7 | 2.5 | 2.3 | 2.7 | 2.7 | 10.5 | 10.8 | 7.6 | 8.5 | 8.2 | 9.5 | 5.8 | 7.2 |
| 6. Cleaning house | 2.6 | 3.4 | 1.4 | 2.2 | 1.5 | 2.5 | 6.9 | 8.0 | 3.9 | 4.5 | 4.5 | 6.0 | 3.2 | 5.0 |
| 7. Laundry | 0.9 | 0.1 | 0.3 | 0.3 | 0.3 | 0.2 | 5.0 | 4.5 | 3.6 | 4.2 | 3.8 | 4.2 | 2.3 | 2.8 |
| 8. Other housekeeping | 4.5 | 3.3 | 2.6 | 1.3 | 2.8 | 2.0 | 1.6 | 0.8 | 0.8 | 0.2 | 0.9 | 0.5 | 1.7 | 1.1 |
| 9. Gardening, pets | 0.8 | 8.6 | 0.3 | 4.7 | 0.4 | 6.3 | 0.3 | 2.7 | 0.1 | 1.2 | 0.2 | 2.0 | 0.3 | 3.3 |
| *Housework* | 12.7 | 19.1 | 7.2 | 10.8 | 7.7 | 13.5 | 24.3 | 26.8 | 16.0 | 18.5 | 17.6 | 22.2 | 13.3 | 19.3 |
| 10. Child care | 1.1 | 2.0 | 1.6 | 1.9 | 1.5 | 1.8 | 9.2 | 5.4 | 3.2 | 3.6 | 4.2 | 4.5 | 3.1 | 3.5 |
| 11. Shopping | 2.1 | 8.2 | 1.8 | 3.1 | 1.8 | 5.0 | 3.4 | 7.1 | 2.9 | 5.4 | 3.0 | 6.0 | 2.5 | 5.7 |
| 12. Non-work trips | 7.4 | 6.3 | 4.6 | 3.1 | 4.9 | 4.1 | 7.0 | 6.4 | 5.0 | 4.0 | 5.1 | 4.3 | 5.2 | 4.8 |
| *Family Tasks* | 10.6 | 16.4 | 7.9 | 8.1 | 8.2 | 10.9 | 19.6 | 18.8 | 11.1 | 13.0 | 12.2 | 14.8 | 10.8 | 14.0 |

| | | | | | | | | | | | | | | |
|---|---|---|---|---|---|---|---|---|---|---|---|---|---|---|
| 13. Sleep | 59.5 | 57.0 | 53.5 | 54.2 | 54.1 | 54.7 | 58.0 | 58.3 | 54.6 | 55.4 | 55.6 | 55.3 | 54.8 | 56.2 |
| 14. Personal care | 7.9 | 7.8 | 6.0 | 7.1 | 6.2 | 7.4 | 6.4 | 7.1 | 6.6 | 6.1 | 6.6 | 6.8 | 6.4 | 6.9 |
| 15. Eating | 7.6 | 10.0 | 5.3 | 7.3 | 5.5 | 8.4 | 7.6 | 10.0 | 5.2 | 7.3 | 5.7 | 8.8 | 5.6 | 8.5 |
| *Personal Needs* | 75.4 | 74.8 | 64.8 | 68.8 | 65.8 | 70.4 | 72.1 | 75.3 | 66.4 | 68.9 | 67.8 | 71.0 | 66.8 | 71.6 |
| 16. Education | 13.3 | 0 | 0.7 | 1.0 | 1.9 | 0.8 | 8.2 | 1.4 | 0.8 | 0.5 | 2.2 | 1.0 | 2.1 | 0.8 |
| 17. Organizations | 0.6 | 0.1 | 1.2 | 0 | 1.1 | | 0.6 | 0.1 | 0.7 | 0.1 | 0.7 | 0.1 | 0.9 | 0.1 |
| 18. Radio | 0.6 | 0.7 | 0.2 | * | 0.3 | * | 0.1 | * | 0.1 | 0 | 0.1 | * | 0.2 | 0.1 |
| 19. Television | 15.9 | 19.2 | 14.5 | 12.6 | 14.6 | 14.7 | 13.6 | 13.5 | 10.7 | 10.6 | 11.2 | 11.8 | 12.7 | 13.0 |
| 20. Reading | 9.8 | 4.5 | 5.8 | 3.1 | 6.1 | 3.6 | 6.1 | 3.8 | 3.5 | 2.2 | 4.0 | 3.0 | 5.0 | 3.1 |
| 21. Social life | 3.8 | 7.9 | 2.6 | 5.4 | 2.7 | 6.2 | 4.0 | 8.3 | 2.1 | 4.2 | 2.5 | 8.0 | 2.6 | 6.2 |
| 22. Conversation | 2.0 | 3.6 | 1.2 | 0.8 | 1.3 | 1.8 | 2.3 | 3.0 | 1.3 | 0.9 | 1.5 | 1.7 | 1.4 | 1.8 |
| 23. Walking | 4.1 | 2.8 | 1.5 | 0.5 | 1.7 | 1.3 | 4.2 | 1.4 | 1.4 | 0.4 | 1.9 | 0.8 | 1.5 | 1.0 |
| 24. Sports | 1.5 | 0.2 | 1.8 | 0.5 | 1.8 | 0.5 | 0.3 | 0.1 | 0.6 | 0.1 | 0.5 | 0.2 | 1.1 | 0.2 |
| 25. Various leisure | 2.3 | 1.3 | 0.8 | 0.5 | 0.9 | 0.8 | 5.7 | 5.5 | 2.3 | 1.6 | 2.9 | 3.4 | 2.1 | 2.5 |
| 26. Spectacles | 2.6 | 0.8 | 0.9 | 0.3 | 1.1 | 0.5 | 0.6 | * | 0.6 | * | 0.6 | * | 0.8 | 0.2 |
| 27. Resting | 6.1 | 5.5 | 3.4 | 4.4 | 5.4 | 4.8 | 5.4 | 5.2 | 2.4 | 4.3 | 3.0 | 4.6 | 3.3 | 4.7 |
| *Total Free Time* | 62.3 | 46.7 | 34.5 | 29.1 | 37.1 | 34.7 | 51.0 | 42.1 | 26.5 | 25.0 | 31.3 | 34.6 | 33.8 | 33.8 |

SOURCE: Americans' Use of Time Project.

NOTE: Figures do not add to subtotals due to rounding.

*Less than 0.5 hours per week.

Pskov women are about the same as in Jackson, more of that care goes for gardening, child care, and shopping among Pskov women, while Jackson women spend more time cleaning house.

Sleeping and meal times are both 1–3 hours higher in Pskov, while grooming and other personal-care times are 2–3 hours higher among Jackson women. The result is that personal-care time is 4–6 hours higher in Pskov, some of which may have been used as a form of free time. Thus, while we might assume that the differences between economic systems would result in differing hours of work, the differences actually occur during nonwork hours.

Whatever the reason, actual free time in Pskov is now about 7 hours a week less for Pskov men and women now than it was 10 years ago in Jackson (and there is no reason to believe that free time has decreased in Jackson since 1986). More than half of that difference is accounted for by the higher television viewing times in Jackson, and another 2–3 hours by increased visiting and conversation time in Jackson. Time spent in organization and religious activities is also now far higher in Jackson, as are movie-going, radio-listening, and outdoor sports. Two activities that used to be far higher in Pskov—reading and walking—have now declined to the point that they are about the same as in Jackson. The one free-time activity now clearly higher in Pskov is rest and relaxation.

While this does not suggest that life has become that much more difficult under the Russian version of capitalism, certain Western behaviors are now more in evidence—for example, shopping, meals, and social life. Russians still manage to get more sleep and now have longer meal times than Americans, two of the more "European" features of daily life found in the Szalai et al. (1972) study. However, the declines since 1965 in such distinctly "Russian" activities as reading, movie attendance, and other cultural/educational activities may not represent advances in the quality of their lives.

## Subjective Time Responses in Russia

The basic differences in American and Russian responses to subjective time questions are shown in Table 30. The data come from a national in-home survey of 1,194 respondents aged 18 and older conducted in June and July of 1993 by the Russian Academy of Sciences.

As in the case with the Japanese comparisons, Americans show far more indicators of time pressure and stress than do Russians. Indeed, the only factor on which Russians appear more time pressured is in terms of amount

**Table 30.** Comparison of U.S.-Russia Differences on Time Pressure Questions

| | Aged 18+ | | Aged 18–55 | |
|---|---|---|---|---|
| | U.S. | Russia | U.S. | Russia |
| *Americans More Time Pressured* | | | | |
| 1. I'd rather be kept busy. | 79% | 49% | 79% | 49% |
| 3. When I need time, I cut back sleep. | 49 | 38 | 51 | 42 |
| 5. Not enough time with family, friends. | 43 | 31 | 45 | 37 |
| 10. Feel stress with not enough time. | 55 | 26 | 57 | 28 |
| 16. I always feel rushed to do things. | 35 | 19 | 39 | 22 |
| 17. Almost never have time on hands. | 68 | 54 | 72 | 53 |
| 20. Less free time than 5 years ago. | 47 | 40 | 55 | 48 |
| 21. Estimated free-time hours. | 19 hrs | 26 hrs | 18 hrs | 25 hrs |
| 22. Ideal free-time hours. | 26 hrs | 34 hrs | 26 hrs | 35 hrs |
| *Russians More Time Pressured* | | | | |
| 23. Actual free time. | 42 hrs | 34 hrs | 37 hrs | 31 hrs |
| *Americans and Russians Equal in Time Pressure* | | | | |
| *4. Not accomplished at end of day. | 44 | 45 | 43 | 48 |
| *6. I feel constantly under stress. | 41 | 35 | 42 | 36 |
| *7. I feel trapped in a daily routine. | 28 | 33 | 30 | 36 |
| *8. Long hours make me feel guilty. | 33 | 27 | 34 | 34 |
| *9. I don't have time for fun anymore. | 23 | 26 | 25 | 28 |
| *10. Spouse doesn't know who I am. | 21 | 15 | 22 | 17 |
| 12. Give up day's pay for a day off. | 49 | 50 | 52 | 52 |
| 14. Experienced great, moderate stress. | 65 | 59 | 69 | 61 |
| 15. Great effect of stress on health. | 12 | 17 | 14 | 19 |
| 18. I enjoy myself more at work. | 15 | 14 | 15 | 12 |

SOURCE: Americans' Use of Time Project.

*Item in time crunch scale.

of free time reported in their time diaries, and even that may not reflect time pressure if the average Russian's longer workweek has considerable leisure built into it, as many observers of working life in Russia have pointed out.

On the other hand, there are actually more items on which Russian and American respondents report almost equal levels of time pressure, again both for the entire sample and for those aged under 55. This indicates ways in which residents of the two countries are more similar than different in that regard.

Turning to the areas of difference in Table 30, we see:

• Some 79 percent of American respondents saying they'd prefer to keep busy rather than have time on their hands, compared with only 49 percent of Russians

- Some 55 percent of Americans saying they feel stress when they don't have time, compared with only 26 percent of Russians
- Some 35 percent of Americans saying they always feel rushed to do things, compared with 19 percent of Russians
- Some 68 percent of Americans reporting they almost never have time on their hands they don't know what to do with, compared with 54 percent of Russians
- Americans estimating 19 hours of free time versus 26 hours for Russians, with ideal hours of free time 7–10 hours higher in both countries, reflecting the same difference as estimated hours

In this latter comparison, then, Russians estimate that they have more free time than Americans estimate, but that does not deter them from wanting still more—even though, as more objectively measured by time diaries, Russians have significantly less free time than Americans (see Table 29). At the same time, it means that Russians are far better at estimating (or being candid about) the free time they actually have than are American (or Japanese) respondents.

Overall, as noted above, there are actually more time attitude areas on which no difference is found than the items on which Americans feel more time pressure (see the end of Table 30). These include items dealing with feeling constantly under stress, trying to handle too much, not having enough time for fun—and being willing to take a day's pay cut to get a day off from work. Levels of reported stress in general are similarly almost equivalent in the two samples.

Thus, the pattern of responses among Russians shows more similarity to the American responses than to the Japanese responses. That makes the Japanese responses stand out even more distinctively in their suggestion of a less stressful and less time-pressured Japanese way of life than American respondents report.

## Demographic Correlates in Russia

As with Japan, there are demographic correlations with the major time pressure and stress measures in the Russian survey (see Appendix R). As with the Japanese results, these tend to identify the same life conditions as related to time pressure and stress in the two cultures, namely:

- Being female rather than male, particularly being an employed female
- Being between the ages of 25 and 44, the major years of family and job commitments
- Being better educated, and particularly a college graduate
- Having a higher income, with these effects not being as strong or consistent as for education

In general, then, it appears that these separate indicators show the same consistent correlates of subjective time pressure across societies, indicating that they are tapping common perceptions and life conditions across societies.

## Canada

To gain a better appreciation of these diary differences across countries, we compare U.S. data with data from Canada, the country that is perhaps most culturally similar to the United States. The contrasts between the 1985 U.S. national results and a 1986 national telephone diary survey conducted in Canada with 9,000 respondents aged 18 and older are shown in Appendix B. (Comparable data from a 1987–88 survey in California in the same appendix also illustrate the similarity of results.)

Comparison with the U.S. national results shows how similar time is spent in these two neighboring countries, with their long common border. Minutes per day on the most time-consuming of activities are remarkably close. Work hours are within about an hour a week. Television numbers are exactly the same. Sleep time is 25 minutes higher in Canada, but Americans make up 7 of those minutes by taking more naps.

Certain differences with Canada can be found, however, even if they are not particularly pronounced:

- More meal preparation, outdoor yard work, and gardening/pet care in the United States
- More shopping time in Canada
- More restaurant meal times in the United States, offset by more home meal time in Canada
- More grooming time in the United States
- More adult educational activity in Canada
- More religious activities in the United States

- More visiting in Canada, but more conversation in the United States (possibly a coding difference)
- More overall travel time in the United States

The two countries therefore do have some distinguishing differences in time use, suggesting some cultural and structural factors that are worth further study.

Whatever the causes of these minor differences, these data indicate that although the United States may be the heaviest television-watching country in the world, it is in good company with its neighbors to the north. U.S. residents may be heavy shoppers, but Canadians have the edge. U.S. residents may do more housework or family care than the Japanese or Russians, but no more than the Canadians. Canadians also match if not surpass U.S. citizens in their socializing and visiting.

## Subjective Time

Canadians also appear similar to their neighbors to the south in terms of subjective time. A 1996 national study of 1,200 Canadian households (Harper, Neider, and Godbey, 1996) that replicated questions from a similar U.S. study done in 1992 (Godbey, Graefe, and James, 1992) found Canadian 1996 attitudes toward time almost exactly mirrored those of U.S. citizens in 1992. When asked if they had more time for recreation and leisure compared with five years ago, Canadians were most likely to say less time—47 percent—while 35 percent said no change and 22 percent said they have more time. The corresponding U.S. numbers were 47 percent less, 31 percent no change, and 22 percent more time respectively.

Canadian women were significantly more likely than men to say they had more time for recreation and leisure—25 percent versus 19 percent—while those between the ages of 15 and 35 were more likely than average to say that their recreation and leisure time was less than it had been five years previously. As in the United States, those with a college education were more likely than those with only a high school education to say that their leisure time had decreased.

Some 43 percent of Canadians in 1996 said their work was more important to them than leisure activities, compared with 35 percent of U.S. residents in 1992. This higher percentage may reflect the comparatively greater impact of the North American Free Trade Agreement on Canada, a country that is much more highly unionized than the United States and that has a much higher percentage of work-dedicated French-speaking people. As in the United States, those aged 55 and over were far more likely to say that their leisure time was more important than their work.

Zuzanek and Smale (1994) report highly similar patterns of response to the time-crunch scale items in Canada (see Chapter 16). Moreover, about one-third (34 percent) of Canadians aged 18–64 said they always felt rushed, within one percentage point of the 1995 U.S. number. In Canada, people with income levels over $60,000 were more likely than the less affluent (42 percent) to always feel rushed, as were those between the ages of 21 and 55. Women (36 percent) were slightly more likely to always feel rushed than men (31 percent). Residents of the Quebec province were more likely than average to feel always rushed (39 percent), while those in the "Lotus land" province of British Columbia were significantly less likely (25 percent) to always feel rushed.

## Summary and Contrasts with Americans

In this exploratory examination of measures of time pressures in other countries, we have been able to show that the concepts can be operationalized in other cultures and that these measures point to the same societal conditions that affect feeling time pressured as in the United States. These are being female (particularly an employed woman being aged 35–44), being more educated, and having a higher income. Regional and city-size factors are not associated with time attitudes, suggesting that conditions of modern life pervade entire societies and are not affected by geography or transportation.

The low scores of Japanese on the time crunch items (Table 28) is particularly surprising and interesting, especially because the agree-disagree format in which the questions were asked might have been thought to induce higher scores on that count alone. In general, then, it appears that whatever the ways the Japanese economy and culture work to constrain the free time of its workers, they have little conscious effect on the workers themselves. The Japanese people may appear overworked to us, but that is apparently not the way they respond to their life conditions. On the other hand, perhaps subtler questions are needed to capture the way time pressures affect Japanese respondents.

The relatively high rates of time pressure among Russian respondents are similarly surprising, although it is clear that the high employment rates and work hours of Russian workers, particularly women workers, mean that they do have less free time than adults in either the United States or Japan. It would be most interesting to see how these questions would have been answered in the Soviet period, particularly the legendary period of stagnation in the later Brezhnev years. At the same time, these benchmark measures can be used to track how continued inroads of Western modernization affect how Russian citizens will respond to the imperatives of the clock.

These data do point to attitudes about time that seem to be uniquely American. Almost twice as many Americans as Japanese or Russians describe their lives as always rushed, and higher percentages of American respondents also agree that they would rather be busy than have time on their hands and that they worry about neglect of family and friends because of long work hours. Future research may show that these are prominent features of the American lifestyle, much as suggested by Alexis de Tocqueville and subsequent observers of American culture.

If there is a pattern of activities that identifies Americans as Americans, it is that Canadians and U.S. citizens sleep a little less and eat fewer meals at home than people in other countries. What also sets Americans apart is the time they spend eating out, going to church, and traveling. Americans and Canadians also seem to share very similar attitudes toward time.

# PART 6

# Only Time Will Tell

# 20

# Issues for the Future

The time is out of joint. O cursed spite
That ever I was born to set it right!
—Shakespeare, *Hamlet,* 1.5.190–91

The range of possibilities for dealing with
restlessness has not been exhausted.
—Theodore Zeldin

Our major conclusions and hypotheses emerging from the material in the previous 19 chapters are organized around the five main topic areas we have been discussing: (1) the methodology of time measurement, (2) the current distributions of how time is spent and the historical changes in time use since the 1960s, (3) the differences and inequalities found within various demographic segments of the American population, (4) comparisons with other countries and other cultures, and, perhaps most important, (5) the lack of fit between how people feel about time and what they report in their time diaries.

# The Methodology of Time Measurement

There are many important discrepancies between what respondents report in their time diaries and what they *estimate* as the time they spend on the same activities. In the case of paid work, the discrepancy is an overestimation of about 10 percent. This is not as serious as the overestimation of household care time, but it is enough to raise serious questions about the measurement of productivity in the United States, given the current methodologies in use by the U.S. Bureau of Labor Statistics. On the other hand, it is a problem that arises in other countries as well, so the United States does not seem to be unique in that respect.

What makes the estimate data pertaining to paid work especially mischievous is that the groups giving the most distorted estimates are the groups who report longer work hours than normal. The people in these groups could be either (a) admired for their dedication to productivity or (b) admonished for losing out on the rest of life. The fact that the workweek times for this "overworked" group are exaggerated serves to relax both concerns, although it does appear that these people *do* work longer-than-normal hours, so that they do have less free time.

Methodologically, it is also instructive to find that those giving the conventional 40-hours response to the work-estimate question may be providing the most accurate information. Ironically, this is the group usually thought to give the laziest or least thoughtful responses (Juster and Stafford, 1985).

At the low end of the work scale, the time diary seems to pick up the paid work time that government surveys tell us does not exist: the paid work of the nonemployed. In this respect, the diary highlights another important problem with traditional government indicators, namely that measurement of unemployment is another aspect of work that also could be improved using diary data.

The time diary also provides what appear to be the most accurate current estimates of all the unpaid work and family care that take place in society. Moreover, the time-estimate method seems to generate even more exaggerated amounts of the time respondents spend doing housework, as described by Marini and Shelton (1993).

The estimate approach generates the most exaggerated numbers for the total free time that are available, but here the bias goes in the opposite direction. Respondents estimate that they have fewer than 20 hours of weekly free time, about half that reported in their time diaries. It is even less than the total weekly hours that they estimate they watch television as a primary *and* secondary activity in their diaries. It thus appears to be socially undesirable in today's society to tell a survey interviewer that you have more than 20 hours of free time a week, and somehow television is not in the forefront of the thought processes involved in these respondent estimates. Whatever the reason, the concept of "free time" is either too fuzzy in respondent's minds for them to give accurate estimates, or too socially undesirable.

In addition, the time diary provides an otherwise unavailable glimpse of *all* the things people do in their free time. Half of free time goes to the media and the other half goes to nonmedia activities, which generally provide more opportunity for self-expression and enjoyment—or more "social capital." The time-diary method indicates that about half of free time is still committed to these diverse activities, although that may be less than social observers would like to see. Thus, less than 5 percent of free time goes to the arts or to organization/community participation. Similarly, helping others is a comparatively rare occurrence.

All the same, there are many aspects of the current time-diary methodology that need improvement and testing. The evidence for validity, while encouraging, needs updating with larger sample sizes and more sophisticated designs. We have found modestly encouraging results in this direction from student class assignments in which students "shadow" someone they know for a waking day, then call on that person the following day to see how they would complete a "cold" diary for that same day (that is, the procedure used in our current national telephone diary surveys). While there is clearly evidence of mistaken reports for individual respondents, the aggregate time-diary measures are quite accurate, much as we found in most earlier validity studies.

There is also a good deal to be learned from using the week rather than the day as the diary period of record. While we have shied away from the weekly approach because of the burden on respondents and the lower response rates involved in such a lengthy reporting period, the results from the two countries that have used the weekly reporting period (England and Holland) are most encouraging.

Take, for example, the reporting of paid work in the diary (Chapter 5). Those analyses are necessarily limited to one-day reports, many of which contained no work at all for the working respondent. In the British and

Dutch weekly diaries, on the other hand, the work schedules of respondents can be seen as quite complex across the entire week.

Figure 13 contains examples of Dutch respondents with regular, somewhat irregular, and very irregular workweeks, as reported in their weekly diaries. Work hours are the hours shaded in black for each day of the week. It is interesting that about one-third of Dutch respondents fit into each category. These graphic schedules help us understand how difficult it must be for respondents with irregular schedules to come up with reasonable estimates of their workweeks, particularly in the short time available to answer the questions in a standard survey. Indeed, there is a significant correlation in the British data between regularity of the workweek and ability to give accurate workweek estimates (Robinson and Gershuny, 1994). This suggests that workers in more recent times may give more inaccurate workweek estimates in recent surveys because of more irregular schedules.

Having diary data for an individual across a week would therefore allow far greater insight into the long-term ways in which people use time, as well as into some of the short-term strategies and trade-offs that are now disguised in their one-day diaries. It would allow more meaningful analyses of individual lifestyles, including typologies of individual ways of spending time and appropriate measures of weekly free time for these individuals.

Even more insightful would be broader qualitative data about respondents' current lifestyles and use of time, such as what goals they are attempting to achieve, what resources they are employing to reach those goals, and how the resource of time fits in with the other resources the respondent has available to reach those goals. How do respondents manage and negotiate time with the significant other people in their lives? To what extent is their time directed toward narrow personal goals rather than purposes that would benefit family, neighbors, community, country, or even humanity in general? How many people dedicate some part of their time to broader social goals, such as the environment or abortion policy?

The variable of time appears to offer an ideal leading indicator of how much of individual energy and effort extends in each of these directions. When cumulated, week-long diaries could provide similar insights into how individual lives map into a society's larger overall agenda. While we have offered several conclusions from the current data, the one-day period is severely limiting.

Thus, while the one-day period may provide the most accurate daily estimates of how much time is spent on various activities, it does so at the expense of achieving a broader understanding of what time means to our

Figure 13. Examples of Workweeks in Dutch Weekly Diary Data

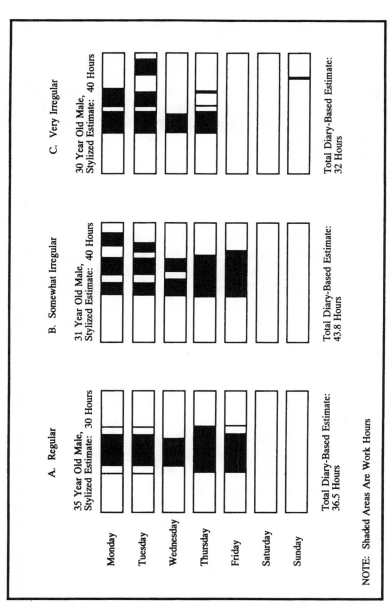

A. Regular

35 Year Old Male,
Stylized Estimate: 30 Hours

B. Somewhat Irregular

31 Year Old Male,
Stylized Estimate: 40 Hours

C. Very Irregular

30 Year Old Male,
Stylized Estimate: 40 Hours

Monday
Tuesday
Wednesday
Thursday
Friday
Saturday
Sunday

Total Diary-Based Estimate:
36.5 Hours

Total Diary-Based Estimate:
43.8 Hours

Total Diary-Based Estimate:
32 Hours

NOTE: Shaded Areas Are Work Hours

SOURCE: 1990 Dutch time-diary data.

respondents—that is, for example, what it *means* to spend 15 hours watching television or 35 hours working. That understanding would allow greater theoretical insights and explanations of *why* people spend time the way they do. Our current one-day data collections mix people with different agendas, different goals, and different resources, and that all but precludes useful theorizing about why people use time as they do. These quantitative accounts, however accurate, still need inputs from anthropology, clinical psychology, leisure studies, and other social sciences in order to be interpreted more readily in both human and scientific terms.

Thus, the next step is to do more qualitative studies of the meaning and role of time in people's lives. Such studies could include the individual judgments people make concerning subtle goals that are important to them and that are the basis for the decisions they make concerning time use. How many Americans just get through each day by "putting out fires," rather than following a controlled life pattern in which activities during the day have been designed to serve some long-term objective? How much of the day's activities are "under control" in the mind of the respondent, as opposed to being dictated by or at the call of others (such as a child or an ailing spouse or parent)? How much is television an escape or an antidote for the pressures of daily living, as opposed to an elevating experience that provides new insights into or appreciation of life? These are aspects of chosen activity that particularly reflect the lifestyles and goals of women, who may feel that they do not have the freedom of time that men do.

The combination of such qualitative insights with the precise diary numbers, such as those in the preceding chapters, would allow us to test the important hypotheses that we have offered from our time-diary analyses.

The data on perceived time pressures, on activity-related satisfactions, and on time outputs (Part Five) generate basic questions about the quality of American life. Are Americans rushing past life, oblivious to the smell of the roses? How many of us are living lives of "quiet desperation"? Do people make best use of the free time they do have available? Are they aware of the apparent mismatches between what they say they like to do and what they actually do? How would they explain or tolerate them?

The questions raised in our *quantitative* journey through the time diaries raise fundamental *qualitative* questions about time and daily life that can be addressed with a directed set of in-depth interviews of a cross-section sample. That would give future time-diary data collections a much clearer sense of purpose and provide a richer set of hypotheses to test.

# How Time Is Spent: Structure and Trends

The major focus of this book has been how people divide their time and how the use of time has been changing historically. Our data indicate that Americans work less on the job and at home than they think they do, and that they therefore have more free time available than they realize.

The time-diary data have revealed many of the balances and symmetries that characterize current daily life. If we subtract sleep and necessary eating and grooming from the 168-hour week for the economically most active segment of 18–64-year-old people in America, what is left are roughly 100 hours a week to divide between work, family care, other personal care, and free-time activities. A little more than half of that 100 hours (53 hours) goes to paid work and family care, a number that is surprisingly close for men and women (Chapter 6). Another 40 hours are given over to free-time activities, almost half of which are devoted to the media, most of it to television; again the gender differences are minimal (Chapter 8). The remaining 7 hours go to other personal-care activities that might be considered discretionary as well, such as the socializing that often extends meal times, the relaxing or luxurious bath, or the grooming that is more vanity than necessity. One could also add here playing with children or window shopping, now coded as family-care time.

Without too much stretching of the data, then, we could argue that Americans currently have close to a 50–50 split of time between work and play, in their waking hours free of other personal care. This may not be consistent with the way most Americans *feel* about their time, but it is a figure implied in the time-diary accounts. The old union slogan heard early in the twentieth century may have arrived unannounced: 8 hours for work, 8 hours for sleep, 8 hours for what we will.

The thought that half of people's waking lives between the ages of 18 and 64 is potentially available for anything they want to do should be an enormously liberating idea. True, the time slots in which this time is available may not be ideal, and people might not have the money or opportunity to do many of the things they want to, but 40–50 hours a week should be adequate time to do things they can really enjoy. The fact that much of that time is devoted to television, even more so among retired people with almost total discretionary time, suggests that Americans are not realizing as much from their free time as they could. That view is confirmed by the higher enjoyment ratings for most of the activities Americans do in the other half of their free time, such as sports, arts, and socializing.

While it is popular and convenient, and even politically correct, to pick on television because of its "couch potato" image and often mindless content, we have discovered behavioral correlates that distinguish TV viewing from other free-time activities, besides its simple predominance over other free-time activities. These do not reflect just our "academic" values, but rather what our respondents tell us about how they evaluate activities and what their lives are about.

For example, television is the first activity people say they would give up if they had to do so during the diary day. In the arts participation data (Chapter 11) and in our time-diary data as well (Robinson, 1981a), television viewing is the one activity that correlates negatively with other, more active forms of leisure, such as arts or sports participation, or almost any activity that takes place outside the home. Putnam (1995a) found much the same phenomenon when he examined the lifestyles of people who participated in organizations. Kubey and Csikszentmihalyi (1990) present evidence of passivity and lack of mental stimulation from television, which ultimately leads to more negative mental states. These are important independent behavioral indicators that reinforce the conclusion that Americans are allocating too much of their time to this most prevalent of free-time activities. Television has become such an accepted way to spend time that we have encountered people who tell us they don't have any free time *because* they are watching television.

Such discussion of overly abundant leisure is quite different from images of "overworked Americans" or of women overwhelmed by the second shift of work they face at home after returning from paid work. In Chapter 3, we described some basic methodological problems about these accounts of where people's time goes. The problems have not diminished as we reviewed different scenarios emerging from the complete accountings of time evident in our full diary accounts.

Millions of Americans are clearly in positions in which time is very scarce—but even those with the greatest role demands, employed mothers, still average almost 30 hours of free time in their diaries (Chapter 8). While this 30 hours is 10 hours less than the 40 hours a week for the rest of society and we need to have weekly diaries to see how that figure applies to individuals, it is substantially more than the 10 hours they estimated in the 1991 Hilton survey.

There may be more time than Americans think, then—particularly when they can afford to spend an average of 20 hours a week of their free time watching television. Television may be the chosen activity because it is the most convenient thing to do in that time slot, but less-convenient, shorter activities, like contemplation or exercise, could fit in that time instead. People's perceptions are involved, but those perceptions may be what define reality more than the actual time available to us.

Samuelson (1995) has argued how much the same perception dominates our feelings about the other major resource in our lives: money. The many ways in which our lives have improved economically are lost on the average American, particularly since new "entitlements" come to Americans in the form of services rather than in dramatic pay raises or price reductions. An October 1996 *Washington Post* poll reflects Americans' overtly pessimistic views of the economy, in which estimated rates of unemployment and inflation are about five times higher than objective government figures. Along with *Newsweek*'s January 8, 1996, bottom-line message of Samuelson's book, we too say that it is time to "Cheer up, America." Unlike these many entitlements, which come to us passively, however, free time requires commitment, imagination, reflection, and discipline if we are to use it wisely.

Americans are not alone in having gained free time since the 1960s. Ausubel and Grubler (1994) found similar trends in most of the time-diary studies in the 12 European and Western countries they examined. They found that, calculated over the lifetime, free time is now greater than time spent working for seven Western countries (see Figure 14). In contrast, work time tended to be greater in the five Eastern European countries, particularly for women. Even more important is the upward slope of most of the trend lines in Figure 14 (a and b), which indicates trends toward increased amounts of free time as a function of both time and income. These slopes suggest that increased free time will continue into the future, both in the United States and elsewhere.

## Narrowing and Widening Gaps by Demographics

Perhaps as important as the gains in free time we have described is the evidence of closing gender gaps (Chapter 13), suggesting that both women and men have come a long way toward a more equitable sharing of the resource of time (although diary studies in the 1920s and 1950s indicate that women then had more free time than men did). With similar evidence of a closing gender gap in the resource of money, as women's pay moves toward that for men, there is solid evidence that America is indeed moving toward a gender-less or androgynous society (Bianchi and Spain, 1996).

Some may look at the inequities that have persisted across this period, such as women's doing more housework, and take them as evidence that women will always be victims of discrimination. But we also note that differences in doing housework are found among *single* men and women, who are not constrained by the demands of marriage. Even among people who live alone, then, single women do twice as much housework as single men. Can one criticize single men for their lack of attention to household chores when they are the ones who must live with the consequences? Is it not appropriate to look at these differences as defining the territory of gender, as Berk (1985) describes in *The Gender Factory*, a way of defining one's gender uniquely? While men may continue to make strides in doing a larger share of housework, the greater gains will probably continue to come from women spending less time on these activities.

Our examination of time diaries of today's male teens does not give much encouragement to those expecting the next generation of men to do significantly more in the way of housework. Nor is it clear that there is great sentiment for this among today's married women. Only about 40 percent of married women in our 1995 survey said they wanted their husbands to do more housework. That same survey also found more men saying they liked doing housework and cooking than in 1975, especially men under 30. More gender blending of housework, therefore, may already be under way.

The trend toward gender equalization in time use is also distinctive in that it occurred in a time when the trend among other social categories has been toward more differentiation. Thus, in Chapter 14, we saw that differences by age-groups are larger than they were in 1965, largely because of earlier retirement among those above age 55. Similarly there are greater differences in certain activities of African Americans and white Americans, particularly in the religious participation and watching television (Chapter 15), and those differences are not due to educational or income differences between the two races, which while closer still remain significant between the races.

Moreover, the trend toward greater differentiation in free time is also found by all three role factors. The differences between the employed and nonemployed, married and unmarried, and parents and nonparents have all become sharper in more recent decades. All were to the disadvantage of those taking on these role responsibilities, indicating a main reason why more people may have just said "no" to taking on these role responsibilities in recent times. This may reflect a greater awareness of their real time costs and related hassles.

In light of these trends toward greater gaps for other social categories, the closing of the gaps between men and women seems even more remarkable. To the extent that it continues, the debates on gender differences may need to focus on issues other than time. Our data provide striking evidence of the convergence of men's and women's lifestyles over the last three decades.

## Comparisons with Other Countries

In the course of our analyses we noted several differences in how Americans use time, compared with time use in other countries. In addition to the usual comparisons with Japan, we encountered examples of more rewarding ways of spending time in other countries.

The allocation of time in Holland has a number of appealing features (Robinson, 1993b), including much lower work times and the work days beginning later and ending earlier than in the United States. This meant that the average Dutch adult had almost 10 hours more free time each week. But that did not mean they watched more television—indeed, they watched notably less television than Americans.

What did occur was a higher expenditure of time among the Dutch on social life, with visiting times perhaps higher than in any other country. Despite the high enjoyment levels associated with visiting in the United States, there has been a decline in that form of social life since 1965. (Americans were distinctively high in visiting time in the 1965 multinational study, but Holland was not a participating country in that study.) In contrast, the Dutch seem to have found a way to keep social life alive in an age of television and high technology.

Another fascinating feature of the Dutch experience is the high amount of time both women and men spend doing housework. In contrast to the declines found in the United States and other Western countries, housework does not appear to be on the wane in Holland. It may be a function of their more intense social life. Nonetheless, the standard of living in Holland still compares favorably with other Western countries.

The Dutch have social buffers and safety nets that are unavailable in the United States. This may go along with another feature of daily life most Americans would not appreciate—substantially higher taxes. They also have far longer vacation periods, which is in keeping with the rest of Europe. On this point we agree with Juliet Schor about Americans being overworked. That most Europeans appear to have twice the vacation time most Americans do, and perhaps more holidays during the year as well, is a startling fact. The downside is that in Europe people have a hard time finding a loaf of bread or an automobile mechanic on a weekend or during the evening, because Europeans are reluctant to work the off-hours Americans routinely do.

When comparing the Japanese with Americans, the time contrasts are not so enviable. Male Japanese workers put in 8 to 10 hours more work a week than their American counterparts. Moreover, male workers do less than 3 hours of housework a week, less than one-fifth as much as American men and one-tenth that of Japanese women. While they have about the same amount of free time, Japanese men and women appear to devote less of that free time to television and much more to rest and relaxation. Indeed, their rest hours may be among the highest in the world. Perhaps that is a main reason that Japanese survey respondents claim to be less harried and stressed than American respondents.

If we are looking for a country to emulate in terms of time use, then, Holland may provide the more appropriate role model. Moreover, in terms of total free time across the year, the Dutch as well as other Europeans enjoy more of it, in the form of vacation days. As we shall see in the next chapter, vacation days are the one time that we see Americans abandoning their television sets for more engaging and enjoyable forms of free time.

## Confronting Our Time Paradoxes

The paradoxes encountered in studying how Americans use time are both numerous and profound. Time devoted to work has declined, but Americans believe it has increased. The increases in free time have been largely devoted to more television viewing, even though that is a free-time activity that Americans rate relatively low in terms of pleasure. They also spend little time doing the free-time activities they rate more pleasurable, such as socializing or playing sports.

There are paradoxes contained within these affective ratings of activity as well. People rate work and child care as more pleasurable in general or in the abstract than in the diary context of "real time." The reverse is found for most free-time activities, including TV viewing, the activity of which we have been most critical. If we are attempting to explain everyday behavior with the hedonistic models that seemed to work well (Chapter 17), these short-term pleasures seem to do a better job of it than the longer-term ratings used in prior research. Thus, the decline in ratings of the general enjoyment from television in 1995 may not portend the decline in viewing that we might hope. We may not enjoy television in general, but the programs we saw last night were pretty good.

There is also the paradox that there is no relationship between time spent and output from such time; doing something for a longer period of time does not necessarily mean that more is accomplished. This is particularly true when technology is involved, such as the "labor-saving" devices of the modern household.

## The More-More Phenomenon, Newton, and the Irrelevance of Time

In combination, these findings suggest the basic irrelevance of time as a measure of accomplishment, welfare, or well-being. Cut the amount of work time in American society, and Americans may believe they are working longer hours. Give Americans more free time, and they devote most of that time to television, an undemanding, unresponsive activity that they now generally rate as lower in pleasure than many household chores. Give Americans the opportunity to purchase labor-saving technology, and they subvert its time-saving features, even though they say they are starved for time and presumably purchase such technology in order to save time.

At a basic behavioral level, we have encountered repeated evidence of what we have called the "more-more" phenomenon. Thus, people who work long hours are also more likely to spend more or the same time engaged in more active free-time activities like arts participation, sports/exercise, or organizational involvement. Women who work seem to have homes that are kept up no less well than women who are full-time homemakers and spend 40 percent more time doing housework. People who lead busier lives are more likely to participate in our diary surveys, and perhaps other surveys as well. These reinforce the popular adage that if you want something done, give it to a busy person.

Such results also fit into what might be called a larger "Newtonian" model of human behavior, following Isaac Newton's classic principle from physics that "Bodies in motion stay in motion, bodies at rest stay at rest." This Newtonian model can also be invoked to cover the "(time) rich get richer" free-time trends discussed in Chapter 8.

**Figure 14.** Free Time to Total Labor Time Ratios vs. Per Capita GDP for Male and Females of Selected Countries, 1961–1986

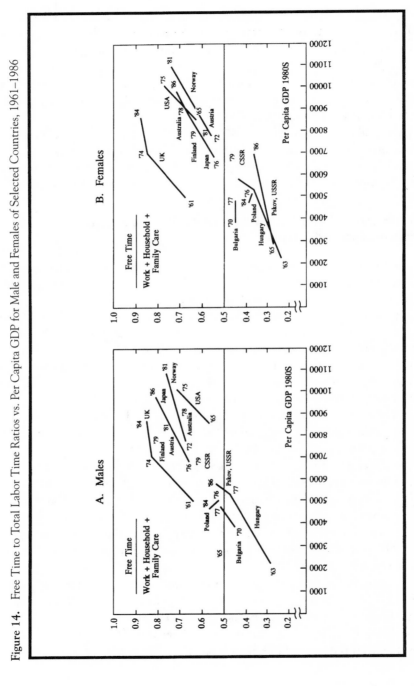

SOURCE: Ausubel and Grubler, 1994.

This basic bifurcation process model is more familiar in other contexts— particularly in economics, in which the rich getting richer has become not only an accepted fact of economic life but also a political issue that has recently been producing strong public resentment and debate. It has also become a staple finding in communications research, in which more information acquisition has been repeatedly found among those who are already well informed. It was first found in the study of campaign effects in Cincinnati about the United Nations (Hyman and Sheatsley, 1948), subsequently for other foreign affairs media information (Robinson, 1968), in local community affairs (Tichenor et al., 1970), for Sesame Street (Cook, 1975), and in a broad array of other contexts (Gaziano, 1983; Robinson and Levy, 1986). Based on the findings in Chapter 10, we suspect that computers and other new information technologies will further serve to separate the information haves from the have-nots.

In the time/behavioral context, most of this more-more evidence thus clearly points to more support for the "spillover" rather than "compensatory" models of free-time activity that were debated in the 1960s and 1970s (Parker, 1972). That is, the activities that people engage in in their free time spill over into their leisure time—at least in terms of time commitment. Those most active in productive activities also seem to be most active in free time, paradoxical as that may seem.

## The Longer View

With these findings in hand, it now seems appropriate to ask harder questions about the ultimate outcomes of how Americans spend their time. Does it make a difference if people reconfigure their day by dropping activities from which they get the least benefit or the least output? Might they have done something more worthwhile? If so, what might that be? Those are questions that foreign observers have long and benignly asked about American culture and the American way of life.

In 1932, American trade unions seriously fought for a 30-hour workweek. At the heart of the movement was the assumption of limited needs. People could need, want, or buy only so many things, and when such limits were reached additional gains in productivity would go toward increasing free time. While few limits have been found, free time has nevertheless increased, confounding the logical assumptions made by many authors that if people want to have more material goods they must put in longer hours of work.

Restructuring everyday life in ways that make free time more meaningful and lives less rushed will take political courage. It will also make us confront the question asked by ancient philosophers concerned with leisure: What is worth doing?

# 21

# Brother, Can You Spare Some Time?

> Will Time say nothing but "I told you so"?
> If I could tell you I would let you know.
> —W. H. Auden

> There is no obligation on us to be richer,
> or busier, or more efficient, or more pro-
> gressive or in any way worldlier or wealth-
> ier, if it does not make us happy.
> —G. K. Chesterton

Implicitly or explicitly, time has become a central concern of American society. We can conclude that time is largely irrelevant and ought to be irrelevant, or at least subservient to the rest of life, but that is a bit like asking the world to stop so we can get off. As Sebastian De Grazia (1962) observed ironically, Americans have rejected the tyranny of man only to accept the tyranny of the clock.

But this is an age where irony and paradox run rampant, and we have added one more paradox to the list: in collective and societal terms, Americans have substantially reduced the number of hours a week that are devoted to work behaviors, but they simultaneously feel more rushed and believe they have less free time. In this chapter we speculate on what such ironies and paradoxes may mean and look at the prospects for change in the near future.

## Diverging Internal and External Worlds

Time, as measured mechanically, seems to have become increasingly divorced from meaning. Internal and external realities diverge in a world that may have become simultaneously more highly ordered and more insane, in which perceptions and behaviors are increasingly out of sync. Increased free time is supposed to slow down the pace of life and make us more tranquil and leisurely, but the opposite appears to be happening. Even as "free" time increases, more people feel they are rushing past life. True leisure is an idea that has been abandoned and is even no longer understood or considered. Many people have developed dysfunctional attitudes toward time as an infinitely expandable resource. Almost by definition, that means one can never have enough time—even though we may really have all we need.

This paradox also means that American society has progressed, in spite of our perceptions of time. Americans in the aggregate have more free time to do as they wish. The "leisure potential" has increased. The dream of more leisure time, time freed from the necessity of labor, has been realized. But we still suffer from a cultural lag and continue to rush, consume, and stay perpetually busy. Negative feelings associated with rushing through life may be overcome only by succeeding generations, just as crowds seem normal to a resident of Tokyo, Hong Kong, or New York.

Feelings of being perpetually rushed represent part of the increasing tendency to feel victimized. The victim mentality is evident even within groups of people who live lives of unparalleled privilege. It has become attractive to think of oneself as a victim: "The mantra of the victims is the same: *I am not responsible; it's not my fault*" (Sykes, 1992, p. xiii). "Paradoxically, this don't-blame-me permissiveness is applied only to the self, not to others; it is compatible with an ideological Puritanism that is notable for its shrill demands of psychological, political and linguistic correctness" (Sykes, 1992, p. 11). In the mind-set of the victim, the message that Americans are working longer hours is very attractive. It is less attractive to point out that people choose to devote their gained free time to watching television.

The "psychology of entitlement" that has emerged in the last few decades (see, for example, Lasch, 1979; Samuelson, 1995) is related to the victimized posture many people increasingly assume. On a recent television show, for instance, three young adults who lived with their parents complained that making it on their own was simply impossible. Among other problems, all three mentioned that they could not afford the cost of dry-cleaning.

As Samuelson (1995) observed, people are not aware of the extent to which their expectations about everyday life have increased or how former expectations have been fulfilled. We have come to expect hassle-free personal relations, limitless material possessions, and a world unfolding to meet our personal agendas, timewise and otherwise. We then feel more rushed than we would prefer when the world does not respond as we expected. The tragic view of life has been rejected by most Americans, although such a view might make us feel better.

## The Expanding Sense of the Necessary

Some of these feelings reflect the advent of the postmodern era, which has led to the "saturated self." As psychologist Kenneth Gergen (1991) observed, the replacement of a mass culture with a more diverse and individualized one has been accompanied by the romantic and modern notions of ourselves being replaced with "postmodern" notions. The romantic view of the self attributes characteristics of personal depth—passion, soul, creativity, and moral fiber—to everyone. "This vocabulary is essential to the formation of deeply committed relationships, dedicated friendships and life purposes" (Gergen, 1991).

Thus, the postmodern era is characterized not only by technological change but also by constant change at both the group level and the individual level. In such a situation, as others are incorporated into one's own self-concept, their desires become ours. "There is an expansion of goals—of 'musts,' 'wants,' and 'needs.'" While people's use of time may not be changed by this condition, *the sense of the necessary is*, with the attendant result that time is made psychologically more scarce. *Free time is expanding, but not as fast as people's sense of the necessary.* This gap results in rushing and in dysfunctional attitudes toward time, as the postmodern proliferation of issues that seem to need attention is almost endless

We are becoming, in the words of poet Theodore Roethke, "perpetual beginners." Such a world cannot be easily translated into specific, delimited meanings. Even "free time" behaviors have less culturally distinct meanings.

As the philosopher Kierkegaard prophetically wrote in the middle of the nineteenth century, "When I behold my possibilities I experience the dread which is 'the dizziness of freedom' and my choice is made in fear and trembling" (quoted in Kaufmann, 1956, p. 17).

In today's postmodern era, the collapse of belief is all around us. The concepts of relative truth and multiple truth take us very far from our ancestors, who willingly killed one another over absolute beliefs about God and the universe.

> We can see, if we look closely at the ideas and events of the postmodern world, a new sensibility emerging—a way of being that puts the continual creation of reality at the heart of every person's life, at the heart of politics, and at the heart of human evolution. (Anderson, 1990, p. xiii)

The postmodern world brings us to a growing suspicion that all belief systems or truths are social constructions. The nature of truth is multiple, or simply a social construction. This kind of freedom can hardly be thought of as leisure:

> Today we are all "forced to be free" in a way that Rousseau could not have imagined when he coined that famous phrase. We have to make choices from a range of different stories—stories about what the universe is like, about who the good guys and the bad guys are, about who we are—and also have to make choices about how to make choices. The only thing we lack is the option of not having to make choices—although many of us try hard, and with some success, to conceal that from ourselves. (Anderson, 1990, p. 8)

Thus, scientists and religious fundamentalists may find themselves on the same side—holding absolute views of what is true based on a single method, belief system, or variable.

Leisure has historically meant undertaking one activity instead of another in the belief that it was superior. The various "rational recreation" movements of the late nineteenth and early twentieth century were based on an absolute belief in what was and was not worthwhile leisure. Such beliefs were articles of faith, usually made at the group level and transmitted to individuals.

As numerous scholars have observed, two modes of human consciousness exist. One perceives reality as separate objects existing in three-dimensional space and linear time. The other, which may be called spiritual, holistic, or transpersonal, views reality as a series of relationships among all things that is part of some universal consciousness. People who subscribe to the first mode typically lead ego-centered, competitive, goal-oriented lives.

> They tend to be unable to derive satisfaction from ordinary activities in everyday life and become alienated from their inner world. For people whose existence is dominated by this mode of experience, no amount of wealth, power or fame will bring satisfaction. They become infused with a sense of meaninglessness, futility and even the absurdity that no amount of external success can dispel. (Grof, 1988, p. 122)

Such a consciousness is related to how time is viewed and to the extent to which pace of life is an issue. Those who cannot derive satisfaction from ordinary activities of everyday life will always be rushed to construct another basis of satisfaction.

While increased free time should lead to *greater potential* for an empathetic time dynamic to take hold, we find little evidence that this has happened. The entrance into the postmodern world has led not only to an expansion of what people perceive as necessary, but also to a diminution of the time available to achieve it.

## Must Time Be the Measure of Things?

If people perceive that it is necessary to achieve more and that there is less time to do those things, it may be natural that time has become the measure. It appears, however, that time is the true measure of very little in work or in leisure. In terms of work, hours spent cleaning a house do not predict how the results are judged, and hours spent studying have little relation to grades.

While time may be a relevant measure of productivity in assembly-line jobs, where humans do manual labor in uniform fashion, such jobs are today few and far between. A more relevant measure may be the extent to which an individual has increased the productivity of information regarding the task and the level of technology brought to bear. In a service economy, there is more emphasis on providing service or getting the job done than on the hours needed to complete it.

In terms of leisure, what is most time-consuming is not most satisfying. Thus, Americans spend more time watching television than any other form of free-time use, but that activity is not rated as most pleasurable or satisfying. In particular, it appears that "free time" and "leisure," as De Grazia (1962) concluded more than three decades ago, will continue to reside in different worlds. Some recent definitions of leisure, returning to ancient concepts, consider leisure in nonquantitative terms:

> Leisure is living in relative freedom from the external compulsive forces of one's culture and physical environment so as to be able to act from internally compelling love in ways which are personally pleasing, intuitively worthwhile, and provide a basis for faith. (Godbey, 1985, p. 9)

In such definitions, leisure represents a way of life rather than a period of time. While our data suggest that there has been a gain of almost one hour a day of "free time," the qualitative aspects of such gained time may be as harried as the time devoted to obligation. Indeed, in a culture that is materially privileged at historically unprecedented levels, obligation has become a notion that is potentially without limit.

## Future Distribution of Free Time Across the Life Cycle

Even if we have not achieved a society of leisure, people *have* gained free time—not only on a daily basis but also as a percentage of their total lives. Ausubel and Grubler (1994) show the relevant calculations for Great Britain projected into the next century (Figure 15). While "free time" in the United States is not presented in their analysis, Owen (1969) calculates that the percentage of all lifetime hours devoted to work has also declined, from 23 percent in 1900 to 15 percent in 1960, and British uses of time generally mirror those in the United States (Gershuny and Robinson, 1988). Ausubel and Grubler's analysis suggests that the percentage has declined further since the 1960s, given people's later entry into the labor force and earlier retirement with longer life expectancy.

The average U.S. worker now retires in his or her late fifties or early sixties, and American men who reach the age of 65 now have a life expectancy of 80 years, while the life expectancy of American women is 84 years. On

**Figure 15.**  Allocation of Lifetime Hours to Different Activities for Male Working Population in Great Britain, 1956–1981, in Fraction of Disposable Lifetime (excluding physiological time).

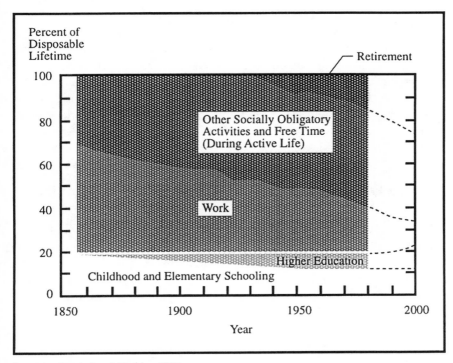

SOURCE: Ausubel and Grubler, 1994.

average, about 12 of these years after age 65 will be relatively healthy. The elderly are no longer disproportionately poor, and if wealth is measured as financial assets they are among the wealthiest groups in society (age 55–64 is the wealthiest group), their potential for free-time use has increased dramatically. It is no wonder that the 55-and-over age-group constitutes a disproportionate share of the traveling public as well as those who dine in fancy restaurants.

The current system hoards huge amounts of free time to be spent only in the last 15–20 years of life. The Prussian bureaucrat who is reputed to have established age 65 as the age of retirement payment is said to have done so completely arbitrarily. He probably never imagined that the institution of retirement he helped establish would today consume almost one-fifth of a person's life. Less than one out of five of the 52 million Americans age 55 and over is in the labor force—a stunning indicator of where free time has grown most quickly. Retirement should be changed to recognize the vastly different rates at which people age and to provide more tranquillity for those in earlier life stages, particularly for parents of young children.

In macro terms, not only retirees but children as well may be considered to have more free time. School-age children attend public school only about 180 days a year (compared with 240 days in Japan), and the amount of time they spend doing schoolwork at home is thought to have declined. It may also be that they spend less time helping parents with housework or other chores.

## Future Distribution of Free Time in Everyday Life

The reorganization of time needs to be rethought for daily life, as well as for the entire life cycle. As our data show, about two-thirds of free time comes on weekdays, not weekends. Much of the free time people gained during the last few decades is during weekdays rather than in larger segments, such as vacations. Free time in larger segments has expanded potential for leisure purposes (see Table 31).

Data from the 1975 University of Michigan time-use study shows how the nature of free time differs dramatically on vacation days. Even though the 7.4 hours of free time on vacation days are barely more than a typical Sunday, there is a dramatic decline in television viewing, to less than 20 minutes a day (see Table 31). In its place, reading time more than doubles and communication time almost doubles as well (although visiting time is cut in half). The biggest increase is in sports, walking, and other outdoor activities— nearly 2 hours. The increases in sleep and meal time, and the decrease in grooming time, also suggest a more leisurely pace. Travel more than doubles.

The finding that vacation periods offer one circumstance in which Americans finally turn off the TV set is an encouraging conclusion from Table 31. More gratifying, perhaps, is that the activities chosen instead—sports, reading, conversation, and sleep—were all rated as more satisfying or enjoyable (see Chapter 17). That is not to say that vacation-day time expenditures are ideal, because many Americans use their vacation days to work or shop (although it may involve more enjoyable types of work or shopping) and there is a marked decline in socializing on vacation days. Nonetheless, it is

**Table 31.**   Vacation Day Differences in Time Use (1975 data, in hours per day)

| | Vacation Days (n = 46) | Nonvacation Days (n = 940) |
|---|---|---|
| *Contracted Time* | | |
| Work | 1.4 | 3.3 |
| Commute | .2 | .3 |
| *Committed Time* | | |
| Housework | 1.4 | 2.5 |
| Child care | .2 | .4 |
| Shopping | 1.2 | .7 |
| *Personal Time* | | |
| Sleep | 9.6 | 8.4 |
| Meals | 1.5 | 1.2 |
| Groom | .6 | 1.3 |
| *Free Time* | | |
| Education | .1 | .1 |
| Religion | * | .2 |
| Organization | * | .3 |
| Events | 1.3 | .2 |
| Visiting | .6 | 1.3 |
| Sports | 2.2 | .3 |
| Hobbies | .6 | .4 |
| Communication | 1.1 | .6 |
| TV | .3 | 1.6 |
| Read | 1.2 | .5 |
| Stereo | * | .1 |
| Total Free Time | 7.4 | 5.5 |
| Travel | 2.7 | 1.2 |

SOURCE: Adapted from M. Hill, 1985, pp. 167–69.

*Less than 0.05 hours per day.

clear that vacation days look more like what philosophers and scholars of leisure in the Athenian tradition would applaud.

In line with these findings, survey respondents generally report they would rather have their increases in free time in the form of 3-day weekends or larger blocks of time. In spite of this, however, the chores of weekdays appear to be expanding into the weekend, even as free time expands during weekdays. The expansion of free time on weekdays may help explain the greater amount of time devoted to television during the last few decades (see Chapter 8).

Larger segments of time, such as vacations, exhibit time uses that in many ways seem healthier and more enjoyable. One can see this extended in the lives of many retired people who take the time to visit other areas, to do volunteer work, and to "smell the roses." They take whatever time is required—something they were not likely do while employed. Still, the lives of most seniors who fill out our time diaries seem to revolve around the television set.

To the extent that "television" is redefined during this generation, free-time use will also be radically reshaped. The computer revolution promises to decentralize TV watching and make it interactive.

> Rather than a system whereby a few "stations" spray images at millions of dumb terminals in real time, computer networks put the customer in control, not settling passively for what is on the "air" but actively seeking and even shaping the customer's first choices. Television will die because it affronts human nature; the drive to self-improvement and autonomy that lifted the race from the muck and offers the only promise for triumph in our current adversities. (Gilder, 1994, p. 16)

A critical question here, in terms of future time use, is the extent to which people want the endless choices computers provide or whether they prefer to have the television decide what to watch for them.

Part of the allure of television is its *freedom from choice*. It is a respite from a complex world. Interactive television, with its capacity to shape what is seen and heard, may actually be less appealing to people who may use future television less if they must invest more energy and imagination. There is also the possibility, in an increasingly have-and-have-not world, that television will evolve into two different forms: (1) a computational instrument of learning and personal growth for a have culture, and (2) an instrument of diversion and control of the have-nots—not unlike the world envisioned by Kurt Vonnegut in *Player Piano* (1952).

Perhaps we need to remember that even though television may be temporarily overwhelming people's use of time, there is historical evidence that discrimination can be learned. Historian Zeldin (1994) observed:

> It needs to be remembered that at the same time as the British invented the consumer society, they also took to drink as never before, and the USA followed suit, but over the last generation there has been a radical change in attitudes to alcohol, with a move to moderate drinking of high-quality wines rather than mass consumption of

anything fermented. Watching television may become addictive but gradually discrimination is learned. (P. 296)

## Prospects for the Further Decline of Work

While much attention has been given to the proposition of decreasing amounts of free time, other analysts believe that working will consume a continuously shrinking percentage of the hours in people's lives. Professionals may enter the labor force later in life after extensive education, work long hours for high pay, and retire or change occupational directions much earlier. These will be what management analyst Charles Handy (1989) called the "core workers," one of three prototypes of workers in organizations of the future. Handy believes professionals will have to work harder, stay on the cutting edge of technological advance, and become even more efficient.

While core workers will shape the organization, much of the actual work will be contracted out to workers outside the organization, who will be paid for what they produce, not for the time they put in. They will be paid in fees, not wages. Finally, workers in the flexible labor force will work in temporary or part-time jobs. The temporary or part-time worker is already the fastest-growing part of the labor scene in most industrial societies. These workers are disproportionately female. They do not always want a full-time job, but sometimes merely seek to supplement the wages of a spouse or other member of their household. They may have more than one job, and in some sense might better be thought of as self-employed. Many of them are young people who move through a variety of work experiences.

Handy projects that the number of lifetime work hours per worker could be cut in half, from 100,000 to 50,000. This could be achieved in different ways. For example, because they need more years of education, core workers might work full-time throughout the year, but only for twenty-five years. Part-time workers might work for forty-five years, but only 25 hours a week across the year; temporary workers would work 45 hours a week, but only for half the year. Other more family-oriented workers could work for ten years, take ten years off to raise children full-time, and return to the work force for fifteen more full-time years. Each of these options would effectively cut lifetime work hours in half. Free-time hours would increase dramatically, providing unprecedented opportunities for true leisure across the lifetime.

## Slowing Down

Changes in the pace of life is a bigger problem than changes in the duration of paid work, housework, or other obligated activity, as we have seen. The issue for the future is therefore less one of reducing work hours than one of slowing down the pace of life. This will be a tall order. As De Grazia (1962) observed, it has taken 200 years for the industrial revolution to speed up the pace of life, so it may take that much time to slow it down.

Part of this slowdown may occur naturally, based merely on the aging of the population. In broadest terms, the aging of the Baby Boom generation may mean the following:

> We will have our national mid-life crisis in this decade. . . . The values that will emerge will be many of the traditional middle-age values; a slowing down (we'll see this in everything from entertain-ment to the pace of our fitness activities); a seeking of quality (this will be present in our evaluation of washing machines as well as in our choice of friends); less acquisition-mindedness; a streamlining of our activities; less time for shopping; more time for both at-home leisure and experiential expenditures away from home. (Editors of *Research Alert*, 1992, p. 14)

They may redirect their patterns of "conspicuous consumption" toward cau-tion and savings. Fortunately, they are in the stage of life in which earnings are greatest. All this, combined with the fact that this group values leisure increasingly, means that Baby Boomers are likely to become more critical about how they spend their time and money. Perhaps they will become more able to find contentment while doing less, owning less, and saying no more often. Their values of competence, control, and concern for improving their health and environment lead away from the time famine. They may also lead toward wellness, defined as:

> . . . [a] balance among physical, emotional, spiritual intellectual and social health. Physical health may be thought of in terms of fitness, nutrition, control of substance abuse, medical self-help, and so on. Emotional health may refer to such areas as stress management and care for emotional crises. Examples of spiritual health are those themes dealing with love, charity, purpose and meditation. Intellec-tual health encompasses topics in the realms of education, achieve-

ment, career development, and others, while subjects concerned with social health may include relationships among friends, families and communities. (Alberta Centre for Well-Being, 1989)

Scientific evidence increasingly supports each of the following interconnections (see, for example, Sobel and Ornstein, 1987; Csikszentmihalyi, 1991; Godbey, 1993b):

- People who have things they love to do are healthier than people who don't.
- People who live with nature are healthier than people who do not.
- People who are optimists are healthier than people who are pessimists.
- People who laugh or sing are healthier than people who don't.
- People who serve as volunteers are healthier than people who don't.
- People who act rather than living lives of vicarious reaction are healthier.
- People who watch small amounts of television are healthier than those who watch constantly.

Many of the satisfying uses of leisure, research increasingly indicates, are those in which an individual develops increasing levels of skill to accept increasingly larger challenges. While such activity may be as diverse as rock climbing, playing chess, or writing music, it all involves learning, acting in ways that produce "effects," and a continuum of involvement. It also involves finding something one loves to do. Addiction researchers frequently find that teenagers who are prone to addiction have in common the belief that they do not have any satisfying way to use their time (Peele, 1989).

Society needs to be prepared and educated for leisure. One goal would be to make people more aware of the vicarious forms of leisure that harm society. The notion of dieting might be applied to television, escapist movies, and other forms of vicarious leisure. The commercialization of leisure can be critiqued and questioned. Alternative tourism concepts such as "green tourism" and "eco-tourism" could be put into practice. Education for leisure should continue throughout the life cycle and involve public support for adult education in subjects not related to work.

## Increasing Appreciation

Perhaps the most critical variable in how satisfying future time use will be revolves not so much around technology, efficiency, or the reorganization of society, but around people's ability to appreciate. We need to reexamine our consciousness of everyday life—to become more aware of and thankful for the good things in life as they occur. Instead of time-saving skills, we need to cultivate *time-savoring* skills, in order to appreciate the simpler delights of life as they are occurring: the taste of good food, the presence of good company, and the delights of good fun and silliness.

To be happier and wiser, it is easier to increase appreciation levels more than efficiency levels. Only by appreciating *more* can we hope to have a sustainable society. While efficiency, at least as envisioned in American society, always starts with *wanting* more, appreciating may start both with *valuing* more what is already here and with wanting less.

We need to recall the extraordinary range of limitations of the past that have been overcome. Less than a century ago, the developmentally disabled were often cast aside or kept out of sight; boys as young as 6 years old were sent into coal mines to do dirty and dangerous work; most women simply did men's bidding; most African Americans lived lives of unbelievable hardship, with little chance to advance regardless of effort or talent; sanitation was so bad that it routinely shortened life by decades. The past was not "the Waltons," but rather a time of huge limitation, discomfort, and inhumanity. People often ignore or forget these conditions, as their soaring expectations cloud their understanding of their own history.

Are we allowing our lives simply to evaporate through time, as steam from a pipe? Has prosperity made us incapable of understanding our own insignificance or of marveling at the great floating cosmos? Without a sense of wonder—the all-important ability to appreciate what we do not understand—we risk being no more than strangers on an inexplicable planet.

More time may mean we have a larger container, but how we fill it is the crucial question. If our spiritual standard of living has eroded, we could use more of our free and nonfree time to reclaim it. While most of us lead lives of unbelievable privilege, we appear no happier than our predecessors. Maybe that is because we directly try to achieve pleasure and happiness, when they are as ultimately as elusive and uncatchable as a rainbow. Maybe it is tied to our trying to do everything for a purpose—walking for fitness, dining for contacts, or playing golf for contracts.

Many things are worth doing simply because they are worth doing. They are not done "in order to." We have forgotten about most of them. Dylan Thomas wrote that he had read about "a shepherd who, when asked why he made, from within fairy rings, ritual observances to the moon to protect his flocks, replied: 'I'd be a damn fool if I didn't.' " The worthwhile things in life are done for this reason—we'd be fools not to.

We agree with Schor's criticism that the "work and spend cycle" represents materialism carried to obscene heights. "Compared to forty years ago, Americans in every income class—rich, middle class, and poor—have about twice as much in the way of income and material goods" (Schor, 1991, p. 109). Where we disagree has to do with how long average Americans now work to support this increasingly materialistic style of life. They are less trapped in "capitalism's squirrel cage," as Schor suggests, than in the endless economic *and* experiential *expectations* created by the culture. They are not so much squirrels running in endless circles as small frogs attempting to swallow the moon.

## The Pace of Life as a Political Issue

Ancient Athenians believed that if leisure was not prepared for it would be misused. During the early twentieth century, several reform movements sought to reshape opportunities for children's play and for adult recreation. The simple assumption was that children needed to be exposed to positive models of play and to play leaders who served as positive role models. Reviving such movements could meet the needs of children in many large urban areas. Such play need not be reshaped into formal instruction or viewed as therapy, but simply guided more.

The privatization of public schools, local recreation and park departments, and other youth-serving agencies means that they respond more to the affluent while the needs of the underclass go unmet. Our recent studies show that use of local recreation and park services *increases* greatly with both income and education level—another example of "the more, the more" phenomenon. People exposed to education for leisure are taught not only skills but also exposure to diverse activities from which they may slowly begin to pick and choose. Through such a process they may finally arrive at and learn to appreciate their own uniqueness.

Part of this involves studying ways in which society can be slowed down and made more leisurely. The ways to slow things down are easy to identify but difficult to implement. For instance, if people really want to slow down they can simply decide to do less, own less, and say no more often.

While such advice seems impractical, this slowing down can be contributed to in a number of ways: We can tax consumption more. We can give tax incentives for durable products. We can reward workers for the excellence and importance of what they discover and accomplish, rather than counting their work hours. We can stop answering unimportant correspondence. We can unplug the telephone. We can sit in the backyard and let it get dark. We can roam around town with no agenda. We can think about justifying our lives less in terms of what other people want us to do and think and more in terms of what we want and need to do to justify our lives to ourselves.

We can, in many ways, simply let go. In the words of novelist Toni Morrison (1996):

> At some point in life the world's beauty becomes enough. You don't need to photograph, paint, or even remember it. It is enough. No record of it needs to be kept, and you don't need someone to share it with or tell it to. When that happens—that letting go—you let go because you can. (P. 93)

Rather than let go, too many of us are clinging tighter and running faster. In the process, we are rushing past life.

We can back up and see what we have missed, accepting the gift of time. There is time for life.

# 22

# A 1990s Update:
# Trends Since 1985

Paradise is exactly like where you are right
now, only much, much better.
—Laurie Anderson

It is in you, my mind, that I measure time.
. . . As things pass by, they leave an impression on you. . . . It is this impression
which I measure. Therefore this itself is
time or else I do not measure time at all.
—St. Augustine

Trends in the way Americans use their time were documented in the first
edition of *Time for Life* (1997), which was based on accounts of daily behavior through 1985, but since then many changes in society have taken place.
Perhaps the major change has been in the economy, particularly during the
late 1980s and early 1990s, when many companies and firms reportedly
"downsized" their operations in the face of competition from other countries
(particularly Japan) and in order to increase corporate profits through greater
efficiency. Hochschild (1997) further argued that workers were staying

longer at work, either as "face time" to impress their bosses or as a way to escape the demands and routines that awaited them at home.

The increased presence of home technologies in consumers' homes since the 1980s has also been a factor. Not only do more households contain dishwashers and microwave ovens, but these appliances now feature more options and conveniences. There has been a parallel growth in home entertainment systems: CD players, VCRs, larger-screen TVs and the like, and cellular phones now allow people to be "on call" and reachable any time, any place.

Perhaps the major change has been the increased diffusion and use of home computers, which were at first used to streamline household accounting and to play more sophisticated computer games, but more recently are allowing people to communicate inexpensively via e-mail and to surf the Internet. Indeed, Chapter 10 is devoted to investigating the time shifts that appear to be associated with the use of home computers, and those results have been replicated with a different and larger data set (see later in this chapter and in Robinson and Kestnbaum [1999]).

Although the analyses of computer users have shown little apparent time shift due to these technologies, it is clear that enough social and technological change has occurred over the last decade to raise serious questions about the current relevance of the original 1985 results. For that reason, it is fortunate that two new time-diary studies were conducted in the 1990s, with a combined sample size of more than 10,000 respondents of all ages—almost double that in 1985. Table 32, an updated version of Exhibit 1 (Chapter 4), contains methodological information about the 1990s studies alongside the methodological information for the earlier diary studies that took place in 1965, 1975, and 1985.

## Methodology

Both of the 1990s time-diary studies were conducted by the University of Maryland's Survey Research Center by national random digit dial (RDD) telephone procedures between September 1992 and December 1995, using the University of California for Computer Assisted Telephone Interviewing (CATI) software. The combined study can be viewed as conducted in two phases: the first between 1992 and 1994, with 9,386 respondents of all ages; the second in 1995, with 1,200 respondents aged 18 and above. All interviews in both phases used the retrospective diary (or "yesterday") method,

**Table 32.** Methodological Features of the National Time-Diary Studies from the Americans' Use of Time Project, 1965–1995

|  | 1965 | 1975 | 1985 | 1992–94 | 1995 |
|---|---|---|---|---|---|
| Funder | NSF | NSF | NSF; ATT | EPA | EPRI |
| Data collector | University of Michigan | University of Michigan | University of Maryland | University of Maryland | University of Maryland |
| Sample size | 1,244 | 2,406 | 5,358 | 9,386 | 1,200 |
| Age range | 18–65 | 18+ | 12+ | 0+ | 12+ |
| Months | Oct.–Nov. | Oct.–Dec. | Jan.–Dec. | Oct.–Sept. | Jan.–Dec. |
| Model/response | Personal (72%) | Personal (72%) | Mail-back (3,340) (51%) Telephone (1,120) (67%) Personal (808) (60%) | Telephone (63%) | Telephone (65%) |
| Diary type | Tomorrow (1,244); Yesterday (130) | Yesterday (2,406) | Tomorrow (3,890); Yesterday (1,468) | Yesterday (9,374) | Yesterday (1,200) |

SOURCE: Americans' Use of Time Project.

NOTE: This table is an updated version of Exhibit 1 (page 72).

in which one respondent per household reported his or her activities for the previous day.

The first (1992–94) phase of the study was conducted for the Environmental Protection Agency (EPA) and included people of all ages, children under the age of 18 among them. (If the child was under the age of 6, the diary was completed by a knowledgeable adult in the household; if the child was between 6 and 9 years old, the diary was completed by the child and with the help of a knowledgeable adult.) The sample was designed as a series of eight independent quarterly surveys of a projected sample size of 1,250 respondents per quarter, to yield 10,000 diaries overall. Interviewers went through a lengthy general training session and a specific training session on the particular features of the diary questionnaire. Special CATI commands were developed to ensure proper reporting of all diary activities, all travel activity, unusually lengthy activities, and the exact location of activities within homes and other locations for EPA needs. Weekend days, especially Sundays, were oversampled relative to weekdays.

The second phase of the study was conducted for the Electric Power Research Institute (EPRI). It used virtually the same procedures as the first phase, except that it involved only 1,200 respondents aged 18 and older and was conducted between January 1995 and December 1995. Specific new diary features and interviewer training were implemented to produce more detailed and numerous activity accounts (also including fewer supplemental questions about the environment, to reduce survey length). This resulted in somewhat different diary estimates for a few activities (discussed below).

The overall response rate for the 1992–94 phase was 63 percent, with 20 percent refusal, 12 percent noncontact, and 5 percent other contact problems. That response rate reached 65 percent during the last seven quarters of the study. The response rate for the second phase of the study was 65 percent, with 18 percent refusal, 12 percent noncontact, and 5 percent other problems. All diaries were coded using the basic diary code described in Table 1 and in Szalai et al. (1972).

To simplify the reporting of results from these different 1992–95 surveys, they are referred to as the "1995" results in the analyses below. In order to streamline the reporting of results further, the hours of employed and nonemployed men and women are usually combined into two categories: all men aged 18–64 and all women aged 18–64. Data on the changing activity patterns of those aged 65 and older during the 1990s have been reported in Robinson, Werner, and Godbey (1997); 1990s data for those under the age of 18 are presented in Robinson and Bianchi (1997).

# Methodological Differences

In preparing data tables from these updates, it has become clear that some major methodological differences in these 1990s time-diary studies make it difficult to treat the data as part of a simple time series—that is, continuous readings that can be linked easily to the earlier studies. First, the focus of these studies, and their sponsors, was quite different, which meant that sociological and trend questions took a back seat to the objectives of these new studies. That focus was the environment, because the Environmental Protection Agency (EPA) sponsored the study and was interested in the extent to which the daily activity patterns of citizens might lead them to unhealthy contact with various pollutants in their daily environments. Thus, a major environmental concern was the extent to which people were exposed to environmental tobacco smoke (ETS) either as active smokers or in the vicinity of smokers—and that question was asked for each activity in the diary (Robinson, Ott, and Switzer, 1996). Respondents were also asked questions about their exposure to pesticides, detergents, and unsafe water, among many other potential pollutants. While care was taken to ensure that the basic diary format was unchanged, respondents who were asked several questions about their potential contact with pollutants in the environment may have had a different reporting frame for thinking about and reporting on their daily activities.

This environmental study emphasis meant that certain variables of primary social science interest were not included in these surveys, most prominent among them marital status and income. These questions were inadvertently excluded because of concern about more direct environmental issues. Further problems arose in the execution of the survey. In particular, as interviewers experienced difficulty in maintaining cooperation in what turned out to be a lengthy and complicated telephone questionnaire, respondents reported *fewer* diary activities. This is not to say that there was a notable decline in the quality of the diary data, or in response rates for the surveys, which were close to 65 percent across the two years of the survey. Several computerized innovations in the EPA study now made it possible to check on and improve that aspect of the diary electronically. Thus, if respondents described two separate and consecutive activities that occurred in different locations (such as "sleeping" followed by "shopping"), an automatic prompt that asked respondents to fill in the missing travel episodes that connected the two activities was activated. Similarly, if any activity (except sleep) lasted more than two hours, interviewers were automatically cued to ask respondents to report whether they had done anything else during that time period.

Despite these precautions, however, there was still no way to ensure that respondents would not try to shorten this long telephone interview by omitting reference to certain activities (perhaps especially short ones) or by combining activities to shorten the interview. For that and other reasons, the EPA diaries contained 15–20 percent fewer activities than the earlier University of Maryland and Michigan studies done by telephone.

Moreover, in examining time-diary results from both the 1990s and earlier studies, it became clear that there was a confounding connection between the number of diary activities reported and the types of activities reported. In less-detailed respondent diaries, more work, more sleep, and more television hours were reported—along with less family care, grooming, travel, and meals. While that could be a function of actual behavior—longer work days, or longer television-viewing episodes, do mean there is less time for family-care activities—less-detailed diaries still represent a confounding factor that limits what can be inferred from the diary data across different historical periods.

Multivariate analyses that attempt to control for this decline in reporting detail do indicate conclusions about the direction of many trends that are different from what might be concluded from the simple data reported below. These multivariate adjustments (using the MCA procedures described on page 78) usually produce results in the direction of reinforcing the earlier trend results, such as the declines in productive activities and the increases in free time, as noted below.

Another way to adjust for fewer activities reported in the EPA diaries was to use the data from the follow-up 1995 EPRI survey in which more-detailed diary reports were obtained. Thus, the tables and figures in the present chapter contain numbers that are the simple arithmetic average of the results from the EPA study and the EPRI study, even though the EPA study is much larger and might on that basis be given more weight. Nonetheless, it is felt that the greater diary detail in the EPRI study justifies its being given equal weight.

At the same time, as in earlier diary surveys using different modes of data collection (see Chapter 4), once again one is impressed by the large number of convergences in the EPA and EPRI data. They are usually within sampling error of each other. In other words, the data generally point in the same direction, usually along the lines suggested in the first edition of *Time for Life*. For that reason, these results are presented in the form of graphs in order to highlight the consistent and gradual nature of the shifts in time use that have characterized American life since 1965 and in the larger context of the quantitative structure of American daily life.

# Recent Changes in Activities

## Paid Work

Figure 16 shows the overall trends in *diary* work hours, for women and for men, between the 1960s and the 1990s as the bottom lines in the figure. These can easily be contrasted with the higher, more consistent, and virtually unchanged figures for *estimated* workweeks as the top lines in both figures. The latter unchanged pattern is found again in the massive estimated workweek data (from 50,000 + respondents per month over the last thirty to fifty years) collected by the Bureau of Labor Statistics (BLS)—as shown in the workweek estimate trend lines in Figure 6 (Chapter 5).

The main work-hours trend noted in the first edition of this book was the generally increased levels of the GAP (see Chapter 5) between estimated and diary work hours for the years 1965–85 for employed women and non-employed men. That value of GAP (between estimated and diary work time) had increased from less than one hour for men in 1965 to nearly 4 hours in 1985, and from less than 4 hours for women in 1965 to more than 7 hours by 1985.

The new 1995 (unadjusted) data now show values of GAP in the 1990s that are more similar—about 5 hours both for men and for women working more than 20 hours a week. This is because of the increase in diary work hours of employed women and not any notable declines in their *estimated* work hours. That these estimated work hours have been remarkably constant since 1965 suggests that respondents continue to be unable to give workweek estimates that match their diary (and presumably their actual) work hours. The paid work hours in women's diaries are now only 5 hours lower than those for employed men, compared with the nearly 10-hour differential found in 1965.

While this shift, found in *both* the EPA and the EPRI data, may signal an important shift away from gender-differentiated work hours in the 1990s (a shift that would be consistent with the "androgyny model" in Chapter 13), one must keep in mind the 1995 methodological problems with diary detail noted above. Indeed, when one adjusts the work-hour figures (by the MCA procedures described in Chapter 4) for number of activities, the 1995 ad-

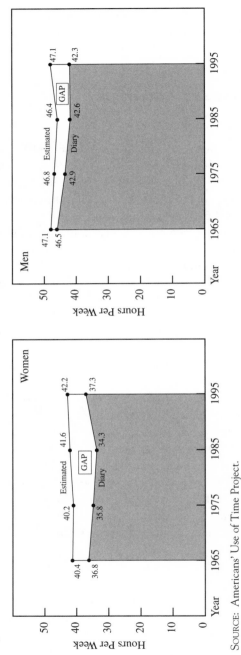

**Figure 16.** Trends in Paid Work Time. Estimated vs. Diaries, 1965–1995 (aged 18–64, employed only, hours per week)

SOURCE: Americans' Use of Time Project.

justed number of diary work hours for women is now *lower* for women than in 1985. Moreover, the diary work hours for employed men decline by about 2 hours a week.

In other words, the MCA-adjusted numbers for both men and women point to an increasing level of GAP since 1985 fueled mainly by a continuation of the 1965–85 slope in diary work hours. Thus, it is still the case that GAP (either adjusted or unadjusted) has become more prominent over time. The ability of workers to provide a consistent fit between their diary work hours and their estimated work hours is a phenomenon that seems not to have survived the 1960s. This conclusion is further confirmed by MCA analyses using GAP rather than diary work hours as the variable of interest. Workers in the 1990s continue to overestimate their diary work hours, particularly if they estimate workweeks of 50 hours or more, much as shown in Figure 7.

The gender gap in the diary work hours of men and women is still apparent in Figure 16, even if women's overall paid work hours have increased since 1985. Thus, it appears that women's gain on men in total work hours is due mainly to the *proportions* of American women working rather than to time actually spent on the job. That seems true for employed men as well. Thus, the adjusted diary work-hour figures for 1995 do not seem that different from the figures from the 1980s.

## Other Demographic Predictors of Work Hours

The pronounced difference in work hours by age (being lowest for those aged 18–24 and 55–64) noted at the end of Chapter 5 is still in place, with the effect most pronounced for employed men aged 55–64 and attributable more to men apparently taking early retirement than cutting back their work hours, if employed. It is well to remember that, in 1965, employed men aged 55–64 worked *longer* hours than men in younger age-groups, as opposed to their dramatically lower hours found in the 1980s and 1990s. More detailed analyses indicate that the decline is due mainly to work structure differences (such as early retirement or not working for other reasons) and not to reduced workweeks among those who are employed—because the work hours for those *employed* men (and women) aged 55–64 are now not that much lower than those for other age-groups.

As in earlier studies, more educated (and presumably more affluent) respondents reported longer diary work hours, but that seems to be mainly a function of their simply being employed in jobs with long work hours. Thus the longer hours of work reported by the more educated can be explained by their higher employment levels, and their employment in long-hour jobs, rather than by their reporting longer work hours in their diaries if they were employed. Also as in previous studies, differences between blacks and whites were minimal, although other minorities reported below-average work hours.

In summary, Figure 16 illustrates the two divergent trends in estimated work hours for employed men and employed women. In contrast to the virtually constant number of estimated work hours since 1965, there is a decline in diary work hours over that same period. The GAP between estimated and diary work hours in 1995 may be less than in 1985, but it is still far larger than in 1965; and the upward bump since 1985 (Figure 16) may simply be a function of less-detailed overall diary-reporting in the 1995 study and of an American economy that was in full bloom.

## Family Care

The bottom line for the women's graph of Figure 17 (left) shows the continued and predictable declines in housework by women across the decades since 1965. Alongside, in the men's graph of Figure 17 (right), one can see the countertrend of *increased* housework time for men. While women's housework hours declined from 27 hours in 1965 to less than 16 in 1995, men's hours have increased from about 5 hours a week to more than 9 hours. Because the decline of more than 10 hours of housework for women is more than double the roughly 4 + -hour increases for men, it is clear that less housework is being done in American homes than in the 1960s. Moreover, that gap does not seem to be made up for by paid help or children's help, since other survey data do not show either paid help or children's help to be more prevalent today.

To some extent, the declines in women's housework are due to the societal demographic shifts noted in Chapter 1. First, women in the 1990s are more likely to be employed, and women who are employed full time have consistently reported about a 40 percent decline in housework. (Gershuny [1992] has found that this "employment effect" can be demonstrated *causally*, using panel data from the United States and Great Britain.) Second, today's women are less likely to be married, and, third, they are less likely to have children in the household to care for. (The extent of lowered housework time associated with each of these three role factors is shown in Appendix I and is graphically illustrated in Figure 18 later in this chapter.)

Nonetheless, as in previous years, only about half the decline in house-

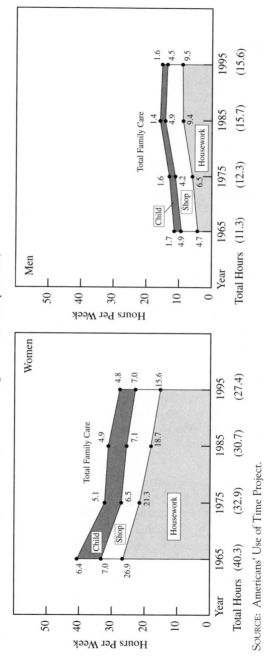

**Figure 17.** Trends in Family-Care Time, 1965–1995 (aged 18–64, hours per week)

SOURCE: Americans' Use of Time Project.

work is explained by these demographic shifts. The rest of the decline seems to be due simply to women reporting less housework in their diaries across time, not to technology for doing housework (see Chapter 18), or to having more outside help. The same is true for the increase for men. Moreover, the trends appear across different types of housework activity, from cooking to cleaning to household management. Two exceptions to that pattern appear in the increased overall time on pet and plant care since the 1960s, and in more time spent maintaining yards or gardens—perhaps reflecting the increased size of the grounds surrounding American homes.

As discussed in more detail in Bianchi et al. (1999), the decline in women's housework time cuts broadly across different categories of women—from the old to the young, from the married to the never married, from those with children to those without, from those with high school education to those with postgraduate education—and among both blacks and whites. The decline is also found among *both* employed women and full-time housewives, although it is not as sharp among employed women as among housewives. (That suggests a further gap between employed and nonemployed women in terms of all productive activity; see Table 33 below.)

The overall trend toward less housework goes counter to certain factors that might have been thought to lead to increased housework now and in the future. First, American homes are getting larger (now averaging more than 700 square feet per person), which means more interior area to keep clean. Second, with the aging of the population and the tendency for older people to do more housework (even as their children leave home), more housework time can be predicted from this demographic change as well. Nevertheless, even in the face of these trends, time spent doing housework continues to decline.

## Other Family-Care Activities

Counter to the declines in housework for women and the increases in housework for men since 1965, few changes are generally in evidence in Figure 17 for the other two categories of family care: shopping and child care. Therefore, the declines in overall family care (housework + shopping + child care) for women are accounted for almost exclusively by the declines in core housework just described. In other words, the hours women spend on child care and shopping over the years have hardly changed: 7 hours for shopping and 5–6 hours for primary-activity child care.

While the 1995 child-care figure for women is more than one hour lower than in 1965, that is explained entirely by the decrease in the number of households with children in the 1990s. The hours for respondents who are mothers with children in the household are virtually unchanged—and, when the greater proportions of working mothers (whose employment seems to reduce child care as well as housework time) are taken into account, as well as the decrease in the number of children in households, those hours have actually *increased* (see Robinson, 1989a). In the case of men, hours spent in child care and shopping are also almost identical to those for 1965, despite the smaller numbers of children. But it is still the case that fathers who have children in the household report spending only one-third of the time on child care that mothers report, in terms of primary activity. As in previous years, most of the fathers' primary-activity child-care time is in the form of interactional time (playing, reading) with children and not the "custodial" time that mothers mainly put in (feeding, dressing) (Robinson, 1989a). In terms of total hours of *contact* with children, moreover, unreplicated 1965 and 1975 data showed fathers spending closer to 25 hours a week with their children, and mothers spending 35 hours.

The converging trends in *total family-care time* for both men and women, then, simply and almost entirely reflect the declines in the housework component of family care. Only housework time has changed much over the years. Ironically, thirty years ago it looked as if nothing would reduce housework time (Robinson and Converse, 1972; Vanek, 1974). The first national time-diary studies found that 1960s women were doing no less housework than more-limited community time-use studies done in the 1920s and 1930s had shown. When compared with women in less-technologically advanced countries, American women in the 1960s were doing only a little less— despite the far greater supply of home appliances available to them. These findings suggested another kind of "invisible hand" that kept women doing the same amount of housework no matter how much modern technology was available in the form of home appliances.

Since the 1960s, however, the grip of this hand has loosened considerably, perhaps as housework cleanliness and production standards have relaxed. Women continue to report doing less and less housework, and that trend has carried over into the 1990s. Since 1985, women are doing 2–3 fewer hours of housework a week, which follows on a 5-hour drop in the 1970s and a 2–3-hour drop in the 1980s. The overall decline comes mainly from women spending less time on traditional "female" chores like laundry and meal cleanup (perhaps attributable to more eating out, pizza deliveries, and disposable dishware) and laundry, rather than on "nonfemale" chores like yardwork and pet/plant care—which have actually increased for women since the 1960s. Core housecleaning itself appears to be affected least, declining only by about 20 percent compared with a nearly 40 percent decline for the other aspects of housework.

Men may not have increased their housework in the last decade, but the hours they spend on housework is still about double the hours men spent in 1965. In contrast to women, the time men spend on both "female" and male tasks has nearly doubled, particularly in terms of basic housecleaning, which for men has increased threefold. The result is that men are doing slightly more of the housework in the 1990s (38 percent) than in the 1980s (34 percent), but still far more than their 15 percent share in the 1960s.

## Predicting Housework Time from Demographics

Figure 18 shows how the three main predictors of housework time— employment, marriage, and parenthood—work together to produce more or less time spent separately for men and women. It shows time spent on house- work in the order in which these predictors usually occur in adult life—from first taking on a paid job, to getting married, and then having children. Each factor plays a different part, depending on the other factors. To increase sample sizes for these analyses (particularly because marital status was not ascertained in the EPA study), the data for the 1980s and for 1995 have been combined.

The center of Figure 18 shows the *overall* difference between the time women and men spend doing housework: 15.6 hours of housework by women, versus 9.5 hours spent by men. Figure 18 first shows that when women become employed they do almost 7 hours less housework, while em- ployed men do only about 4 hours less housework than nonemployed men (although the percentage drop is about the same as for women).

At the next stage—getting married—employed women increase their housework by about 5 hours a week, while housewives show approximately a 12-hour increase over nonemployed women who are not married. That aver- ages nearly 7 hours a week, the same difference as for becoming employed. In contrast, married employed men show only a one-hour increase over un- married men—although nonemployed men (a small minority) show a 9-hour increase. This amounts to an overall increase of a little more than 2 hours a week difference for married men versus nonmarried men. In sum, when women get married their housework increase is more than three times that of men who get married.

**Figure 18.** Segmented Housework Time, 1985–1995 (aged 18–64, hours per week, by gender and parental, marital, and employment status)

Children  Married  Employed          Employed  Married  Children

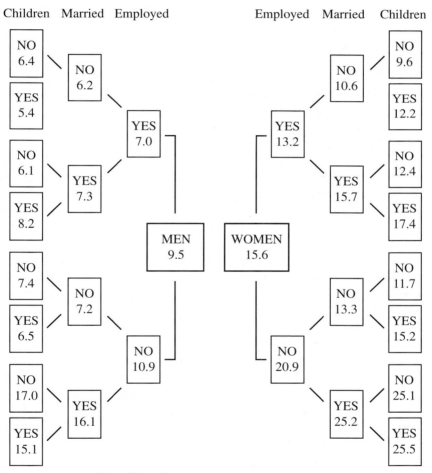

SOURCE: Americans' Use of Time Project.

When there are children in the family, it is again the mothers whose schedules change the most. Under these circumstances, women average about 3 hours more housework than when there are no children. Fathers, on the other hand, show almost no difference from nonfathers; indeed, some groups of men report less housework when there are children in the household than when there are no children. Only nonemployed married men put in more than 10 hours a week of housework—and they are the only group of males for whom there is less than a 2-to-1 ratio of female-to-male housework time.

In other words, the amount of housework time for women rises rather predictably as more role responsibilities are added to their lives. For men, however, only marriage and lack of a job consistently increase their time on housework. These different patterns for men and women underscore the subtle and perplexing nature of the "invisible hand" metaphor we use below to describe what keeps the productive time and free time of men and women in near parity. These patterns do not result merely from simple trade-offs, such as husbands filling in when their wives go to work or have children. For reasons that remain multidetermined and somewhat mysterious, changes in the productive hours of men and women stay in close proximity.

In summary, women continue to do more than 60 percent of the family care in America, but that is well below the 85 percent figure for 1965, and men have made small gains in their relative contribution since 1985. Here, however, the gains come from the reduced time women spend rather than from increased housework time spent by men. Nor have men reported any increase in child care or shopping since 1965, despite the recent reports that men are finding less strenuous jobs or reducing workloads "to spend more time with the kids," or that men are spending more time shopping for cars and high-tech equipment. Figure 17 reflects the nature and consistency of these trends in the various components of family care quite directly.

Multivariate MCA analyses indicate that the trends shown in Figure 17 may be affected by the same diary-reporting factors as for paid work. Here, however, the effect is in the opposite direction from paid work: the fewer the activities, the less the reported time spent in total family care and in each of its components. When this confounding factor is taken into account, it results in men increasing their housework time by one hour a week in 1995 over 1985, while women decrease their time from 3 hours a week to 2 hours over the same period. The trends found in the latest comparisons of 1995 with 1985, then, are consistent with the trends found in comparisons for the years in 1965–85 (see Chapter 6). The hours women spend doing housework are decreasing faster than men's housework hours are increasing.

## Total Productive Activity

As in Table 4 (Chapter 6), we can use the Figure 16 and Figure 17 total calculations (along with the work commute) to derive the estimate of "total productive activity" shown in Table 33. When that is done, the figures of 62.9 hours for employed women in 1995 is 3 hours greater than the 59.8-hour figure for 1985, although it remains 3–4 hours *below* the 66.6-hour figure for 1965.

By contrast, we find a continued decline in productive activities for full-time housewives: almost 12 hours a week fewer than in 1965. Put another way, in their 1965 time diaries employed women reported 13 hours more productive activity time than housewives, but by 1995 that gap had grown to 21 hours a week. In percentage terms, housewives in 1965 did 80 percent of the productive activity of employed women, but the figure was only 67 percent in 1995; part of this might be attributed to a reduction in the average number of residents per household, which has shrunk to 2.6 today.

Compared with employed men, however, the long-term 1965–95 decline of 3.7 hours a week in productive activities for employed women (from about 67 to 63 hours) is still larger than the 1.6-hour decrease (from 62.5 to 61 hours) that employed men experienced. Unlike nonemployed women, however, nonemployed men spent slightly *more* time in total productive activity than nonemployed men in 1965 did. Nonetheless, nonemployed men in

**Table 33.** Trends in Total Productive Activity (in hours per week), 1965–1995 (Paid Work + Work Commute + Family Care)

|  | 1965 | 1975 | 1985 | 1995 | 1995–65 Difference |
|---|---|---|---|---|---|
| Women |  |  |  |  |  |
| Employed | 66.6 | 62.1 | 59.8 | 62.9 | − 3.7 hrs/wk |
| Nonemployed | 53.6 | 44.2 | 43.2 | 42.0 | − 11.6 hrs/wk |
| Total women | 59.4 | 52.3 | 53.2 | 55.7 | − 3.7 hrs/wk |
| Men |  |  |  |  |  |
| Employed | 62.5 | 58.6 | 58.7 | 60.9 | − 1.6 hrs/wk |
| Nonemployed | 26.8 | 25.9 | 32.1 | 28.1 | + 1.3 hrs/wk |
| Total men | 59.1 | 53.7 | 53.1 | 54.2 | − 4.9 hrs/wk |

SOURCE: Americans' Use of Time Project.

1995 still spent almost 14 fewer hours in such activity (28 hours) than non-employed women (42 hours).

For 1995 this amounts to an overall reported 55.7 hours of productive activity for women aged 18–64, compared with 54.2 hours for men. The "invisible hand" that keeps the male-female work time equivalent, noted at several points in Chapters 1–14, appears to be at work again in the 1990s data, despite the complex pattern of gender determinants of housework time shown in Figure 18.

## Personal Care and Travel Time

In Chapter 7, personal care was characterized as the least interesting as well as the most consistent set of time-diary activities across time. That characterization now needs to be changed. Changes in personal-care activities over the last decade now appear to be the least expected and most dramatic of recent changes that have taken place.

Figure 19 shows that this is *least* true for personal activity that takes up the most time—sleep—which from 1965 to 1995 has shown only a one-hour increase *overall* from 1965 to 1995 (mainly among women). For the last decade, then, women report almost a 3-hour-a-week edge in sleep time over men, instead of the roughly one-hour edge in previous studies.

In contrast to the increase in sleep, hours spent eating showed more *decline* than increase, and that roughly one-hour decrease since 1985 was evident among both men and women. Whether people were eating faster or eating less food (or snacking in periods that were too short to report), the diary meal-time figures showed the first decline for women since 1965, with an even larger decrease shown among men. The decline was found for both eating at home and eating out, and as well among both the employed and the nonemployed and among men and women. Overall, then, the decrease in eating time can be seen as more or less canceling out the small increase in sleep.

The third personal-care category—grooming—showed the greatest overall change since 1985: almost a 2-hour decrease over the last decade. That finding is consistent with the trend toward "dressing down" and more casual attire that has been reported in the media. Whether it reflects less-frequent bathing or hygiene, or less time getting dressed up, the nearly 20 percent decline in diary grooming time was found both among men and women and among the employed and the nonemployed.

This decline was surprising too because previous surveys had shown steady

**Figure 19.** Trends in Personal-Care Time, 1965–1995 (aged 18–64, hours per week)

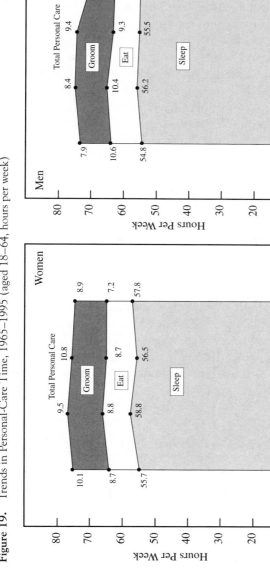

SOURCE: Americans' Use of Time Project.

*increases* in grooming time, from about 9 hours overall in 1965 to 9.5 hours in 1975 to more than 10 hours in 1985. The drop back to 8 hours a week overall thus represents a notable turnaround in grooming time from previous surveys. Women, however, continue to spend almost 2 hours more a week grooming than men, even if grooming time has declined.

The net decline in total personal care (or grooming) is important because it represents the first notable change in activities other than work, housework, and free time. Until 1995, it appeared that Americans were simply trading reduced work and family care for more free time (or, alternatively, were finding free-time activities that were more attractive than productive activities). Now it appears that Americans are trading time spent on personal care activities like eating and grooming in order to find time either for more paid work or for more enjoyable activities in their free time.

While the decline in eating/mealtime hours could indicate busier lifestyles, it is more difficult to argue that Americans are cutting back on grooming as a way to reduce stress. Again, the value of the zero-sum diary approach noted in Chapter 1 is that it can accommodate such new and more complex interchanges across the four types of time. Time use in American life has become more than a simple tug-of-war between work and leisure.

*Travel.* Time spent traveling in 1995 was generally unchanged from 1985 for both men and women. The 10-to-11-hour-a-week total travel time was about the same reported by men in 1965, but it is 2 hours higher than the travel time reported by women in 1965. As noted in Chapter 7, then, women have shown gains in their travel time (mainly due to employment) while men stayed the same. What is different in the 1990s is that nonemployed women are joining employed women in going out of the home, having registered the greatest gains since 1985. Whatever the dynamics, travel represents another activity in which women have continued to close the time gap with men.

## Free Time

The decreases in family care and personal/grooming times noted in Figure 17 and Figure 19, respectively, are generally larger than the increases in work time in Figure 16. Given the zero-sum nature of time and diary time, that means there must have been some increase in diary-reported free time over the last decade. The extent of that increase in free time, and how it gets divided up among our four gender-employment categories, is shown in Table 34.

Since 1985, men have shown more of a gain in free time than women. Employed men reported a 3-hour increase in free time, which is consistent with earlier trends toward more free time. The gain by nonemployed men, on the other hand, represents a recouping of about one hour of free time a day in 1985, which is 2 hours more than in the 1960s.

For 1995, nonemployed women also reported an increase in free time of 3 hours over 1985, from about 46 to 49 hours (which is still more than 13 hours less than men who are not in the paid labor force). By contrast, employed women showed a one-hour decrease in their free time (probably reflecting their increased work hours).

Taking in the longer picture, nonemployed women since 1965 have picked up more than 10 hours of free time, compared with 5-to-6-hour increases for employed women and employed men. In percentage terms, employed women have increased their free time by 20 percent, compared with 26 percent for nonemployed women. But while employed women may have gained less free time than the rest of the population since 1985, today's employed woman still enjoys significantly more free time than her 1960s counterpart.

Moreover, the free-time situation of women is slightly enhanced when the methodological factor of number of activities is taken into account for the 1995 data. The MCA-adjusted figure for the free time of employed women goes *up* an additional hour—as it does for employed men as well. For housewives, there is a *decline* of about one hour from the 1995 figure after MCA adjustment. Overall, then, while the figures for total free time (Table 34) are not as affected by the methodological fact that fewer diary activities were

**Table 34.** Trends in Free Time (in hours per week, for those aged 18–64)

|  | 1965 | 1975 | 1985 | 1995 | 1995 minus 1965 |
|---|---|---|---|---|---|
| Women |  |  |  |  |  |
| Employed | 27.2 | 30.0 | 34.0 | 32.8 | +5.6 |
| Nonemployed | 39.2 | 45.4 | 46.4 | 49.5 | +10.3 |
| Total women | 34.0 | 38.4 | 38.9 | 38.5 | +4.5 |
| Men |  |  |  |  |  |
| Employed | 33.0 | 35.3 | 36.3 | 38.9 | +5.9 |
| Nonemployed | 61.1 | 61.6 | 55.6 | 63.0 | +1.9 |
| Total men | 35.7 | 39.2 | 40.4 | 43.6 | +7.9 |
| Total sample | 34.8 | 38.7 | 39.6 | 41.0 | +6.2 |

SOURCE: Americans' Use of Time Project.

reported in the 1995 diaries, they do indicate 1985–95 increases in free time that are slightly larger than those shown in Table 34.

It is important to note that the recent increase in free time is not solely an American phenomenon. In Chapter 20 (Figure 14) we show the movements toward increased free time in European countries in the 1980s as documented by Ausubel and Grubler (1994). In a more recent publication, Bittman (1999) found 1990s increases in Australia across two decades similar to those in Table 34. Bittman also calculated the changes in MCA-adjusted free-time averages across nineteen countries (mainly European, and not including the 1990s U.S. data) since the 1960s (see Table 35) and found a pattern that is remarkably consistent with the pattern in Table 34, including, as in the United States, that the largest shifts occurred between the 1960s and 1970s. Thus, the U.S. free-time increases in Figure 20 noted here do seem to reflect what is happening in other Western countries as well.

**Table 35.**   Changes in Free Time Across Nineteen Countries, 1960–Present (MCA-adjusted averages)

|         | 1960–1970 | 1971–1977 | 1978–1982 | 1983–1991 | 1992 onward | 1990s–1960s |
|---------|-----------|-----------|-----------|-----------|-------------|-------------|
| Men     | 30.0      | 34.0      | 36.4      | 35.0      | 37.1        | + 7.1 hrs   |
| Women   | 28.3      | 31.2      | 33.1      | 32.6      | 33.9        | + 5.6 hrs   |

SOURCE:   Adapted by the authors from Bittman, 1999.

## Television and Other Media

Following the pattern described in Chapter 9, we would expect that television-viewing would increase as free time increased. In the 1990s, however, the gained free time is not entirely given over to the television set. In contrast to the 2-to-3-hour gains in free time, television-viewing increased only about an hour and a half a week between 1985 and 1995 (Figure 20). Parallel gains were found for men and women, but the gain for nonemployed men and women was higher than for employed men and women, whose television-viewing increased less than one hour a week (Figure 20). Among employed men, then, free-time gains were for the first time mainly devoted to nonmedia activities (fitness activities, computer time, etc.), as described below.

Nonetheless, Figure 20 makes it clear that when viewed from the perspective of the last third of the twentieth century the gains in free time have

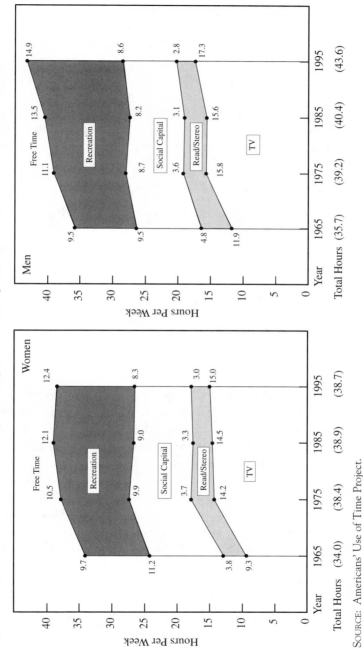

**Figure 20.** Trends in Free Time and Its Components (aged 18–64, hours per week)

SOURCE: Americans' Use of Time Project.

been largely turned over to gains in television-viewing—for both men and women. Figure 20 also shows the small declines in reading over the years, and the small declines in radio/recording use as well (although, as noted in Chapter 9, radio time as a secondary activity has recently risen to more than 10 hours a week). At the same time, Figure 20 illustrates how television continues to play an increasingly central role in the use of free time, in relation to reading, to other media use, and to other free-time activities. When combined with television-viewing as a secondary activity, more than half of Americans' free time is now spent in the company of television.

## The Home Computer

The rapid spread and increased use of home computers have been viewed as main factors influencing changes in daily life in the 1990s. However, there is not much evidence of that in time-diaries, as of 1995, because the primary activity time reported in those diaries as computer use is only about one hour a week. That is not large enough to indicate much of an effect on other activities, although there is reason to believe that the real increase in computer/Internet use has occurred after the time of the 1995 survey. Future studies that examine more intensive and longer-range computer use time will be needed to see which activities will be most affected.

Chapter 10 contains results from a 1995 *nondiary* survey of computer and Internet usage that examined the use of such technologies in far more detail. That analysis revealed that, rather than displacing "functionally equivalent" information media, computer and Internet users generally reported *higher* daily use of both print and broadcast media than nonusers. There was somewhat lower usage of television for entertainment, but it was not significant and could be explained largely by the lower educational level of nonusers.

Another large survey has recently investigated computer use in the context of a wide variety of other free-time behaviors: the 1997 update of the Survey of Public Participation in the Arts (SPPA) described in Chapter 11. SPPA97 interviewed a national telephone sample of more than 6,000 adults aged 18 and older about their computer and Internet use. Again, after MCA adjustments, the more-more pattern noted in Chapter 10 was repeated—not just for reading and media activity, but also for exercise, outdoor activities, volunteer work, and attending sports events (Robinson and Kestnbaum, 1999). It was also positively related to increased attendance at arts events, such as concerts and plays, as well as to personal participation in arts activities, such as painting or writing.

Computer and Internet use, then, can be added to the list of activities that largely follow the more-more pattern of participation. It is not possible, however, for this to extend to all activity, because time's zero-sum property means that if time on computer activity goes up, time on some other activity must go down. Future diary studies will be needed to clarify exactly which trade-offs in activities will be involved.

## Social Capital and Recreation Time

For the first time in this diary data series, then, the gains in free-time activities other than television almost kept pace with those for television-viewing time. Table 36 shows that there has been a gain of 2 hours a week since 1965 and that the 1995 gain came from free-time activities, especially recreation.

These nonmedia activities continue to consume more than 20 hours a week of Americans' free time since 1965 (Table 36). The recent gains have come from fitness activities, which have tripled over the last thirty years, from 1 to 3 diary hours a week. This seems to be mainly a result of the media/ health professional push for healthier lifestyles and of an economy in which most jobs are now in the service sector (rather than manufacturing), thereby providing inadequate physical activity. Communication in the family and by telephone has declined some, while attending college and taking other adult education courses have gained about half an hour a week. No gain was found

**Table 36.** Trends in Recreation and Social Capital Activities, 1965–1995 (in hours per week, for those aged 18–64)

|  | 1965 | 1975 | 1985 | 1995 | 1995 minus 1965 |
|---|---|---|---|---|---|
| Recreation |  |  |  |  |  |
| Communication | 3.6 | 3.4 | 4.4 | 3.7 | +0.1 |
| Sports/exercise | 1.0 | 1.6 | 2.2 | 3.0 | +2.0 |
| Hobbies | 2.2 | 2.8 | 2.8 | 2.6 | +0.4 |
| Sports/cultural events | 1.2 | 0.6 | 0.9 | 1.3 | +0.1 |
| Adult education | 1.8 | 2.3 | 2.2 | 2.7 | +0.9 |
| Social capital |  |  |  |  |  |
| Socializing | 8.2 | 7.1 | 6.7 | 7.3 | −0.9 |
| Religion | 0.9 | 0.9 | 0.9 | 0.9 | 0.0 |
| Other organizations | 1.3 | 1.5 | 1.2 | 0.9 | −0.4 |
| Total | 20.2 | 20.2 | 21.3 | 22.4 | +2.2 |

SOURCE: Americans' Use of Time Project.

for hobbies, which now mainly take the form of computer use instead of needlework activities; the latter are done more by women, while the former are popular among men.

The second set of nonmedia free-time activities in Table 36 includes the three "social capital" activities, to which Putnam's (1995a, 1995b) research has drawn considerable attention. And, as Putnam has argued, we do find an overall decline in these activities since 1965. The largest decline, of about one hour a week, is in the time spent for socializing, which would be expected from the Table 8 finding of activities initially affected by television. With the 1995 gain, however, *social and visiting time* is still at about the same level as in 1975. In other words, social life may be making a comeback from the impact television apparently made on it—even as e-mail and the cellular telephone might have been thought to render person-to-person interaction more obsolete.

The decline of *organizational and formal volunteer time* in 1995 (to less than one hour a week), on the other hand, is the first clear indication of decreased social capital in this form of behavior. The finding that less than one hour a week is spent on these organizational activities (and little of that on actual "volunteering") contrasts sharply with the recent poll estimate data in which Americans estimate spending an average of 4 to 5 hours a week on volunteer activities (Gerson, 1997, p. 27).

Time spent on the third indicator of social capital—*religious practice*—has remained remarkably stable across time, at just under one hour a week: about the same amount of time as for other organizational activity. But here the data on hours of time involved hide an important countertrend. As Presser and Stinson (1996) have shown from the same diary data, the *proportion* of Americans attending weekly religious services has significantly declined in recent years—again counter to what respondents in other national surveys report in response to estimate questions. What our constant figures in religious observance convey, then, is that for those who do attend services, *time per attender* has increased across time. In this case, then, the greater attendance times per attender provide another example of our Newtonian model, in that it is the religiously rich who are getting richer, or becoming more dedicated, in their beliefs.

Adding the hours of all three of these social capital activities together totals just over 9 hours a week of social capital, compared with about 10.4 hours in the 1960s. That represents a decline of almost 15 percent in such activities. While that might not be as dramatic a decline as sometimes reported, it stands in marked contrast to the free-time increases in television, exercise, home communication, and adult education. In that way, then, *any* decline in social capital takes on added importance, as well as irony, given that these are among the most enjoyable of the activities people report doing (see Chapter 17).

## Trend Summary

The 1995 data continue to tell much the same story as the 1965–85 data. Diary hours of paid work in 1995 are notably lower than in 1965, while women are doing less housework and men more. This situation has provided the American public with increased free time, as has the increased free time made possible by decreased marital and parental responsibilities (but separate from them as well). A new wrinkle to the added free time of Americans in the 1990s comes from the time freed because of reduced time for personal care in the form of meals, dressing, and personal hygiene.

Unlike earlier gains in free time, the most recent gains are not completely dominated by television. Indeed, the increased times Americans now report spending in fitness, education, and outside event activities are healthy signs in that Americans are not only now more active but also engaging in activities that they themselves report as more enjoyable than television-viewing. At the same time, we cannot overlook the finding that television hours continue to go up (despite recent short-term trends) and that television remains the focus of up to 50 percent of free-time activity. The decline in social capital activities is another trend that is of concern.

Table 37 simplifies and recapitulates the complicated nature of the above major trends and patterns between the 1965 and 1995 data. The 5–8 hours a week of increased free time for women and men was arrived at by different routes. The increase for men has come mainly from about 10 hours a week less paid work, while the increase for women has come mainly from about 13 hours less unpaid work.

In the case of men, decreased paid work time comes from two sources: more earlier retirements (particularly of those aged 55–64) and almost 4 hours less weekly work for those who remain in the labor force. Together these total nearly 10 hours less paid work for all men aged 18–64, from roughly 45 to 35 hours for all men aged 18–64, about 10 percent of whom were not working in 1965 and closer to 20 percent of whom are not working in the 1990s. Men have also reduced their eating and grooming time by almost 3 hours since 1965. On the other hand, they have taken on almost 5 more hours of housework during that time, leading to a net gain of about 8 hours (that is, from 10 hours less paid work, plus 3 hours less grooming, minus their 5 hours of increased housework).

**Table 37.**    Summary of Trends, 1965–1995

|  | 1965–85 | 1985–95 | 1965–95 |
|---|---|---|---|
| **WOMEN** | | | |
| Work time (employed only) | Down 3.0 hrs | Up 3.0 hrs | Same |
| Work time (all women) | Up 3.0 hrs | Up 5.0 hrs | Up 8.0 hrs |
| Housework | Down 8.0 hrs | Down 3.0 hrs | Down 11.0 hrs |
| Child care | Down 2.0 hrs | Same | Down 2.0 hrs |
| Shopping | Same | Same | Same |
| *Total family care* | Down 10.0 hrs | Down 3.0 hrs | Down 13.0 hrs |
| Sleep | Up 1.0 hr | Up 1.0 hr | Up 2.0 hrs |
| Eat | Same | Down 1.0 hr | Down 1.0 hr |
| Groom | Up 1.0 hr | Down 2.0 hrs | Down 1.0 hr |
| *Total personal care* | Up 2.0 hrs | Down 2.0 hrs | Same |
| Television | Up 5.0 hrs | Up 1.0 hr | Up 6.0 hrs |
| Read/listen | Down 1.0 hr | Same | Down 1.0 hr |
| Social capital | Down 2.0 hrs | Down 1.0 hr | Down 3.0 hrs |
| Recreation | Up 3.0 hrs | Same | Up 3.0 hrs |
| *Total free time* | Up 5.0 hrs | Same | Up 5.0 hrs |
|  | **1965–85** | **1985–95** | **1965–95** |
| **MEN** | | | |
| Work time (employed only) | Down 4.0 hrs | Same | Down 4.0 hrs |
| Work time (all men) | Down 10.0 hrs | Same | Down 10.0 hrs |
| Housework | Up 5.0 hrs | Same | Up 5.0 hrs |
| Child care | Same | Same | Same |
| Shopping | Same | Same | Same |
| *Total family care* | Up 5.0 hrs | Same | Up 5.0 hrs |
| Sleep | Up 1.0 hr | Down 1.0 hr | Same |
| Eat | Down 1.0 hr | Down 2.0 hrs | Down 3.0 hrs |
| Groom | Up 2.0 hrs | Down 2.0 hrs | Same |
| *Total personal care* | Up 2.0 hrs | Down 5.0 hrs | Down 3.0 hrs |
| Television | Up 4.0 hrs | Up 2.0 hrs | Up 6.0 hrs |
| Read/listen | Down 2.0 hrs | Same | Down 2.0 hrs |
| Social capital | Down 1.0 hr | Same | Down 1.0 hr |
| Recreation | Up 4.0 hrs | Up 1.0 hr | Up 5.0 hrs |
| *Total free time* | Up 5.0 hrs | Up 3.0 hrs | Up 8.0 hrs |

SOURCE: Americans' Use of Time Project.

Employed women, on the other hand, have not decreased their work hours since 1965 and have closed the GAP noted in Figure 7 since 1985. Since a higher percentage of women are now working than in 1965, women's overall paid work hours have increased 8 hours because of their increased participation in the labor force (from about 40 percent of women aged 18–64 in 1965 to more than 60 percent in 1995). Their sleep times have also gone up 2 hours a week, but that has been offset by decreased meal and grooming time. It is women's 11 hours of decreased housework, then, that has mainly allowed them to see an increase of almost 5 hours of free time a week—that is, 13 hours less family care plus one hour less personal care to offset the 8-hour increase in paid work.

When it comes to free time and what happens in that free time, the patterns and trends are much the same for both men and women. The largest increase in their 5–8 hours of greater free time has been television: 6 hours a week more television-viewing since 1965. There have been gains in more active recreational pursuits, particularly fitness activities, which have increased from 1 to 3 hours a week. Offsetting these increases are declines in two types of free-time activities: other media (particularly reading newspapers) and social capital (especially visiting and socializing, although these showed some resurgence in the 1990s).

While men now have 5 hours more free time than women (Table 34), women register 4–5 hours more weekly hours than men in grooming and sleeping. Whether this reflects a need for rest and preparation due to more complex and tiring role demands for women in the 1990s, or women's preference for sleep and appearance over free time, is an issue to attend to more closely as the new century begins.

Figures 16–20 show the consistencies and continuities in these trends and largely in proportion to the amounts of time in question. Our revised and updated version of Figure 21 tells a more sobering story—that despite all the events, technologies, and turmoil over the last thirty years, the broad outlines of American daily life are not that different from what the 1965 study found. It takes a long time for daily life to change.

## Demographic Differences

With few exceptions, the patterns of demographic correlates of activities shown in Table 17 are found again in the 1995 data, so attention is concentrated on changes in two of the main background variables of interest: age and gender.

**Figure 21.** Trends in Different Types of Time for Women and Men, 1965–1995

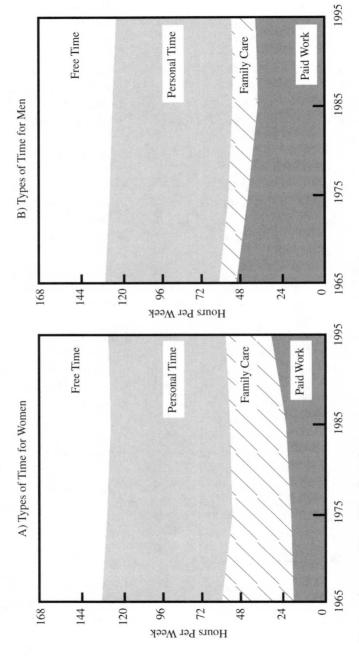

A) Types of Time for Women

B) Types of Time for Men

SOURCE: Americans' Use of Time Project.

The changes in *age* patterns are relatively minor, but it is important to note how age differences have become more pronounced over time as more workers opt for early retirement or shorter workweeks. As they work fewer hours, older people put in more time doing housework and sleeping. They also have more free time and use more of that free time for television, reading, and other media. But it is encouraging to see that, like the younger preretirement aged Americans in Table 36, senior citizens are also involved in more active, nonmedia activities like fitness and socializing (Robinson, Werner, and Godbey, 1997).

In the case of *gender*, we have seen some significant changes over the last decade. Women's diary work hours are now closer to men's, and closer to the work hours those women estimate they put in. (However, while the GAP for women is now smaller than that for men in the 50–65-hour workweek range, it continues higher for 70+ estimated workweeks.) Women have also continued their trend of reduced time spent doing housework, and 1990s men show less evidence of continuing to pick up the resulting slack.

When all the trends are added together in Table 33, however, women still end up with 55.7 weekly hours of productive time, compared with 54.2 hours for men, both of which totals are 5 hours fewer than in the 1960s. Where women differ increasingly from men in the 1995 data is in personal care. Unlike earlier years, women now report almost as much time eating meals as men. While women's grooming time has declined, it is still almost 2 hours a week longer than for men (see Figure 19). Notable differences are now also found for sleep, with women reporting almost 3 hours more sleep time than men in 1995.

That difference in personal care accounts for the 5-hour gap in free time by gender that emerges for the first time from the 1995 data. One could argue either that women have opted to use their increased discretionary time for sleeping or grooming, or that they are so tired from their productive activities and more complex and extended lifestyles that they now require extra rest to recuperate. Whatever the reason, the "invisible hand" that kept men's and women's *free* time in rough parity through the 1980s seems to have relaxed a bit in the 1990s.

However, over the longer term, the 1990s data also provide continuing evidence of the converging androgynous lifestyles of men and women. Chapter 13 discusses how men's and women's activities became more similar between 1965 and 1985 on fifteen of twenty-two activities. When the 1995 data are added to produce an updated version of Table 18—Table 38—most of the "more androgynous" trends are even stronger in 1995 than they were in 1985. Using a more quantified and recognized measure of activity similar-

**Table 38.**    Ratio of Men's to Women's Time on Various Activities Across Time

| | 1965 | 1975 | 1985 | 1995 | 1995–65, Toward Gender Homogeneity |
|---|---|---|---|---|---|
| Contracted time | | | | | |
| Work | 2.50 | 2.10 | 1.70 | 1.40 | More |
| Commute | 2.60 | 2.30 | 1.70 | 1.45 | More |
| Committed time | | | | | |
| Housework | 0.18 | 0.31 | 0.50 | 0.56 | More |
| Child care | 0.27 | 0.31 | 0.29 | 0.32 | Same |
| Shopping | 0.73 | 0.65 | 0.67 | 0.61 | Less |
| Personal time | | | | | |
| Sleep | 0.98 | 0.96 | 0.99 | 0.97 | Same |
| Meals | 1.21 | 1.18 | 1.08 | 1.05 | More |
| Groom | 0.78 | 0.88 | 0.87 | 0.85 | More |
| Free time | | | | | |
| Education | 2.70 | 1.50 | 1.30 | 1.39 | More |
| Religion | 0.67 | 0.63 | 0.57 | 0.62 | Same |
| Organizations | 0.79 | 0.66 | 0.75 | 1.04 | More |
| Events | 1.50 | 1.00 | 1.00 | 1.16 | More |
| Visiting | 0.82 | 0.96 | 1.06 | 0.97 | More |
| Sports | 2.60 | 2.90 | 1.90 | 1.70 | More |
| Hobbies | 0.58 | 0.57 | 0.85 | 1.11 | More |
| Communication | 0.56 | 0.78 | 0.78 | 0.78 | More |
| Television | 1.28 | 1.12 | 1.09 | 1.11 | More |
| Read | 1.24 | 0.91 | 0.90 | 0.95 | More |
| Stereo | 1.45 | 1.19 | 1.66 | 1.76 | Less |
| *Total free time* | 1.04 | 1.01 | 1.03 | 1.09 | Same |
| Travel | 1.36 | 1.27 | 1.13 | 1.08 | More |

SOURCE: Americans' Use of Time Project.

NOTE: This table is an updated version of Table 18.

ity, Bianchi et al. (1999) have calculated that the Euclidean "distance" between male-female patterns gradually dropped from 24 hours in 1965 to 12 hours in 1995. On this measure, the gap between men's and women's activities has been cut almost in half in the latter third of the twentieth century. The evidence of an increasingly androgynous society, therefore, not only is replicated but also can be quantitatively documented to be part of an important long-term trend.

# Perceptions of Time Pressure

One of the other obvious long-term trends documented in Table 34 is the increase in free time, as highlighted in Chapter 7. At the same time, it is also documented in Chapter 16 that Americans believed they had less free time than previously, using several different measures of subjective time pressure. Two of these measures were feelings of being rushed (inquired about in the original 1965 study) and feelings of being stressed (inquired about first in the 1985 study of Healthy People 2000 of the National Health Interview Survey [NHIS]). Among the great virtues of the NHIS survey are the large sample sizes (at least 15,000 respondents a year), the use of identically worded questions, and the very high response rate obtained (at least 80 percent of those selected into the sample).

The end of Chapter 16 notes how the "always rushed" question response apparently peaked in the mid-1990s, along with responses to other questions related to feeling more pressured for time. Was this perhaps a bellwether for a slowdown in the pace of American life? In 1996, the General Social Survey (GSS) also asked the "rushed" question, and the GSS showed results almost identical to those in the 1995 survey. The larger sample size and higher response rate in the GSS therefore make it possible to be more confident that there has been a slight turnaround in public attitudes about feeling rushed.

Stronger corroborating evidence has come from the 1998 release of data from the 1995 NHIS on responses to its questions about stress, asked of a sample of more than 17,000 respondents. From earlier analyses, some leveling of stress feelings was expected, but not a decline. It is therefore quite surprising to find that the proportion of American adults saying they had experienced substantial stress in the previous two weeks (48 percent) was not only lower than that reported in 1993 (56 percent), but also lower than the 50 percent level reported in the first 1985 survey.

The 8-percentage-point decline in feelings of stress in the 1995 survey was not concentrated in certain groups like the elderly, the college educated, or the more affluent (Robinson and Godbey, 1999). Virtually all groups in the survey registered a decline, and at about the same level, both the elderly and young adults, the unemployed and the nonemployed, etc. It is interesting that women continued to report greater stress than men, but that gap also declined in the 1995 data. Moreover, parallel declines were found in the two other stress questions in the NHIS—one dealing with stress felt in the last year, the other dealing with the effects of stress on one's health—so that the decline was not confined to a single survey question.

Could it be that Americans have learned to slow the pace of their lifestyles, which many foreign observers consider fast to the point of ridicule? Have they become aware that they may in fact have more free time than previous generations (as in Table 34), or more familiar with other mass media accounts advising them to take life easier? Will they be taking more time to "smell the roses" in the future?

Hopeful signs that Americans are taking their free time more seriously are apparent in time-diary data as well. Table 36 shows gains in nonmedia free-time activities (like socializing and fitness) over the last decade, as well as gains in television-viewing. The decline in grooming time may signal less concern with fashion and formality and more concern with dressing comfortably and naturally. The decline in time spent at mealtime may reflect greater concern about diet and nutrition. The increase in sleep time may indicate that Americans have become more concerned about restoring their energies and their bodies. The decline in housework may be disturbing to some, but is there any reason to think that the less-tidy homes that may result have any serious life-threatening consequences?

Observers of American life, including the authors, have expressed concern about the unbridled materialism of American culture, the slavish following of the whims of advertising, more sedentary lifestyles, and the mindless content of television and feature movies. In the face of mass advertising, however, the data in this chapter point to signs that more Americans are appreciating and taking advantage of the greater free time they now have. Whether that set of choices will be revealed more clearly in the time-diary data from the next century is something worth anticipating.

# Appendixes

**Appendix A.**   Activity Differences Between 1965, 1975, and 1985 National (Jackson, Michigan) Studies (in minutes per day for age 18–64)

| | | 1965 | (J) | 1975 | 1985 | (J) |
|---|---|---|---|---|---|---|
| | n = | (1,222) | (788) | (1,993) | (3,704) | (740) |
| **00–49 Non-Free Time** | | | | | | |
| **00–09 Paid Work** | | | | | | |
| 00 | (not used) | — | — | — | — | — |
| 01 | Main job | 236 | (234) | 217 | 216 | (197) |
| 02 | Unemployment | 0 | (4) | 1 | 1 | (1) |
| 03 | Travel during work | NA | (3) | NA | NA | (3) |
| 04 | (not used) | — | — | — | — | — |
| 05 | Second job | 5 | (5) | 4 | 3 | (1) |
| 06 | Eating | 11 | (10) | 8 | 8 | (10) |
| 07 | Before/after work | 4 | (4) | 3 | 2 | (1) |
| 08 | Breaks | 8 | (8) | 4 | 3 | (3) |
| 09 | Travel to/from work | 26 | (19) | 21 | 26 | (18) |
| **10–19 Household Work** | | | | | | |
| 10 | Food preparation | 44 | (41) | 41 | 39 | (36) |
| 11 | Meal cleanup | 21 | (21) | 12 | 10 | (12) |
| 12 | Cleaning house | 33 | (29) | 31 | 27 | (26) |
| 13 | Outdoor cleaning | 3 | (5) | 7 | 7 | (8) |
| 14 | Clothes care | 25 | (24) | 15 | 12 | (10) |
| 15 | Not used | — | — | — | — | — |
| 16 | Repairs | 5 | (7) | 11 | 9 | (11) |
| 17 | Plant/animal care | 3 | (4) | 5 | 7 | (4) |
| 18 | (not used) | — | — | — | — | — |
| 19 | Other household | 12 | (11) | 6 | 13 | (7) |
| **20–29 Child Care** | | | | | | |
| 20 | Baby care | 13 | (12) | 8 | 7 | (6) |
| 21 | Child care | 9 | (8) | 7 | 8 | (9) |
| 22 | Helping/teaching | 2 | (2) | 1 | 2 | (2) |
| 23 | Talking/reading | 2 | (1) | 2 | 1 | (2) |
| 24 | Indoor playing | 3 | (4) | 3 | 4 | (4) |
| 25 | Outdoor playing | 1 | (*) | 1 | 1 | (1) |
| 26 | Medical care (child) | 1 | (1) | 1 | 1 | (1) |
| 27 | Other child care | 2 | (1) | 4 | 2 | (2) |
| 28 | (not used) | — | — | — | — | — |
| 29 | Travel/child care | 4 | (4) | 4 | 5 | (5) |
| **30–39 Obtaining Goods and Services** | | | | | | |
| 30 | Everyday shopping | 28 | (25) | 20 | 24 | (21) |
| 31 | Durable/house shop | 1 | (2) | 2 | 1 | (2) |
| 32 | Personal services | 2 | (2) | 1 | 1 | (1) |
| 33 | Medical appointments | * | (1) | 2 | 2 | (2) |

**Appendix A.**  Continued.

|        |                            | 1965 (1,222) | (J) (788) | 1975 (1,993) | 1985 (3,704) | (J) (740) |
|--------|----------------------------|--------------|-----------|--------------|--------------|-----------|
|   34   | Govt/financial service     | 1            | (*)       | 1            | 2            | (3)       |
|   35   | Repair services            | *            | (3)       | 2            | 1            | (3)       |
|   36   | (not used)                 | —            | —         | —            | —            | —         |
|   37   | Other services             | 1            | (2)       | 1            | 2            | (2)       |
|   38   | Errands                    | 0            | (0)       | *            | 1            | (0)       |
|   39   | Travel goods & services    | 18           | (18)      | 16           | 19           | (18)      |
| **40–49 Personal Needs and Care** |  |  |  |  |  |  |
|   40   | Washing, etc.              | 51           | (48)      | 39           | 53           | (56)      |
|   41   | Medical care               | 1            | (1)       | 2            | 1            | (1)       |
|   42   | Help and care              | 6            | (6)       | 8            | 5            | (5)       |
|   43   | Meals at home              | 58           | (58)      | 54           | 50           | (48)      |
|   44   | Meals out                  | 11           | (9)       | 19           | 19           | (18)      |
|   45   | Night sleep                | 457          | (466)     | 475          | 463          | (456)     |
|   46   | Naps/day sleep             | 16           | (19)      | 21           | 16           | (18)      |
|   47   | (not used)                 | —            | —         | —            | —            | —         |
|   48   | NA activities              | 14           | (9)       | 14           | 15           | (19)      |
|   49   | Travel/personal care       | 8            | (8)       | 12           | 12           | (13)      |
| **50–99 Free Time** |               |              |           |              |              |           |
| **50–59 Education and Training** |  |  |  |  |  |  |
|   50   | Students' classes          | 2            | (2)       | 5            | 7            | (8)       |
|   51   | Other classes              | 3            | (1)       | 3            | 2            | (3)       |
|   52   | (not used)                 | —            | —         | —            | —            | —         |
|   53   | (not used)                 | —            | —         | —            | —            | —         |
|   54   | Homework                   | 4            | (4)       | 6            | 7            | (5)       |
|   55   | Library                    | —            | (3)       | —            | —            | (*)       |
|   56   | Other education            | 1            | (*)       | *            | *            | (*)       |
|   57   | (not used)                 | —            | —         | —            | —            | —         |
|   58   | (not used)                 | —            | —         | —            | —            | —         |
|   59   | Travel/education           | 2            | (1)       | 2            | 2            | (2)       |
| **60–69 Organizational Activities** |  |  |  |  |  |  |
|   60   | Professional/union         | *            | (2)       | 1            | 1            | (1)       |
|   61   | Special interest           | 0            | (*)       | 1            | 1            | (1)       |
|   62   | Political/civic            | 0            | (1)       | *            | *            | (2)       |
|   63   | Volunteer/helping          | 2            | (*)       | *            | 1            | (1)       |
|   64   | Religious groups           | 2            | (3)       | 4            | 2            | (2)       |
|   65   | Religious practice         | 8            | (7)       | 9            | 7            | (12)      |
|   66   | Fraternal                  | 0            | (0)       | 1            | *            | (0)       |
|   67   | Child/youth/family         | 2            | (2)       | 2            | 1            | (1)       |
|   68   | Other organizations        | 2            | (1)       | 2            | 1            | (2)       |
|   69   | Travel/organizations       | 4            | (4)       | 4            | 4            | (5)       |

| | 1965 | (J) | 1975 | 1985 | (J) |
|---|---|---|---|---|---|
| n = | (1,222) | (788) | (1,993) | (3,704) | (740) |

**70–79 Entertainment/Social Activities**

| | | | | | | |
|---|---|---|---|---|---|---|
| 70 | Sports events | 1 | (2) | 2 | 3 | (2) |
| 71 | Entertainment/events | 4 | (1) | 1 | 1 | (1) |
| 72 | Movies | 3 | (1) | 2 | 2 | (1) |
| 73 | Theatre | * | (1) | 1 | 1 | (1) |
| 74 | Museums | * | (0) | * | * | (*) |
| 75 | Visiting | 39 | (41) | 37 | 29 | (34) |
| 76 | Parties | 15 | (12) | 4 | 6 | (3) |
| 77 | Bars, lounges | 3 | (5) | 4 | 6 | (6) |
| 78 | Other social | 1 | (1) | 2 | 1 | (1) |
| 79 | Travel/events & social | 12 | (15) | 12 | 16 | (12) |

**80–89 Recreation**

| | | | | | | |
|---|---|---|---|---|---|---|
| 80 | Active sports | 5 | (5) | 4 | 10 | (12) |
| 81 | Outdoor | 1 | (4) | 7 | 5 | (2) |
| 82 | Walking/hiking | 1 | (2) | 2 | 4 | (3) |
| 83 | Hobbies | 2 | (1) | 2 | 1 | (2) |
| 84 | Domestic crafts | 7 | (6) | 8 | 7 | (3) |
| 85 | Art | 1 | (1) | 1 | 1 | (1) |
| 86 | Music/drama/dance | 1 | (1) | 1 | 1 | (1) |
| 87 | Games | 5 | (5) | 5 | 6 | (12) |
| 88 | Computer use/other | 2 | (2) | 3 | 3 | (4) |
| 89 | Travel/recreation | 2 | (2) | 4 | 5 | (4) |

**90–99 Communication**

| | | | | | | |
|---|---|---|---|---|---|---|
| 90 | Radio | 4 | (3) | 2 | 3 | (5) |
| 91 | TV | 89 | (97) | 129 | 129 | (158) |
| 92 | Records/tapes | 1 | (1) | 3 | 1 | (1) |
| 93 | Read books | 5 | (3) | 4 | 7 | (6) |
| 94 | Reading magazines/other | 8 | (8) | 10 | 9 | (12) |
| 95 | Reading newspaper | 21 | (22) | 13 | 8 | (15) |
| 96 | Conversations | 18 | (16) | 18 | 24 | (19) |
| 97 | Writing | 5 | (4) | 2 | 5 | (3) |
| 98 | Think/relax | 4 | (5) | 9 | 9 | (5) |
| 99 | Travel/communication | 3 | (3) | 1 | * | (*) |

| | 1965 | (J) | 1975 | 1985 | (J) |
|---|---|---|---|---|---|
| Total Travel (Codes 09, 29, 39, 49, 59, 69, 79, 89, 99) | 79 | (74) | 76 | 89 | (77) |

SOURCE: Americans' Use of Time Project.

* = Less than 0.5 min. per day.

**Appendix B.**   Activity Differences Between Canadian, California, and U.S. National
Studies (in minutes per day for age 18 + )

| | | Canada | | California | National |
|---|---|---|---|---|---|
| | | 1986 | 1992 | 1987–88 | 1985–87 |
| | n = | (9,000) | (9,000) | (1,579) | (4,939) |
| **00–49 Non-Free Time** | | | | | |
| **00–09 Paid Work** | | | | | |
| 00 | (not used) | — | — | — | — |
| 01 | Main job | 182 | 182 | 205 | 193 |
| 02 | Unemployment | 2 | 2 | 1 | 1 |
| 03 | Travel/during work | 4 | 1 | 7 | NR |
| 04 | (not used) | — | — | — | — |
| 05 | Second job | 3 | 2 | 3 | 3 |
| 06 | Eating | 9 | 8 | 5 | 7 |
| 07 | Before/after work | 2 | 2 | 1 | 2 |
| 08 | Breaks | 4 | 5 | 2 | 3 |
| 09 | Travel to/from work | 19 | 18 | 26 | 22 |
| **10–19 Household Work** | | | | | |
| 10 | Food preparation | 34 | 34 | 30 | 41 |
| 11 | Meal cleanup | 14 | 12 | 11 | 11 |
| 12 | Cleaning house | 28 | 27 | 21 | 29 |
| 13 | Outdoor cleaning | 5 | 6 | 9 | 8 |
| 14 | Clothes care | { 10 | 11 | 7 | 11 |
| 15 | Car repair/maintenance (by R) | { — | 3 | 5 | NR |
| 16 | Other repairs (by R) | 9 | 7 | 8 | 9 |
| 17 | Plant care | 2 | 4 | 3 | 4 |
| 18 | Animal care | — | 2 | 3 | 4 |
| 19 | Other household | 7 | 4 | 7 | 14 |
| **20–29 Child Care** | | | | | |
| 20 | Baby care | 6 | 6 | 3 | 6 |
| 21 | Child care | 8 | 6 | 6 | 7 |
| 22 | Helping/teaching | 2 | 2 | 2 | 1 |
| 23 | Talking/reading | 2 | 2 | 1 | 1 |
| 24 | Indoor playing | { 5 | { 6 | 2 | 3 |
| 25 | Outdoor playing | { — | { — | 2 | 1 |
| 26 | Medical care (child) | 1 | 1 | 0 | 1 |
| 27 | Other child care | 1 | 4 | 2 | 2 |
| 28 | At dry cleaners | NR | NR | 1 | NR |
| 29 | Travel/child care | 2 | 4 | 3 | 4 |
| **30–39 Obtaining Goods and Services** | | | | | |
| 30 | Everyday shopping | { 33 | 8 | 8 | 7 |
| 31 | Durable/house shop | { — | 14 | 18 | 17 |

| | | n = | Canada | | California 1987–88 (1,579) | National 1985–87 (4,939) |
|---|---|---|---|---|---|---|
| | | | 1986 (9,000) | 1992 (9,000) | | |
| 32 | Personal services | | 1 | 1 | 1 | 1 |
| 33 | Medical appointments | | 2 | 2 | 3 | 2 |
| 34 | Govt/financial service | | 1 | 1 | 3 | 2 |
| 35 | Car repair services | | 1 | * | 1 | NR |
| 36 | Other repair services | | — | — | 0 | 3 |
| 37 | Other services | | 1 | 3 | 2 | 1 |
| 38 | Errands | | 1 | 1 | 1 | 1 |
| 39 | Travel/goods & services | | 15 | 16 | 24 | 19 |
| 40–49 | Personal Needs and Care | | | | | |
| 40 | Washing, etc. | | 40 | 41 | 36 | 48 |
| 41 | Medical care | | 2 | 2 | 4 | 1 |
| 42 | Help and care | | 1 | 3 | 4 | 4 |
| 43 | Meals at home | | 74 | 68 | 47 | 54 |
| 44 | Meals out | | 13 | 14 | 27 | 19 |
| 45 | Night sleep | | 490 | 483 | 480 | 465 |
| 46 | Naps/day sleep | | 12 | 14 | 17 | 19 |
| 47 | Dressing, etc. | | — | — | 1 | — |
| 48 | NA Activities | | 3 | — | 2 | 15 |
| 49 | Travel/personal care | | 8 | 4 | 21 | 12 |
| 50–99 | Free Time | | | | | |
| 50–59 | Education and Training | | | | | |
| 50 | Students' classes | | 10 | 14 | 8 | 6 |
| 51 | Other classes | | 2 | 1 | 1 | 2 |
| 52 | (not used) | | — | — | — | — |
| 53 | (not used) | | — | — | — | — |
| 54 | Homework | | 14 | 14 | 8 | 7 |
| 55 | Library | | NR | NR | 0 | 1 |
| 56 | Other education | | 3 | 3 | 1 | 1 |
| 57 | (not used) | | — | — | — | — |
| 58 | (not used) | | — | — | — | — |
| 59 | Travel/education | | 3 | 4 | 2 | 2 |
| 60–69 | Organizational Activities | | | | | |
| 60 | Professional/union | | 1 | * | 0 | 0 |
| 61 | Special interest | | 0 | * | 0 | 1 |
| 62 | Political/civic | | 1 | * | 0 | 0 |
| 63 | Volunteer/helping | | 4 | 4 | 1 | 1 |
| 64 | Religious groups | | 2 | 2 | 1 | 2 |
| 65 | Religious practice | | 5 | 5 | 5 | 9 |
| 66 | Fraternal | | 1 | 1 | 0 | 0 |
| 67 | Child/youth/family | | * | 1 | 1 | 1 |
| 68 | Other organizations | | 0 | 1 | 2 | 1 |
| 69 | Travel/organizations | | 2 | 4 | 2 | 4 |

**Appendix B.**    Continued.

| | | Canada | | California | National |
|---|---|---|---|---|---|
| | | 1986 | 1992 | 1987–88 | 1985–87 |
| | n = | (9,000) | (9,000) | (1,579) | (4,939) |
| 70–79 Entertainment/Social Activities | | | | | |
| 70 | Sports events | 2 | 3 | 2 | 2 |
| 71 | Entertainment/events | 1 | 2 | 4 | 1 |
| 72 | Movies | 2 | 1 | 2 | 2 |
| 73 | Theatre | * | * | 1 | 1 |
| 74 | Museums | 0 | * | 1 | 1 |
| 75 | Visiting | ⎰ 49 | 36 | 25 | 31 |
| 76 | Parties | ⎱ — | 16 | 6 | 5 |
| 77 | Bars/lounges | 6 | 5 | 4 | 5 |
| 78 | Other social | 7 | 4 | 1 | 1 |
| 79 | Travel/events/social | 12 | 14 | 13 | 16 |
| 80–89 Recreation | | | | | |
| 80 | Active sports | 9 | 14 | 8 | 10 |
| 81 | Outdoor | 2 | 4 | 3 | 5 |
| 82 | Walking/hiking | 4 | 8 | 5 | 5 |
| 83 | Hobbies | 4 | 6 | 1 | 1 |
| 84 | Domestic crafts | 9 | 6 | 4 | 8 |
| 85 | Art | ⎰ 2 | ⎰ 2 | 0 | 1 |
| 86 | Music/drama/dance | ⎱ — | ⎱ — | 3 | 2 |
| 87 | Games | 8 | 9 | 5 | 8 |
| 88 | Other computer use | 3 | 3 | 3 | 3 |
| 89 | Travel/recreation | 4 | 7 | 5 | 5 |
| 90–99 Communication | | | | | |
| 90 | Radio | 3 | 3 | 2 | 3 |
| 91 | TV | 139 | 131 | 131 | 139 |
| 92 | Records/tapes | 2 | 2 | 2 | 1 |
| 93 | Read books | ⎰ 16 | 14 | 5 | 7 |
| 94 | Reading magazines/other | ⎱ — | 3 | 17 | 11 |
| 95 | Reading newspaper | 11 | 13 | 11 | 11 |
| 96 | Conversations | 14 | 14 | 15 | 24 |
| 97 | Writing | 4 | 2 | 9 | 5 |
| 98 | Think, relax | 17 | 15 | 9 | 11 |
| 99 | Travel, communication | * | * | 4 | * |
| Total Travel (Codes 09, 29, 39, 49, 59, 69, 79, 89, 99) | | 70 | 71 | 107 | 84 |

SOURCE: Americans' Use of Time Project.

NR = not recorded.

* = Less than 0.5 min. per day.

**Appendix C.**    Activity Differences Between Survey Techniques (1985 data in minutes per day for age 18 + )

| | n = | Mailback (2,921) | Telephone (1,210) | Personal (808) |
|---|---|---|---|---|
| **00–49 Non-Free Time** | | | | |
| **00–09 Paid Work** | | | | |
| 00  Regular work | | 195.3 | 191.5 | 172.4 |
| 02  Unemployment | | 0.7 | 0.6 | 1.5 |
| 05  Second job | | 3.6 | 2.5 | 0.9 |
| 06  Meals at work | | 7.0 | 9.0 | 4.8 |
| 07  At work/other | | 2.0 | 1.2 | 1.8 |
| 08  Work breaks | | 2.0 | 3.2 | 2.0 |
| 09  Travel to/from job | | 23.0 | 24.2 | 18.0 |
| **10–19 Household Work** | | | | |
| 10  Food Preparation | | 36.7 | 43.9 | 48.9 |
| 11  Meal cleanup | | 11.7 | 7.2 | 12.6 |
| 12  Clean house | | 24.9 | 38.5 | 30.3 |
| 13  Outdoor chores | | 7.7 | 10.2 | 8.5 |
| 14  Laundry/ironing | | 11.2 | 11.4 | 12.6 |
| 16  Other upkeep | | 9.4 | 9.2 | 7.2 |
| 17  Gardening/animal care | | 9.5 | 6.3 | 1.9 |
| 19  Other duties | | 12.8 | 16.1 | 16.6 |
| **20–29 Child Care** | | | | |
| 21  Child care | | 4.4 | 9.8 | 10.9 |
| 22  Help on housework | | 0.9 | 2.1 | 2.0 |
| 23  Talk to children | | 1.1 | 1.3 | 1.5 |
| 24  Indoor playing | | 2.7 | 4.0 | 2.7 |
| 25  Outdoor playing | | 0.9 | 0.5 | 0.5 |
| 26  Child health | | 0.4 | 0.5 | 0.8 |
| 27  Babysitting | | 1.3 | 2.1 | 2.1 |
| 29  Travel with child | | 3.4 | 5.4 | 6.4 |
| **30–39 Obtaining Goods and Services** | | | | |
| 30  Marketing | | 22.8 | 25.9 | 23.6 |
| 31  Shopping | | 0.8 | 0.6 | 0.3 |
| 32  Personal care | | 1.1 | 1.4 | 0.9 |
| 33  Medical care | | 2.3 | 1.2 | 1.5 |
| 34  Admin. service | | 1.6 | 1.0 | 1.7 |
| 35  Repair service | | 1.2 | 1.2 | 1.2 |
| 37  Other services | | 2.6 | 1.0 | 1.7 |
| 38  Errands | | 1.3 | 2.3 | 1.5 |
| 39  Travel/service | | 19.9 | 16.3 | 18.8 |

**Appendix C.** Continued.

| | Mailback (2,921) | Telephone (1,210) | Personal (808) |
|---|---|---|---|
| n = | | | |
| **40–49 Personal Needs and Care** | | | |
| 40    Personal hygiene | 55.7 | 49.5 | 48.0 |
| 41    Personal medical | 0.9 | 0.7 | 0.8 |
| 42    Care to adults | 3.9 | 4.1 | 5.4 |
| 43    Meals/snacks | 53.0 | 56.6 | 59.0 |
| 44    Restaurant meals | 20.2 | 16.1 | 14.4 |
| 45    Night sleep | 467.8 | 457.7 | 471.6 |
| 46    Naps and resting | 19.4 | 14.7 | 20.6 |
| 48    Private/other | 20.6 | 4.4 | 32.2 |
| 49    Travel/personal | 11.9 | 10.3 | 12.3 |
| **50–99 Free Time** | | | |
| **50–59 Education and Training** | | | |
| 50    Students' classes | 6.9 | 8.3 | 2.9 |
| 51    Other classes | 2.2 | 1.5 | 1.4 |
| 54    Homework | 6.5 | 10.2 | 3.3 |
| 56    Other education | 0.5 | 0.0 | 0.0 |
| 59    Travel education | 2.0 | 2.0 | 1.8 |
| **60–69 Organizational Activities** | | | |
| 60    Professional/union | 0.8 | 0.3 | 0.2 |
| 61    Special interest | 1.0 | 0.1 | 0.0 |
| 62    Political/civic | 0.1 | 0.0 | 0.3 |
| 63    Volunteer/helping | 1.4 | 0.6 | 1.9 |
| 64    Religious | 2.0 | 1.3 | 1.7 |
| 65    Religious practice | 7.3 | 10.6 | 9.7 |
| 66    Fraternal | 0.2 | 0.2 | 0.1 |
| 67    Child/youth/family | 0.1 | 0.2 | 2.2 |
| 68    Other organizations | 1.4 | 0.8 | 0.6 |
| 69    Travel/organizations | 3.9 | 3.6 | 3.8 |
| **70–79 Entertainment/Social Activities** | | | |
| 70    Sports events | 3.0 | 2.3 | 0.7 |
| 71    Entertainment/events | 1.1 | 1.8 | 1.3 |
| 72    Movies | 2.5 | 1.8 | 0.6 |
| 73    Theatre | 0.7 | 0.3 | 0.1 |
| 74    Museums | 0.2 | 0.8 | 0.1 |
| 75    Visiting with friends | 25.7 | 41.5 | 33.8 |
| 76    Parties | 4.8 | 6.3 | 5.5 |
| 77    Bars/Lounges | 5.4 | 5.8 | 3.5 |
| 78    Other social | 1.4 | 1.7 | 0.2 |
| 79    Travel/social and events | 15.3 | 17.5 | 10.9 |

|  | n = | Mailback (2,921) | Telephone (1,210) | Personal (808) |
|---|---|---|---|---|
| **80–89 Recreation** | | | | |
| 80 Active sports | | 11.4 | 8.0 | 5.5 |
| 81 Outdoors | | 6.1 | 3.7 | 3.2 |
| 82 Walking/hiking | | 4.4 | 5.0 | 2.9 |
| 83 Hobbies | | 1.7 | 0.4 | 0.5 |
| 84 Domestic crafts | | 6.2 | 8.3 | 14.6 |
| 85 Art work | | 1.1 | 0.8 | 0.6 |
| 86 Music/drama/dance | | 1.1 | 2.3 | 1.3 |
| 87 Games | | 7.7 | 7.1 | 5.9 |
| 88 Other | | 2.9 | 2.5 | 3.3 |
| 89 Travel/recreation | | 6.0 | 4.2 | 1.9 |
| **90–99 Communication** | | | | |
| 90 Radio | | 3.2 | 1.7 | 3.6 |
| 91 Television | | 136.9 | 140.5 | 152.6 |
| 92 Records/tapes | | 1.1 | 1.1 | 1.6 |
| 93 Read books | | 6.7 | 8.6 | 4.8 |
| 94 Read magazine | | 9.8 | 11.5 | 11.4 |
| 95 Read newspaper | | 10.6 | 9.1 | 10.2 |
| 96 Conversation | | 25.5 | 14.2 | 28.8 |
| 97 Writing | | 6.0 | 3.4 | 3.7 |
| 98 Relaxing/thinking | | 7.6 | 17.3 | 9.8 |
| 99 Travel/communication | | 0.2 | 0.1 | 0.2 |

SOURCE: Americans' Use of Time Project.

**Appendix D.**    National Study Location Codes (1985)

A.  At Respondent's Home (00–19)
   00  Respondent's home/yard (general)
   01  Basement/cellar
   02  Bathroom
   03  Bedroom
   04  Dining room
   05  Computer room
   06  Den
   07  Family room / front room / living room
   08  Game room / recreation room
   09  Garage
   10  Kitchen
   11  Laundry / utility room
   12  Office
   13  Porch
   14  Hall

   19  Other home

B.  Travel (20–29)
   20  Transit (NA mode)
   21  Car transit

   29  Other transit

C.  Other (30–89)
   30  Work
   40  Friends/relative home
   50  Restaurant / bar / fast food
   60  Indoor place of leisure
   70  Outdoor place of leisure
   80  School
   81  Church
   82  Store, etc.
   83  Banks/office/library
   89  Other

   99  NA/Ref

Source: Americans' Use of Time Project.

**Appendix E.**  Diary Work Hours for Different Workweek Estimates
(in average hours per week)

| Estimated Hours (Est) | 1965–85 Totals | Diary Hours at Work | | | GAP (Est.) − (Work) | GAP 1965–85 |
|---|---|---|---|---|---|---|
| | | 1965 | 1975 | 1985 | | |
| 0 | 2.8 | 0.5 | 1.7 | 6.2 | −3 | +5.7 |
| 1–19 | 17.2 | 20.5 | 14.6 | 16.6 | −6 | −3.9 |
| 20–29 | 24.3 | 27.1 | 24.5 | 21.3 | 2 | −5.8 |
| 30–34 | 30.1 | 30.9 | 30.0 | 29.4 | 2 | −1.5 |
| 35–39 | 30.8 | 31.6 | 32.6 | 28.1 | 7 | −3.5 |
| 40–44 | 38.6 | 41.3 | 38.2 | 36.2 | 2 | −5.3 |
| 45–49 | 44.3 | 49.8 | 41.5 | 41.7 | 3 | −8.1 |
| 50–54 | 44.6 | 49.9 | 42.4 | 41.6 | 9 | −8.3 |
| 55–59 | 47.9 | 42.5 | 57.9 | 43.2 | 10 | +0.7 |
| 60–64 | 50.7 | 55.7 | 52.1 | 44.2 | 14 | −11.5 |
| 65–74 | 55.2 | 57.6 | 55.1 | 52.8 | 15 | −4.8 |
| 75+ | 54.9 | 46.2 | 63.5 | 54.9 | 25 | +8.7 |
| Average Estimated Workweek (20+ hrs) | | | | | | |
| Men | | 47.1 | 46.8 | 46.4 | | |
| Women | | 40.4 | 40.2 | 41.6 | | |

SOURCE:  Robinson and Bostrom, 1994; Americans' Use of Time Project.

**Appendix F.**  Variations in GAP by Estimated Workweek, Year, Day of Week, and Gender (in hours per week, for those estimating 20+ hour workweeks)

|  |  | Before MCA | After MCA Adjustment |
|---|---|---|---|
| Grand Mean |  | +5.0 hrs | +5.0 hrs |
| Estimated Workweek (Midpoint) |  |  |  |
| 20–29 (25) | (296) | 0 | −1 |
| 30–34 (32) | (248) | 1 | 0 |
| 35–39 (37) | (394) | 6 | 4 |
| 40–44 (42) | (2,083) | 3 | 3 |
| 45–49 (47) | (533) | 3 | 4 |
| 50–54 (52) | (466) | 7 | 8 |
| 55–59 (57) | (183) | 9 | 9 |
| 60–64 (62) | (262) | 12 | 14 |
| 65–74 (69) | (149) | 15 | 14 |
| 75+ (80) | (110) | 29 | 30 |
|  |  | .17 | .19[a] |
| Year |  |  |  |
| 1965 | (816) | 1 | 1 |
| 1975 | (1,305) | 4 | 4 |
| 1985 | (2,602) | 7 | 6 |
|  |  | .07 | .06[a] |
| Sex |  |  |  |
| Male | (2,702) | 4 | 3 |
| Female | (2,022) | 6 | 7 |
|  |  | .04 | .08[a] |
| Day |  |  |  |
| Weekday | (3,336) | −4 | −4 |
| Saturday | (720) | 23 | 23 |
| Sunday | (668) | 30 | 30 |
|  |  | .52 | .52[a] |

SOURCE: Robinson and Bostrom, 1994; Americans' Use of Time Project.

[a]Difference statistically significant at .001 level.

**Appendix G.** Diary-Estimate Differences (GAP) by Estimated Work Hours by Country (in hours per week)

| Years (n = ) | 1979 Australia (1,276) | 1980 Canada (1,845) | 1987 Denmark (2,389) | 1979–87 Finland (2,268) | 1975 France (4,633) | 1981 Norway (4,309) | 1975–85 U.S. (1,753) | 1974–87 U.K. (3,897) | 1975–85 Netherlands (5,469) |
|---|---|---|---|---|---|---|---|---|---|
| Hours/week | | | | | | | | | |
| 0 | -1 | -16 | -6 | -3 | -2 | -2 | -4 | -4 | -1 |
| 1–9 | — | — | — | -3[a] | -1[a] | — | -9 | 1 | 1 |
| 10–19 | 5[a] | -2[a] | -6 | -3 | 2 | -2 | -5 | 1 | 4 |
| 20–29 | 3 | -7 | 0 | 0 | 2 | — | 0 | 3 | 7 |
| 30–34 | 9 | -2[a] | 2 | 3 | 1 | 6 | 1 | 4 | 11 |
| 35–39 | 4 | 0 | 3 | 3 | 2 | 3 | 6 | 2 | 5 |
| 40–44 | 2 | 3 | 6 | 2 | 5 | 5 | 3 | 3 | 4 |
| 45–49 | 1 | -3[a] | 8 | 7 | 4 | 5 | 4 | 6 | 6 |
| 50–54 | 8 | 6 | 15 | 12 | 8 | 12 | 6 | 7 | 8 |
| 55–59 | 7 | 1 | 12[a] | 11 | 13 | 10 | 13 | 8 | 13 |
| 60–69 | 15[a] | 20[a] | 4 | 9 | 11 | 9 | 9 | 11 | 14 |
| 70+ | — | 47[a] | 25[a] | 20 | 19 | 21 | 17 | 25[a] | 28[a] |
| Average | 2 | 2 | 3 | 2 | 3 | 2 | 3 | 3 | 4 |

SOURCE: Robinson and Godbey, 1994.

[a]Fewer than 50 respondents.

—Fewer than 10 respondents.

**Appendix H.**   Proportionate Time Spent on Various Aspects of Household and Family Care (1985 data, in percentages of hours per week)

|  | Women | | Men | |
|---|---|---|---|---|
|  | Employed | Not | Employed | Not |
| Sample size          n = | 1,234 | 814 | 1,327 | 354 |
| Hours per week | 25.6 hrs. | 38.9 hrs. | 14.5 hrs. | 20.4 hrs. |
| Cooking | 21% | 22% | 12% | 13% |
| Cleaning | 20 | 23 | 10 | 11 |
| Laundry | 7 | 7 | 2 | 3 |
| Management, paperwork | 6 | 4 | 10 | 10 |
| Animal, plant care | 2 | 2 | 5 | 6 |
| Repairs, maintenance | 2 | 1 | 12 | 12 |
| Yard, outdoor work | 1 | 2 | 8 | 10 |
| Child care | 13 | 18 | 11 | 5 |
| Shopping | 13 | 10 | 12 | 10 |
| Services | 5 | 4 | 6 | 9 |
| Travel | 9 | 7 | 12 | 12 |
| Total | 100% | 100% | 100% | 100% |

SOURCE: Americans' Use of Time Project.

**Appendix I.**  Differences in Women's Housework Time by Year and Role Factors, 1965–1985 (in hours per week, before and after MCA adjustment)

|  |  |  | Before Adjustment (n = 3,855) | | After Adjustment (n = 3,855) | |
|---|---|---|---|---|---|---|
| TOTAL: | | | 21 hrs/wk | | 21 hrs/wk | |
| Year | (n = ) | | | | | |
| 1965 | ( 692) | | 27 | | 26 | |
| 1975 | (1,125) | | 21 | | 20 | |
| 1985 | (2,038) | | 19 | | 20 | |
| | | Eta | | .18 | | .11 |
| Employed | | | | | | |
| No | (1,808) | | 27 | | 26 | |
| Yes | (2,047) | | 14 | | 15 | |
| | | Eta | | .34 | | .28 |
| Married | | | | | | |
| No | (1,295) | | 14 | | 16 | |
| Yes | (2,560) | | 23 | | 23 | |
| | | Eta | | .24 | | .22 |
| Children | | | | | | |
| None | (1,972) | | 18 | | 20 | |
| One | (709) | | 20 | | 20 | |
| Two | (660) | | 24 | | 22 | |
| Three | (308) | | 27 | | 24 | |
| Four + | (206) | | 32 | | 28 | |
| | | Eta | | .23 | | .13 |

SOURCE: Americans' Use of Time Project.

**Appendix J.**   Differences Between TV Owners and Nonowners in Selected Secondary Activities, at Various Locations and in Contact with Various Types of People (in minutes per day across 13 survey sites)

|  | Owner-Nonowner Difference |
|---|---|
| *Secondary activities:* | |
| Mass Media | |
| Radio | − 22  min/day |
| TV, home | + 19 |
| TV, away | − 5 |
| Read paper | 0 |
| Read magazine | 0 |
| Read book | − 1 |
| Nonmedia | |
| Child care | 0 |
| Social, at home | 0 |
| Social, away | 0 |
| Conversation | + 3 |
| *Location:* | |
| At home, inside | + 32 |
| At home, outside | − 13 |
| Others' homes | − 10 |
| Work | − 1 |
| Streets | − 4 |
| Stores, business | − 2 |
| Indoor leisure | − 3 |
| Outdoor leisure | + 1 |
| Restaurant | − 2 |
| Other | 0 |
| *Company:* | |
| All alone | − 36 |
| Alone in a crowd | − 5 |
| With spouse | + 12 |
| With children | + 10 |
| Spouse and children together | + 30 |
| Other household adults | + 4 |
| Friends, relatives | − 14 |
| Neighbors | − 9 |
| Work colleagues | + 7 |
| Organization members | 0 |
| Formal contacts | + 3 |
| Other | − 3 |

SOURCE: Robinson, 1972b.

NOTE: Data are weighted to ensure equality of days of the week and number of eligible respondents per household.

**Appendix K.**   Media Use and Longer-Term Use of Home Computers, After MCA Adjustment, 1995 (in minutes per day)

| Use: | Every Day | 3–5 Week | 1–2 Week | Once, Few | Less Often | Never | Don't Have | | Original Correlation |
|---|---|---|---|---|---|---|---|---|---|
| Use PC | (281) | (395) | (352) | (171) | (83) | (147) | (2,672) | = | (3,603) |
| Newspapers | 27 | 22 | 23 | 24 | 18 | 20 | 19 | | .07[a] Yes |
| Magazines | 18 | 16 | 14 | 11 | 15 | 14 | 13 | | .10[a] Yes |
| Books | 25 | 24 | 23 | 20 | 15 | 18 | 16 | | .13[a] Yes |
| Movies | 4 | 4 | 3 | 2 | 4 | 2 | 2 | | .13[a] Yes |
| Word process | (72) | (230) | (393) | (286) | (114) | (182) | (2,321) | | |
| Newspapers | 25 | 27 | 22 | 22 | 19 | 29 | 19 | | .08[a] Yes |
| Books | 22 | 26 | 27 | 19 | 19 | 16 | 15 | | .13[a] Yes |
| Financial | (65) | (115) | (266) | (231) | (63) | (559) | (2,321) | | |
| Newspapers | 30 | 23 | 22 | 24 | 16 | 21 | 20 | | .06[b] Yes |
| Games | (85) | (146) | (286) | (245) | (156) | (363) | (2,321) | | |
| Books | 30 | 25 | 22 | 20 | 18 | 26 | 15 | | .10[a] Yes |

SOURCE:  Based on Kohut, 1995; *Times-Mirror* Survey.

[a]Correlation significant at .01 level.
[b]Correlation significant at .05 level.

Yes—Significant after MCA adjustment.
No—Not significant after MCA adjustment.

**Appendix L.**   Mass Media Use and Computer Use, for On-Line Users Only (entries are Pearson correlation coefficients, comparable to Tables 11 and 12)

| | Yesterday Use (Table 11) | | Longer-Term Use (Table 12) | | | | |
|---|---|---|---|---|---|---|---|
| | Personal Computer | On-Line | Personal Computer | Word Processing | Finance | Games | CD-ROM |
| TV time | −.01 | −.03 | .00 | −.02 | .01 | .03 | .00 |
| TV news | −.04 | −.01 | −.01 | .02 | .07 | −.02 | .05 |
| Radio news | .04 | −.00 | .04 | .00 | .02 | −.01 | .04 |
| Newspapers | .05 | −.03 | .07 | .12[a] | .08[a] | −.01 | .00 |
| Magazines | .10[a] | −.01 | .09[a] | .06 | .00 | .03 | .06 |
| Books | .02 | .04 | .05 | .08[a] | −.03 | .04 | .02 |
| Movies | .02 | .06 | .02 | .08[a] | −.06 | .02 | .01 |

SOURCE:  Based on Kohut, 1995; *Times-Mirror* Survey

[a]Significant at .05 level.

**Appendix M.**   Difference in Bi-Weekly Fitness Participation Occasions by Age and Sex, 1985–1990 (average occasion over prior two weeks)

| Ages | Men 1985 | 1990 | 1985–90 Difference | Women 1985 | 1990 | 1985–90 Difference | Male/Female Ratio 1985 | 1990 | 1985–90 Changes |
|---|---|---|---|---|---|---|---|---|---|
| 18–24 | 12.7 | 11.4 | − 1.3 | 8.2 | 6.9 | − 1.3 | 65% | 61% | − 4 |
| 25–34 | 8.7 | 8.0 | − 0.7 | 6.9 | 5.8 | − 1.1 | 79 | 73 | − 6 |
| 35–44 | 7.0 | 6.8 | − 0.2 | 5.3 | 5.2 | − 0.1 | 76 | 76 | 0 |
| 45–54 | 5.0 | 5.3 | + 0.3 | 4.7 | 3.9 | − 0.8 | 94 | 74 | − 20 |
| 55–64 | 4.9 | 4.6 | − 0.3 | 4.4 | 3.9 | − 0.5 | 90 | 85 | − 5 |
| 65–74 | 5.1 | 5.0 | − 0.1 | 3.8 | 3.6 | − 0.2 | 75 | 72 | − 3 |
| 75–97 | 1.9 | 2.3 | + 0.4 | 1.7 | 1.5 | − 0.2 | 89 | 65 | − 24 |
| Total Sample | 7.3 | 6.7 | − 0.6 | 5.4 | 4.7 | − 0.7 | 74 | 70 | − 4 |

SOURCE: Robinson and Godbey, 1993a; National Center for Health Statistics, National Health Interview Survey.

**Appendix N.** Comparisons of the 1989–1990 California Children's Data with Those from the 1980–1981 University of Michigan National Study of Time Use (Data in hours per week)

| | Ages 3–11 | | | | Age (Boys and Girls Combined) | | | | | | Total | |
| | Boys | | Girls | | 3–5 | | 6–8 | | 9–11 | | | |
| | National (n = 118) | Cal (n = 452) | National (n = 111) | Cal (n = 442) | National (n = 67) | Cal (n = 335) | National (n = 69) | Cal (n = 278) | National (n = 93) | Cal (n = 281) | National (n = 229) | Cal (n = 894) |
|---|---|---|---|---|---|---|---|---|---|---|---|---|
| Paid work (05,08) | 1.4 | 0.2 | 0.1 | 0.1 | 0.0 | 0.1 | 1.3 | 0.1 | 1.0 | 0.3 | 0.8 | 0.2 |
| Housework (10–19) | 2.5 | 3.2 | 3.2 | 3.6 | 1.7 | 2.1 | 2.2 | 3.6 | 3.0 | 4.7 | 2.8 | 3.4 |
| Eating (44,44,06) | 9.4 | 9.1 | 9.3 | 9.2 | 9.5 | 10.3 | 9.4 | 9.0 | 8.7 | 7.9 | 9.4 | 9.2 |
| Sleeping (45) | 69.5 | 71.7 | 69.8 | 72.7 | 73.6 | 74.1 | 71.0 | 72.7 | 65.5 | 69.3 | 69.6 | 72.2 |
| Other personal care (40,41,42,47,48) | 5.0 | 4.3 | 5.3 | 4.7 | 5.0 | 4.9 | 5.6 | 5.0 | 4.8 | 3.6 | 5.1 | 4.5 |
| School (50,51,42 53,56,57,58) | 21.0 | 12.3 | 21.6 | 14.0 | 11.4 | 8.8 | 24.3 | 16.3 | 26.3 | 15.3 | 21.3 | 13.2 |
| Studying (54,55) | 1.3 | 1.4 | 1.6 | 1.5 | 0.2 | 0.2 | 0.7 | 2.0 | 2.8 | 2.4 | 1.4 | 1.5 |
| Church (60) | 2.3 | 0.5 | 2.4 | 0.3 | 2.2 | 0.2 | 2.6 | 0.6 | 2.5 | 0.6 | 2.3 | 0.4 |
| Visiting (78–78) | 2.1 | 0.7 | 2.0 | 1.2 | 1.5 | 0.5 | 1.5 | 0.4 | 1.3 | 2.0 | 2.1 | 0.9 |
| Sports (80) | 3.2 | 8.2 | 1.8 | 5.9 | 0.5 | 4.6 | 3.0 | 7.9 | 3.2 | 9.2 | 2.5 | 7.0 |
| Outdoors (81,82) | 1.8 | 8.6 | 1.4 | 7.8 | 0.6 | 10.2 | 1.7 | 8.3 | 2.0 | 5.7 | 1.6 | 8.2 |
| Hobbies (83–84) | 0.3 | 0.1 | 0.5 | 0.1 | 0.1 | 0.0 | 0.3 | 0.2 | 0.3 | 0.2 | 0.4 | 0.1 |
| Art activities (85–86) | 0.5 | 1.6 | 0.5 | 2.2 | 0.6 | 2.4 | 0.5 | 1.8 | 0.4 | 1.5 | 0.5 | 1.9 |
| Playing indoors (87,875–879) | 17.3 | 10.3 | 18.5 | 8.9 | 31.5 | 13.9 | 15.3 | 7.8 | 8.5 | 6.3 | 17.9 | 9.6 |
| TV (91,914,915) | 19.1 | 19.8 | 14.7 | 18.6 | 13.0 | 16.3 | 12.8 | 18.9 | 18.3 | 23.1 | 16.9 | 19.2 |
| Reading or Being read to (93,94, 95,937,949) | 1.2 | 1.4 | 0.9 | 1.4 | 0.9 | 1.2 | 1.0 | 1.6 | 1.1 | 1.4 | 1.1 | 1.4 |
| Conversation (96) | 1.3 | 1.3 | 1.2 | 0.9 | * | 1.4 | * | 1.0 | * | 0.9 | 1.3 | 1.1 |
| Other leisure (98) | 1.3 | 0.5 | 1.6 | 0.8 | 1.0 | 0.5 | 0.4 | 0.6 | 0.4 | 0.9 | 1.4 | 0.7 |
| Not ascertained (1) | 2.5 | 0.2 | 3.1 | 0.1 | 4.2 | 0.3 | 1.4 | 0.1 | 2.4 | 0.2 | 2.8 | 0.2 |
| Other activities[a] | 5.0 | 12.1 | 8.5 | 13.7 | * | 15.6 | * | 10.1 | * | 12.4 | 6.9 | 12.9 |

SOURCE: Wiley et al., 1991; Juster and Stafford, 1985, tables 14.3–14.6.

*Not available for National Survey.

[a]Not strictly comparable. For the California survey, includes the following codes: Travel 09,29,39,49,59,69,79,89,99,199, child care 20–27; shopping 20–38; naps 46; entertainment 70–74, 711; watching others recreate 88; radio, records, letters 90,92,97.

**Appendix O.**    Ratings of Detailed Activities on Enjoyment Scale (1985 Diaries)

| | Work/House Activities | Personal/ Shopping Activities | Organization Activities | Education Activities | Free Time |
|---|---|---|---|---|---|
| 10.0 (*Like*) | | | | | |
| 9.3 | | Sex | | | |
| 9.2 | | | | | Play sports |
| 9.1 | | | | | Fishing |
| 9.0 | | | | | Art, music |
| 8.9 | | | | | Bars, lounges |
| 8.8 | Play with kids | Hug and kiss | | | |
| 8.7 | | | | | |
| 8.6 | Talk/read to kids | | | | |
| 8.5 | | Sleep | Church | | Attend movies |
| 8.4 | | | | | |
| 8.3 | | | | | Book, walk |
| 8.2 | Work break | Meals away | | | Relax, magazines, visit |
| 8.1 | | | | | |
| 8.0 | Talk with family | | | | Listen to stereo |
| 7.9 | Lunch break | | | | |
| 7.8 | Home meal | | | | TV, read paper |
| 7.7 | | | | | Knit, sew |
| 7.6 | | | | | |
| 7.5 | | | | | Recreational trip |
| 7.4 | | | | | |
| 7.3 | | Trip meal | Planning trips | | Radio, hobbies |
| 7.2 | Baby care | | Meetings | | Phone, exercise |
| 7.1 | Gardening | | Social trips | | Correspondence |
| 7.0 | Work, homework help | Bathe | | | |
| 6.9 | | | | | |
| 6.8 | | | | | |
| 6.7 | Second job | | | | |
| 6.6 | Cook, work at home | Shop | | | |
| 6.5 | | | | | |
| 6.4 | Child care | Help adults | | | |
| 6.3 | Work commute | | | | |
| 6.2 | | | | School commute | |
| 6.1 | | Dress | | | |
| 6.0 | Pet care | | | Classes | |
| 5.9 | Errands | | | | |
| 5.8 | Housework | | | | |
| 5.7 | Personal service | | | | |
| 5.6 | Unpaid work | | | | |
| 5.5 | Home repair, serve meal | Grocery shop | | | |
| 5.4 | | | | | |
| 5.3 | | | | Homework | |
| 5.2 | Pay bills, iron | | | | |
| 5.1 | | Shop for necessities, bank, post office | | | |
| 5.0 | Yardwork | | | | |
| 4.9 | Clean house, dishes | | | | |
| 4.8 | Laundry | Personal medical | | | |
| 4.7 | Child health | Doctor, dentist | | | |
| 4.6 | | Car repair shop | | | |
| 0.0 (*Dislike*) | | | | | |

SOURCE: Americans' Use of Time Project.

**Appendix P.** Items in Seven Time Zones of Zimbardo

**Factor 1: Future, work motivation—perseverance**
A.* Meeting tomorrow's deadlines and doing other necessary work comes before tonight's partying.
B. I meet my obligations to friends and authorities on time.
C. I complete projects on time by making steady progress.
D. I am able to resist temptations when I know there is work to be done.
E. I keep working at a difficult, uninteresting task if it will help me get ahead.

*All items are listed in order of their significance within each factor.

This factor embodies a positive work motivation and a stereotypically Protestant work ethic of finishing a task despite difficulties and temptations.

**Factor 2: Present, fatalistic, worry-free, avoid planning**
A. If things don't get done on time, I don't worry about it.
B. I think that it's useless to plan too far ahead because things hardly ever come out the way you planned anyway.
C. I try to live one day at a time.
D. I live to make better what is rather than to be concerned about what will be.
E. It seems to me that it doesn't make sense to worry about the future, since fate determines that whatever will be, will be.

People with this orientation live one day at a time, not to enjoy it fully but to avoid planning for the next day and to minimize anxiety about a future they perceive as being determined by fate rather than by their efforts.

**Factor 3: Present, hedonistic**
A. I believe that getting together with friends to party is one of life's important pleasures.
B. I do things impulsively, making decisions on the spur of the moment.
C. I take risks to put excitement in my life.
D. I get drunk at parties.
E. It's fun to gamble.

In contrast with the present-oriented people described by Factor 2, hedonists fill their days with pleasure-seeking, partying, taking risks, drinking and impulsive action of all kinds. Many teenagers fall into this category. Among older hedonists, gambling is often an important element.

**Factor 4: Future, goal seeking and planning**
A. Thinking about the future is pleasant to me.
B. When I want to achieve something, I set subgoals and consider specific means for reaching those goals.
C. It seems to me that my career path is pretty well laid out.

Compared to future Factor 1, the items here center less on work per se and more on the pleasure that comes from planning and achieving goals.

**Appendix P.**  Continued.

### Factor 5: Time press
A.   It upsets me to be late for appointments.
B.   I meet my obligation to friends and authorities on time.
C.   I get irritated at people who keep me waiting when we've agreed to meet at a given time.

*This factor doesn't fall neatly into a present or future orientation (although it does correlate positively with the future factors). It centers on a person's sensitivity to the role time plays in social obligations and how it can be used as a weapon in struggles for status.*

### Factor 6: Future, pragmatic action for later gain
A.   It makes sense to invest a substantial part of my income in insurance premiums.
B.   I believe that "A stitch in time saves nine."
C.   I believe that "A bird in the hand is worth two in the bush."
D.   I believe it is important to save for a rainy day.

*These people act now to achieve desirable future consequences. The item "A bird in the hand is worth two in the bush" is less characteristic of present orientation, than as advice to do or have something concrete now rather than gambling on an uncertain outcome. Thus it is a conservative strategy to safeguard future options.*

### Factor 7: Future, specific, daily planning
A.   I believe a person's day should be planned each morning.
B.   I make lists of things I must do.
C.   When I want to achieve something, I set subgoals and consider specific means for reaching those goals.
D.   I believe that "A stitch in time saves nine."

*Factor 7 describes individuals obsessed with the nitty-gritty of getting ahead. They adopt a somewhat compulsive attitude toward daily planning, make lists of things to do, set subgoals and pay attention to details.*

Source: Zimbardo, 1985.

**Appendix Q.**    Differences in Responses to Time Crunch/Stress Items by Demographic Groups in Japan

| | | Time Crunch (Q1a–h) | Day Off (Q2) | Stress (Q4) | Rushed to Do (Q5) | Free Time (hrs) (Q7) | Less Free Time (Q10) |
|---|---|---|---|---|---|---|---|
| Total Sample | (1,475) | 2.4 | 64% | 40% | 17% | 19.5 | 30% |
| Sex, Employment | | | | | | | |
| Men, nonemployed | (109) | 2.0 | NA | 29 | 12 | 29.3 | 29 |
| Men, employed | (604) | 2.4 | 55 | 42 | 19 | 29.3 | 30 |
| Women, nonemployed | (366) | 2.1 | NA | 35 | 14 | 21.5 | 24 |
| Women, employed | (386) | 2.7 | 74 | 44 | 20 | 16.5 | 36 |
| Age | | | | | | | |
| 18–24 | (178) | 2.4 | 64 | 44 | 19 | 28.3 | 57 |
| 25–34 | (259) | 2.7 | 70 | 52 | 22 | 17.8 | 54 |
| 35–44 | (343) | 2.6 | 65 | 45 | 17 | 16.3 | 32 |
| 45–54 | (311) | 2.4 | 63 | 36 | 19 | 17.2 | 18 |
| 55–64 | (230) | 2.1 | 57 | 31 | 13 | 19.0 | 13 |
| 65 + | (144) | 1.6 | 62 | 20 | 10 | 27.4 | 8 |
| Marital Status | | | | | | | |
| Married | (1,143) | 2.4 | 66 | 38 | 17 | 17.5 | 26 |
| Separated | (20) | 2.4 | 63 | 35 | 10 | 21.5 | 20 |
| Divorced | (45) | 2.2 | 60 | 37 | 11 | 24.9 | 11 |
| Unmarried | (264) | 2.4 | 64 | 48 | 20 | 27.0 | 53 |
| Education | | | | | | | |
| Elementary | (255) | 2.1 | 61 | 28 | 11 | 18.3 | 14 |
| Secondary | (682) | 2.4 | 64 | 39 | 16 | 19.4 | 30 |
| Special | (126) | 2.5 | 71 | 47 | 18 | 22.1 | 36 |
| College | (125) | 2.5 | 66 | 42 | 18 | 18.7 | 43 |
| University | (273) | 2.6 | 63 | 49 | 26 | 20.2 | 38 |
| Income | | | | | | | |
| Low | (237) | 2.4 | 64 | 38 | 17 | 21.7 | 23 |
| Low middle | (300) | 2.5 | 60 | 38 | 13 | 17.3 | 30 |
| Middle | (308) | 2.3 | 66 | 41 | 15 | 19.1 | 30 |
| High Middle | (208) | 2.4 | 66 | 43 | 24 | 19.9 | 31 |
| High | (275) | 2.5 | 63 | 42 | 24 | 21.1 | 34 |

SOURCE: Americans' Use of Time Project.

NOTE: Q = Question. See Table 28.

**Appendix R.**   Differences in Responses to Time Crunch/Stress Items by Demographic Groups in Russia

| | | Q1–10 Time Crunch | Q12 Day Off | Q14 Stress | Q16 Rushed to Do | Q21 Free Time (hrs) | Q20 Less Free Time |
|---|---|---|---|---|---|---|---|
| Total Sample | (1,196) | 2.9 | 54% | 59% | 19% | 25.6 | 30% |
| Sex, Employment | | | | | | | |
| Men, nonemployed | (155) | 2.1 | NA | 46 | 14 | 31.4 | 17 |
| Men, employed | (316) | 2.7 | 49 | 49 | 18 | 26.7 | 43 |
| Women, nonemployed | (356) | 2.5 | NA | 67 | 18 | 26.5 | 34 |
| Women, employed | (367) | 3.6 | 56 | 65 | 23 | 21.7 | 52 |
| Age | | | | | | | |
| 18–24 | (121) | 2.7 | 68 | 53 | 22 | 33.4 | 50 |
| 25–34 | (218) | 3.1 | 56 | 59 | 23 | 24.0 | 56 |
| 35–44 | (257) | 3.6 | 59 | 65 | 24 | 23.6 | 46 |
| 45–54 | (191) | 2.9 | 41 | 62 | 17 | 23.3 | 41 |
| 55–64 | (285) | 2.6 | 45 | 58 | 17 | 27.7 | 31 |
| 65 + | (202) | 2.0 | 53 | 54 | 10 | 25.8 | 16 |
| Marital Status | | | | | | | |
| Married | (669) | 2.7 | 50 | 59 | 18 | 25.8 | 33 |
| Divorced/separated | (338) | 3.4 | 57 | 62 | 21 | 22.1 | 50 |
| Never married | (112) | 2.2 | 57 | 55 | 18 | 37.3 | 44 |
| Education | | | | | | | |
| Elementary | (226) | 2.4 | 51 | 56 | 11 | 25.9 | 19 |
| Secondary | (102) | 2.9 | 41 | 61 | 15 | 24.8 | 30 |
| Technical school | (248) | 3.0 | 49 | 52 | 15 | 27.1 | 42 |
| Some college | (323) | 2.8 | 53 | 57 | 22 | 25.8 | 44 |
| University grad | (287) | 3.2 | 62 | 69 | 28 | 24.9 | 52 |
| Income | | | | | | | |
| Low | (242) | 2.4 | 65 | 58 | 13 | 26.1 | 23 |
| Low Middle | (291) | 3.1 | 58 | 61 | 17 | 24.3 | 42 |
| Middle | (236) | 2.7 | 50 | 58 | 20 | 25.9 | 42 |
| High Middle | (115) | 3.3 | 44 | 56 | 19 | 24.8 | 47 |
| High | (177) | 3.1 | 56 | 65 | 27 | 25.5 | 51 |

SOURCE: Americans' Use of Time Project.

NOTE: Q = Question. See Table 30.

**Appendix S.**    How to Read Table 17

Each entry in Table 17 (page 190) indicates the extent of correlation between a background factor and the activity in question. The more the +'s or −'s in the entry, the stronger the correlation between that background factor and that group's way of spending time. Thus, the − − − entry for gender and paid work means that men spend much more of their time on paid work than women do. The direction of the relationship is denoted by whether + or − signs are used. For gender, the + sign means women do more of the activity than men. The number of +'s or −'s reflects how strong the relation is. For example, for work (the first row) the largest differences are obviously found by estimated length of the workweek and days of the week. Men work much longer hours a week than women (9 hours a week overall). People with higher education, income, and occupation work slightly more hours, while those with preschool children work less. Differences in work time by race, marital status, children under 18, season, housing, and urbanicity are negligible.

In general, a single + (or −) indicates values for that group that are about 50 to 100 percent above or below average; two +'s indicate figures roughly 100 to 200 percent above average; 3 +'s, 200 to 300 percent above, and 3 +'s indicate figures more than 300 percent above average. (In correlational terms, one + indicates a correlation roughly in the +.05–.09 range, two correlations of .10–.19, three correlations of .20–.29 and four correlations of .30 and above.) (For sleep and other less invariant activities, differences of 10 to 20 percent above average may be noted, because of the large amounts of time involved.) The positive or negative sign refers to the direction of the correlation as noted in the second row of the table. Thus, a + entry denotes more time spent by women, by older people, by blacks, by those with more education, higher income, higher status jobs, the married, parents with more children, rural residents, during the summer and on weekends.

# References

ACTION. 1975. *Americans Volunteer*. Washington, D.C.: Government Printing Office.

Alberta Centre for Well-Being. 1989. *Newsletter*. Edmonton: University of Alberta.

Allen, C. 1968. "Photographing the TV Audience." *Journal of Advertising Research* 8, no. 1:8.

Anderson, W. T. 1990. *Reality Isn't What It Used to Be*. San Francisco: HarperCollins.

Andrews, F., and J. Robinson. 1991. "Measures of Psychological Well-Being." In J. Robinson, P. Shaver, and L. Wrightsman, eds., *Measures of Personality and Social Psychological Attitudes*. San Diego: Academic Press.

Andrews, F., and S. B. Withey. 1976. *Social Indicators of Well-Being in America*. New York: Plenum.

Andrews, F., J. Morgan, J. Sonquist, and L. Klem. 1973. *Multiple Classification Analysis: A Report on a Computer Program for Multiple Regression Using Categorical Predictors*. Ann Arbor: Institute for Social Research, University of Michigan.

Aschoff, J. 1974. "Free-Time Within the Framework of Biological Program(me)s." In *Leisure Activities in the Industrial Society*, 125–44. Brussels: Foundation Van Cle.

Ausubel, J., and A. Grubler. 1994. "Working Less and Living Longer: Long-Term Trends in Working Time and Time Budgets." Working Paper 94–99. Laxenburg, Austria: International Institute for Applied Systems Analysis.

Barker, R., and L. Barker. 1961. "Behavior Units for the Comparative Study of Cultures." In B. Kaplan, ed., *Studying Personality Cross-Culturally*. Evanston, Ill.: Row, Petersen.

Barker, R., and H. Wright. 1948. *One Boy's Day*. New York: Harper.

Bates, T. 1988. "Book Review: *Blacks and Whites: Narrowing the Gap?*" *Review of Black Political Economy* 16 (Winter): 115–20.

Bechtel, R., C. Achepohl, and R. Akers. 1972. "Correlates Between Observed Behavior and Questionnaire Responses in Television Viewing." In E. A. Rubenstein, G. A. Comstock, and J. P. Murray, eds., *Television and Social Behavior, Reports and Papers*, vol. 4: *Television in Day-to-Day Life: Patterns and Use*, 274–344. Washington, D.C.: Government Printing Office.

Becker, G. S. 1965. "A Theory of the Allocation of Time." *Economic Journal* 75:493–517.

———. 1975. "The Clock Watchers: Americans at Work." *Time*, September 8, 55.

Bell, D. 1976. *The Coming of the Post-Industrial Society: A Venture in Social Forecasting*. 2d ed. New York: Basic Books.

Bellah, R., et al. 1985. *Habits of the Heart: Individualism and Commitment in American Life*. Berkeley and Los Angeles: University of California Press.

Bem, S. 1974. "The Measurement of Psychological Androgyny." *Journal of Consulting and Clinical Psychology* 42:155–62.

Berk, R. A., and S. F. Berk. 1979. *Labor and Leisure at Home: Content and Organization of the Household Day*. Beverly Hills, Calif.: Sage Publications.

Berk, S. F. 1985. *The Gender Factory: The Apportionment of Work in American Households*. New York: Plenum.

Berry, Leonard. 1990. "Market to the Perception." *American Demographics* 12 (February 1990): 32.

Bianchi, S., et al. 1999. "Is Anyone Doing the Housework?" Paper presented at the Annual Meeting of the American Sociological Association, August.

Bianchi, S., and D. Spain. 1996. "Women, Work, and Family in America." *Population Bulletin* 51, no. 3. Washington, D.C.: Population Reference Bureau.

Bishop, D., C. Jeanrenaud, and K. Lawson. 1975. "Comparison of a Time Diary and Recall Questionnaire for Surveying Leisure Activities." *Journal of Leisure Research* 7:73–80.

Bittman, M. 1998. "The Land of the Long Lost Weekend: Trends in Free Time Among Working Age Australians, 1974–1992." *Society and Leisure* 21, no. 2:353–79.

Blum, A. 1964. "Lower-Class Television Spectators." In A. Shostak and W. Gomberg, eds., *Blue-Collar World*, 429–35. Englewood Cliffs: N.J.: Prentice-Hall.

Bond, M. J., and N. T. Feather. 1988. "Some Correlates of Structure and Purpose in the Use of Time." *Journal of Personality Social Psychology* 55, no. 2:321–29.

Bose, C. 1979. "Technology and Changes in the Division of Labor in the American Home." *Women's Studies International Quarterly* 2:295–304.

Bourdieu, P. 1977. *The Inheritors: French Students and Their Relation to Culture*. Chicago: University of Chicago Press.

Bower, R. 1973. *Television and the Public*. New York: Holt.

Branch, E., and C. Williams. 1988. "20 Years After Kerner: Two Separate Societies— Still." *Black Enterprise* 18 (May 10): 35.

Bryce, H. 1973. Letters from Readers. "On the Nature of Black Progress." *Commentary* 56 (August): 4–19.

Bureau of Labor Statistics. 1965. *Marital and Family Characteristics of the Labor Force*. Special Labor Force Report No. 64. Washington, D.C.: Government Printing Office.

———. 1976. *Employment and Earnings*, vol. 23, no. 3 (September). Washington, D.C.: Government Printing Office.

———. 1986. *Monthly Labor Review* 109, no. 1 (November).

Burke, P. J., and S. L. Franzui. 1988. "Studying Situations and Identities Using Experiential Sampling Methodology." *American Sociological Review* 53 (August): 359–68.

Burns, L. 1993. *Busybodies—Why Our Time-Obsessed Society Keeps Us Running in Place*. New York: Norton.

Campbell, A., P. Converse, and W. Rodgers. 1976. *The Quality of American Life*. New York: Russell Sage.

Chapin, S. 1974. *Human Activity Patterns in the City: Things People Do in Time and Space*. New York: Wiley.

Chase, D., and G. Godbey. 1983. "The Accuracy of Self-Reported Participation Rates: A Research Note." *Leisure Studies* 2:231–33.

Clarke, J., and C. Critcher. 1985. *The Devil Makes Work: Leisure in Capitalistic Britain*. Champaign: University of Illinois Press.

Coffin, T. 1955. "Television's Impact on Society." *American Psychologist* 10 (October): 630–41.

Cohen, E. 1972. "Toward a Sociology of International Tourism." *Social Research* 39, no. 1:1–19.

Coleman, J. 1982. *Foundations of Social Theory.* Cambridge, Mass.: Harvard University Press.

Converse, P. 1972. "Country Differences in Time Use." In A. Szalai et al., *The Use of Time,* 145–79. The Hague: Mouton.

Cook, T. 1975. *Sesame Street Revisited.* New York: Russell Sage.

Coontz, S. 1992. *The Way We Never Were: American Families and the Nostalgia Trap.* New York: HarperCollins, 1992.

Cotton, J. 1989. "The Declining Relative Economic Status of Black Families." *Review of Black Political Economy* 18 (Summer): 75–85.

Cross, G. 1990. *A Social History of Leisure Since 1600.* State College, Pa.: Venture.

———. 1993. *Time and Money: The Making of Consumer Culture.* London: Routledge.

Csikszentmihalyi, M. 1991. *Flow: The Psychology of Optimal Experience.* New York: HarperCollins.

de Beauvoir, S. 1974. *The Second Sex.* New York: Knopf.

De Grazia, S. 1962. *Of Time, Work, and Leisure.* New York: Twentieth Century Fund.

Deem, R. 1986. *All Work and No Play? The Sociology of Women and Leisure.* Milton Keynes, Eng.: Open University Educational Enterprises.

Editors of *Research Alert.* 1992. *Future Vision: The 189 Most Important Trends of the 1990s.* Naperville, Ill.: Sourcebooks Trade.

Etzioni, A. 1991. *The Consumption of Time and the Timing of Consumption.* New York: North-Holland.

———. 1993. *The Spirit of Community: Rights, Responsibilities, and the New Communitarian Agenda.* New York: Crown.

Farley, R. 1984. *Blacks and Whites: Narrowing the Gap?* Cambridge, Mass.: Harvard University Press.

Felder, H. 1984. *The Changing Patterns of Black Family Income, 1960–1982.* Washington, D.C.: Joint Center for Political Studies.

Fenstermaker, S. 1991. "Gender Inequalities, New Conceptual Terrain." In R. L. Blumberg, C. West, and D. Zimmerman, eds., *Gender, Family, and Economy: The Triple Overlap,* 289–307. Beverly Hills, Calif.: Sage Publications.

———. 1996. "The Dynamics of Time Use: Context and Meaning." *Journal of Family and Economic Issues* 17, no. 4, 231–43.

Ferber, M. A., and B. G. Birnbaum. 1977. "The New Home Economics: Retrospect and Prospects." *Journal of Consumer Research* 4:19–28.

Ferber, R., ed. 1981. "Consumption of Time," *Journal of Consumer Research* 7 (special issue): 4.

Fisher, S. 1992. *From Margin to Mainstream: The Social Progress of Black Americans.* 2d ed. Lanham, Md.: Rowman & Littlefield.

Fitzgerald, F. S., quoted in R. Boyle. 1962. "The Bizarre History of American Sport." *Sports Illustrated,* January 8, 62.

Fraisse, P. 1964. *The Psychology of Time.* English trans. London: Eyre & Spottiswoode.

Fraser, J. T. 1987. *Time: The Familiar Stranger.* Redmond, Wash.: Microsoft Press.

Freeman, R. 1976. *Black Elite: The New Market for Highly Educated Black Americans.* New York: McGraw-Hill.

Galbraith, J. K. 1984. *The Affluent Society.* 4th ed. Boston: Houghton-Mifflin.

Gaziano, C. 1983. "The Knowledge Gap. An Analytical Review of Media Effects." *Communication Research* 10, no. 4, 447–86.

Gerbner, G., L. Gross, M. Morgan, and N. Signiovelli. 1980. "The Mainstreaming of America: Violence Profile #1." *Journal of Communications* 30 (Summer): 10–29.

Gergen, K. 1991. *The Saturated Self—Dilemmas of Identity in Contemporary Life*. New York: Basic Books.

Gershuny, J. 1990. "The Multinational Longitudinal Time Budget Data Archive." European Foundation for the Improvement of Living and Working Conditions, Dublin.

———. 1992. "Are We Running Out of Time?" *Future*, January–February.

Gershuny, J., et al. 1986. "Time Budgets: Preliminary Analyses of a National Survey." *Quarterly Journal of Social Affairs* 2.

Gershuny, J., and J. Robinson. 1988. "Historical Changes in the Household Division of Labor." *Demography* 25, no. 47: 537–53.

Gerson, M. 1997. "Do Do-Gooders Do Much Good?" *U.S. News & World Report*, April 28, 25–34.

Giddens, A. 1987. "Time and Space in Social Theory." *Social Science* 72 (Fall): 99–103.

Gilder, G. 1994. *Life After Television: The Coming Transformation of Media and American Life*. New York: Norton.

Gitlin, Todd, ed. 1986. *Watching Television*. New York: Pantheon.

Glazer, N. 1978. *Affirmative Discrimination: Ethnic Inequality and Public Policy*. New York: Basic Books.

Godbey, G. 1985. *Leisure in Your Life: An Exploration*. 2d ed. State College, Pa.: Venture.

———. 1989. "Anti-Leisure and Public Recreation Policy." In Fred Coalter, ed., *Freedom and Constraint: The Paradoxes of Leisure*, 74–87. London: Routledge.

———. 1993a. "Time, Work, and Leisure: Trends That Will Shape the Hospitality Industry." *Hospitality Research Journal: The Futures Issue* 17, no. 1: 49–59.

———. 1993b. "What Does Leisure Mean?" *Issues in Science and Technology*, Fall, 13–14.

———. 1994a. *Leisure in Your Life: An Exploration*. 4th ed. State College, Pa.: Venture.

———. 1994b. "The Problem Is Not Too Little Time, It's That People Want Too Much." *Baltimore Sun*, June 26, 4.

Godbey, G., and A. Graefe. 1993a. "Rapid Growth in Rushin' Americans." *American Demographics*, April, 26–27.

———. 1993b. "Reality and Perception—Where Do We Fit In?" *Parks and Recreation*, January, 76–98.

Godbey, G., A. Graefe, and S. James. 1992. *The Benefits of Local Recreation and Park Services: A Nationwide Study of the Perceptions of the American Public*. National Recreation and Park Association. Arlington, Va.

Goldschmidt-Clermont, C., and E. Pagnossin-Aligisakis. 1995. "Measures of Unrecorded Activities in Fourteen Countries." In *Human Development Report #20*. New York: United Nations Development Report Office.

Goodale, T., and G. Godbey. 1988. *The Evolution of Leisure: Historical and Philosophical Perspective*. State College, Pa.: Venture.

Gottlieb, N. 1957. "Neighborhood Taverns and Cocktail Lounges." *American Journal of Sociology* 62 (May): 559–62.

Graham, E., and C. Crossan. 1996. "Too Much to Do, Too Little Time." *Wall Street Journal*, March 8, R1–R4.

Grof, S. quoted in Capra, F. 1988. *Uncommon Wisdom: Conversations with Remarkable People*. New York: Simon & Schuster.

Gruenberg, B. 1974. "How Free Is Free Time? An Analysis of Some Determinants of Leisure Activity Patterns." Ph.D. diss., University of Michigan.

Gutenschwager, G. 1973. "The Time-Budget-Activity Systems Perspective in Urban Research and Planning." *Journal of the American Institute of Planners* 39:378–87.

Hadaway, C. I., P. Marler, and M. Chaves. 1993. "What the Polls Don't Show: A Closer Look at U.S. Church Attendance." *American Sociological Review* 58:741–52.

Hamilton, R. 1991. "Work and Leisure: On the Reporting of Poll Results." *Public Opinion Quarterly* 55:347–56.

Handy, C. 1989. *The Age of Unreason*. London: Arrow Books.

Harding, V. 1981. *There Is a River: The Black Struggle for Freedom in America*. New York: Vintage.

Harper, J., D. Neider, and G. Godbey. 1996. *The Use and Benefits of Local Government Recreation and Park Services: A Canadian Perspective*. Winnipeg: University of Manitoba.

Harris, L. 1987. *Inside America*. New York: Vintage.

Harris and Associates. 1988. "Americans and the Arts, V." Study 871009. New York: Harris & Associates.

Harvey, A., and D. Elliot. 1983. *Time and Time Again*. Ottawa-Hull: Employment and Immigration Commission.

Hawes, D., W. Talarzyk, and R. Blackwell. 1975. "Consumer Satisfactions from Leisure Time Pursuits." In M. Schlinger, ed., *Advances in Consumer Research*. Chicago: Association for Consumer Research.

Hedges, J. 1992. "The Overworked American: A Book Review," *Monthly Labor Review* 51 (May): 2.

Heirich, M. 1964. "The Use of Time in the Study of Social Change." *American Sociological Review* 29:386–97.

Henderson, K., M. D. Bialeschki, S. M. Shaw, and V. Freysinger. 1989. *A Leisure of One's Own: A Feminist Perspective on Women's Leisure*. State College, Pa.: Venture.

Hill, D. 1985. "Implications of Home Production and Inventory Adjustment Processes for Time-of-Day Demand for Electricity." In F. T. Juster and F. P. Stafford, eds., *Time, Goods, and Well-Being*, 493–513. Ann Arbor: Institute for Social Research, University of Michigan.

Hill, D. H., ed. 1982. "Analysis of Residential Response to Time-of-Day Prices." Palo Alto, Calif.: Electric Power Research Institute.

Hill, M. 1985. "Patterns of Time Use." In F. T. Juster and F. P. Stafford, eds., *Time, Goods, and Well-Being*, 133–76. Ann Arbor: Institute for Social Research, University of Michigan.

Hill, R. B. 1978. *The Illusion of Black Progress*. Washington, D.C.: National Urban League, Research Department.

———. 1981. *Economic Policies and Black Progress: Myths and Realities*. Washington, D.C.: National Urban League, Research Development.

Hilton Organization. 1991. "Americans Want More Time." Los Angeles: Hilton Hotel Corporation.

Hochschild, A. 1989. *The Second Shift: Working Parents and the Revolution at Home*. New York: Viking.

———. 1997. *The Time Bind*. New York: Henry Holt & Company.

Howe, N., and B. Strauss. 1993. *13 gen—Abort, Retry, Ignore, Fail?* New York: Random House.

Hunnicutt, B. 1988. *Work Without End: Abandoning Shorter Hours for the Right to Work.* Philadelphia: Temple University Press.

Hyman, H., and P. Sheatsley. 1948. "Some Reasons Why Information Campaigns Fail." *Public Opinion Quarterly* 11, 412–23.

Jaynes, G., and R. Williams Jr., eds. 1981. *A Common Destiny: Blacks and American Society.* Washington, D.C.: National Academy Press.

Johnson, A., and O. Johnson. 1978. "In Search of the Affluent Society." *Human Nature,* September, 50–59.

Juster, F. T. 1985. "The Validity and Quality of Time Use Estimates Obtained from Recall Diaries." In F. T. Juster and F. P. Stafford, eds., *Time, Goods, and Well-Being,* 63–92. Ann Arbor: Institute for Social Research, University of Michigan.

Juster, F. T., and F. P. Stafford, eds. 1985. *Time, Goods, and Well-Being.* Ann Arbor: Institute for Social Research, University of Michigan.

Kaufmann, W. 1956. *Existentialism from Dostoevsky to Sartre.* New York: Meridian Books.

Kelly, J., and G. Godbey. 1992. *The Sociology of Leisure.* State College, Pa.: Venture.

Kerner, O., et al. 1968. *Report of the National Advisory Commission on Civil Disorders.* Washington, D.C.: National Advisory Commission on Civil Disorders.

Kerr, W. 1962. *The Decline of Pleasure.* New York: Simon & Schuster.

Kohut, A. 1995. *Technology in the American Household.* Washington, D.C.: Times-Mirror Center for the People and the Press.

Kolbert, E. 1993. "Racial Gap in Television Viewing Habits Widened." *New York Times,* April 5, D7.

Kubey, R., and M. Csikszentmihalyi. 1990. *Television and the Quality of Life.* Hillsdale, N.J.: Erlbaum.

Kunstler, J. H. 1993. *The Geography of Nowhere: The Rise and Decline of America's Man-Made Landscape.* New York: Simon & Schuster.

Lappe, F., and P. DuBois. 1994. *The Quickening of America: Rebuilding Our Nation, Remaking Our Lives.* San Francisco: Jossey-Bass.

Lasch, C. 1979. *The Culture of Narcissism.* New York: Warner Books.

Leete, L., and J. Schor. 1994. "Assessing the Time-Squeeze Hypothesis: Hours Worked in the United States, 1969–89." *Industrial Relations* 33 (January): 25–43.

Levine, R. 1984. "The Type-A City: Coronary Heart Disease and the Pace of Life." *Journal of Behavioral Medicine* 12, no. 6:24–33.

———. 1985. "Social Time: The Heartbeat of Culture." *Psychology Today,* March, 28–35.

———. 1990. "The Pace of Life." *American Scientist,* September–October, 449–60.

———. 1993. "Cities with Heart." *American Demographics,* October, 46–54.

Lewin, R. 1980. "An Introduction of Affluence." In J. Cherfas and R. Lewin, eds., *Not Work Alone: A Cross Cultural View of Activities Superfluous to Survival,* 14–16. Beverly Hills, Calif.: Sage Publications.

Liebow, E. 1967. *Talley's Corner: A Study of Negro Streetcorner Men.* Boston: Little, Brown.

Light, P. 1988. *Baby Boomers.* New York: Norton.

Linder, S. 1970. *The Harried Leisure Class.* New York: Columbia University Press.

Lundberg, G., M. Komavovsky, and M. McInerny. 1934. *Leisure: A Suburban Study.* New York: Columbia University Press.

Marini, M., and B. A. Shelton. 1993. "Measuring Household Work: Recent Experience in the United States." *Social Science Research,* 361–85.

Masnick, G., and Bane, M. 1980. *The Nation's Families: 1960–1990*. Cambridge, Mass.: Joint Center for Urban Studies of MIT and Harvard University.

Mata-Greenwood, A. 1992. "An Integrated Framework for the Measurement of Working Time." STAT Working Paper No. 92. Geneva: International Labor Organization.

Mattox, W. 1990. "America's Family Time Famine." *Children Today*, November–December 9.

McLuhan, M. 1964. *Understanding Media: The Extensions of Man*. New York: McGraw-Hill.

McSweeney, B. 1980. "Lack of Time as an Obstacle to Women: The Case of Upper Volta." *Comparative Education Review* 24, no. 2, 124–39.

Mead, M. 1958. "The Patterns of Leisure in Contemporary American Culture." In E. Larrabee and R. Meyersohn, eds., *Mass Leisure*, 11–12. Glencoe, Ill.: The Free Press.

Meyersohn, R. 1968. "Television and the Rest of Leisure." *Public Opinion Quarterly* 32:102–12.

Michael, R., et al. 1994. *Sex in America: A Definitive Survey*. Boston: Little, Brown.

Michelson, W., ed. 1978. *Public Policy in Temporal Perspective*. The Hague: Mouton.

Morgan, J. N., I. Sirageldin, and N. Baerwaldt. 1966. *Productive Americans*. Ann Arbor: Institute for Social Research, University of Michigan.

Morrison, T. 1996. "Let Go." *Utne Reader Almanac*. Minneapolis: Utne Reader Press.

Moynihan, D. P. 1972. "The Schism in Black America." *Public Interest* 27:3–24.

Myrdal, G. 1944, 1962. *An American Dilemma*. New York: Harper & Row.

Nakanishi, N. 1982a. "Changes in Mass Media Contact Times: Analysis of Results of National Time Use Survey." Tokyo: Public Opinion Research Institute, Japan Broadcasting Corporation (Nippon Hoso Kyokai).

———. 1982b. "A Report on the 'How Do People Spend Their Time' Survey in 1980." Reprinted from *Studies of Broadcasting*, no. 18:93–113.

Neuman, R. 1982. "Television and American Culture: Multiple Messages and Pluralistic Audiences." *Public Opinion Quarterly* 46:471–87.

Nielsen Organization. 1975. *Nielsen Television '75*. Northbrook, Ill.: A. C. Nielsen.

———. 1976. *The Television Audience: 1976*. New York: A. C. Nielsen.

Niemi, I. 1983. "Systematic Bias in Hours Worked?" Prepared for the 1982 Workshop on Time Budgets, Institute for Social Research, University of Michigan, Ann Arbor. Published in *Statistisk Tidakrikt* (Statistical Review), vol. 4 (Stockholm).

———. 1990. *Measuring Work Activities and Hours Worked*. (International Labor Office Workshop on Household Surveys of Labor Force for Eastern and Central Europe) Geneva: International Labor Organization.

Ornstein, R., and P. Erlich. 1989. *New World, New Mind: Moving Toward Conscious Evolution*. New York: Doubleday.

Ostrow, R. J. 1993. "New Report Echoes 'Two Societies' Warning of 1968 Kerner Commission." *Los Angeles Times*, February 28.

Owen, J. 1969. *The Price of Leisure*. Rotterdam: Rotterdam University Press.

———. 1976. "Workweeks and Leisure: An Analysis of Trends, 1948–75." *Monthly Labor Review* 99, no. 4:3–8.

Owen, J. 1979. *Working Hours: An Economic Analysis*. Lexington, Mass.: D. C. Heath.

———. 1988. "Work-Time Reduction in the U.S. and Western Europe." *Monthly Labor Review* 3:41–45.

———. 1989. *Reduced Workhours: Cure for Unemployment or Economic Burden?* Baltimore: Johns Hopkins University Press.

Parker, S. 1972. *The Future of Work and Leisure*. New York: Praeger.

Parkinson, C. N. 1962. *Parkinson's Law; or, The Pursuit of Progress*. New York: Penguin.

Peele, S. 1989. *Diseasing of America: Addiction Treatment Out of Control*. New York: Lexington Books.

Pinkney, A. 1984. *The Myth of Black Progress*. Cambridge: Cambridge University Press.

Postman, N. 1985. *Amusing Ourselves to Death: Public Discourse in the Age of Show Business*. New York: Viking.

Presser, H. 1995. "Are the Interests of Women Inherently at Odds with the Interests of Children or the Family? A Viewpoint." In K. Mason and A. Jensen, eds., *Gender and Family Change in Industrialized Countries*, 279–319. New York: Oxford University Press.

Presser, S., and L. Stinson. 1996. "Estimating the Bias in Survey Reports of Religious Attendance." *Proceedings of the American Association of Public Opinion Research* (in press).

Putnam, R. 1995a. "Bowling Alone: America's Declining Social Capital." *Journal of Democracy* 6 (January): 65–78.

———. 1995b. "Tuning In, Tuning Out: The Strange Disappearance of Social Capital in America." *P.S.*, December.

*Random House College Dictionary, Revised Edition*. 1988. New York: Random House.

*Random House Thesaurus, College Edition*. 1989. New York: Random House.

Reiss, A. 1959. "Rural-Urban and Status Differences in Interpersonal Contacts." *American Journal of Sociology* 75:182–95.

Rheingold, H. 1993. *The Virtual Community: Homesteading on the Electronic Frontier*. New York: HarperCollins.

Riesman, D. 1953. *Thorstein Veblen: A Critical Interpretation*. New York: Scribner's.

———. 1958. "Leisure and Work in Post-Industrial Society." In E. Larabee and R. Meyersohn, eds., *Mass Leisure*. Glencoe, Ill.: The Free Press.

Rifkin, J. 1987. *Time Wars: The Primary Conflict in Human History*. New York: Holt.

———. 1995. *The End of Work*. New York: Tarcher-Putnam.

Robinson, J. 1968. "World Affairs Information and Mass Media Exposure." *Journalism Quarterly* 44 (Spring): 23–30.

———. 1969. "Television and Leisure Time: Yesterday, Today, and (Maybe) Tomorrow." *Public Opinion Quarterly* 33 (Summer): 210–22.

———. 1971a. "The Audience for National TV News Programs." *Public Opinion Quarterly* 35:302–405.

———. 1971b. "Mass Media Usage by the College Graduate." In Stephen Withey, ed., *A Degree and What Else*. New York: McGraw-Hill.

———. 1972a. "The Impact of Television on Mass Media Usage." In A. Szalai et al., *The Use of Time*, 491–807. The Hague: Mouton.

———. 1972b. "Television's Impact on Everyday Life: Some Cross-National Evidence." In E. Rubinstein et al., *Television and Social Behavior*, 410–31. Washington, D.C.: Government Printing Office.

———. 1976. *Changes in Americans' Use of Time, 1965–1975*. Cleveland: Communication Research Center.

———. 1977a. *How Americans Use Time: A Social-Psychological Analysis of Everyday Behavior*. New York: Praeger. (More detailed calculations and documentation are in "How Americans Used Time in 1965–75." Ann Arbor: University of Michigan, University Microfilms, Monograph Series.)

———. 1977b. "The New Household Economics: Sexist, Unrealistic, or Simply Irrelevant?" *Journal of Consumer Research* 4 (December): 178–81.

———. 1978a. "Massification and Democratization of the Leisure Class." *Annals of the American Academy of Political and Social Science*, January, 206–25.

———. 1978b. "Time Use as a Social Indicator." In William Michelson, ed., *Public Policy in Temporal Perspective*, 103–12. The Hague: Mouton.

———. 1980a. "British-American Differences in the Use of Time." *Loisir et Société* 3, no. 2:281–98.

———. 1980b. "Household Technology and Household Work." In S. F. Berk, ed., *Women and Household Labor*, 53–67. Beverly Hills, Calif.: Sage Publications.

———. 1981a. "Television and Leisure Time: A New Scenario." *Journal of Communication* 31, no. 1:120–30.

———. 1981b. "The Changing Reading Habits of the American Public," *Journal of Communication*, January, 141–52.

———. 1981c. "Will the New Electronic Media Revolutionize Our Daily Lives?" In Robert Haigh et al., eds., *Communications in the Twenty-First Century*, 66–67. New York: Wiley-Interscience.

———. 1982. "Of Time, Dual Careers, and Household Productivity." *Family Economics Review* 3:26–30.

———. 1983. "Environmental Differences in How Americans Use Time: The Case for Subjective and Objective Indicators," *Journal of Community Psychology*, April, 171–80.

———. 1984. "Work, Free Time, and Quality of Life." In M. Lee and R. Kanungro, eds., *Management of Work and Personal Life*, 133–42. New York: Praeger.

———. 1985a. "Changes in Time Use: An Historical Overview." In F. T. Juster and F. P. Stafford, eds., *Time, Goods, and Well-Being*, 289–312. Ann Arbor: Institute for Social Research, University of Michigan.

———. 1985b. "The Validity and Reliability of Diaries versus Alternative Time Use Measures." In T. F. Juster and F. P. Stafford, eds., *Time, Goods, and Well-Being*, 33–62. Ann Arbor: Institute for Social Research, University of Michigan.

———. 1987a. "Microbehavioral Approaches to Monitoring Human Experience." *Journal of Nervous and Mental Disorders* 175, no. 9:514–18.

———. 1987b. "The Arts in America." *American Demographics*, September, 434–37.

———. 1988. "Who's Doing the Housework?" *American Demographics*, December, 24–28.

———. 1989a. "Caring for Kids." *American Demographics*, July.

———. 1989b. "Survey Organization Differences in Estimating Public Participation in the Arts." *Public Opinion Quarterly* 53 (Fall): 397–414.

———. 1989c. "Television and Children's Activity Patterns." In *Television and Children*. New York: Children's Television Workshop.

———. 1989d. "Time for Work." *American Demographics*, April, 68.

———. 1989e. "Time's Up." *American Demographics* 13 (July): 33–35.

———. 1989f. "When the Going Gets Tough." *American Demographics*, February, 50.

———. 1990. "Television's Effect on Families' Use of Time." In Jennings Bryant, ed., *Television and the American Family*, 195–209. Hillsdale, N.J.: Erlbaum.

———. 1991a. "Quitting Time: Activity Patterns of Older Americans." *American Demographics*, March, 34–36.

———. 1991b. "Your Time or Your Money." *American Demographics*, November, 22–26.

———. 1993a. "As We Like It." *American Demographics*, February, 26–28.

———. 1993b. "Life's Good in Holland." *American Demographics*, September, 36–42.

———. 1993c. "Rapid Growth in Rushin' Americans." *American Demographics*, April, 26–28.

———. 1993d. " 'Round Midnight." *American Demographics*, June, 44–49.

———. 1993e. "Arts Participation in America, 1982–1992." Washington, D.C., National Endowment for the Arts (Research Report no. 27).

———. 1994. *The Demographics of Time*. Ithaca, N.Y.: American Demographics.

Robinson, J., and S. Bianchi. 1997a. "What Did You Do Today? Children's Use of Time, Family Composition, and the Acquisition of Social Capital." *Journal of Marriage and the Family* 59 (May).

———. 1997b. "Children's Hours." *American Demographics* 19 (October): 20–24.

Robinson, J., and J. Blair. 1995. *The National Macroenvironmental Activity Pattern Survey (Preliminary Report)*. Washington, D.C.: Environmental Protection Agency.

Robinson, J., and A. Bostrom. 1994. "The Overestimated Workweek? What Time Diary Measures Suggest." *Monthly Labor Review*, August, 11–23.

Robinson, J., and P. Converse. 1972. "Social Change as Reflected in the Use of Time." In A. Campbell and P. Converse, eds., *The Human Meaning of Social Change*, 17–86. New York: Russell Sage Foundation.

Robinson, J., and D. Davis. 1989. "News Flow and Democratic Society in an Age of Electronic Media." In *Public Communication and Behavior* 2:60–102. New York: Academic Press.

Robinson, J., and J. Gershuny. 1994. "Measuring Hours of Paid Work: Time-Diary vs. Estimate Questions." *Bulletin of Labor Statistics*, xi–xvii. Geneva: International Labor Office.

Robinson, J., and G. Godbey. 1978. "Work and Leisure: How We Spend Our Time." *Leisure Today*, October, 27–28.

———. 1993a. "Sports, Fitness, and the Gender Gap." *Leisure Sciences* 15, no. 4:291–308.

———. 1993b. "Has Fitness Peaked?" *American Demographics*, September, 36–43.

———. 1995. "Are Americans Really Overworked?" *American Enterprise*, September–October, 43.

———. 1996. "The Great American Slowdown." *American Demographics*, June, 42–48.

———. 1998. "No Sex Please . . . We're College Graduates." *American Demographics* 20 (February): 18–23.

Robinson, J., and L. Jeffres. 1980. "Participation in Mass Media Consumption." In D. Smith and J. Macaulay, eds., *Participation in Social and Political Activities*, 257–77. San Francisco: Jossey-Bass.

———. 1981. "The Great Age-Readership Mystery." *Journalism Quarterly* 58, no. 2:219–24.

Robinsin. J., and M. Kestnbaum. 1999. "The Personal Computer, Culture, and Other Uses of Free Time." *Social Science Computer Review* 15 (Summer): 209–16.

Robinson, J., and M. Levy. 1986. *The Main Source: Learning from Television News*. Beverly Hills, Calif.: Sage Publications.

Robinson, J., and F. Nicosia. 1991. "Of Time, Activity, and Consumer Behavior." *Journal of Business Research* 22:171–86.

Robinson, J., and H. Sahin. 1981. "Beyond the Realm of Necessity: Television and the Colonization of Leisure." *Media, Culture, and Society* 3:85–95.

Robinson, J., V. Andreyenkov, and V. Patrushev. 1989. *The Rhythm of Everyday Life: How Soviet and American Citizens Spend Time*. Boulder, Colo.: Westview.

Robinson, J. R., Athanasiou, and K. Head. 1969. *Measures of Occupational Attitudes*. Ann Arbor: Institute for Social Research, University of Michigan.

Robinson, J., P. Converse, and A. Szalai. 1972. "Everyday Life in Twelve Countries." In A. Szalai et al., *The Use of Time*, 113–44. The Hague: Mouton.

Robinson, J., S. Levin, and B. Hak. 1998. "Computer Time." *American Demographics* 20 (August): 18–23.

Robinson, J., W. Ott, and P. Switzer. 1996. "Daily Exposure to Environment Tobacco Smoke." *American Journal of Public Health* 86 (September): 1303–5.

Robinson, J., P. Shaver, and L. Wrightsman. 1991. *Measures of Personality and Social Psychological Attitudes*. New York: Academic Press.

Robinson, J., T. Triplett, et al. 1985. *Americans' Participation in the Arts*. Washington, D.C.: National Endowment for the Arts Research Division.

Robinson, J., P. Werner, and G. Godbey. 1997. "Freeing Up the Golden Years." *American Demographics* 19 (October): 20–24.

Roper, B. J. 1975. *Trends in Public Attitudes Toward Television and Other Media, 1959–1974*. New York: Television Information Office.

Roper Reports. 1995. No. 95-10. New York: Roper Starch Worldwide.

Rybczynski, W. 1991. *Waiting for the Weekend*. New York: Viking.

Sahlins, M. 1972. *Stone Age Economics*. New York: Aldine Atherton.

Samuelson, R. 1995. *The Good Life and Its Discontents: The American Dream in the Age of Entitlement, 1945–1995*. New York: Times Books.

Scheuch, E. 1972. "The Time-Budget Interview." In A. Szalai et al., *The Use of Time*, 69–89. The Hague: Mouton.

Schor, J. 1991. *The Overworked American*. New York: Basic Books.

Schuman, H., et al. 1985. "Effort and Reward: The Assumption That College Grades Are Affected by Quantity of Study." *Social Forces*, 945–66.

Smith, J. P., and F. R. Welch. 1986. *Closing the Gap: Forty Years of Economic Progress for Blacks*. Santa Monica, Calif.: Rand Corporation.

Sobel, J., and R. Ornstein. 1987. *Healthy Pleasures*. New York: Addison-Wesley.

Sorokin, P., and C. Berger. 1939. *Time-Budgets of Human Behavior*. Cambridge, Mass.: Harvard University Press.

Sowell, Thomas. 1981. *Ethnic America*. New York: Basic Books.

Spring, J. 1993. "Seven Days of Play." *American Demographics*, March, 50–56.

Stone, P. J. 1972a. "Child Care in Twelve Countries." In A. Szalai et al., *The Use of Time*, 249–65. The Hague: Mouton.

———. 1972b. "Models of Everyday Time Allocation." In A. Szalai et al., *The Use of Time*, 179–91. The Hague: Mouton.

Swinton, D. 1988. "Economic Status of Blacks 1987." *The State of Black America, 1988*. Washington, D.C.: National Urban League.

Sykes, C. 1992. *A Nation of Victims: The Decay of the American Character*. New York: St. Martin's.

Szalai, A. 1966. "Trends in Comparative Time Budget Research." *American Behavioral Scientist* 29:3–8.

Szalai, A., et al. 1972. *The Use of Time*. The Hague: Mouton.

Szalai, A., S. Ferge, et al. 1966. "The Multinational Comparative Time-Budget Research Project: Report on the Organization, Methods, and Experiences of the Pilot Study,

1965–1966, and the Preliminary Results of 13 Parallel Time-Budget Surveys." Contributions to the Round Table on Time-Budgets at the VIIth World Congress of Sociology, Evian, September 1966. Also published in *American Behavioral Scientist* 10 (December 1966): 1–31 and under the title "Recherche comparative internationale sur les budgets-temps," in *Etudes et Conjectures*, September, 103–88.

Tichenor, P., G. Donohue, and C. Olien. 1970. "Mass Media Flow and Differential Growth in Knowledge." *Public Opinion Quarterly* 34:159–70.

Tyler, B., 1992. *From Harlem to Hollywood: The Struggle for Racial and Cultural Democracy.* New York: Garland.

United States, Department of Transportation. 1994. *1990 Nationwide Personal Transportation Survey.* Washington, D.C.: Bureau of Transportation Statistics and Federal Highway Administration.

Vanek, J. 1974. "Time Spent in Housework." *Scientific American* 11:116–20.

Veblen, T. 1899. *The Theory of the Leisure Class.* New York: Heubsch.

Verbrugge, L., and D. Gruber-Baldine. 1993. *Baltimore Study of Activity Patterns.* Ann Arbor: Institute of Gerontology, University of Michigan.

Vonnegut, K., Jr. 1952. *Player Piano.* New York: Dell.

Waksberg, J. 1978. "Sampling Methods for Random Digit Dialing." *Journal of the American Statistical Association* 73:45–46.

Walker, K. 1969. "Homemaking Still Takes Time." *Journal of Home Economics* 61 (October): 621–24.

Walker, K., and M. Woods. 1976. *Time Use: A Measure of Household Production of Family Goods and Services.* Washington, D.C.: American Home Economics Association.

Wattenberg, B., and R. Scammon. 1973. "Black Progress and Liberal Rhetoric." *Commentary* 55 (April): 35–44.

Wilensky, H. 1961. "The Uneven Distribution of Leisure: The Impact of Economic Growth on Free Time." *Social Problems* 9:32–56.

Wiley, J., J. Robinson, T. Piazza, K. Garrett, K. Cirksena, Y. Cheng, and G. Martin. 1991. "Activity Patterns of California Residents." Final Report Under Contract No. A6-177-33, California Air Resources Board. Sacramento, Calif.

Yanai, T. 1995. *1992 Survey on Time Use and Leisure Activities in Japan.* Tokyo: Statistics Bureau, Management and Coordination Agency.

Zeldin, T. 1994. *An Intimate History of Humanity.* New York: Harper Perennial.

Zerubavel, E. 1984. *Hidden Rhythms: Schedules and Calendars in Social Life.* Chicago: University of Chicago Press.

Zimbardo, P. 1985. "Time in Perspective." *Psychology Today*, March, 20–27.

Zuzanek, J. 1974. "Society of Leisure, or the Harried Leisure Class: Leisure Trends in Industrial Society." *Journal of Leisure Research* 6:293–304.

Zuzanek, J., and B. J. Smale. 1994. "Uses of Time and Changing Perceptions of Time Pressure by Different Life-Cycle Groups: Recent Trends in Canada (1986–92)." Paper presented to the 13th World Congress of Sociology. Bielefeld, Germany, July.

# Index

## DATE DUE

| MAR 1 3 2006 | | | |
|---|---|---|---|
| | | | |
| | | | |
| | | | |
| | | | |
| | | | |
| | | | |
| | | | |
| | | | |
| | | | |
| | | | |
| | | | |
| | | | |
| | | | |
| | | | |
| | | | |
| | | | Printed In USA |